MILITARISM AND ISRAELI SOCIETY

An Israel Studies Book

Israel Studies is sponsored by the Ben-Gurion Research Institute for the Study of Israel and Zionism, Ben-Gurion University of the Negev, and the Schusterman Center for Israel Studies, Brandeis University.

Militarism and Israeli Society

EDITED BY

Gabriel Sheffer & Oren Barak

Indiana University Press

Bloomington & Indianapolis

This book is a publication of

Indiana University Press
601 North Morton Street
Bloomington, IN 47404-3797 USA

www.iupress.indiana.edu

Telephone orders   800-842-6796
Fax orders   812-855-7931
Orders by e-mail   iuporder@indiana.edu

♾The paper used in this publication
meets the minimum requirements of
the American National Standard for
Information Sciences—Permanence
of Paper for Printed Library Materials,
ANSI Z39.48-1992.

Manufactured in the United States of
America

Library of Congress Cataloging-in-
Publication Data

Militarism and Israeli society / edited by
Gabriel Sheffer and Oren Barak.
    p. cm. — (Israel studies book)
    Includes bibliographical references and
index.
    ISBN 978-0-253-35441-9 (cloth : alk.
paper) — ISBN 978-0-253-22174-2
(pbk. : alk. paper) 1. Civil-military
relations—Israel. 2. Militarism—Israel.
3. Israel—Politics and government—
1993– I. Sheffer, Gabriel. II. Barak,
Oren.
    JQ1830.A38C5853 2010
    355'.03305694—dc22

                                        2009028692

1 2 3 4 5   15 14 13 12 11 10

CONTENTS

ACKNOWLEDGMENTS

The editors extend our sincere thanks to the Van Leer Jerusalem Institute, and especially to its former director, Shimshon Zelniker, for their help that has facilitated the successful operation of the Workshop on Israeli Security and Society and the 2006 international conference. We thank Ilan Troen and Natan Aridan, the editors of *Israel Studies,* for their wholehearted encouragement and assistance in the various stages of the publication of the special volume of *Israel Studies* and the preparation of this book, and Janet Rabinowitch of Indiana University Press for her confidence in the entire project that includes the special volume of *Israel Studies* and this book. Last but not least, we thank Assaf Shapira for his help in preparing the appendices to this volume.

MILITARISM AND ISRAELI SOCIETY

INTRODUCTION

GABRIEL SHEFFER AND OREN BARAK

Although "security" is probably the most central issue pertaining to the lives of all Israeli citizens, it is usually dealt with by politicians, academics, and media commentators using traditional and conventional theoretical and analytical tools. Thus, the study of the various aspects of the relationship between Israel's "civil" and "military–security" spheres and actual sectors more often than not focuses on its *formal* facets while overlooking its more *informal* features, which are most influential in these relationships. It is thus not surprising that most of these traditional conventional studies[1] contend that, despite some deviations from an ideal democratic model, the civilian sector in Israel has maintained its predominance over the security sector since the state's independence in 1948. This has been the prevalent view with regard to all of Israel's political and military relative successes and major failures, including, most recently, the Israel–Hizbullah War in 2006 (the "Second Lebanon War").

The essays included in this book challenge this premise by critically and systematically reexamining the relationship between Israel's civil and security sectors and providing a deeper and more nuanced view of the actual situation in this regard. They throw light on the *formal and informal* arrangements, connections, and dynamic relations between Israel's security sector, on the one hand, and the country's civilian sector—the cultural sphere, political system, society, the economy, and the public discourse—on the other hand.

To critically and systematically reexamine this important subject the editors of this volume (together with Amiram Oren) established the

1

Workshop on Israeli Security and Society (hereafter: the Workshop) under the provocative title *An Army Who Has a State?* at the Van Leer Jerusalem Institute. The goal of the Workshop was twofold: first, to discuss and present new and innovative ideas regarding the relationship between Israel's security and civilian sectors, and to do so from a critical and interdisciplinary perspective; second, to expose Israeli politicians, academics, professionals, and the general public to the resultant new insights regarding these issues. The Workshop participants, who included Israeli scholars and practitioners interested in these questions, critically examined: 1) the concept of "security" in Israel; 2) the various components of Israel's large and powerful security sector; 3) the roles and influence of serving and retired security officials; and 4) the impact of security policies on the political, social, economic, and cultural spheres both generally and in particular instances.

The book, an expanded version of a special volume of the journal *Israel Studies* 12.1 (2006), presents the main findings discussed within the framework of the Workshop and in an international conference organized by the editors to further discuss and publicize the findings of the participants in the Workshop and specialists in civil–security relations whom we invited from abroad. The fifteen chapters provide innovative and critical perspectives on the changing roles of the politically, bureaucratically, and discursively dominant security sector in Israel and its relationship with the civilian sector.[2]

After more than sixty years of Israeli statehood, the contributors to this volume feel that it is high time to reconsider old analytical and normative notions of "what ought to be?" with regard to Israel's security sector and patterns of civil–security relations, and to focus instead on "what is actually there?" Most contributors view the situation in this regard in Israel as highly complex, fluid, and under constant change, but at the same time it exhibits a degree of continuity, particularly as far as the nonseparation and significant overlapping of Israel's civilian and security spheres and sectors are concerned.

In order to clarify the existing complicated reality, and to do so in a fresh, interdisciplinary fashion, the contributors deal not only with the role of the security sector in Israel's politics and society—which is the main focus of previous contributions on this topic[3]—but also discuss other facets of Israel's civil–security relationship, including the role of the security sector vis-à-vis the country's culture, civil society, bureau-cracy, economy, educational system, gender relations, internal territory, and the media. This reflects the overall goal which is not only to provide a broader and more nuanced understanding of Israel's civil–security relationship but also to suggest how this issue could be further explored theoretically, analytically, and empirically and applied to other states that face similar situations.

On the theoretical level, most of the chapters suggest that "classic" theories of civil–military relations are insufficient when trying to comprehend the Israeli case. These theories may certainly be valid, al-though it is worth adding that some of their basic premises are under challenge even with regard to the "effective democracies" in the West.[4] However, these theories cannot fully grasp the Israeli case, or even its most important characteristics. Incidentally, studies presented in a sec-ond international conference that we, the editors, organized in 2008, suggest that these theories do not apply to other smaller democratic and democratizing states that, like Israel, face (or have faced) real or imagined "continuous existential threats." Hence, there is a need to ex-pand the scope of inquiry to include not only "effective democracies" in the West, which presumably exhibit more satisfactory patterns of civil–military relations, but also non-Western states that are "formal democracies," "partially democratic," "democratizing," or "nondemo-cratic" states where the situation is pretty different in this respect, and more similar to the Israeli case. We hope that the study of these cases, including Israel, which is discussed in the book, and the other cases, which are addressed in a second volume soon to be published as the re-sult of the second international conference, will contribute to the theory in this academic field.

One of the main points suggested in this book is that in order to better understand the current situation in Israel, studies on the security sector ought to expand beyond the military and its relations with the country's various civilian spheres to include those arrangements and ter-ritories in which the Israel Defense Forces (IDF) and the other security agencies are dominant but which are on the borders of, or outside, Israel "proper." These include Israel's "Separation Barrier," the wall/fence that separates Israel from parts of the West Bank and the Gaza Strip; Israel's self-declared "Security Zone" in South Lebanon (until 2000); and the security sector's "territorial kingdom" within Israel itself. Additional studies are needed in order to fully comprehend the role of the IDF and the other security agencies in the occupied West Bank and the Golan Heights as well as Israel's military industries, nuclear and chemical agencies, arms exports, security cooperation with other states including other "existentially threatened" states, and so forth.

In the same vein, the question of how the security sector in Israel, and especially the IDF, encourages and helps reinforce prevailing political, social, and cultural norms and patterns of intersectoral relations is warranted. Three chapters in this volume specifically address these questions with regard to gender relations; the relationship between Ashkenazi and Oriental Jews; and the relationship between national religious Jews and the IDF. However, there is still a need for more studies on other relationships, especially between Israel's Jewish majority and its Palestinian Arab minority, as well as on normative-cultural issues.[5]

The "flip side" of the dominant role of Israel's security sector, especially the IDF, which is acknowledged by most, though not all, contributions to this volume, is the perpetual weakness of Israel's civilian actors, including government agencies (e.g., the Ministry of Finance and the Ministry of Foreign Affairs); the political system, including the major political parties; civil society groups, such as those operating in the political, socioeconomic, educational, and environmental realms; and the media. At the same time, the present volume includes two chapters that demonstrate that civil society groups in Israel can operate in the realm of national security, and are even successful at times, and a third chapter discusses mechanisms for improving the Treasury's control over security expenditures. By the same token, one chapter discusses the role of the media in matters of national security in Israel, and the security sector's control over vast territories in Israel,[6] and suggests ways to improve the situation. It should be noted, however, that at least some of the book's chapters posit that the civil–political sector is still predominant in Israel.

The main goal of Oren Barak and Gabriel (Gabi) Sheffer in "The Study of Civil–Military Relations in Israel: A New Perspective" is threefold: 1) to define and examine the major approaches to the study of the relationship between Israel's security sector and civilian realms (cultural, political, social, economic, and discursive), which they refer to as the "traditional," "critical," and "new critical" approaches; 2) to emphasize the theoretical and empirical "gaps" that exist in the scholarly treatment of the relationships between actors operating within both types of spheres, and particularly with regard to the more informal aspects of their interplay; 3) to suggest ways to overcome the lack of adequate treatment of these highly informal exchanges by employing insights from the expanding literature on "policy networks" and demonstrating how these networks, which can be identified in the Israeli case, influence general and concrete policymaking on both the local and national levels.

In "Military Knowledge and Weak Civilian Control in the Reality of Low Intensity Conflict—The Israeli Case," Kobi Michael argues that the changes in the nature of warfare and its transformation toward intrastate conflicts (also known as Low-Intensity Conflicts) pose a challenge to the nature of the interaction between the political and the military echelons in general and in Israel in particular. While in these instances political supremacy is maintained on the institutional and formal levels, on the substantial level, which requires reliance on knowledge and systematic staff work, the political position is weakened and substantive civilian control is wanting. Michael characterizes the interactions between the political and the military echelons in Israel during the last half-decade as a "discursive space" imbued with military content and characterized by a blurred political directive. Employing the concept of "epistemic authority," borrowed from the field of social psychology, he shows how Israel's military echelon has become an "epistemic authority" with regard to the confrontation with the Palestinians in the eyes of both the general public and the political echelon in Israel. He also elucidates both the nature of the political–military interaction in this period and the weakness of civilian control of the military.

Avraham Sela argues in "Civil Society, the Military, and National Security: The Case of Israel's Security Zone in South Lebanon" that Israel's unilateral withdrawal from South Lebanon in 2000 was a unique case in the state's history of national security. For the first time since 1948, a small grassroots movement challenged Israel's security establishment and played a key role in turning on its head a longstanding concept of national security—the "Security Zone" in South Lebanon.

He examines the process that led to Israel's withdrawal from Lebanon as a reflection of Israel's pattern of civil–military relations and as a case of the blurred boundaries between these social sectors, demonstrated by networks of officers in uniform and their retired colleagues in key positions of political decision making. Sela explains the origins of the concept of the "security zone" in South Lebanon in the mid-1980s, the military-based decision-making process that led to its adoption by the government, and the deliberate avoidance of any public debate or even reconsideration of this concept by the IDF itself, despite the entanglement of the "Security Zone" in a limited war of attrition with Lebanese guerrilla movements. The "Security Zone" was a typical example of military blunder underlining the dangerous monopoly of the IDF on shaping the national security policy, especially in the absence of civil institutions capable of providing alternative policies. The main achievement of civil society in this case was its success in triggering a public debate on this issue, offering an alternative security discourse, and questioning the military and political logic of the "Security Zone." At the same time, he argues that the case of the "Security Zone" in South Lebanon may indicate the *limits* of civil society in Israel in affecting decision making on national security.

In "Intractable Conflict and the Media," Yoram Peri focuses on the relationship between the media and military–security affairs in Israel, arguing that this relationship has been dramatically altered since 1973 and more so since the early 1990s. Media outlets have transformed from being subservient and deferential into adopting a confrontational model, and the military ceased to be a "sacred cow." If in the past the media were only a tool of the state, now they are also regarded as reflecting Israeli society and individuals. At the same time, a deconstruction of media and news texts reveals deep structures that have not changed. As in the past, the media continue to be a major agent in the development of the Israeli military ethos. They also play a significant role in the construction of the image of the enemy (be it the Arabs, the Palestinians, or non-Jews at large) while nourishing the positive image of the Jewish hero and of war ethos. Finally, they transfix *Macht* (power) values and contribute to the construction of gender structure of Israeli society. Eventually, the media nourish the aspired model of Israel as a warring society. Therefore, as research of civil–military relations in Israel historically focused on the modes by which the media assisted the survival of a besieged society under conditions of prolonged war, while keeping its democratic spirit,

Peri demonstrates how the media has restrained the development of civilian ethos and impeded the development of a postwar society *in spite of* the accelerating process of decolonization.

In "Tensions between Military Service and Jewish Orthodoxy in Israel: Implications Imagined and Real," Stuart A. Cohen argues that recent years have witnessed a significant rise in the numbers of "national religious" soldiers in the IDF's combat units. As a result, their sociological and cultural profile has become a matter of considerable public and academic interest. Particular attention has been focused on the strains that might be placed on the military loyalties of national religious troops, should they be required to carry out missions that they interpret as being contrary to Jewish religious teachings. In this context, when confronted with orders to dismantle Jewish settlements in the territories, their behavior has generally been considered as constituting the litmus test of their allegiance. He contends that national religious soldiers in the IDF often sense a conflict of loyalties between their military duties and their Jewish religious obligations. Yet, such tensions cannot be attributed solely, or even mainly, to factors associated with their commitment to possession of the Land of Israel (Eretz Israel). Rather, the principal sources of tension between religious observance and military service in Israel lie elsewhere: in matters of an essentially ritual and behavioral dimension. From that perspective, he argues that the near-complete absence of conscientious objection on the part of national religious IDF troops during Israel's 2005 Disengagement from the Gaza Strip was by no means an aberration.

The military–society interface is also the focus in "From 'Obligatory Militarism' to 'Contractual Militarism'—Competing Models of Citizenship" by Yagil Levy, Edna Lomsky-Feder, and Noa Harel. Since the Arab–Israel War of 1973, secular Ashkenazi middle-class groups in Israel, which traditionally had constituted the "backbone" of the IDF, have displayed a lack of enthusiasm to continue to bear the military burden, a phenomenon that was publicly portrayed as a "motivation crisis." They conceptualize this process as a shift from an "obligatory militarism" that perceived the military service as an unconditional, mandatory national duty to a "contractual militarism," according to which military service is stipulated by the fulfillment of the individual's ambitions and interests, although it remains a formal obligation. Socialization—school memorial ceremonies and preparation for the military service—serves as a mediating mechanism between the structural, social change and the social agency. Both have been utilized by Israel's dominant social groups to reshape the military ethos in a manner that redefines their relations vis-à-vis the military in contractual terms.

Amiram Oren contends in "Shadow Lands: The Use of Land Resources for Security Needs in Israel" that Israel's security sector controls and influences in manifold ways more than half (!) of the state's territory, not including the occupied West Bank, while also dictating the use of Israel's aerial and maritime spheres. This situation is facilitated by Israeli laws that accord the security sector a different status from the civilian sector, leaving the security sector with ample room for maneuver. In the territorial sphere, the security sector behaves like a "separate framework," operating aside and sometimes separated from the civilian spheres.

Despite this situation, the modus operandi of the security sector in the territorial realm and its relationship with the relevant civilian spheres have received inadequate attention, manifest in the relatively small number of issues discussed by academics and researchers and by the general public in Israel. The government, media, and general public there rarely show interest in land use for security purposes and related issues. Oren accounts for this state of affairs, its significance, and broader implications.

In "'The Battle over Our Homes': Reconstructing/Deconstructing Sovereign Practices around Israel's Separation Barrier on the West Bank," Yuval Feinstein and Uri Ben-Eliezer suggest that during the Second Palestinian Intifada, Israel started to construct a "Separation Barrier," officially aimed at preventing armed Palestinian activists from penetrating its territory. Previous Palestinian attacks not only caused the death and injury of many innocent civilians, but also challenged Israel's sovereignty and created a sense of indignation toward its government and security forces. The construction of the "Separation Barrier," however, raised some objections based on the argument that it was not built on the Green Line (the Armistice line between Israel and Jordan delineated in 1949) and that it both expropriated extensive Palestinian agricultural lands and de facto annexed many Israeli settlements that had been built in the territories since 1967.

They show that, in general, protests along the "Separation Barrier" have been conducted through the cooperation of Israeli peace and human rights activists, local Palestinians, and international activists. Given the well-known theoretical assumption that states are weakening in the era of global restructuring and that both local and global social movements are gaining more political influence, the authors raise the question of why the broad and intensive activity to hinder the construction of the "Separation Barrier" has failed. They trace the various practices, representations, discourses, and arenas in which the clashes between the state and its official agents and the protestors have occurred.

Zalman F. Shiffer explains in "The Debate over the Defense Budget in Israel" that Israel has invested large quantities of human and material resources in the development of a strong army to confront threats emanating from the fact that it is a small state whose very existence has been repeatedly challenged by its neighbors. Although Israel has achieved peace with two of its neighbors, Egypt and Jordan, its security predicament has not disappeared and its many facets continue to affect its society in many ways. He highlights one important aspect of Israel's security issue: the debate regarding the allocation of budgetary resources to the security sector. He characterizes the defense expenditures—their definitions, their importance in both absolute and relative terms, and their development over time; presents the major actors involved in the debate over the defense budget; reviews the major arguments and disagreements regarding the quantity of resources allocated to defense and the defense budget management; and deals with the development of this debate in recent years.

Samy Cohen argues in "Civilian Control over the Army in Israel and France" that the problem of civilian control over the armed forces is of major concern in all democracies, and is even more acute in those countries that have a large army and/or are engaged in a protracted international conflict. This is particularly the case, or was the case, in countries such as France and Israel. It usually involves worrying about the excessive influence the army might gain over legitimately elected civil authorities who are not in a position to exercise their prerogatives knowledgeably. Comparing France and Israel is a useful way to understand and better assess the characteristics of the Israeli case. The two countries have a number of characteristics in common. Both are what can be called "medium-sized military powers," and both have a large army and have experienced, or continue to experience, repeated wars. Both have experienced the problem of conquest and colonization (as well as decolonization) of a territory. In particular, Cohen focuses on the decisions to use force in the course of external military operations. His main argument is that in each of these states the civilian sector has been dominant in such decision-making processes.

The nature of Amir Bar-Or's "The Making of Israel's Political–Security Culture" is more historical. Like other contributors to this volume, he argues that complexity is the key feature of civil–military relations in Israel and mentions that many explanations have been offered for this phenomenon. However, he proposes another approach, which explores the broader ramifications of the term "political–security culture" on the supremacy of the political leadership led by David Ben-Gurion over the military power that the Yishuv (the Jewish community in Palestine prior to the establishment of the State of Israel) had developed in the critical period of its evolution to a state. The starting point is the adaptation of the term *national security system* to the security system of the Yishuv. This system includes two subsystems—one political and the other military. According to Bar-Or, the scope of the activity of these bodies and the pivotal role that they played in the Yishuv allow us to regard them as its political and military subsystems, and although these subsystems' objectives were, essentially, similar, there were differences in their approach to attaining them. There have also been conflicts related to the political–strategic and military–operational spheres regarding agreed-upon policies, policymaking procedures, and policy implementation. He concludes that the term "political–security culture," which enables us to examine the connection between the terms *political culture* and *security culture,* is the best course for understanding these phenomena.

Edna Lomsky-Feder and Eyal Ben-Ari show in "The Discourses of 'Psychology' and the 'Normalization' of War in Contemporary Israel" how psychological discourses contribute to the construction of traumatic imagery of war and military service and work to incorporate such ideas into the routines of social life in Israel. Within this context, they explore how war and military service are socially "normalized"—turned into "natural" albeit important—parts of society. Concretely, the authors examine three discourses: the first, a developmental one, focuses on how military service is constructed as a "natural" stage in progression toward adulthood and manhood; the second, which is therapeutic, centers on the traumatic influences of war on warriors and, more recently, on civilians, and thereby blurs the power relations between Israelis and Palestinians; the third, rooted in organizational psychology, deals with the army's effectiveness by likening it to other organizations, thus obscuring its unique character as specializing in the organized use of violence.

In "Visual Representations of IDF Women Soldiers and 'Civil-Militarism' in Israel," Chava Brownfield-Stein focuses on the visual representations of IDF women soldiers and addresses the role of the visual field and the significant impact of photographs of such soldiers on the "militaristic" character of Israeli society. She contends that if the militarization of society is achieved through the naturalization of militaristic values, the study of Israeli militarism would be incomplete without considering the visual ramifications of Israel's Security Service Law and the unique phenomenon of women's conscription, and without discussing visual representations of women soldiers in army camps, city streets, and military parades. Brownfield-Stein analyzes the army's penetration throughout Israeli culture and draws attention to the visual aspects of the evasive and ever-changing processes of militarization of Israeli society. By focusing on the visual aspects of the unique phenomenon of women's conscription, she calls attention to the pleasurable dimension of the connections between "technologies of the self" and "technologies of domination" (what Michel Foucault termed *governmentality*) and illuminates the militaristic links between the constitution of the subject and the state's formation. Building on Cynthia Enloe's theoretical framework and definition of militarism, Brownfield-Stein defines the unique phenomenon of cultural militarism in Israel as "erotic militarism."

Yuval Benziman describes in "Contradictory Representation of the IDF in Cultural Texts of the 1980s" the representation of the IDF in Israeli cultural texts of the 1980s dealing with the Israeli-Arab conflict, in which the IDF is represented as both determining and implementing Israeli policy toward the Palestinians, and as shaping Israeli society from within. The army is described as an organization that possesses unconstrained power, that acts harshly and abusively, that determines who can and who cannot be part of Israeli society, and that performs the unpleasant task of excluding Arabs from Israeli society. Although these

representations criticize the role of the army in Israeli society, Benziman explains that the texts in fact express the human tendency known
as "ultimate attribution error." Thus, although they describe the army
disapprovingly, they also show that it has no other choice but to act the
way it does. Nevertheless, despite its unfavorable depiction, the army
is represented as conducting itself in the least damaging way possible,
considering the position it has gained in Israeli society, a position that,
according to these cultural texts, it had been forced into.

Christopher Dandeker's concluding chapter, "Military and Society
since 9/11: Retrospect and Prospect," argues that democracies across the
world, Israel included, face the challenges of "hybrid wars" and need
to design armed forces that are fit to face them and to invest in their
military's capacity so as to become useful contributors to coalitions of
the willing. Military investments pose difficult choices in terms of the
level and shape of public expenditure and the functioning of the armed
forces. Hence, governments need to think about how best to integrate
military and nonmilitary instruments when they intervene in hybrid
wars (to balance use of force, "hearts and minds," or state construction
or reconstruction efforts, for instance). Furthermore, governments have
to clearly define for their domestic and international publics why they
are intervening, what constitutes the basis of achieving success in these
interventions, and how long they plan to engage in missions to counter
threats posed by hybrid wars.

In this regard they will need to acquire and nurture in their own
public "strategic patience." Operations may take longer and be more
difficult than both publics and governments may foresee, and they will
need resilience in the face of terrorist objectives to unnerve, as well as a
facility for controlling strategic narratives. In a fast-moving media environment, with a diversity of providers and media of communications,
it is important that military and other security agencies are surefooted
and able to provide effective, proactive counter-responses to terrorist
information operations: to ensure that successes on the ground are converted into successes in the information war. As outrages from 2001 to
2008 illustrate, an essential response to them is not confined to military
means but engages in the struggle for ideas. Thus this struggle should not
be restricted to ends (defending the values of democracy) but must extend to the means through a convincing narrative, including short- and

longer-term steps about how the struggle is being waged, how setbacks are being dealt with, and how political will is being deployed on objectives that can be achieved as well as being valuable in their own terms.

Notes

1. See the chapter by Oren Barak and Gabriel (Gabi) Sheffer.

2. Unlike previous studies on Israel, we regard Israel's security sector as consisting of serving and retired officials and officers of the Ministry of Defense, the IDF, the secret services, the police, and the military industries.

3. The major scholarly approaches to the Israeli case are presented and discussed in this book by Oren Barak and Gabriel (Gabi) Sheffer.

4. Douglas Bland, "A Unified Theory of Civil-Military Relations," *Armed Forces and Society* 26.1 (1999): 7–26; James Burk, "Theories of Democratic Civil-Military Relations," *Armed Forces and Society* 29.1 (2001): 7–29.

5. One understudied topic is the role of ambiguity in the realm of Israel's national security and also more generally.

6. See the chapter by Amiram Oren.

ONE

The Study of Civil–Military Relations in Israel: A New Perspective

OREN BARAK AND GABRIEL SHEFFER

Because of its theoretical and practical significance and implications, in recent decades civil–military relations in Israel have been the focus of extended debates among analysts from different academic disciplines.[1] That more than a half-century after its establishment, Israel lacks clearly defined and internationally recognized borders; that it is still engaged in an unending conflict with its neighbors; that many of its citizens continue to believe that it is facing existential threats; and that its security sector[2] and especially the Israel Defense Forces (IDF) play a major role in almost all spheres—all these have made this topic perennially relevant and debatable. In fact, various writers imply clear causal links between some or all of these factors.

In view of the questions and quandaries raised by these debates, which extend beyond academic studies into the public discourse in Israel, the purpose of our chapter is twofold: first, to critically examine the major existing approaches to the study of the relationship between Israel's security sector, on the one hand, and the country's various civilian spheres—political, social, economic, and cultural—on the other hand. We refer to these approaches as the Traditional Approach, the Critical Approach, and the New Critical Approach. In particular, we wish to draw attention to the theoretical and empirical gaps that exist in these scholarly analyses of the relationships between actors that operate within both types of spheres, and especially with regard to the more comprehensive, deeper, and essentially informal aspects of their interplay; and second, to suggest ways to overcome the lack of adequate treatment of these highly informal intertwining relationships and exchanges that have tremendous influences on public policymaking concerning both critical attitudinal and practical matters. We suggest that this can be attained by employing insights from the literature on "policy networks," defined as "clusters of actors, each of which has an interest, or 'stake' in a given policy sector and the capacity to help determine policy success or failure."[3]

The chapter has three parts. First, we examine the main attributes of each of the previous three approaches to the Israeli case. Then, we analyze and compare these characteristics, and emphasize the conceptual and empirical gaps that exist in their treatment of the various facets of the Israeli case. Finally, we present our own approach and explain how it can enhance the understanding of the Israeli case and, if developed further, contribute to the study of civil–military relations in general.

Existing Approaches to the Israeli Case

As noted above, we distinguish between three major approaches to the study of the relationships between Israel's civilian and military spheres.[4] These approaches represent three generations of Israeli scholars whose work has been influenced and inspired by broader theoretical developments in Israel and the West, especially as far as the relationship between the civilian and military spheres of the State are concerned.

THE TRADITIONAL APPROACH

The first of these approaches, the Traditional Approach, has focused on institutional and formal aspects of the relationship. Generally speaking, in the study of the Israeli case, this approach has drawn on traditional theories of civil–military relations, and especially on the works of Morris Janowitz[5] and Robin Luckham.[6] The perspective adopted by this school, whose proponents followed structural-functional theories that dominated Israeli social sciences until the 1980s, has been the examination of the structural and functional features of what they regarded as two clearly distinguishable civilian and military subsystems. Thus, the emphasis in these studies was on formal institutions, functions, and policymaking, and on the consequent relations between two essentially separate subsystems—the civilian and the military—whose mutual interactions remained to a great extent confined to the sphere of Israel's national security. The underlying premise of the proponents of this approach was that the civilian sector in Israel has been, traditionally, the dominant between the two.[7]

More particularly, those authors depicted Israel as a "nation-in-arms" par excellence. As mentioned above, according to the adherents of this approach, two clearly distinguishable subsystems—a civilian one and a military one—have existed in Israel; the former was strong and more powerful than the latter.[8] However, due to necessity and especially because of the military's significant role in the realm of national security, the boundaries between these two subsystems became somewhat fragmented. This fragmentation allowed interaction between the two subsystems, which mainly meant that the military was able to engage in civilian tasks such as settlement, agriculture, and education, and could participate in policymaking in the area of national security but without undermining civilian control. Indeed, although these scholars have argued that a limited "partnership" concerning policymaking and policy implementation in the area of national security existed between Israel's civilian and military elites, they emphasized that, as in other democratic nations-in-arms, it was the former that explicitly controlled the latter.[9]

These writers have deduced such conclusions not only from the IDF's purported continuous dependence on the civilian sector for material resources and manpower, especially for its continuation, enlargement, and maintenance of reserves components, but also from the dominance of Israel's civilian leaders, such as prime ministers David Ben-Gurion, Levi Eshkol, and Menachem Begin, and from the social networks formed between civilians and security personnel that, in their view, ultimately reinforced the military's civilianized nature.[10]

To explain the endurance of Israel's democratic regime despite its preoccupation with security issues, the proponents of this first approach have applied civil–military relations theories and argued that, in this case, the boundary separates not civilian and military institutions per se, but a military sphere, on the one hand, and the societal, economic, and cultural spheres, on the other hand. Thus, the argument of this school has been that while the IDF and secret services have acquired a de facto monopoly over most matters pertaining to Israel's national security, they have generally abided by the civilian norms in other areas of domestic politics.[11]

If one accepts this analysis, the conclusion is that Israel has completed the process of state formation[12] and social integration, including the differentiation of its civil and military realms and the imposition of effective control of the latter by the former.[13] We contend that this is not an adequate depiction of the Israeli case, especially since 1967.

THE CRITICAL APPROACH

The second approach, which we call the Critical Approach, has been part of a general trend in the Israeli social sciences, beginning in the 1980s and 1990s, to present more critical examinations of the Yishuv and Israeli history, as well as of the societal and political arrangements that influenced the relations and the policy role of the state's civilian and security sectors. However, although, to a certain extent, the adherents to this approach have dealt critically with the underlying sociopolitical, cultural, and ideological positions of each of these sectors, they still regarded them as two clearly distinguishable sectors. Similarly, they also focused on the formal institutional relations between the two sectors, while paying some, but by no means sufficient, attention to "softer" behavioral and informal aspects and factors.

Like the previous school, the Critical Approach also followed institutional–organizational theories, but did so in a more critical fashion. Its major departures from the previous paradigm are the depiction of both civilian and military subsystems as essentially heterogeneous entities, and the contention that the location of the boundary between these spheres, particularly when it is fragmented, "is not fixed, but shifts according to the interaction between the military and civil sub-systems."[14]

From this standpoint, which allows for a somewhat more dynamic analysis of the development of the Israeli case, this approach has been able to define different types of relationships that have existed between various civilian actors, on the one hand, and the security sector, on the other. Thus these analysts have argued that the security sector intruded more into certain civilian spheres than into others. Concomitantly, "rivalries between political groups [were] reflected inside the military establishment,"[15] and the policymaking process has witnessed the participation of "a coalition of officers and politicians versus another coalition of officers and politicians."[16]

Like the adherents to the previous approach, the writers of this school argued that civil–military relations in Israel have been characterized by a "political–military partnership" between its separate military and civilian elites, which is manifested in clearly defined spheres. Yet, in their view, this pattern, which prevailed in most periods in Israel's history, has in fact prevented the imposition of effective civilian control of the military in "pure" military matters.[17] The continuous involvement of political parties in running the IDF since 1948, most notably Mapai under the leadership of David Ben-Gurion, has also been stressed, like the military's own growing intervention in politics in later periods, especially since 1967.[18] They have also attached importance to the IDF's expanded control of the occupied West Bank and Gaza Strip and the "Security Zone" in South Lebanon (until its withdrawal in 2000)[19] and to its increased role in shaping the perceptions and discourse of Israel's political elite toward the Israeli–Palestinian conflict, particularly during the second Palestinian Intifada.[20]

Unlike the first approach, which focused on the IDF's reservists and their role in its continuously being "civilianized," this approach has argued that such a view ". . . tends to obscure the equally important facts that, in order to maintain such an army, it is also necessary to have a core of long-service professionals to ensure its capability between military campaigns, and that this puts them in a position to play a major role in influencing such highly important matters as the size of the military budget and even, on occasions, the resort to war itself."[21]

The third factor that this approach brought up is the ways in which Israel's political society has turned into a lodestone for retired security officials.[22] While correctly identifying some attributes of the Israeli case, this approach is still far from offering a coherent and satisfactory explanation for the continued predominance of serving and retired security officials, their complex connections with elites in other sectors, and hence their substantial impact on numerous aspects of Israeli politics, society, economy, and culture.

THE NEW CRITICAL APPROACH

The third approach to the study of the relationship between Israel's civil and military realms is that which we termed the New Critical Approach.

Its adherents, who are influenced by the postmodernist tradition in the social sciences, pay a great deal of attention to cultural aspects of Israeli society, and they are highly critical of the powerlessness of Israeli civil society, which allows its security sector to play a hegemonic role in shaping the state's behavior.

Unlike the first two approaches, this approach has not followed civil–military relations theories, claiming that these constitute a field of knowledge imbued with Western ethnocentrism. Such theories, these writers have contended, are applicable to other democratic states, including Israel, only in a very limited fashion.[23] However, according to them, that is not the only drawback of previous studies on the Israeli case. They argue that earlier writers "endeavored to rid Israel of the stigma of militarism" by defining it as a "nation-in-arms," a term with positive connotations, instead of a "garrison state" or a "praetorian society," terms that are more pertinent to its true nature.[24] From this perspective, even the term "military democracy,"[25] coined by an author from the Critical Approach, could be regarded as a sort of euphemism.

Some authors within this third approach have criticized previous works for not trying "to ascertain whether civility as such even exists in Israel; and if so, what its essence and character might be."[26] Their conclusion was that Israeli society had clear militaristic attributes, which have impinged on its democratic character.[27] Yet, these writers themselves understood the term "militarism" in quite different ways (they thought about it in cultural, materialist terms, and so forth) and their assessment of its long-term effects on Israeli politics and society varied. While some suggested that the militarization of politics and society in Israel precluded civilian control of the military,[28] others posited that this process did in fact allow for the state's civilian institutions to establish mechanisms for control of the military by making the IDF "dependent on the state's resources" in return for legitimacy and prestige accorded to the civilian institutions.[29] Still others identified "agreement and cooperation among the military, the political elites, and the citizenry," which precluded military intervention in Israeli politics.[30]

Finally, unlike the previous approaches, which viewed the IDF mainly as a political actor, the New Critical Approach treated the military also as a major arena for social exchanges (ethnic, cultural, class, gender, etc.), thus providing a more complex and nuanced assessment of its place in the state and society. However, in our discussion we limit ourselves to the political aspects of the civilian–military interface.

Comparison of the Three Approaches

In the following more detailed discussion of the three approaches to the Israeli case, we address nine issues dealt with by these approaches, in a comparative manner. We identify the gaps in their treatment of the Israeli case, and suggest what we think should be done in order to comprehend the latter more fully and deeply. These issues are: 1) the main theoretical emphasis of these approaches, 2) the theoretical and analytical models that they employ to analyze the Israeli case, 3) their characterization of the nature of the relationship between these spheres, including the boundaries that exist between them, 4) their conceptualization of the structure and relationship between the two sectors, 5) the assessment of the strength of the civilian sphere in Israel, 6) the assessment of the level of civilian control of the military in Israel, 7) the assessment of the strength of the security sector in Israel, 8) the view of the relationship between the civilian and military spheres in a broad historical perspective, and 9) the overall conclusions regarding the process of state formation in Israel and whether it has been completed. We summarize these issues, including our own approach, in the table presented at the end of this chapter (Table 1.1).

THE THEORETICAL PERSPECTIVE

Generally speaking, the theoretical perspectives of the three approaches can be described as follows. The Traditional Approach has adopted a formal–structural–institutional standpoint that views the relationship between Israel's civil and military spheres as a relationship between two established subsystems that perform their expected formal roles in a fundamentally democratic fashion. The main perspective of the Critical Approach is also formal–institutional, but some writers who belong to this school have given attention to certain informal aspects that they thought characterized the relations between the two subsystems. Finally, the main emphasis of the New Critical Approach is on cultural aspects of the relationships between the two spheres: that is, on highly informal exchanges.

In our view, the main contributions of the Critical Approach and the New Critical Approach are that they have gradually moved away from the emphasis of the Traditional Approach on formal–structural–institutional aspects of the Israeli case, calling attention to its highly significant informal aspects. Indeed, while the Critical Approach has been interested in highlighting the informal political and social relationships between actors within the civilian and military spheres, the New Critical Approach has stressed the cultural dimensions of this interface as well as the disagreements and debates concerning values, ideologies, and positions regarding the solution of the conflicts in which Israel is involved.

We agree that to fully understand the power and roles of the security sector in Israel, the deeper and continuous connections between serving and retired IDF officers and officials of the various agencies in the security sector, on the one hand, and actors operating in the civilian sector, on the other hand, are more meaningful than the formal aspects of their relationship. However, we contend that the informal exchanges, which concern various patterns of public policymaking and behavior, are by no means random and haphazard but are routinized and have assumed a continuous nature. What is still lacking, however, is a more systematic inquiry of these factors in the Israeli case. As we suggest below, the vast literature on "policy networks" can be employed to elucidate and conceptualize the relationships between these closely linked individuals and groups.

The existing literature on the Israeli case does include certain allusions to the existence of such networks. While some authors have spoken of a partnership between Israel's distinguishable civil and military subsystems or of a connection between its military and political elites,[31] others have identified something resembling a military-industrial complex in this state.[32] Nevertheless, no attempt has been made to broaden this characterization to deal with the complex informal networks that emerged among various actors operating within Israel's security sector, on the one hand, and the political, social, economic, and cultural spheres on the other, which substantially influence policymaking and major policies in this state.

THE THEORETICAL MODELS FOR THE
ANALYSIS OF THE ISRAELI CASE

Despite certain disagreements, the Traditional Approach and the Critical Approach were influenced by existing analytical models of civil–military relations that were developed in, and applied to, the established Western democracies. Since theorists of civil–military relations, too, regarded Israel as an example for Western modes of such relations, the adoption of this perspective was understandable.[33]

However, the New Critical Approach, which was informed by more critical assessments of the process of state formation, rejected the paradigm of civil–military relations, which was "based on the desire to protect democracy and to sustain the stability of regimes" and "neglected the relation between external conflicts . . . and domestic social and political arrangements."[34] Instead, these authors emphasized Israel's incomplete process of state formation, which, in their view, precluded a discussion of its separate civilian and military realms. It is interesting to note, however, that while some writers who adhere to the New Critical Approach did compare Israel to Western democracies in periods of severe domestic crisis (e.g., France during the Algerian War),[35] they did not make any attempt to compare Israel to non-Western democratic and democratizing states.[36]

Our own view is that the use of Western models of civil–military relations to analyze the Israeli case, which was problematic from the outset, became particularly unhelpful after 1967. One reason for this is Israel's undefined boundaries as a result of that war, which impinged on the relationship between its civil and military realms, among others, and the process of state formation as a whole. Another is the considerable expansion of Israel's "Security Network"—the informal and hybrid policy network in the realm of the state's national security—and its significant impact over the entire Israeli scene (see below). We would like to emphasize here that not only military officers are active participants in this network. In addition, civilians who are, or were, employed in various agencies of the security sector are very active members of this network.

It can thus be concluded that the Critical Approach and the New Critical Approach, despite their attempts to present an alternative reading of the Israeli case, did not pay enough attention to the wider aspects and implications of the activities of this Security Network.

Our own suggestion in this matter is twofold. First, we propose that thinking in terms of "policy networks" would result in a much better understanding of the informal aspects of the various roles of Israel's security sector in this country's politics, society, economy, and culture. More specifically, we call for the systematic examination of the various impacts of Israel's Security Network on this state's behavior, and especially with regard to the perceived existential threat to its security; its enduring conflict with its Arab neighbors; its relations with, and actions in, the occupied territories under its control; the uncertainty concerning its economy; and its public discourse.

We also propose that the scope of comparison be significantly broadened to include other "new states" that have not completed their process of state formation as well as other states that perceive themselves to be under existential threat and/or are engaged in protracted conflicts with their neighbors.

CHARACTERIZATION OF THE ISRAELI CASE

As mentioned, the Traditional Approach has characterized Israel as a "nation-in-arms," or, in the words of one author, as a "civilianized military in a partially militarized society."[37] The Critical Approach, while also using the notion of a "nation-in-arms," spoke of a "partnership" between some members of the security and civilian sectors and claimed that in the earlier decades after Israel's establishment, the pattern of civil–military relations in the state was characterized by "apparat control" by Ben-Gurion's Mapai party over the security sector.[38] Finally, the New Critical Approach questioned the traditional and quite simplistic concept of Israel as a "nation-in-arms" and portrayed it as a "garrison state" or as a "praetorian state" that is imbued with a "militaristic" spirit. As we have stated, few writers regarded Israel as being dominated by a "military-industrial complex."

It appears, then, that the Critical Approach and the New Critical Approach represent far less idealistic images of Israel than the Traditional Approach. However, their conceptualization of the Israeli case, too, is problematic. The Critical Approach, consistent with its emphasis on the treatment of both the political and military spheres as essentially hetero-geneous, draws attention to the informal linkages between the military and the political parties, especially Mapai, which was the dominant party in Israel until 1977. However, the notion of "apparat control" with regard to the earlier decades of Israel's independence is questionable in view of the heightened role of the security sector in that period as well, though it could be argued that the latter's dominant position in later decades—probably with the exception of Ariel Sharon's five years of premiership (2001–2005) during which he himself, to a great extent because of his personal military background and connections to the security network, attained almost full control of the military and government—was related to the *absence* of one hegemonic party that controlled all aspects of life in Israel. The New Critical Approach, for its part, seems to have replaced one blurred concept (nation-in-arms) with another (militarism).

Therefore, we suggest that there is a need for a new approach that would emphasize the dynamic processes occurring in Israeli politics, society, economy, and culture. This observation also applies to the re-lationship between security officials and actors operating within the above-mentioned spheres. Again, we suggest that the most beneficial way of analyzing the Israeli case is by thinking in terms of the existence of a highly variegated and changing security network whose members are very deeply involved in almost all aspects of public life in Israel.

THE STRUCTURE OF THE TWO SECTORS AND THEIR RELATIONSHIPS

The Traditional Approach posits that there are homogeneous, autono-mous, and separate civilian and security sectors in Israel and that ba-sically the boundaries between them have been, and continue to be, fragmented. The view of the Critical Approach is that while there are indeed two separate sectors, each is heterogeneous, a factor that allows for different types of boundaries and interdependence. Finally, the New Critical Approach maintains that the question of structure and relation-ship is virtually meaningless because a civilian sector as such virtually does not exist in Israel or lacks substantial coherence and power.

The valuable analytical insights that the Critical Approach and the New Critical Approach have provided are their criticism of the widely

accepted traditional depictions of the structural homogeneity and hierarchical relationship between the civilian and military sectors in Israel.
In fact, the two approaches regard these spheres as made up of various
actors that pursue quite different types of interactions. From a theoretical perspective, this represents a break from traditional strict theories
of civil–military relations concerning such structures and interactions
which, according to members of both approaches, are not applicable to
the Israeli case.

Our approach is to view these sectors as consisting of many actors
that intermingle very closely and form a highly informal policy network—the Security Network. This analytical and theoretical approach
takes into consideration the increased penetration of active and retired
personnel of the security sector into most of the civilian sphere, which
it seems has no parallel in effective democratic states, and which, moreover, is not balanced by the latter's control of the state's security sector.
The result of this process is that in Israel there is very little civilian influence over the military, as stipulated by Janowitz's sociological approach,
but, rather, the other way around: military values penetrate and influence most civilian spheres. It is also clear that Huntington's political
approach, which prescribed a professional army separated from society
by clearly defined borders that are supervised by civilian institutions,
cannot be applied to Israel due to the weakness of its political society.[39]

In sum, Western "ideal-types" of civil–military relations are inapplicable to Israel since they presuppose a predominant civilian sector.
What is needed, hence, is a more down-to-earth approach that would
start from the premise that the civilian sector in Israel is weak compared
to its security counterpart and that explains the causes for this situation,
its various manifestations, and the ways in which it could be reversed.

THE POWER OF THE CIVILIAN SECTOR

As noted, there is disagreement between the three approaches concerning this aspect, also. The proponents of the Traditional Approach argue
that the political and social power of the civilian sector in Israel sub-
stantively supersedes that of the security sector. However, the Critical
Approach contends that the power of the civilian sector has been on
the decline, especially since 1967. Analysts adhering to the New Critical

Approach suggest that the civilian sector in Israel lacks much power compared to the security sector; some question its actual existence.

Basically we agree with the view expressed by the Critical Approach that clear processes have occurred whereby the pure civilian sector in Israel has been relatively weakened through the years, especially since 1967. This can be ascribed to the rising power of the security sector in Israel, to its success in evading continuous attempts to control it, as well as to the growing penetration of security officials into many civilian spheres.

At the same time, and unlike some adherents to the New Critical Approach, we suggest that it is impossible to discard the total existence of the civilian sphere in Israel. While one should wonder about the existence of truly civilian values among the state's intertwined political and military elites, as well as among the general public, at least some civilian values surely exist and have some impact on Israeli politics, though this is sometimes difficult to articulate and detect. As a proof, one could mention the views expressed by peace movements, by civil rights organizations, by anticorruption movements, by environmental organizations, and even by individual "whistle-blowers" such as Mordechai Vanunu, who stood up against the Israeli nuclear program and weapons. Hence, it can be argued that while the civilian sphere in Israel is generally and relatively weak—part of this weakness should be attributed to its considerable fragmentation, manifested in the decline of political parties, the failings of the Knesset and to an extent also of the Israeli courts—and has to share power with the security sector especially in matters concerning national security, sometimes it is capable of asserting itself and influencing public policy.

CIVILIAN CONTROL OF THE MILITARY IN ISRAEL

The Traditional Approach suggests that civilian control of the military in Israel is firm. Not only are the state's civilian institutions paramount, but the IDF is also "civilianized" due to the important role played by its reserves. The Critical Approach maintains, by contrast, that the scope and level of civilian control, which has been exercised through whichever was the dominant political party, is insufficient, especially during perceived security emergencies. The New Critical Approach, which underscores the role of social factors in civilian control of the military, argues that this is difficult, if not impossible, due to the inherent weakness of Israel's civilian sector.

The valuable contributions of the Critical Approach and the New Critical Approach are, again, their reconsideration of the relationship between Israel's civilian and military realms, especially in view of the situation since 1967. Rather than a firm control, their works suggest a very problematic civilian control of the military; these approaches believe that, in fact, the security sector wields considerable influence over the civilian spheres.

We argue that in view of the accumulated power of the Security Network, the imagined continuous existential threats (which, to a large extent, are propagated by the security sector), and the incomplete process of state formation in Israel, civilian control of the military and the other security agencies is indeed weak and problematic. It seems, moreover, that attempts to impose civilian control without solving Israel's cardinal problems are ineffective, and could even backfire, as they do in the United States—where the "postmodern army" envisaged by some authors[40] became largely overshadowed following the events of September 11, 2001.

THE INTERESTS AND POWERS OF
THE SECURITY SECTOR IN ISRAEL

There are two aspects to this issue: the interests of the security sector and its relative power and influence. Concerning the interests of Israel's security sector, the first approach does not identify any particular interests of that sector, especially the IDF, and argues that its goals have been determined by the predominant Civilian Sector. The third approach, for its part, emphasizes the influence of class, ethnic, and educational relations in Israeli society on shaping the military's interests.[41] Only the second approach tries to deal to some extent with the corporate interests of the security sector.

We concur that these interests, especially those of the IDF, are essentially similar to those of military institutions elsewhere.[42] However, and due to structural factors, especially the chronic weakness of the civilian sector in Israel, these interests have gradually come to be shaped by a complex game between the various components of the country's more extensive Security Network.

The positions of the three approaches concerning the relative powers and influences of the two sectors are also very different. The Traditional Approach suggests that the power of the security sector is far from substantial and claims that it gains its strength from the reserve system and from social contacts between its own officials and the civilian policymakers. The Critical Approach argues, by contrast, that the power of the security sector has been increasing since 1967, especially due to the increase in size and budgets of the IDF and the penetration of senior army officers into politics. The New Critical Approach maintains that because of the weakness of the civilian sector, the military is hegemonic in many public spheres.

Though they do not elaborate on this phenomenon, the important contributions of the Critical Approach and the New Critical Approach in this connection are their emphases on the considerable strengthening of the security sector since 1967, and especially on the growing penetration of senior security officials into Israel's political society. Our own empirical findings reaffirm the occurrence of this trend.[43]

The Critical Approach is attentive to the corporate interests of the military, and has differentiated between the regular army, which has long-standing and long-range interests and considerations; the reservists; and the conscripts. The latter two categories are effectively under the regular army's control and influence—the IDF can place them where it desires. Thus, for example, to prevent severe public criticisms and objections, the IDF did not station reserves in Israel's self-proclaimed Security Zone in South Lebanon in the period 1985–2000. The New Critical Approach, for its part, is right when emphasizing the hegemonic power of the security sector in Israel, yet it raises the question of whether this supremacy represents a continuous phenomenon or one that could be accelerated by dramatic events such as the wars of 1967, 1973, and 1982. Indeed, our own findings show that during and after each of these conflicts, both the number of retired security officials in the Israeli cabinet and the functions they assumed had shown a marked increase.[44]

We suggest that on most occasions the security sector, especially the IDF, gets its way through the Security Network and leads in policymaking in matters of national security especially during periods of crisis, which constitute the usual situation in Israel. Of course, this raises the question whether, and to what extent, it is in the military's interest to initiate and perpetuate such crises in order to further empower itself or maintain its power. We will return to this issue.

THE RELATIONSHIPS BETWEEN THE TWO SPHERES IN A HISTORICAL PERSPECTIVE

As could have been expected, the three approaches offer differing perspectives on the historical pattern of the relationship between Israel's civilian and military spheres. The Traditional Approach argues that the civilian sector has been strengthened over time and that its penetration into and control of the security sphere has increased. Thus the proponents of this approach maintain that over the years the military has withdrawn from civilian areas where it has been active and that civilian control of its activities has intensified, especially through the judicial system and the media. The Critical Approach maintains that the process was affected by the unending and repetitive crises facing Israel, especially since 1967. This approach presents evidence showing that while in the early decades after its establishment Israel witnessed a substantial penetration of party politics into the military, this process was later reversed and it is the army that has become increasingly involved in politics. The third approach stresses that militarism is intrinsic to Zionism and that the ongoing nature of militarism in Israel "tends to serve as one of the *organizational principles* of the society" (emphasis in text)[45] or, alternatively, traces a process whereby militarization has led to the imposition of civilian control of the military.[46]

We suggest that the problem with the attitude of the Critical Approach concerning this issue is its emphasis on crises while it avoids the structural problem that underpins them. In other words, we think that the crises are the symptoms of the disease rather than its causes. In some of its assertions, the New Critical Approach is insensitive to changes and transformations that have occurred in this sphere, as evinced by the diametrically opposing outcomes that it ascribes to Israel's militarism.

Unlike these approaches, we maintain that what has actually happened were growing mutual suspicions and competition over resources and policymaking between civilian and security actors, which reached their pinnacle in 1967, with the ascendance of the Security Network to a hegemonic position in the country ever since.[47]

THE PROCESS OF STATE FORMATION IN ISRAEL

Although the Traditional Approach attributes some significance to the impact of the 1967 War on the development of the Israeli State, mainly because of the occupation of additional territories and the expansion of Israel's de facto borders, it does suggest that basically the process of state formation has been completed and that consequently one can speak of two distinct stable spheres in this state: the civilian and the military. Therefore, the adherents to this approach can define the relative positions of each of the two sectors and their interactions. Contrarily, the Critical Approach and the New Critical Approach—explicitly and implicitly—assert that Israel's state-formation process is still under way. Yet, all three approaches more or less assume that there have been no major changes in the relations between the various sectors in Israel society and politics. This means that these approaches demonstrate a rather static conception concerning the dual processes of state formation and social integration in Israel since its establishment in the late 1940s.

Still, the implicit or explicit acceptance by the second and third approaches of the incompleteness of the process of state formation in Israel is important because it makes this state comparable to other new states in the Third World that are engaged in establishing various systems of governance, and not only to established states in the West. As mentioned earlier, this has implications for the application of Western theories and models of civil–military relations to the Israeli case.

As far as the historical perspective is concerned, we suggest that a static conception and analysis is inappropriate for the study of the Israeli case and for other cases, for that matter. This is because the security sector, and its relationship with the relevant civilian spheres, changes over time. Thus the dramatic change in the role of the security sector in the United States after the events of September 11, 2001, is, again, a case in point. Accordingly, a more penetrating discussion of the Israeli dynamic and changing case should focus on the following questions: first, in what ways is the process of state formation in Israel incomplete; second, what are the implications of this incompleteness for the various sectors under consideration here; third, what has been the impact of the chaotic transformation that Israeli society and politics have been experiencing in recent years, most notably since the first Intifada, on the composition, policymaking, and actual functioning of the Security Network and its relations with the civilian sector; fourth, what are the informal cultural, political, economic, and discursive exchanges between the Security Network concerning major as well as less significant public policies; fifth, what kinds of corporate interests has the security component of Israel's Security Network (i.e., actors in the security sector) been pursuing, and how do these interests enmesh, or overlap, with those of other actors; and sixth, when and to what extent can the civil sector control the security components of the Security Network? Essentially, the issue here is whether the relationship between security and civilian actors comprising the Security Network is one of power sharing or control, and its corollary, who leads Israel in periods of crisis. Two other questions remain: seventh, what are the means through which the amalgamation of the Security Network occurs; and, finally, what is the degree of mutual acceptance, cooperation, and even commitment and loyalty among the various components of the Security Network?

We will address these questions, but at this point we would like to emphasize that we regard the process as a chaotic transformation of many factors, aspects, and characteristics of the Israeli state. As mentioned above, we presume that this is a continuous process, but one that is not necessarily linear. For example, the year 1967 represented a step backward in the process.

As far as the theoretical issue is concerned, we argue that the chaotic process of state formation in Israel, which, among other things, impinged on its democratic character, has produced only nominal separation between its national-security realm and its cultural, political, social, and economic spheres. In our view, what has emerged in this case is, in effect, a tightly knit policy network characterized by intimate ties between acting or retired security officials—including officers who serve in the army's reserves, politicians on the national and local levels, civilian bureaucrats, private entrepreneurs, and journalists. As noted, we refer to this network as a Security Network, and we have emphasized its common features.

From the empirical viewpoint we suggest that after more than five and a half decades of independence, this complex and informal Security Network has acquired a predominant status in major areas of public life and public policy in Israel. Although the security sector is, of course, an actor with its own corporate interests, various elements within it have gradually become intertwined with influential actors in Israel's civilian spheres. As we demonstrate elsewhere,[48] Israel's Security Network, which had existed in an embryonic form since 1948, has been strongly influenced—and to a large extent transformed—by the 1967, 1973, and 1982 wars and by later events such as the two Palestinian Intifadas of 1987 and 2000.

A New Approach to the Israeli Case

Summing the discussion above, it is adequate to specify here some of our general views concerning the study of the position, power, and role in policymaking of Israel's Security Network.

First, we would like to elaborate and clarify what we mean by the term *Security Network* and what differentiates it from a political–military partnership,[49] or, alternatively, from the military's role expansion and role contraction,[50] terms used by proponents of other approaches. Whereas these terms imply the existence of at least two clearly delineated and stable subsystems that are more or less equal in strength and that interact voluntarily, we regard the Security Network as an informal hybrid arrangement involving a range of different actors, including some representing nongovernmental institutions and firms that are inherently involved in public policymaking and implementation.

Our concept of Israel's Security Network thus connotes a complex and fluid type of relationship between security and civilian actors, but one that is ultimately capable of shaping the policymaking process as well as determining concrete policies. The boundaries between these actors are utterly blurred; significant overlapping areas are created; and the civilian actors are neither equal in their power to the security actors nor able to exercise effective control of them or to reduce significantly their impact on policymaking. In addition, movement between the defense establishment and each of the civilian spheres remains frequent, if not natural. Probably most importantly, actors from both types of realms who are members of the network share values, interests, goals, discipline, and behavioral patterns.

Hence, and in contrast to the ideas of fragmented boundaries between autonomous security and civil sectors, a partnership between them, or a weak or even nonexistent civil realm, in fact, Israel's Security Network works against the systemic differentiation and professionalism of the military and the other security agencies as well as against efficiency in them and in the relevant civilian spheres. Instead, there has been a high level of mutual penetration and interdependency between the two sectors. The persistence of this dynamic state of affairs renders the notion of the military's role expansion or role contraction inapplicable; the same pertains to the notion of a crisis in civil–military relations in Israel.[51]

In a much wider sense, but still somewhat resembling the concept of the military-industrial complex, the Security Network connotes a highly potent fusion of security and civilian interests that comes at the expense of the interests and needs of the Israeli public. As we have argued above, our approach is different from previous conceptualizations of the Israeli case in that it underscores the relationship between actors within the state's security sector and a large number of civilian actors, including many senior reservists, the unremitting flow of security personnel into utterly civilian spheres, and the ways all these affect policymaking and concrete policies.

In the Israeli case, the continued existence of the Security Network, especially since 1967, has prevented the emergence of more differentiated civilian and military spheres, thus impeding the completion of the process of state formation and the emergence of a truly democratic regime. Indeed, unlike the notion of partnership, which has a positive connotation, our notion of a Security Network reflects a critical appraisal of the current situation in Israel. Finally, the focus on a Security Network reflects our emphasis on informal aspects of the relationship between security and civilian actors.

As we suggest elsewhere,[52] Israel's Security Network stems not from the militaristic nature of Zionism, as claimed by the New Critical Approach, but rather from the particular power structure established by the state's founding fathers and their successors, who paradoxically sought to use the security sector, and especially the IDF, to promote the processes of state formation and social integration. Yet, in their quest to guarantee the corporate interests of their institutions, actors from within the security sector later cast a shadow on the civilian leaders, and as an informal collective entity, became the single most influential political actors in Israel. The boundaries between the state's security and civilian spheres, which were deliberately kept porous, allowed these security officials to penetrate utterly civilian realms and forge alliances with influential actors within them, thus enhancing the mutual links between these spheres.

As argued above, our own reconceptualization of the highly complex relationship between actors within Israel's security sector, on the one hand, and influential actors within the state's cultural, political, social, and economic spheres, on the other hand, is aimed at explaining the current situation, filling the gaps in and between previous analyses, and laying the basis for a new theoretical approach to this issue in Israel and in similar cases, not necessarily in the West.

Conclusion

In this essay we have discussed the major existing approaches to the study of the relationship between Israel's civilian and security sectors and presented the main features of our own approach, which focuses on what we have termed the Security Network. By critically dealing with these approaches to the relationship between these realms and by being attentive to both its formal and informal aspects, we have offered some clues as to how the considerable "gaps" in the study of this topic—in Israel and perhaps elsewhere—may be addressed.

In the remainder of this essay, we will briefly discuss some of the questions related to Israel's Security Network that warrant further investigation: first, who are the members of the network and how do they organize to advance their shared interests and goals; second, what are the values and perceptions shared by network members and how do these become accepted by Israeli society at large; and finally, what are the sources of the network's power, the resources that it employs to attain its goals, and the factors that facilitate its continued existence?

The first question requires more in-depth studies of Israel's security elite, the informal interactions between its members and actors from the country's civilian spheres, and an inquiry into those areas where its activities have become institutionalized. Thus, a recent study has traced the informal networks between Middle East specialists including members of the security sector and scholars who teach and do research at Israel's leading universities, and discusses their cumulative impact on how Israelis have come to view their Arab neighbors.[53] By identifying additional spheres where such interactions take place, and by assessing their long-standing impact on Israeli politics, society, economy, and culture, the understanding of this phenomenon would be enhanced. At the same time, an exploration of the institutional aspects of the network would promote our understanding of its impact and persistence. Elsewhere we mention the existence and activities of organizations such as *Tzevet,* the IDF Veterans Association, which serves as a sort of lobby or pressure group that promotes the collective interests of former security officials.[54] This and other similar groups warrant additional attention.

The second area that needs to be addressed concerns the values and perceptions that are shared by members of Israel's Security Network and how they have shaped the worldview of other Israelis. In our view, the discussion of these issues could be significantly enhanced by referring to recent theoretical advances in the fields of political science and international relations. These include works that suggest that the definition of security ought to be expanded to include economic, environmental, and cultural threats, and that security itself should be treated not as an *objective* condition but, rather, as the outcome of a specific social process whereby certain issues are "securitized."[55] A second pertinent area is the expanding discussion of "communities of practice," and particularly the notion of "epistemic communities" that are networks of experts who share a common understanding of the scientific and political nature of particular problems (in our case, security-related issues) and whose influence on policymakers, especially under real or imagined conditions of uncertainty—including the existence of an imagined existential threat—stems from the fact that they are considered to be authorities in their areas of specialization.[56] It would be interesting to ask, for instance, how both critical *and* mundane issues and areas in Israel have become "securitized," and whether its Security Network has, in fact, become a type of epistemic community. A related question, which is more prescriptive in nature, is how to create *civilian* epistemic communities that would serve

Table 1.1. Approaches to the Study of Civil–Military Relations in Israel

Area/Approach	Traditional	Critical	New Critical	Security Network
Theoretical Emphasis	Institutional-formal	Institutional-formal but attention to some informal aspects	Cultural and informal	Informal exchanges within a highly variegated Security Network
Paradigm for Analysis of Israeli Case	Civil-Military Relations	Civil-Military Relations (but more critical)	State-Building (Civil-Military Relations theories are ethno-centrist)	Policy Networks
Conceptualization of Relationship	Nation-in-arms; "civilian-ized military in a partially militarized society"	Partnership; Nation-in-arms but also Apparat Control in the earlier decades	Garrison State or Praetorian State; militarism; Military-Industrial Complex	A highly variegated Security Network with political, social, economic, and cultural facets
Nature of Relationship between Spheres	Homogeneous separate spheres; fragmented boundaries	Heterogeneous separate spheres; different types of boundaries	Meaningless since civilian sphere is weak or nonexistent	Intermingling between actors from both spheres; increased penetration of retired security into civilian realms into civilian realms
Strength of Civilian Sphere in Israel	High, supersedes that of of military sphere	On the decline (especially since 1967)	Civilian sphere weak or even nonexistent in Israel	Generally weak; sharing power with the security sector; sometimes capable of asserting itself
Strength of Military Sphere in Isreael	Intermediate; emphasis on reserves and social relations between civilian and military spheres	Increasing since 1967; emphasis on regular army and penetration of senior army officers into politics	Military sphere hegemonic and exclusive	Security sector (especially IDF) leads in crises and gets its way through the Security Network
Civilian Control of Military	Extensive	Incomplete, especially during emergencies	Non-existent	Inherently problematic
Relationship between Spheres in Historical Perspective	Civilian sphere strengthened and its penetration into military sphere increased	Riddled with crises, especially since 1967; increased penetration of army into civilian sphere	Inherently problematic; militarism intrinsic to Zionism; continuous phenomenon	Mutual suspicion and competition over resources and policy-increase in defense establishment's power since 1967
State Formation in Israel	Complete	Incomplete	In progress	Chaotic transformation

as a counterweight to Israel's Security Network and how "securitized" issues in this country could be "de-securitized."[57]

Finally, there are the sources of the network's power and the resources available to its members. Here one could mention external factors such as the generous American military aid to Israel, which enhances the domestic stance of its security sector, and the Arab–Israeli conflict, which "justifies" its continued preeminence. A second set of factors, which can be termed internal/external, are Israel's blurred boundaries with its neighbors, the Arab territories that have been, or still are, under Israeli occupation (these are administered by the security sector), and the massive fortifications built by Israel in and around these areas, including the current security barrier. The third set of factors, which are domestic in nature, includes the continued state of emergency in Israel and the various exemptions granted to the security sector in areas such as planning, safety, and taxes, which, too, serve to legitimize its role in the country. Current debates on the state of exception in democratic regimes[58] can help elucidate these aspects of the Israeli case, which, as with the other factors mentioned, have not been adequately addressed.

Acknowledgments

An earlier draft of this chapter was presented at the meeting of the Workshop on Israeli Security and Society, Neve Ilan, in March 2005. We thank the members of the workshop, and especially Yagil Levy, for their useful comments. We also thank Einat Vaddai for research assistance. Research was made possible by a grant from the Harvey L. Silbert Center for Israel Studies at The Hebrew University of Jerusalem.

Notes

1. Yoram Peri, *Between Battles and Ballots* (Cambridge, 1983); Dan Horowitz and Moshe Lissak, *Trouble in Utopia* (Albany, N.Y., 1989); Rebecca Schiff, "Civil-Military Relations Reconsidered: Israel as an 'Uncivil' State," *Security Studies* 1 (1992): 636–58; Baruch Kimmerling, "Patterns of Militarism in Israel," *European Journal of Sociology* 34 (1993): 196–223; Avner Yaniv (ed.), *National Security and Democracy in Israel* (Boulder, Colo., 1993); Uri Ben-Eliezer, "A Nation-in-Arms: State, Nation, and Militarism in Israel's First Years," *Comparative Studies in Society and History* 37 (1995): 264–85; Yehuda Ben-Meir, *Civil-Military Relations in Israel* (New York, 1995); Yoram Peri, "The

Radical Social Scientists and Israeli Militarism," *Israel Studies* 1 (1996): 230–66; Daniel Maman and Moshe Lissak, "Military-Civilian Elite Networks in Israel: A Case Study in Boundary Structure," in Benjamin Frankel (ed.), *A Restless Mind* (London, 1996), 49–79; Eva Etzioni-Halevi, "Civil-Military Relations and Democracy: The Case of the Military-Political Elites' Connection in Israel," *Armed Forces and Society* 22 (1996): 401–417; Yagil Levy, "How Militarization Drives Political Control of the Military: The Case of Israel," *Political Power and Social Theory* 11 (1997): 103–133; Uri Ben-Eliezer, *The Making of Israeli Militarism* (Bloomington, Ind., 1998); Martin Van Creveld, *The Sword and the Olive* (New York, 1998); Alan Dowty, *The Jewish State* (Berkeley, Calif., 1998); Edna Lomsky-Feder and Eyal Ben-Ari (eds.), *The Military and Militarism in Israeli Society* (Albany, N.Y., 1999); Uri Ben-Eliezer, "Do the Generals Rule Israel?" in Hanna Herzog (ed.), *A Society in the Mirror* (Tel-Aviv, 2000) [Hebrew]; Eyal Ben-Ari, Zeev Rosenhek, and Daniel Maman, "Military, State and Society in Israel: An Introductory Essay," in Daniel Maman, Eyal Ben-Ari, and Zeev Rosenhek (eds.), *The Military, State and Society in Israel* (New Brunswick, N.J., 2001), 1–39; Yoram Peri, "Civil-Military Relations in Israel in Crisis," in Maman, Ben-Ari, and Rosenhek, *The Military, State and Society,* 107–136; Uri Ben-Eliezer, "From Military Role Expansion to Difficulties in Peace-Making: Israel Defense Forces 50 Years On," in Maman, Ben-Ari, and Rosenhek, *The Military, State and Society,* 137–72; Yoram Peri, *The Israeli Military and Israel's Palestinian Policy* (Washington, D.C., 2002); Majid Al-Haj and Uri Ben-Eliezer (eds.), *In the Name of Security* (Haifa, 2003) [Hebrew]; Yoram Peri, "The Democratic Putsch of 1999," in Al-Haj and Ben-Eliezer, *In the Name of Security,* 125–43; Zeev Rosenhek, Daniel Maman, and Eyal Ben-Ari, "The Study of War and the Military in Israel," *International Journal of Middle East Studies* 35 (2003): 461–84; Ofer Shelah, *The Israeli Army: A Radical Proposal* (Or Yehuda, 2003) [Hebrew]; Yagil Levy, *The Other Army of Israel* (Tel-Aviv, 2003) [Hebrew]; Uri Ben-Eliezer, "Post-Modern Armies and the Question of Peace and War: The Israeli Defense Forces in the 'New Times'," *International Journal of Middle East Studies* 36 (2004): 49–70.

2. By security sector we mean not only the armed forces (or the military) but also other law-enforcement agencies such as the police and paramilitary forces, the border guards and coast guard, the intelligence and internal security services, and the military industries. In this paper, however, we will mainly relate to the armed forces, which are the most significant security service in terms of their size, roles, and close association with the process of state formation.

3. John Peterson, *Policy Networks* (Vienna, 2003), 1; David Marsh and Martin Smith, "Understanding Policy Networks: Towards a Dialectical Approach," *Political Studies* 48 (2000): 6. See also Bernd Marin and Renate Mayntz, "Studying Policy Networks," in Bernd Marin and Renate Mayntz (eds.), *Policy Networks* (Frankfurt, 1991); David Marsh and Rod Rhodes (eds.), *Policy Networks in British Government* (Oxford, 1992); David Marsh and Gerry Stoker, "Conclusions," in David Marsh and Gerry Stoker (eds.), *Theory and Methods in Political Science* (London, 1995), 292–94.

4. For a useful albeit not exhaustive discussion of some of these approaches, see Ben-Ari et al., "Military, State and Society in Israel." For trends in research, see Rosenhek, Maman, and Ben-Ari, "The Study of War." See also Peri, "Radical Social Scientists."

5. Morris Janowitz, *The Military in the Political Development of New Nations* (Chicago, 1964).

6. Robin Luckham, "A Comparative Typology of Civil-Military Relations," *Government and Opposition* 6 (1971): 5–35.

7. Dan Horowitz, "The Israel Defense Forces: A Civilianized Military in a Partially Militarized Society," in Roman Kolkowicz and Andrzej Korbonski (eds.), *Soldiers, Peasants, and Bureaucrats* (London, 1982), 77–106; Shmuel Noah Eisenstadt, *Israeli Society* (London, 1967); Shmuel Noah Eisenstadt, *The Transformation of Israeli Society* (Boulder, Colo., 1985); Horowitz and Lissak, *Trouble in Utopia*.

8. This agrees with Luckham's definition of the "nation-in-arms." Luckham, "Comparative Typology," 24.

9. Horowitz, "The Israel Defense Forces," 78–79.

10. Maman and Lissak, "Military-Civilian Elite Networks in Israel."

11. Horowitz quoted in Peri, *Between Battles and Ballots*, 8.

12. By this term we mean the cumulative product of three interrelated and often-overlapping subprocesses: 1) *state-building,* which consists of measures that produce "territorial consolidation, centralization, differentiation of the instruments of government, and monopolization of the means of coercion"; 2) *statecraft*—or state-construction—defined as the "processes or mechanisms whereby a state enhances its power and authority" using its formal agencies but also an array of informal, including cultural, means; and 3) *national integration,* which involves centrally based efforts to inculcate the state's entire populace with a common identity. The first quotation is from Charles Tilly, "Reflections on the History of European State-Making," in Charles Tilly (ed.), *The Formation of National States in Western Europe* (Princeton, N.J., 1975), 42. See also Timothy Mitchell, "The Limits of the State: Beyond Statist Approaches and Their Critics," *American Political Science Review* 85 (March 1991): 77–96; George Steinmetz (ed.), *State/Culture* (Ithaca, N.Y., 1999). The second remark is from Eric Davis, "Theorizing Statecraft and Social Change in Oil-Producing Countries," in Eric Davis and Nicholas Gavrielides (eds.), *Statecraft in the Middle East* (Miami, 1991), 12. See also Benedict Anderson, *Imagined Communities,* 2nd ed. (New York, 1991); Eric Hobsbawm, *Nations and Nationalism since 1780* (Cambridge, 1990); Ernest Gellner, *Nations and Nationalism* (Oxford, 1983); Anthony Smith, *The Ethnic Origins of Nations* (Oxford, 1986).

13. Amos Perlmutter, *Military and Politics in Israel* (New York, 1969); Horowitz and Lissak, *Trouble in Utopia*; Ben-Meir, *Civil-Military Relations;* Moshe Lissak, "Uniqueness and Normalization in Military-Government Relations in Israel," in Maman, Ben-Ari, and Rosenhek, *The Military, State and Society,* 395–422.

14. Peri, *Between Battles and Ballots,* 15.

15. Ibid., 7–11.

16. Peri, *The Israeli Military,* 13.

17. Peri, *Between Battles and Ballots;* Peri, *The Israeli Military,* 12; Roger Owen, *State, Power, and Politics in the Making of the Modern Middle East,* 2nd ed. (London, 2000), 216.

18. Peri, *Between Battles and Ballots,* 8–9.

19. Avraham Sela, "Civic vs. the Military: The Case of Israel's Security Zone in South Lebanon (1997–2000)," paper presented to the Annual Conference of the Association for Israel Studies, Jerusalem, June 2004.

20. See the contribution of Kobi Michael to this issue.

21. Owen, *State, Power, and Politics,* 215.

22. Peri, *Between Battles and Ballots,* 9; Peri, "Democratic Putsch."

23. Rebecca Schiff, "Civil-Military Relations Reconsidered: A Theory of Concordance," *Armed Forces and Society* 22 (Fall 1995): 8; Uri Ben-Eliezer, "Is a Military Coup Possible in Israel? Israel and French-Algeria in Comparative Historical-Sociological Perspective," *Theory and Society* 27 (1998): 311–49.

24. Kimmerling, "Patterns of Militarism in Israel," 197–98; for criticism, see Gabriel Sheffer, "Has Israel Really Been a Garrison Democracy?" *Israel Affairs* 3 (1996): 13–38.

25. Peri, *Between Battles and Ballots,* 286.

26. Ben-Eliezer, "From Military Role Expansion," 138; Schiff, "Civil-Military Relations"; Schiff, "Civil-Military Relations Reconsidered," 9.

27. Kimmerling, "Patterns of Militarism in Israel"; Ben-Eliezer, "A Nation-in-Arms"; Ben-Eliezer, "From Military Role Expansion."

28. Kimmerling, "Patterns of Militarism in Israel"; Ben-Eliezer, "A Nation-in-Arms"; Ben-Eliezer, "From Military Role Expansion."

29. Levy, "How Militarization Drives Political Control of the Military," 104–106.

30. Schiff, "Civil-Military Relations Reconsidered," 17–19.

31. Etzioni-Halevi, "Civil-Military Relations and Democracy."

32. Alex Mintz, "The Military-Industrial Complex: American Concepts and Israeli Realities," *Journal of Conflict Resolution* 29 (1985): 623–39; Yoram Peri and Amnon Neubach, *The Military-Industrial Complex in Israel* (Tel-Aviv, 1985).

33. See, e.g., Luckham, "Comparative Typology," 24, and the sources he cites.

34. Ben-Eliezer, "Is a Military Coup Possible in Israel?" 339–40.

35. Ibid.

36. Peri attributes this failure to these authors' uncritical use of the concept of militarism. See his "The Radical Social Scientists and Israeli Militarism."

37. Horowitz, "The Israel Defense Forces."

38. Peri, *Between Battles and Ballots.*

39. For an overview of these approaches, see David Segal, "Civil-Military Relations in Democratic Societies," in Jurgen Kuhlmann and David Segal (eds.), *Armed Forces at the Dawn of the Third Millennium* (Munich, 1994), 37–48. A book that argues for a professional army in Israel is Shelah, *The Israeli Army.*

40. Charles Moskos, "Towards a Postmodern Military: The United States as a Paradigm," in Charles Moskos, John Allen Williams, and David Segal (eds.), *The Postmodern Military* (New York, 2000), 14–31.

41. Levy, *The Other Army of Israel,* and his notion of a "materialist militarism."

42. Owen, *State, Power, and Politics,* 199.

43. Oren Barak and Gabriel Sheffer, "Israel's 'Security Network' and Its Impact on Policymaking: An Exploration of a New Approach," *International Journal of Middle East Studies* 38 (2006): 235–61.

44. Barak and Sheffer, "Israel's 'Security Network'."

45. Kimmerling, "Patterns of Militarism in Israel," 199. For an analysis of recent events in Israel from this perspective, see Ben-Eliezer, "Post-Modern Armies."

46. Levy, "How Militarization Drives Political Control of the Military."

47. For details, see Barak and Sheffer, "Israel's 'Security Network'."

48. Ibid.

49. Peri, *The Israeli Military,* 12.

50. Lissak, "Uniqueness and Normalization," 403–405.

51. Yoram Peri, "Civil-Military Relations in Israel in Crisis."

52. Barak and Sheffer, "Israel's 'Security Network'."

53. Gil Eyal, "Dangerous Liaisons between Military Intelligence and Middle Eastern Studies in Israel," *Theory and Society* 31 (2002): 653–93.

54. Barak and Sheffer, "Israel's 'Security Network'."

55. See especially Ole Wæver, "Securitization and Desecuritization," in Ronnie Lipschutz (ed.), *On Security* (New York, 1995), 46–86; Barry Buzan, Ole Wæver, and Japp De Wilde, *Security: A New Framework for Analysis* (Boulder, Colo., 1998); Michael Williams, "Words, Images, Enemies: Securitization and International Politics," *International Studies Quarterly* 47 (2003): 511–31.

56. Peter Haas, *Saving the Mediterranean* (New York, 1990), 55; Peter Haas, "Introduction: Epistemic Communities and International Policy Coordination," in Peter Haas (ed.), *Knowledge, Power and International Policy Coordination* (Columbia, S.C., 1997), 1–35; Emanuel Adler, "The Emergence of Cooperation: National Epistemic Communities and the International Evolution of the Idea of Nuclear Arms Control," in *Knowledge, Power and International Policy Coordination,* 101–145; Emanuel Adler, *Communitarian International Relations* (New York, 2005).

57. See the contribution of Kobi Michael to this issue.

58. Carl Schmitt, *Political Theology,* trans. George Schwab (Cambridge, Mass., 1985); Giorgio Agamben, *State of Exception* (Chicago, 2005).

TWO

Military Knowledge and Weak Civilian Control in the Reality of Low Intensity Conflict—The Israeli Case

KOBI MICHAEL

The reality of wars and violent conflicts brings the military to the front of the stage and empowers its presence in public discourse. It also has influence over public opinion due to its expertise and professional responsibility for exercising military power. Under such circumstances, the challenge of maintaining civilian control over the military increases dramatically.

Civilian control has troubled many scholars since the end of World War II. During that time and the four decades following it, war was mostly characterized by armed conflict between statist entities. Those conflicts can be described as High Intensity Conflicts (HIC) or inter-state conflicts, but since the collapse of the USSR and the end of the Cold War, the nature of warfare has changed dramatically and most violent conflicts have been characterized as ethno-national conflicts. Those can be described as Low Intensity Conflicts (LIC) or intrastate conflicts[1] with major components of terror and guerrilla warfare. This is the kind of conflict that Israel has faced with the Palestinians since 2000. The military's implicit influence over the conflict's management has severely challenged the political echelon in Israel regarding its relations with the military echelon and the efficiency of its substantive civilian control.

The uniqueness of the LIC as a multifaceted conflict[2] forced the military echelon to develop a sophisticated knowledge infrastructure, going far beyond the traditional and declared fields of military professionalism, and positioning the military echelon as an important and critical actor in the conflict theater. This developed knowledge became one of the military establishment's key assets, enhancing its centrality in managing the conflict and leading toward its "functional expansion."

The systematic development of military knowledge turned the military echelon into an "epistemic authority" in the eyes of the public and the political echelon in Israel regarding the conflict's management. In the absence of both similar processes of knowledge development among civilian institutions (which basically are less appreciated by the public and the political echelon) and the lack of a permanent professional staff in the Israeli government, the knowledge gap between the military and the political echelons was broadened. The discourse between the echelons became an "unequal dialogue," but contrary to the inequality claimed by A. Eliot Cohen,[3] which is based on the superiority of the political echelon, the interaction between the echelons in Israel was characterized by asymmetry in favor of the military echelon and by the latter's domination over the "discourse space" between the echelons.[4]

I examine the source of this knowledge and its influence over the interactions between the echelons in the reality of LIC, assessing the necessity of knowledge as a crucial resource for efficient civilian control. I attempt to prove the premise that as long as the political echelon was unable or unwilling to provide clear and distinct directives defining their political goals, the military echelon's "conceptual distress" was increased, pushing it to develop an alternative "conceptual system" and a more sophisticated "knowledge infrastructure." Due to this course of developments, the knowledge gap between the echelons was broadened; the military echelon enhanced its position as an "epistemic authority" and its influence over the "discourse space" nature.

I begin by presenting the "discourse space" concept, utilizing it later as an organizing concept to describe the main argument. I then describe the development process of Israeli military knowledge since 1998, clarifying the meaning of the process as a conceptual revolution in the military's organization. I emphasize the principle of civil control and its implications by describing the main literature about this concept and conclude with a description of the interactions between the echelons as a "discourse space," explaining how the knowledge gap between the military and political echelons weakens the efficiency of civil control.

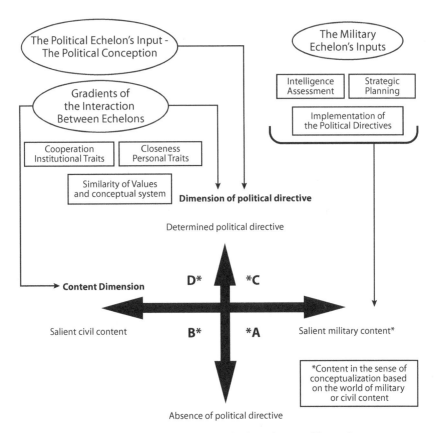

Chart 2.1. The Discourse Model and the impact of independent variables on the dimensions of the discourse space.

The Discourse Space and the
Political–Military Echelons' Interactions

The discourse space is the organizing concept used here to describe the interaction between the political and the military echelons. In introducing this concept,[5] I suggested that its essence is the exchange of information, knowledge, and insights between levels concerning a specific subject. The influence exercised by the echelons is a function of the inputs that each of them contributes to the discourse space.

The nature and character of the discourse can be described as having two dimensions: that of content and that of political directive. These dimensions create a matrix of four main types of discourse spaces (A, B,

C, and D), and are determined by three independent variables: inputs of the political echelon, inputs of the military echelon, and the gradients of interaction between the two. The interaction that takes place between the echelons in the discourse space is, in fact, an intellectual encounter between statesmanship and military strategy and reflects the relative power of each of the echelons and its influence on the examined context.

The military's influence is expressed by the content–conceptualization dimension, while the political echelon's influence is expressed by the political directive dimension. The more the content dimension is characterized as military (in the sense of concepts based on military knowledge), the more the military's influence is increased. On the other hand, the more clear and distinctive the political directive dimension, the more the political echelon's influence is increased.

The discourse space enables each level to gain a better understanding of the limitations of the operative space of the other level, and facilitates the articulation of directives by the political level. In a situation of coherent, consecutive discourse, there is a better prospect that the circles of knowledge of the two levels will be broadened. Such a dialogue also generates a type of shared responsibility[6] of the levels for the success of the process.

The Main Argument

The changes in the nature of warfare and its transformation toward intrastate conflict (which is known as low intensity conflict) have challenged the patterns of interaction between the political and the military echelons, in general, and in Israel, in the protracted reality of such a conflict, in particular. It seems that the political echelon's superiority is maintained at the institutional and formal levels; but on the substantive level, which demands relying on knowledge and systematic staff work, the political echelon's position is weakened and the substantive civilian control loses its validity. The years of violent confrontation indicate that the discourse space between the echelons was characterized by military content and a blurred political directive.

Elaborating my main argument and introducing the military echelon in Israel as an epistemic authority regarding the violent confrontation (in the eyes of the public and the political echelon) might clarify some fundamental issues about the characteristics of the interactions between the echelons and the weakness of the civilian control. I argue that the military echelon arranged the discourse space and affected the way it was conducted by using knowledge and a sophisticated conceptual system developed under the circumstances of conceptual distress in the absence of clear and distinct political directives.[7] In addition, the military echelon influenced security and public discourse in Israel and even arranged and shaped ("burned," in IDF jargon) the Israeli public consciousness.

The IDF's social status and the trust it earns from the Israeli public (to distinguish from the mistrust the political echelon earns)[8] leads the Israeli public to appraise the military echelon as a certified knowledge source that is professional, reliable, and impartial, and to adopt the military echelon's views. In other words, military knowledge affects societal judgment regarding management of the core issues of the violent confrontation.

The military is a task-oriented entity that acts toward defined goals and cannot operate in a vacuum.[9] Due to the blurred political directive, or its absence, the military echelon found itself in a blurred and unbearable reality. In order to ensure the efficiency of military force and its effectiveness, the military echelon was forced to interpret the political echelon's intentions and directives and to create the political context for the violent confrontation by developing and elaborating relevant knowledge.[10] Those military operations that were exercised according to the military's interpretation of political intentions shaped the violent conflict environment and the conflict management strategy, and were perceived by the political echelon as well as by most of the public as justified. The military's hegemonic performance in the conflict theater and its implicit influence are both a result and an indication of weak political control, which is the result of a breakdown in political thought. This weakness is a threat to the substantive superiority of the civilian level and its ability to delimit the military's influence over the political process and the conflict management strategy.

What Is Epistemic Authority?

The source of the concept of "epistemic authority" is found in social psychology. Arie W. Kruglanski,[11] based on the early research of Carl Iver Hovland and W. J. McGuire[12] about learning theory, presented it as a unique perspective that can be used to assess the implications of social judgment. He attributes supreme importance to the information sources that are adopted by the individual and that influence his positions and judgment regarding different issues. Kruglanski defines epistemic authority as the information source that the individual relies on while trying to acquire and internalize knowledge about defined issues. Individuals tend to believe that experts are right because they are experts. Consequently, individuals tend to appraise expert views as valid and reliable. A certain overlap can be found between Kruglanski's premise and Foucault's argument that social discourse is composed of propositions that function as a means for defining the truth: "not everyone can produce propositions. . . . Some propositions are more authoritative than others in the sense that they are related with those who hold institutional positions of power."[13]

The epistemic authority's influence will increase when it functions as what Kruglanski calls a "stopping mechanism."[14] This mechanism affects the individual's cognition; individuals tend to freeze their quest for information and information sources to solidify their attitude regarding an issue. They prefer relying on what they perceive as an epistemic authority.

Epistemic authority affects public opinion and therefore has unique importance and social implications in democratic societies that face violent conflict and social and security crises. The importance increases when individuals and groups suffer from cognitive and mental difficulties from being exposed to diverse and contradicting information. In such situations, the epistemic authority can block individuals from accessing alternative information to create an "informational dependence," leaving the individual dependent on the epistemic authority as the only reliable source of information. The dependence creates a psychological convenience that leads to positions and behavior consistent with the recommendations of the epistemic authority.[15]

Trying to find the political implications of the concept, Daniel Bar-Tal and Kruglanski[16] pointed to similar findings regarding the tendency of right-wing voters and self-defined conservatives to rely on epistemic authorities. Their findings indicate a tendency for decreased critical appraisal of the epistemic authority as well an increase in "closure." This is the reason why Kruglanski and others attribute significance and even meta-cognitive importance to epistemic authority as an information source and as a convincing factor.

An interesting conceptual development was added by Eran Halperin and Bar-Tal,[17] who analyzed Ehud Barak's influence over public opinion and the peace camp in Israel. They clarify the influence of "major events" on public opinion but conclude that this is not enough to generate dramatic changes, or "psychological earthquakes" in their terminology. In order to generate such changes in public opinion, there is need for a communicator who is regarded by the public as reliable and can be considered an epistemic authority on the information and its interpretation and implications. They conclude that Prime Minister Barak was perceived by the public in Israel as such an authority and for that reason he was able to engender a turnaround in Israeli perceptions toward the Oslo process.

Ehud Barak was able to enjoy a positive public perception because of, inter alia, his military service and his former position as the IDF Chief of General Staff (CGS). Furthermore, his strict position and explanations about Arafat's refusal of his generous offers at Camp David were robustly backed by the military echelon, at least until the beginning of 2003.[18]

The military echelon in Israel, maybe even more than Barak, benefits from a good public reputation. It is perceived by most of the public as professional, expert, reliable, and impartial to partisan interests. Its involvement in political processes is perceived by the public as legitimate and even required.[19] In the terms of concordance theory,[20] there is an agreement between the military, the civilian authorities, and the citizenry about the active participation of the military establishment in the political decision-making process. It can be deduced that the military echelon in Israel is perceived by the public as an epistemic authority regarding the violent conflicts. The political echelon acknowledges this fact and even relies on and is dependent on the military echelon as a knowledge authority in decision-making processes.

Military Knowledge Development since 1998
and the Characteristics of Its Methodology

The buds of military knowledge development in the context of LIC can be found at the end of 1998 in the IDF's Central Command.[21] The process began as a result of severe conceptual distress. In 1998, Maj. General (MG) Moshe Ya'alon, as the Central Command General Officer Commanding (GOC), understood that the Estimation of the Situation (EOS) process, which should have been the most important component in knowledge creation for the decision-making process, was practically irrelevant:

> I felt that we were missing tools; I felt that the discourses in the Central Command as well as in other places were not deep enough. They dealt with foam on water . . . I felt it was wrong . . . I understood that we had to build a different process of EOS. (Ya'alon, personal interview, July 10, 2005)

Ya'alon internalized the idea that the Israeli–Palestinian conflict does not occur in a vacuum, but in a political and international context. In an independent process, almost subversive (in the sense of swimming against the tide)—without direction or initiative from IDF headquarters—Ya'alon decided to begin developing methodology and tools for a different kind of EOS, which would later be found to be revolutionary.

Ya'alon established a think tank composed of some senior officers from the Central Command Headquarters as well as from the subordinated field divisions' headquarters. He began training them to acquire the new methodology and tools, actually a new language and concepts. After some months, the newly established think tank began leading the EOS process.

The EOS process was characterized as a knowledge-generation and analysis process, based on brainstorming. Effort was devoted to clarifying, interpreting, and conceptualizing the changing reality on the ground. Its declared objective was to "look for phenomena that are not seen by the binoculars and are not connected to the tactical dimension, but in the end cause violent outbreaks" (Ya'alon, personal interview). The assumption was that if it were possible to locate these phenomena and conceptualize them, they could be used as indicating signs and even as an intelligence alert to prevent violent outbreak.

The thinking process led toward the development of an understanding about the nature and the characteristics of different phenomena in the conflict theater and to classifying them into two major groups: "Phenomena that influence events and can be influenced (by the IDF) were designated inside campaign boundaries, while phenomena that influence events but cannot be influenced, were designated as phenomena within the system boundaries." The traditional borders between the military and the political spheres became more permeable by defining the system boundaries as a relevant parameter for the estimation of the situation: "You, as the military commander, should make these classifications and clarifications knowing that essentially this process is a knowledge-generation process" (Ya'alon, personal interview). From this stage, the elections in the United States, the EU positions regarding the Palestinian Authority, and international political and economic trends become relevant inputs in the military EOS processes at all levels.

The knowledge-generation procedures facilitated the conceptualization of phenomena in the conflict arena. The conceptualization process compelled continuing brainstorming; in order to assure its effectiveness, the process had to be released from the military's organizational hierarchy as well as from the traditional military approach to the EOS processes.

The brainstorming process took place in regular gatherings of the think tank every few days and, in exceptional times, every day or even several times a day. This dynamic led to the development of a rich conceptual system and deep insights regarding the reality of a political process in the shadow of a conflict. Those capabilities were translated to military operations at the territorial command level and later on in the General Headquarters.

The new thinking and EOS processes were gradually adopted by the territorial divisions and brigade levels throughout the central command. This was done through advanced studies, special guiding and training events, and by developing the command discourse framework and unique language. The ideas and concepts were presented as "knowledge maps," a sophisticated graphic expression, sometimes too complicated and unclear for the unskilled reader.

In its new form, the EOS engendered the systematic development of knowledge and anchored fundamental concepts in the military language and training methodologies. When Ya'alon began his duty as the CGS Deputy, he turned the process into "the main axis of the General Headquarters' EOS." After his nomination as the CGS of the IDF, he decided to create a new role in his bureau: the CGS Assistant for Analytic Processes. Together, they acted vigorously to diffuse the new EOS methodology to all General Headquarters' levels, "not only regarding force operation dimensions, but force building processes as well" (Ya'alon, personal interview). One salient outcome of the process was a mandatory methodology training booklet (about the limited conflict) published by the General Headquarters' Training Division.

Many in the Central Command and the IDF perceived the new language as arrogant, meaningless, and even irrelevant. EOS documents that were written in the new language and that relied on the new conceptual frameworks were found to be obtuse and esoteric.[22] Col. (Ret.) Yehuda Vagman warned about the dangers of the new language and its resulting faulty operational patterns. He deemed it a strategic failure that would endanger the IDF's deterrence ability and its ability to determine the campaign against Palestinian terror:

> The most prominent expression of the [new] systematic training of the IDF officers was not in their operational success against terror, but mostly in their ability to use the concepts. . . . This language enabled manipulations in presenting the reality . . . false presentations of success. . . . The more those ideas were more blurred, incomprehensible and nonimplementable, the more creative they were considered, and accordingly, the more they enhanced their producer's status in the organization.[23]

Ya'alon was aware of the criticism, but viewed the process as a conceptual and organizational revolution, which drastically improved the IDF's performance in LIC. He agrees that the language was sometimes esoteric and that "language should be understood, and there is no need to invent new words if there are words that can be used for the same purpose" (Ya'alon, personal interview).

According to Ya'alon, the characteristics of LIC compel an understanding of the broader context. Military operations on the tactical level have strategic implications. Under the conditions of LIC, "even the soldier at the roadblock is a strategic soldier. If he doesn't understand the context, he might make a tactical mistake that will become a strategic problem." Thus, it was necessary to expand the new knowledge-generation process to all levels: "I expect that the brigade commander will provide the division commander and me with relevant knowledge in order to enable us to make the right decisions; therefore, the knowledge generation is at every level" (Ya'alon, personal interview).

Whether the revolution led by Ya'alon will last remains to be seen, but it seems there is no doubt that he had a strong impact on the military establishment in Israel. This influence is visible in procedural outcomes (concepts, insights, language, and knowledge) as well as in the military echelon's inputs to the discourse spaces with the political echelon and the public. The military's knowledge infrastructure, developed during the years of violent confrontation, has gone beyond the traditional professional military sphere and has become richer and multidimensional; it has been a unique input that has deepened the knowledge gaps between the echelons and between the military establishment and civilian institutions. This process established the military echelon as an epistemic authority and deepened its involvement in the political process in parallel with the increasing weakness of the substantive civilian control.

The Essence of Civilian Control

As the following review of the concept of civil control will demonstrate, most scholars explain and analyze the interaction between political and military echelons under the assumption of civil control ascendancy. Civil control is thought of as the theoretical organizing concept of the discipline of civil–military relations, with different scholars focusing on different angles and aspects.

The spectrum of definitions, broadened since the beginning of the discipline in the early 1950s,[24] can be characterized by the transition from absolute[25] and structural[26] definitions toward softer and more dynamic ones. The latter identify civil control as a process or an expression of partnership[27] or shared responsibility[28] between the echelons. Civil control is seen as a dialogue, albeit an unequal one,[29] and as an intellectual encounter between the two, meaning that statesmen take part in the military's policy formulation process only "as far as they can contribute substantial inputs in thought and directive."[30]

It seems that the common denominator of all the definitions is the expectation that civilian control provides aim and objective, that it sets limits to the military's influence and ensures concordance between that influence and the political echelon's objectives. This is done in a way that also insures the elected political echelon's superiority and the implementation of its defined goals. Civil control can be defined as a process whose efficiency is best measured by evaluating the relative influence of military officers and civilians over state decisions.[31]

Civil control can be defined as a means for establishing the "rules of the game": the mechanisms of accountability that enable control of the way authority is activated and the way the game will be run.[32] In fact, civil control arranges the division of responsibility between the echelons while the political echelon defines national interests and goals and controls their implementation by allocating security resources, including the authority to use force; the military has the authority to determine military doctrine regarding the management of that force. This definition can be considered a normative one that establishes order in the democratic state. The Israeli case is an exception in that civil control becomes blurred. Many times we find the military echelon present in decisions regarding national policy, far beyond the boundaries of military doctrine.

Peter Feaver[33] would claim in this regard that civilian control efficiency is a function of the possible combinations between the variables of work and shirk (on the military's part) and its identification or nonidentification (on the political echelon's part). The least effective civilian control according to this matrix occurs when the military shirks its duties and the political level does not identify the shirk. However, civil control can also be maintained through the principal's use of punishment; when the political echelon, the principal, recognizes that the military echelon, the agent, is shirking its duties, it can punish the military echelon, thus reinforcing civil control.

The challenge of democratic governance is to exercise civil control while providing for the military's legitimate needs in the context of national security, facilitating its ability to function effectively. This is a challenge as the military establishment naturally tends to maximize its autonomy in order to achieve the resources it considers necessary for successfully carrying out its operational missions. The conflict between internal needs and defense and security needs obliges decisions regarding priorities. Such decisions are political in their essence; therefore, it is elected representatives (politicians in the executive branch as well as in the legislative) who should make them, not those in uniform. Referring to the Israeli case, Yehuda Ben-Meir described at length the problematic and negative implications and consequences of a civil control that lacks sufficient parliamentary control over the IDF because of the weaknesses in the Israeli parliament's Foreign Affairs and Security committees.[34]

The characteristics of civil–military interaction are determined as well by the boundaries between the military and civilian spheres. These boundaries should be drawn by the civil control. As will be demonstrated in the next section of this chapter, evidence shows that the existing distinctions are not entirely clear, and in most cases we find blurred boundaries between them. Politicians are involved in military strategy and officers are involved in politics.

Because open discourse between the political and the military echelons has significant importance regarding issues of war and peace, the expectation is not to limit the military's freedom of thought and expression: ". . . the line between the civil and the military echelons . . . passes in the spheres of authority and responsibility and not in the districts of spirit and mind."[35] However, when the military echelon approaches the discourse with both professional and psychological advantages that generate information dependence within the political echelon, open discourse between the echelons can blur the boundaries between the spheres of responsibility and authority. J. Allen Williams[36] warned about the danger of the military's professional strategy domination over the designation of national interests and objectives. Such blurring of boundaries can easily lead to the intervention of the military echelon in civilian spheres and to a weakening of the latter's authority.

It seems that civil control effectiveness in general, and specifically in the context of violent confrontation, is a function of four major elements: 1) contextual knowledge and historical perspective; 2) public legitimatization in the sense of trust in the political leadership in terms of its abilities, skills, qualifications, and capabilities in the decision-making processes; 3) governance culture; and 4) political leadership that presents a comprehensible vision, defined by clear political directives, to the military echelon regarding the implementation of its political goals.[37]

The political directive is the organizing mechanism of substantive civil control. Its distortion or absence will broaden the military echelon's interpretation of its scope of action in relation to the political echelon's intentions.[38] The political echelon in Israel lacks the capability and institutional infrastructure to generate the kind of systematic knowledge that can produce viable alternatives to the military's recommendations for managing violent conflict. Actually, military knowledge becomes a shared knowledge basis for the political and military echelons:

On important issues regarding the military such as the annual estimation of the situation or defense policy, the discussion doesn't exceed the military presentation and questions about it. The military's ability to prepare a nice and convincing presentation provides its position with an a priori advantage.[39]

Therefore, the knowledge becomes a significant input in the discourse spaces between the echelons and affects the nature of the discourse space and the civil control, as will be described in the following section.

Civilian Control and the Nature of Discourse under the Shadow of Developed Knowledge

Since the country's establishment, the interaction between Israel's echelons has been characterized by permeable borders. It is common for senior officers to enter the political arena after retiring from military service,[40] which in practice makes it sometimes difficult to discern just who belongs to which group. The political echelon in the Israeli context shrinks to the political-security cabinet and primarily to the triangle of the Prime Minister (PM), Defense Minister (DM), and Minister of Foreign Affairs (MFA),[41] although in many cases even this definition is not totally accurate and remains only formal. In some coalitional compositions, we find the PM holding the position of DM. In other cases, the DM or MFA, or both of them, are the PM's political adversaries or each others' political adversaries.[42]

Due to Israel's governance culture, its lack of a tradition of staff work at the political level,[43] and the absence of professional civilian staff other than the government (although in recent years the status of the National Security Council has been elevated) there occurs a reversal of the normal order; the military echelon, with detailed preparations for the possible political–security contexts in hand, precedes the political echelon. The military echelon tries to understand and interpret the political echelon's intentions and directives and, in some cases, the political directives only become clear as the political echelon relates to the military echelon's plans.

Such an order shapes the discourse space between the echelons and releases the political echelon from the obligation to develop knowledge infrastructures of its own as alternatives to the military's. The unbal-

anced encounter between the echelons leads to military domination over
the discourse space, which becomes Type A discourse space (e.g., characterized by military contents) in the model, presented earlier,[44] and the
perpetuation of an "intellectual vacuum":

> When I generate this knowledge and reach insights, I bring them to the
> political level. The political level will not do it by itself. It is not familiar
> with this knowledge, and I have to provide the knowledge . . . what I found
> there was a vacuum and, therefore, the things I brought dominated the
> discourse . . . eventually, my recommendations were accepted. I dominated
> the discourse. (Ya'alon, personal interview, July 10, 2005)

The developed military knowledge infrastructure includes information and knowledge about dimensions and domains that prima facie
are perceived as external to the military's professional realm. The military echelon takes into consideration political, media, economic, and
societal concerns as it relates to the spectrum of options for military
operations in the conflict arena. Trying to understand the broad context of the violent conflict, the military echelon is pushed to introduce
plans and recommendations that contain salient political elements.
As it does so, the military becomes the political echelon's partner or
antagonist, rather than its instrument, and the discourse space takes
on characteristics that deviate from the military's traditional realm of
responsibility:

> At the highest political-military levels, there were disputes . . . Ya'alon
> supported more openness during Abbas's term as Palestinian Prime Min-
> ister. He objected to the attack on the Muqata'a . . . He rejected Sharon's
> suggestion regarding shelling the Gaza Strip and succeeded in influencing
> the Prime Minister. Ya'alon didn't reject the disengagement plan but the
> way it was conducted. He claimed that by negotiating correctly we could
> get a return for such a move.[45]

The GCS is a respected public figure in Israel who often appears in
civilian public forums, using these occasions to introduce assessments
and express professional positions. These appearances are also another
kind of discourse, external and parallel to the political–military discourse but with indirect influence on it. This other space becomes, on
some occasions, a ramming tool used by the military echelon to pressure
and influence the political echelon. By influencing and even shaping the

public consciousness, the GCS generates public pressure that undoubtedly influences the political level:

> In a short piece that was leaked from his speech at the Institute for Democ-
> racy, Ya'alon stung those who see the disengagement as "Messiah Now."
> . . . Ya'alon doesn't see any prospect for permanent agreement but only a
> potential for interim agreement, but [thinks] that even such an outcome
> should be promoted.[46]

In the discourse between the military echelon and the public in
Israel, the former defined the violent confrontation as the continuation
of the War of Independence,[47] the Palestinian Authority as a terrorist
entity,[48] and expressed the need to "burn" the Palestinian consciousness,
and the need to ensure the hardening of Israeli society as a necessary
key for resisting Palestinian terrorism. In such a reality, with the Israeli
public experiencing fear and threat, the internalization of such an interpretation became easier, especially coming from a source perceived
by the public as a reliable expert. In this sense, the public developed
informational dependence on the military echelon, causing it to perceive
the latter as an epistemic authority as well. Moreover, the military echelon succeeded in generating informative influence and facilitating the
"burning" of the Israeli consciousness: portraying terror as an existential
threat[49] and the confrontation as an inescapable but just war. It seems
that the military echelon had more success in "burning" the Israeli consciousness than the Palestinian one.

Some senior civilians severely criticized the salient presence of the
military echelon in this discourse, arguing that civilian institutions
should be more involved in the political process. Ya'alon tends to accept
this criticism and adds that there exists a shortcoming in this regard:
"Such strong centers of knowledge should be everywhere: the NSC, the
Foreign Affairs Ministry and all of those who complain that the military
is too strong, let them strengthen themselves." He adds that with the
absence of additional centers of knowledge, government and cabinet
discussions remain at the operational level, lacking sufficient depth: "Is
this the way that a discussion should be held in the government, in the
cabinet? Are they approving an operation or not? This is a tactical discussion . . . they come to the discussions without insights, without basis"
(Ya'alon, personal interview).

The encounter between the echelons, which should be conducted as an intellectual discourse characterized by the merging of different ideas, becomes one in which the military echelon presents its "knowledge map," with inlaid interpretations of the political echelon's intentions and its directives formulated through inference: "The politicians avoid direct, clear and compelling wording . . . the IDF is pushed to decode the political echelon's intentions by guesswork and information garnered from media interviews and indirect citations in newspaper articles."[50]

Ya'alon concurs with Oren's description, explaining that "there is no doubt that there are such cases. The political echelon avoids clear wording and taking responsibility." On the other hand, Ya'alon perceives this reality as given and even natural: "We have to assume that in a democratic state, we will not hear clear wording from the political echelon, especially in the Israeli reality. I term it fuzziness, yes creative fuzziness." Ya'alon thinks that fuzziness is a political tool that affords the political echelon flexibility: "Once you say something clear, it is done. When you leave it open it is in flux." He thinks that sometimes "there is a need to only signal direction and not an objective because you cannot be sure that you can achieve it. This is the reason we call it political directive, and I can accept it." However, the Israeli case shows that there are many instances in which the directive is not there. "Sometimes they hold the cards so close to their chests that even they don't know what cards they hold" (Ya'alon, personal interview).

In Ya'alon's view, the discourse between the echelons is the means to clarify what should be done. He assumes that even if the political echelon decides that something should be done, it does not necessarily know if the military can do it "because it doesn't really know the military's capabilities." The responsibility of the military echelon in this regard is to present the political echelon with the possible implications of the military operations that are required to implement its objectives. Military knowledge should combine with civilian knowledge, and the outcome should be new knowledge:

> [The combination] generates knowledge by itself, and this is a fertilizing process. This is what I term "creative fuzziness." While everyone contributes their own knowledge, it creates a new knowledge that enables the political echelon to reach an understanding about what is achievable and what

is not. Then we can reach an agreement on objectives. (Ya'alon, personal interview)

This definition shows that Ya'alon tends toward the concept of civil control following the "shared responsibility" approach.[51] He, much like Yehoshafat Harkabi,[52] expects the active participation of the political echelon in formulating thought and directive. However, his remarks leave a definite impression of a flawed partnership between the echelons; the political echelon is not deeply involved in formulation of thoughts and directives. It seems that in the absence of an alternative to military knowledge, the discourse space shrinks to operational dimensions, and the burden of defining objectives inside the conflict falls squarely on the IDF's shoulders. Once again, the discourse space becomes a Type A discourse.

Ya'alon agrees that the political echelon is in a state of "strategic helplessness," a term used to denote a situation brought about by a conflict stalemate in which an actor simply does not know what to do and how to react to create desired change.[53] This situation, according to Ya'alon, is exacerbated by the absence of civilian knowledge centers. Ya'alon criticizes the political echelon for failing to provide real partners in the intellectual running and, therefore, finds it difficult to define the discourse between the echelons as an intellectual encounter:

When you come with this knowledge to the political echelon . . . with such strategic helplessness, the political echelon is happy to buy what you offer it. Then you look for partners that will challenge you intellectually, and you don't find them. To call the encounter between the echelons an "intellectual encounter" is too pretentious. (Ya'alon, personal interview)[54]

The discourse space between the echelons is conducted without a "discourse culture." Ya'alon seeks a richer and broader discourse that is not focused only on the operational level. He thinks that such a discourse cannot be conducted with delineations of the boundaries of responsibility between the civil and the military spheres that are too sharp and focused:

The discourse must be much broader. It should refer to the broad context. I definitely don't see here cut and clear boundaries [between the echelons]; there should be a fusion [of knowledge]. Eventually, you cannot discuss only military issues without taking into account their political aspects and context. (Ya'alon, personal interview)

The result is that the military echelon introduces political ideas and recommendations regarding the way the Palestinian Authority should be treated and even suggests ways to strengthen it.[55] The political echelon in this situation tends to accept these recommendations, mostly without reservations regarding the military's involvement in the political process: "When I came to him [PM Sharon] with the idea about Abu-Mazen [Abu Mazen's nomination for the role of Palestinian Prime Minister], he immediately adopted it" (Ya'alon, personal interview). Sometimes the administration does have reservations, but usually they are not significant. Ya'alon himself does not feel comfortable with such a discourse; he thinks its content is too militaristic and should have been more civilian: "I think it is bad that there are too many participants in these discussions who wear military uniforms, and I definitely think that in many cases the discussions were too military-oriented, immediately going to the force operation. It should be more civilian [in its contents]" (Ya'alon, personal interview).

In the reality since 2003, the military echelon has been a restraining force that believes the military option alone cannot remain the only means, nor even the major means, of managing the conflict: "These things require answers other than using force. Using force should be the last alternative." This point of view leads the military echelon to embark upon "political operations": "I, as the CGS, conducted many political operations together with the Foreign Affairs Ministry. I thought that including Hizbullah on the terror list was worth more than a thousand attacks in Lebanon. This is a political operation, not a military one." It seems that even here the military echelon finds itself almost alone in the campaign: "Why wasn't the cabinet sitting and discussing the strategy that should be used? I expect such discussion to be conducted by the NSC. This is a matter that demands coordination between military, political, and diplomatic bodies on one hand and economic and social ones on the other" (Ya'alon, personal interview).

The political operations mentioned by Ya'alon are an outcome of thought processes conducted by the military that include such inputs as the influence of U.S. elections, U.S. moves in Iraq, and the EU's position toward Israel. All of those issues became relevant for the military EOSs. The EOSs resulted in unique knowledge and insights that were introduced by the military echelon in front of the political echelon as part of what the former perceived as its professional duty: "I should know to come to my superiors, to the political level, and to explain to them how the elections in the States might influence military aspects in the conflict theater" (Ya'alon, personal interview).

The findings regarding the discourse space characteristics indicate the salient hegemony of military knowledge and the weakness of civilian knowledge. The reversal of the "normal order" was institutionalized. In the absence of political directives, the military was forced to expand its domain of interests and developed ideas and alternatives for the conflict's management.

Such interaction fits the Type A discourse space, characterized by military conceptualization and blurred and undetermined political directives. These findings are indicative of the military's hegemony over the discourse space, or, in other words, the military's deep involvement in the political process. The military echelon shaped the nature of the discourse space by using its broad and rich knowledge, which was created systematically in the intellectual vacuum left by the political echelon. The nature of the discourse between the echelons, characterized by military hegemony, is a reflection of the substantive civil control's weakness.

Conclusion

The unique characteristics of the violent confrontation with the Palestinians led the military echelon toward an understanding of the importance and necessity of developing multidimensional knowledge that is more sophisticated and reaches beyond the traditional sphere of military professionalism. The outcome of this process was a conceptual revolution in the military establishment, but not only there.

Following the continued weakness of civilian institutions in Israel, the military echelon's revolution gave it a significant advantage over the political echelon in generating the required knowledge for managing the violent confrontation. The fact that the military establishment earned the appreciation of the public in Israel facilitated the transformation of the military echelon to an epistemic authority in the eyes of the public as well as in the eyes of politicians, and created an informational dependency on the military echelon. The military echelon's ideas and viewpoints were clearly reflected in the discourse space between the echelons. The nature of the discourse became Type A discourse, indicating military hegemony.

This hegemony is an expression of the military's influence over the political process, and such an influence enhances, in its turn, the existing functional arrangement in which the military echelon is responsible for conceptualizing strategy, planning and executing all matters related to the management of the violent confrontation. It is true that all of the military's activities are done with the permission and the authorization of the political level, but in most cases, the political directives are derived from the military knowledge infrastructure, hegemonic knowledge that has almost no competitors.[56]

In Foucault's terms, the military echelon becomes the "truth agent" regarding information and knowledge about violent confrontation. In every society, institutions exercise practices that internalize among the society members what they perceive as the "truth" and use other practices to exclude from the discourse the propositions they perceive as untrue.[57] Knowledge, according to Foucault, is a kind of social "truth regime," which enables the domination of some people or institutions over themselves and others. The social discourse is a reflection of the knowledge structure, and the knowledge structure is a reflection of the power structure, because it is impossible to use knowledge without power and because knowledge necessarily generates power.[58]

If the political echelon really seeks to effectively control the military and to balance its influence over decision-making processes, it must generate knowledge and provide challenging alternatives to the military's ideas. It has to establish its position as an epistemic authority in the eyes of the Israeli public and should lead toward the construction of a strategic thought culture among the civilian institutions. Such a change would facilitate the government's ability to release itself from dependence on military knowledge and will strengthen the substantive civil control.

Acknowledgments

The author thanks David Kellen for his comments and support, and Yagil Levy, Daniel Bar-Tal, Tamar Herman, Gabi Sheffer, and Oren Barak for their useful comments.

Notes

1. G. Allen Sens, "From Peace-Keeping to Peace-Building: The United Nations and the Challenge of Intrastate War," in Richard M. Price and Mark W. Zacher (eds.), *The United Nations and Global Security* (New York, 2004), 141–60; Martin van Creveld, "The Transformation of War Revisited," in J. Robert Bunker (ed.), *Non-State Threats and Future Wars* (London, 2003).

2. For detailed descriptions regarding the LIC, see Shmuel Nir, *"The Nature of the Limited Conflict,"* in Hagay Golan and Shaul Shay (eds.), *The Limited Conflict* (Tel-Aviv, 2004), 19–44 [Hebrew], and Ido Hecht, "The Limited Conflict—Some General Characteristics of Unique Warfare," in Hagay Golan and Shaul Shay (eds.), *The Limited Conflict* (Tel-Aviv, 2004), 45–68 [Hebrew].

3. A. Eliot Cohen, "The Unequal Dialogue: The Theory and Reality of Civil-Military Relations and the Use of Force," in D. Peter Feaver and Richard H. Kohn (eds.), *Soldiers and Civilians: The Civil-military Gap and American National Security* (Cambridge, Mass., London, 2001).

4. Kobi Michael, "The Military's Influence on the Transition Process from War to Peace—the Israeli Case—Focused Comparison: The Peace Process with Egypt and Oslo Process," Ph.D. diss., The Hebrew University of Jerusalem, 2004; Kobi Michael, "The Dialectic Interaction between the Military and the Political Echelons during the Israeli-Palestinian Conflict," in Yaacov Bar Siman-Tov (ed.), *The Israeli-Palestinian Conflict: From Peace Process to Violent Confrontation 2000–2005* (Jerusalem, 2005).

5. Ibid.

6. Douglas L. Bland, "A Unified Theory of Civil-Military Relations," *Armed Forces & Society* 26.1 (1999): 7–25.

7. Former Central Command GOC, MG Yitzhak Eitan said, "We have never gotten a clear mission [from the political echelon] and things required interpretations and trials in order to understand the mission," *Ma'ariv,* March 29, 2002. GCS Ya'alon said, "to demand the political echelon to give the military echelon a clear political directive is naivety" at an Operational Theory Research Institute (MALTAM) seminar about civil–military relations in the reality of LIC, February 24, 2003.

8. Asher Arian, David Nachmias, Doron Navot, and Daniel Shani, *2003 Democracy Index* (Jerusalem, 2003); Ephraim Ya'ar and Tamar Hermann, "The Peace Index," *Ha'aretz,* February 7, 2005: "IDF is the entity which earns the highest trust among the Israeli Public and the common appraisal is that its influence on national policy making is appropriate. . . . The data indicate that the military earns the highest trust of the Jewish population: 73 percent feel full trust and 21 percent trust, [for a] total of 94 percent" [Hebrew].

9. In a personal interview with the author on May 27, 2003, former minister Dan Meridor said: "Sometimes the military echelon has to fill the space left by the political echelon. In most cases, the political echelon doesn't determine a position or has no position."

10. "The politicians avoid direct and compelling formulation of their political platform and avoid using civilian tools like the National Security Council. As a con-

sequence the IDF is pushed to decode the political echelon's intentions. . . . In the IDF the process works upside down; it begins in the IDF and then it goes up for the approval of the political echelon." Amir Oren, *Ha'aretz,* July 15, 2005 [Hebrew].

11. Arie W. Kruglanski, *Lay Epistemic and Human Knowledge: Cognitive and Motivational Bases* (New York, 1989).

12. Carl Iver Hovland, Irving L. Janis, and Harold H. Kelley, *Communication and Persuasion: Psychological Studies of Opinion Change* (New Haven, Conn., 1953); W. J. McGuire, "The Nature of Attitudes and Attitude Change," in Gardner Lindzey and Elliot Aronson (eds.), *Handbook of Social Psychology* (Reading, Mass., 1969).

13. Sara Mills, *Michel Foucault,* trans. Ohad Zehavi (Tel-Aviv, 2005) [Hebrew].

14. Arie W. Kruglanski, Amiram Raviv, Daniel Bar-Tal, Alona Raviv, Keren Sharvit, Shmuel Ellis, Ruth Bar, Antonio Pierro, and Lucia Manneti, "Says Who? Epistemic Authority Effects in Social Judgment," in Mark P. Zanna (ed.), *Advances in Experimental Social Psychology* (San Diego, 2005), 346–92.

15. Ibid.

16. Daniel Bar-Tal, Amiram Raviv, and Alona Raviv, "The Concept of Epistemic Authority in the Process of Political Knowledge Acquisition," *Representative Research in Social Psychology* 19 (1991): 1–14; Arie W. Kruglanski, "Motivated Social Cognition: Principles of the Interface," in E. Tory Higgins and Arie W. Kruglanski (eds.), *Social Psychology: Handbook of Basic Principles* (New York, 1996), 493–520.

17. Eran Halperin and Daniel Bar-Tal, "The Fall of the Peace Camp in Israel: The Determinative Influence of Prime Minister Ehud Barak on Israeli Public Opinion—July 2000–February 2001," *Megamot* 45.3 [Hebrew].

18. Yaakov Bar-Siman-Tov (ed.), *The Israeli-Palestinian Conflict: From Peace Process to Violent Confrontation 2000–2005* (Jerusalem, 2005).

19. Ya'ar and Hermann, "The Peace Index," *Ha'aretz,* February 7, 2005.

20. Rebecca L. Schiff, "Civil-Military Relations Reconsidered: A Theory of Concordance," *Armed Forces & Society* 22.1 (1995): 7, 18.

21. Lt.-Gen. Ya'alon has a major role in this process and therefore the description in this chapter is mostly based on a comprehensive personal interview with him on July 10, 2005. Furthermore, this chapter is based on the personal experience of the author, who was a member of the mentioned think tank.

22. Col. (Res.) Yehuda Vagman wrote one of the most critical essays in this regard: "The 'Limited Conflict'—The Failure," in Hagay Golan and Shaul Shay (eds.), *The Limited Conflict* (Tel-Aviv, 2004), 251–98 [Hebrew].

23. Ibid.

24. Morris Janowitz, *The Professional Soldier: A Social and Political Portrait* (New York, 1971); Samuel Huntington, *The Soldier and the State: The Theory and Politics of Civil-Military Relations* (New York, 1957).

25. H. Richard Kohn, "How Democracies Control," *Journal of Democracy* 8.4 (1997): 140–53, 142. Kohn argues that civil control should be absolute and comprehensive, although he understands that it can never actually be absolute. His definition can be considered normative.

26. E. Claude Welch (ed.), *Civilian Control of the Military Theory and Cases from Developing Countries* (New York, 1976), found the basis for effective civil control in the strength of the governmental mechanisms and the legitimacy they earn from the public.

27. Yoram Peri, *The Israeli Military and Israel's Palestinian Policy from Oslo to the Al Aqsa Intifada* (Washington, D.C., 2002).

28. Bland, "A Unified Theory of Civil-Military Relations."

29. Cohen, "The Unequal Dialogue: The Theory and Reality of Civil-Military Relations and the Use of Force."

30. Yehoshafat Harkabi, *War and Strategy,* 4th ed. (Tel-Aviv, 1994), 526.

31. Kohn, "How Democracies Control," 143.

32. Bland, "A Unified Theory of Civil-Military Relations."

33. Peter D. Feaver, *Armed Servants: Agency, Oversight, and Civil-Military Relations* (Cambridge, Mass., 2003) and "Crisis as Shirking: An Agency Theory Explanation of the Souring of American Civil-Military," *Armed Forces & Society* 24.3 (1998): 407–435.

34. Yehuda Ben-Meir, *Civil-Military Relations in Israel* (New York, 1995).

35. Israel Tal, *Few against Many* (Tel-Aviv, 1996), 107 [Hebrew].

36. J. Allen Williams, "The Military and Modern Society: Civilian-Military Relations in Post–Cold War America, *World and I* 14.9 (1999), 306.

37. Michael, "Dialectic Interaction."

38. Ibid., and Michael, "The Military's Influence on the Transition Process."

39. Aviezer Ya'ari, *The Civil Control over the Military in Israel* (Tel-Aviv, 2004), 34.

40. Yoram Peri, *Between Battles and Ballots—Israeli Military in Politics* (Cambridge, 1983); Peri, *The Israeli Military and Israel's Palestinian Policy;* Uri Ben-Eliezer, "Do the Generals Rule in Israel? The Military-Political Integration and the Legitimacy for War in Nation in Arms," in Hanna Herzog (ed.), *Society in the Mirror* (Tel-Aviv, 2000); Eva Etzioni-Halevy, "Civil-Military Relations and Democracy: The Case of the Military-Political Elites' Connection in Israel," *Armed Forces & Society* 22.3 (1996): 401–417.

41. Peri, *Between Battles and Ballots;* Michael, "The Military's Influence on the Transition Process."

42. "The problem, as usual in Israel, begins with definitions. Who is the political echelon? The prime minister? The minister of defense? The cabinet? The government? What if there is no agreement between all of those?" Amir Oren, "There Will Always Be Terror," *Ha'aretz,* July 15, 2005.

43. Ben Meir, *Civil-Military Relations in Israel;* Michael, "The Military's Influence on the Transition Process"; Ya'ari, *The Civil Control over the Military in Israel.*

44. Michael, "The Military's Influence on the Transition Process."

45. *Ha'aretz,* May 13, 2005. Similar examples: Alex Fishman, Interview with Ya'alon, *Yediot Aharonot,* December 25, 2003; *Ma'ariv,* November 14, 2003; *Ha'aretz,* April 22, 2005.

46. *Ha'aretz,* April 22, 2005.

47. "I have no doubt that with historical perspective, people will say that the War of Independence was the most important event in our national history and this war was the second-most important one. . . . The Palestinians returned us to the War of Independence." Ari Shavit, interview with the GCS, *Ha'aretz,* August 29, 2002.

48. The updated IDF premises claimed that Arafat did not accept the existence of Israel as a Jewish state; that he perceived the violent confrontation as the main means to promote his political goals; that he was a terrorist, that the PA is a terrorist entity, and the conflict is the "war for a home." For additional details, see Yaacov Bar

Siman-Tov (ed.), *As the Generals See It: The Collapse of the Oslo Process and the Violent Israeli-Palestinian Conflict* (Jerusalem, 2003).

49. "The key point here is the Israeli society's hardening . . . this is what the campaign is about. Because here it is a matter of existential threat." Ari Shavit, interview with the GCS, *Ha'aretz,* August 29, 2002.

50. *Ha'aretz,* July 15, 2005.

51. Bland, "A Unified Theory of Civil-Military Relations."

52. Harkabi, *War and Strategy.*

53. Michael, "Dialectic Interaction," 226.

54. Similar things were said by MG Eiland; see Kobi Michael, "The End of the Deterministic Distinction—the Low Intensity War Era as a Paradigmic Challenge for Civil-Military Relations in the Democratic State," in Hagay Golan and Shaul Shay (eds.), *The Limited Conflict* (Tel-Aviv, 2004), 201–238, 226.

55. "[O]fficers speak about the crucial importance of international legitimacy. . . . Washington, said a senior officer is maybe the most important actor in the disengagement operation. Indeed, the IDF in 2005 has flanked the Foreign Affairs Ministry from the left, trying to strengthen Abu-Mazen and the internal Hamas." Amir Oren, *Ha'aretz,* July 15, 2005.

56. Following the Rubenstein Committee's recommendations (December 2004) regarding the improvement of civil control, MK Yossi Sarid said, "indeed, the implementation of the committee's recommendations will improve the current control of the Knesset over the military, but even these . . . recommendations do not ensure that the Knesset will hear alternative positions," *Ha'aretz,* December 29, 2004.

57. Mills, *Michel Foucault,* 83.

58. Michel Foucault, "Prison Talk," in Colin Gordon (ed.), *Power/Knowledge 1972–1977* (Brighton, UK, 1980), 147–65, 152.

THREE

Civil Society, the Military, and National Security: The Case of Israel's Security Zone in South Lebanon

AVRAHAM SELA

Israel's unilateral retreat from South Lebanon on May 23–24, 2000, represents a unique case of security policymaking in Israeli history. For the first and only time in its history, an ex-parliamentary grassroots movement played a key role in reshaping the national security agenda in defiance of the state's potent military establishment, despite its practical monopoly on shaping the national security policy. Moreover, the policy change was effected within a relatively short time and by a movement whose nucleus of activists hardly exceeded a few hundreds.[1]

This chapter explains the circumstantial conditions, strategies, and means that enabled this unique shift from a quarter-century-long concept of maintaining a "security zone" in South Lebanon as a necessary buffer protecting the northern Galilee, to the government decision on unilateral withdrawal from South Lebanon in March 2000. Indeed, the main achievement of civil society in this case was in mobilizing the media to develop a public debate that questioned the validity and necessity of the "security zone" and confronted the security establishment with an alternative rationale and discourse.

Theoretical Aspects

THE POLITICAL-MILITARY NEXUS

Israel's geopolitical and strategic conditions underpinned its concept as a "nation in arms," in which the civil–military interface is marked by permeable and floating boundaries. While this interface theoretically enables "civilianization" of the military no less than "militarization" of civil society,[2] in effect the military institution's impact on society and policymaking often exceeds its strictly legal boundaries. This is mainly the result of Israel's security conditions of frequent and intense military threats; the scope of military penetration into society and the political system by virtue of practically dominating the military forces, regular and reservist alike; the immense part of the national budget swallowed by the military; the variety of military and social roles carried out by the military; and the latter's symbolic status.

Especially under conditions of a low-intensity conflict, as in the case of Israel, civil–military relationships tend to be symbiotic in nature; according to the military establishment, they maintain the status of partnership rather than being strictly subordinate to political leaders in the decision-making process.[3] Moreover, in view of the IDF monopoly on tactical and strategic intelligence and planning, and the absence of a significant alternative capable of countering the IDF analyses and recommendations, the political system is entirely dependent on the professional opinion of the military leadership, especially the Chief of the General Staff (CGS).[4] The latter's access to the inner core of policymaking—as the government's military adviser—renders him one of the three most powerful figures in the Israeli political system, and enables him to take part in ad hoc civil–military alignments with or against the Defense Minister (DM) or the Prime Minister (PM).[5]

Students of Israeli civil–military relations agree that Israel cannot be considered a "praetorian" or "garrison state,"[6] although some point to its endangered democracy and civil nature of policymaking.[7] Indeed, it is especially in the epistemological context that the IDF poses serious constraints on the political system in shaping security policies in times of war and peace, and constructs public discourse of security in theory and practice.[8] The complex military interface with society, economy, and politics; its myriad roles in education; settlement in frontier areas; military government rule over the Arab population in Israel (1948–1966) and the Occupied Territories (since 1967); strategic intelligence and planning; and the pervasive presence of senior military officers with or without uniform in advisory and policymaking core institutions, all combine to shape a "cultural code of a civilian militarism" with institutional violence as an "organizing principle."[9] The IDF further shapes public opinion through regular off-the-record briefings on security and Arab affairs provided to the civil media, which enables the former to disseminate its own interpretations and perceptions of events directly, as well as through the inputs of former senior military officers in civil think tanks.[10] It is in this context of perceptions, concepts, and schemes of action that the IDF's shortcomings in handling complex political affairs is most apparent, as will be demonstrated in the case of the "security zone" in South Lebanon.

CIVIL SOCIETY AND THE MILITARY IN ISRAEL

Despite the differing meanings philosophers and political theorists have attributed to "civil society" since its advent in the late seventeenth century, it is broadly understood to be those individuals, social groups, voluntary associations, and institutions located in an independent space beyond the close control of, and largely in contrast to, the state. The core of civil society is what Jürgen Habermas defined as the "public space," the domain where a free, pluralist, and rational discourse is conducted for the common good through communicative action and mediation of civil interest groups. Despite differences of status, interests, and goals among these groups, a civil society has at its core a common agreement on the collective moral order and continuous process of constructing collective consensus on common goals and means, which in turn can affect the patterns of official policymaking and shape individual and collective identities.[11]

Whether a set of autonomous groups constitutes a "civil society" depends largely on the latter being both passive and active vis-à-vis the state: "passive, in the acceptance of a certain order, and active, in its volitional element, which creates, maintains, and reproduces the moral order through institutions and individual behavior."[12] A civil society is thus marked by its willingness to limit the scope of state action and expand the public space to include other civic discourses and practices, and less by its legitimization of the state. In reality, however, state–society relations seem less a dichotomy and more a complex web of moral and practical interactions among social players in the quest for prestige and legitimacy where identities and loyalties are constantly reproduced.[13]

In the first two decades of independence, Israeli society was passive in response to the all-embracing rule of the political system, the political parties, and constitutive institutions of the organized Yishuv (the pre-state Jewish community in Palestine). Israeli society was led by a rela-tively coherent ruling elite that utilized state instruments to assimilate the newcomers into a hegemonic Israeli culture marked by a high level of mobilization and a strong claim for collectivity. The highly central-ized economy and land resources—mostly owned by the state—further underlined the dominant role of the state in society. With national se-curity being continuously threatened, the issue of security occupied the core collective consciousness urging solidarity and national cohesion in which military service played a primary role.[14]

Since the early 1970s, Israeli society has undergone processes of social and ideological polarization and the rise of distinct interest groups as a result of wars, structural economic reforms toward free market economy, and immigration, especially from the former Soviet Union.[15] This period witnessed a transformation of Israeli society from collective to individual orientation, social segmentation, and multiculturalism, which became apparent in the 1990s. The declining political hegemony of secular Israe-liness represented by the Labor movement and its institutions gave way to separate multicultural autonomies with their particular institutional systems, concepts of rules, and the desirable resource allocation.[16]

These changes gave rise to a burgeoning civil society, hitherto content with the passive role of legitimizing and constituting the state regime, willing to assume an increasingly active role in manifesting expectation for accountability and moral behavior on the part of the political system. Yet, interest groups, voluntary associations, and institutions preferred to address their grievances through exclusive channels of communication rather than in broad civic frameworks. Many of these activities have been based on particular networks of kinship and friendships, which preclude certain segments of society and thus fail to expand the domain of civil society. Indeed, public protests and demonstrations became more frequent and massive in scope, especially at the time of the Lebanon war in 1982, but they were aimed at ad hoc objectives and thus disappeared from the public arena after a relatively short burst of activity without creating a permanent public space beyond state control. Moreover, this mode of action set civil society on adversarial terms with the state as the appropriate address for its complaints, instead of constituting civic norms and patterns of action.[17]

Thus, in spite of the broadening participation of Israelis in professional and communal associations, civil society in Israel remained essentially established or corporative, fragmented and passive, with some segments demonstrating intolerance toward other civil sectors and organizations. Moreover, official regulative apparatuses further weakened the civil society, restricting its freedom of action and encouraging its members to prefer unity and avoid disagreements. These characteristics are particularly apparent in the almost total absence of protest movements from the Israeli political arena, despite deep social frustrations.[18] Nonetheless, since the early 1990s, the proliferation of privatized media, the mushrooming of think tanks, human rights associations, NGOs, and organizations of intercultural dialogue, in addition to long-term protest movements, all contributed to an open and critical public discourse. It is against this backdrop that civil protest against the "security zone" emerged and influenced public discourse and policymaking.

Civil society in Israel is particularly strained in affecting policymaking on national security, which had traditionally been kept out of the public sphere and discourse, including by the law of military censorship. Israeli society largely complied with these restrictions in the name of "rallying around the flag," especially at times of crisis and war.[19] Although this consensus seriously eroded in the controversy over the Lebanon War of 1982 and the apparent bankruptcy of the military "Civil Administration" in the Occupied Territories during the first Intifada (1987–1991), it remained a major character trait of Israeli society.[20] Similarly, despite the blows to IDF prestige as a result of major military crises since the Yom Kippur War, sustained threats to Israel's collective and individual security rejuvenated the public's esteem toward the military leaders and helped the IDF preserve its status as the ultimate guarantor of sovereign Jewish survival, a national symbol and the most credible state institution. Moreover, the decline of traditional constitutive social and political institutions since the early 1970s allowed senior military officers to become an integral part of the social and political elite. This is best manifested in the recruitment of senior officers by political parties and their rapid attainment of key official positions in the government and legislature, and executive positions in the private economy, local government, and the educational system.[21]

Nonetheless, the growing civil activism in Israeli society and the deepening disagreement over norms and policies toward the Occupied Territories—with the IDF caught between contradictory policing assignments toward the Jewish settlers and the Palestinian population—all accounted for turning the security–military discourse into the essence of the social–political debate. The media revolution and the Middle East peace process in the 1990s accounted for a growing critique of the military institution in Israel, calling for reconsidering its structural concept, roles, and relations with society. New protest movements challenged hitherto sacrosanct issues of national security, calling for refusal of military service in the Occupied Territories and defying the military's monopoly of security information.[22]

In the process, growing public pressures were exerted on the political system to subordinate the military institution to legislative and normative restrictions, urging transparency concerning the IDF budget and questioning the credibility of its reports on military operations and moral conduct of the officer corps. The Israeli–Arab peace process legitimized calls for reconsidering the desirable nature and structure of the armed forces with a view to shifting the IDF from a "people's army" to a professional one.[23] It is in this context of changing civil–military relations that the debate on the "security zone" broke into public awareness in 1997 and reverberated among hitherto passive sectors of civil society.

The "Security Zone" in South Lebanon

ORIGINS AND FIXATION

Israel's geopolitical situation dictated from its very birth a security concept that sought to constantly broaden the state's strategic depth. Confronted by guerrilla warfare across borders, Israel adopted a retaliatory policy of inflicting painful costs on states allowing or sponsoring such warfare from their territories. This policy was indeed effective in forcing Egypt and Jordan in the 1950s, and Jordan again in the late 1960s and early 1970s, to coerce Palestinian militant groups and impose law and order within their own borders. In the case of Lebanon, however, as of the late 1960s, this policy of retaliation against both Palestinian guerrilla organizations operating in Lebanon and purely Lebanese targets not only failed to achieve its goals but expedited the deterioration of Lebanon into a civil war which erupted in 1975.

The post-1973 years witnessed an escalation of Palestinian guerrilla attacks against Israeli civilians, mostly from Lebanese territory. These attacks assumed a spectacular type of terrorist operation launched across the border or the sea, where hostages were taken and used as a bargaining chip to release Palestinians imprisoned in Israel.[24] Israel's refusal to negotiate with the kidnappers and resorting to the use of force to release the hostages often ended with widely broadcast scenes of a bloodbath of innocent civilians. It was this specter of atrocities that motivated the IDF efforts in the following years to distance military threats from the Jewish settlements along the Lebanese border by creating a buffer zone in South Lebanon.

The "security zone" was born of the Lebanese civil war and the growing Palestinian military threats to the Christian villages of South Lebanon which, in the absence of an effective government, turned to Israel for support. Israel's interest in cooperation with the Christian population of South Lebanon (and, consequently, also with the Lebanese Forces, the umbrella organization of the Christian coalition led by Bashir Gemayel)[25] drew on a traditional quest for regional allies, be they non-Arab ethnic minorities or peripheral non-Arab states.[26] More specifically, it represented the growing perception of Lebanon among Israeli analysts and decision makers as a "non-state state," which justified Israel's interference in that country's affairs as a necessary evil. Thus, toward the Syrian military invasion of Lebanon, Israel defined the area stretching from the Mediterranean, south of Sidon straight to Lebanon Valley in the east (about 40 km from the border), as a "red line," strictly vital for its national security.[27]

The parameters of Israel's involvement in South Lebanon were shaped by decisions of senior IDF officers of the Northern Sector Command aimed at keeping armed Palestinian guerrillas away from Israel's territory by "helping the Christian border villages to help themselves." These decisions often exceeded the government's generally cautious policy on this matter but were later adopted as fait accompli. By late 1977, Israel had officially stated and practically assumed a military patronage over the Christian enclaves and their militias, including a growing presence of IDF officers and armored units in South Lebanon, in addition to extending civil services on Israel's side of the border to Lebanese villagers.[28] Thus, despite the government's initial refusal to take responsibility for the fate of Christians in South Lebanon, it was gradually dragged into the fray by the dynamics of events affected by foreign actors, miscommunication and poor coordination between local IDF officers and Lebanese commanders, and competition and rivalries among local Lebanese factions and commanders.[29]

The "security zone" in South Lebanon was consolidated in the wake of Israel's Litani Operation, launched in March 1978 in response to a seaborne attack perpetrated by Fatah, which resulted in the killing of thirty-two citizens just a few miles north of Tel-Aviv. The operation enabled Israel to secure a contiguous belt north of the Israeli–Lebanese border with nearly 1,500 men, mostly Christian Maronites with a minority of Shiites and Druze, under the command of Major Saad Haddad. With Israel's backing, Haddad sought to distance the UN Interim Forces in Lebanon (UNIFIL)—established by Security Council Resolution 425 to be deployed along the border and prevent future attacks from Lebanon on Israeli territory—restricting these forces to the area north of the "security zone." In the following years, UNIFIL's mode of deployment and ineffectiveness became a constant source of friction with Haddad's militia and, indirectly, with Israel.[30]

The continued Lebanese crisis and de facto division of the country among various militias seemed to vindicate the Israeli concept of defending its border from within the Lebanese territory, rendering the "security zone" an indivisible part of Israel's security doctrine. Israel took comprehensive responsibility for administering the "security zone's" civil life while underwriting all of its financial and infrastructural military needs. Israel also sought to "normalize" the region's social and economic life, including the movement of people and goods across the region's lines. Similarly, residents of the "security zone" were allowed to cross the border into Israel for work, medical treatment, and visits.[31]

The "security zone" was established to prevent Palestinian guerrilla infiltrations into Israeli territory and—given its limited depth (8–12 km) —was unable to prevent shelling and rocket launching into Israel's territory, which indeed continued, including from the UNIFIL-controlled zone.[32] The tension between Israel and the Palestinian military buildup across the "security zone" peaked in the heavy artillery exchange that erupted in the summer of 1981. Although the confrontation was brought to an end by a U.S.-mediated cease-fire, Israel's military and political leaders were far from acquiescing in the continued buildup of the Palestinian artillery threat to Israeli territory,[33] paving the road to Israel's Lebanon War of 1982.

Nothing in Israel's history of civil–military relations represents the danger to civil policymaking more vividly than the excessive power of the military–security establishment as demonstrated in the latter's secretive preparations and manipulative conduct of the "Peace of Galilee" Operation. That the political system allowed the operation to expand beyond the promised limits of 45–50 km into a full-fledged war, including a confrontation with the Syrian forces in Lebanon and the siege of Beirut, before questioning the military's conduct, attests to the blindness and ignorance of the politicians when confronted by a determined coalition of generals—retired and in uniform—in the IDF and Ministry of Defense.[34]

The "Security Zone" Concept Reaffirmed

Despite the initial public consensus about the Peace of Galilee Operation and the expulsion of the PLO headquarters and armed personnel from Beirut, the Lebanon War soon became resented by growing segments of the Israeli public, especially in the wake of the massacre of Palestinians in Sabra and Shatila conducted by Israel's Lebanese allies. The "war by choice" shattered Israel's public consensus on national security and war as a last resort, and seriously tarnished the IDF's prestige and image. Henceforth, growing public protest and criticism of the war's scope and conduct, including by senior army officers, indicated a continued downturn of support for the war on both political and public levels.[35]

Although the war attained its main goal of practically eliminating the semi-autonomous territorial base of the Palestinian Resistance, the Israeli government was captive of its own grandiose political aspirations in Lebanon which substantiated the IDF's continued deployment in large parts of the country. Yet these aspirations were frustrated by a Syrian-backed coalition of Shiite and Druze militias determined to weaken the legitimacy and effective authority of Lebanese President Amine Gemayel and decimate the peace agreement he had signed with Israel on May

17, 1983. Pressured at home and on the Lebanese battlefield, in September 1983 Israeli forces withdrew from the predominantly Druze Chouf district and deployed along the Awali River, which was tantamount to admitting the failure of the agreement with Lebanon. In March 1984, Gemayel abrogated the agreement and accepted Syria's patronage at a time when Israel had become bogged down in a hopeless war of attrition in an area of topography ideal for guerrilla warfare conducted by Amal, the main Shiite militia, and Hizbullah, an Iranian-backed revolutionary offshoot of Amal.

By mid-January, the official toll of Israeli casualties in Lebanon since June 1982 had reached 609 and the annual cost of continued occupation was $240 million, all of which exacerbated domestic criticism of the government and added to the growing disenchantment with the stalemated economy and hyperinflation. On the eve of the August 1984 general elections, there seemed to be a consensus on both public and official levels that Lebanon was a lost case for Israel and ought to be addressed as a strictly terrorist arena, namely, through maintaining a "security zone" of 25–40 km into Lebanon to prevent future attacks against Israel. Indeed, the question was only "when and how far to withdraw."[36]

With the formation of a national coalition government with Labor leaders Shimon Peres and Yitzhak Rabin as PM and DM, respectively, the IDF was instructed to submit its recommended alternatives for the defense of northern Galilee. In the following months, the IDF leadership considered three main alternatives, of which two required continued deployment of large Israeli forces along the existing lines south of the Awali River, or at an interim line south of the Zahrani River. A third alternative maintained a redeployment of the IDF along the international border while preserving the "security zone."[37] Interestingly, the option of full withdrawal to the international border without a "security zone" was initially excluded at the CGS's instructions. Although it was added later due to pressure from senior members of the General Staff, triggered by persistent intelligence assessments disseminated by the chief of military intelligence, it failed to win the CGS's support. Not surprisingly, and in view of the Labor Party's commitment to "bring the IDF back home," the IDF and the defense ministry's Coordinator of Israel's Activities in Lebanon, Uri Lubrani, strongly supported the third alternative.[38]

The unequivocal preference of preserving the South Lebanon Army (SLA) and the "security zone" indeed dominated the Israeli position in the military talks with Lebanon held in late 1984 and early 1985 at the border town of Naqura under the UN auspices in an effort to forge an accord on Israeli withdrawal and security arrangements in South Lebanon. Operating under Syrian pressure and interfactional tensions, the Lebanese delegation insisted on full Israeli withdrawal to the international border and abolishing the "security zone" while refusing any security arrangements save the deployment of UNIFIL along the border, in accordance with its original mandate, and restoring the 1949 Armistice Agreement between the two states. The Israeli delegation, while unequivocally recognizing Lebanon's sovereignty over the whole territory held by Israeli forces, refused to entrust the security of the northern Galilee settlements to the Lebanese Army and UNIFIL. Instead, Israel suggested a gradual and coordinated withdrawal of its forces, deployment of UNIFIL north of the Litani River, with the South Lebanese militia deployed along the border and officially acknowledged as a legitimate and integral "territorial brigade" in the Lebanese Army.

The failure of the Naqura talks paved the road to the decision by the Israeli government in January 1985 to redeploy the IDF along the northern border "while maintaining a zone in southern Lebanon where local forces will operate with IDF backing."[39] Meanwhile, the death of Haddad and the search for a competent successor forced Israel to accept the condition presented by the designated SLA commander, Gen. Antoine Lahad, to expand the SLA deployment to the Christian town of Jezzin, as a detached enclave deep into the northeastern sector. In retrospect, the extent by which this decision stretched the Israeli "security zone" to the north in the eastern sector was to account for most of the Israeli casualties in the following years.

That the government decision on withdrawal was approved only by a margin of one vote indicates that the fourth alternative had no realistic chance. In retrospect, however, the assumptions on which the IDF preference was based, with the "security zone" at its core, confirm the common wisdom that old beliefs die slowly and that established concepts tend to survive long after they have become obsolete. Indeed, not only had these assumptions already been anachronistic, but the security establishment even adhered to them for years regardless of significant changes in the Lebanese political system and institutions.

First, the IDF overlooked the radical change in the nature of the threat to Israel from Lebanon since 1982. True, some Syrian-backed Palestinian factions remained active in the Biqa and the south, but by late 1984, their threat to Israel was significantly minimized as this area had become dominated by the Shiite militias that emerged as central players in Lebanon.[40] Moreover, in analyzing the potential threat to the northern Galilee settlements, no distinction was made between the Palestinian raison d'être of *liberating Palestine* and the Shiite guerrilla attacks aimed at *liberating the occupied Lebanese territory*. From the IDF viewpoint, they all represented a "terrorist" threat that Israel had to confront regardless of their political identity and motivation.

Second, the Israeli policymakers overlooked the hostility of the Shiite Amal movement toward the Palestinians and its determination to prevent their return to the south. A few months after the Israeli withdrawal began, the Amal militia placed the Palestinian refugee camps from southern Beirut to Tyre in the south under siege, which was only removed following the eruption of the first Intifada.

Third, the assumption that the SLA could maintain the "security zone"—with outside backup from the IDF—went against intelligence estimates and turned out to be utterly mistaken. It still remains unclear whether this evaluation had been put before the government when the decision on the "security zone" was made. In any case, within less than a year it became clear that the SLA failed to repel Hizbullah's attacks, forcing Israel to rush its own forces into the area to prevent a total collapse of the SLA.[41]

Fourth, despite warnings by intelligence analysts, the IDF leaders failed to appreciate the inevitable commitment of the Shiite militias to fight for the "security zone," especially in view of the Amal–Hizbullah competition over the Shiite community in Lebanon. Indeed, Hizbullah adopted the fighting against the "security zone" as a compelling rallying cause of holy war against the Israeli occupation of Lebanon's territory, which boosted the movement's rise to a mass social movement.[42]

Fifth, as in the years 1978–1982, the limited depth of the "security zone" restricted its role to preventing infiltrations into Israel's territory while being useless in preventing Katyusha rockets from being launched into Israel's territory. By late 1993, attempts to infiltrate Israel's territory came completely to a halt while a massive use of rockets against civilians in northern Israel was employed in the course of the 1990s, highlighting the irrelevant and obsolete nature of the "security zone" concept.

Finally, the decade-long mutual interest and collaboration with the SLA and the Christian Lebanese population along the border through routine encounters rendered the option of giving up on this ally inconceivable to the CGS and the DM. This aspect was to surface again in the late 1990s, when retired military commanders in key political positions expressed their sense of commitment to, and personal bond with, the SLA in explaining their adherence to the "security zone."

The process of evaluation of the operational alternatives by the GS underlined the IDF leadership's failure to see beyond the limits of purely military issues or to thoroughly discuss dissenting views regardless of hierarchical relations. The final decision was typically affected by prevailing perceptions and images of the "enemy," and led to a preference for experienced military strategies and means—strongholds, patrols, fences, etc.—over shaping strategies in accordance with the "enemy's" political and military realities, which in the long run could have reduced friction and stabilized relations with that enemy.

The Cost Effectiveness of the "Security Zone"

In retrospect, adherents of the "security zone" concept argued that it was the best military option and that the cost of civilian and military casualties must be seen as reasonably justified because it distanced Hizbullah and the Palestinians from the border and prevented infiltration into Israeli territory.[43] However, this conclusion is flawed mainly because it perceives the threats not as a dynamic dependent variable but as an independent reality, divorced from Israeli policies and activities, primarily the very existence of the "security zone." In the period from June 1985 to September 1997, the SLA sustained 358 fatalities and 1,210 injuries. In the same period of time, the IDF lost 212 soldiers with 677 others injured (6 killed and 170 injured civilians) in addition to 73 soldiers killed in the helicopters crash on their way to Lebanon in February 1997. In comparison, during the twelve years that preceded the Lebanon War, the IDF lost 54 soldiers at the Lebanese front with 297 injuries (compared to 40 killed and 380 injured civilians).[44] Thus, in the post-1985 years, the civilian population of the northern Galilee suffered fewer casualties, while the military paid a much higher price in both absolute and relative respects for maintaining the "security zone." Yet, in the post-1985 withdrawal from Lebanon, the routine life of the civilian population in northern Israel was frequently impeded by Katyusha rockets launched mainly by Hizbullah from within or north of the "security zone," which accounted for all the civilian casualties.[45]

The severity and psychological impact of the Katyusha weapon on the civilian population along the Lebanese border is demonstrated by two Israeli operations of heavy and continuous bombing and shelling of Lebanese targets, including villages and towns in South Lebanon in 1993 ("Accountability") and 1996 ("Grapes of Wrath"). Apart from failing to attain their objective of forcing Syria—through the Lebanese government—to put an end to Hizbullah's attacks against Israel, and the damage to Israel's image in the international arena, they clearly indicated the bankruptcy of the "security zone." Moreover, these operations resulted in international mediation and binding "understandings" between Israel and the Lebanese government which, apart from according Hizbullah a tacit international recognition, effectively enabled Hizbullah to continue operating from populated areas, while Israel's defensive and offensive capabilities were seriously restricted.[46]

The "security zone" was apparently successful in preventing guerrilla infiltrations into northern Galilee: only nine guerrilla infiltrations into the Galilee were executed—the last one, in December 1993—all by Palestinian groups, causing no casualties among civilians.[47] Yet this statistic tells only part of the truth because, as a matter of fact, in late 1993 Syria blocked the routes of Palestinian penetration into Israel.[48] Also, neither in 1985–2000 nor from the time of the full Israeli withdrawal from Lebanon until 2006 was an attempt by Hizbullah to cross the border into Israel discerned, although its combatants had reportedly reached the security fence along the border dozens of times, but systematically avoided crossing it into Israel's territory. For years, then, the IDF and Israeli decision makers chose to ignore the facts that indicated the futility of the "security zone."

True, during the years of the "security zone," Hizbullah leaders maintained an ambiguous position regarding their objective in the war against Israel, moving between a commitment to liberate Lebanon's occupied territory and another to keep fighting Israel itself for liberating Palestine. Effectively, Hizbullah's military activities largely reflected its domestic and regional objectives, especially the impact of Syria's interests and the ups and downs in its negotiations with Israel.[49] Thus, Hizbullah clearly stated its understanding that a Syrian–Israeli agreement would also include Lebanon and commit Hizbullah to cease its armed resistance.[50]

Challenging the "Security Zone" Concept: The Impact of Civil Society

The 1990s witnessed a reconstruction of war-torn Lebanon, while the region as a whole entered a decade of peace process. Under Syria's patronage, the Lebanese political system was reformed on the basis of the Ta'if agreement of national conciliation: all the militias—save Hizbullah's—were disarmed and dismantled and their members were largely incorporated in the renovated army; the economy was revitalized and soon attracted foreign investments; and the army, triple in size and with reinforced authority, demonstrated its ability to impose law and order, including by the use of violence.

Regardless of these changes, until 1997 the Israeli public had been effectively oblivious of the situation in South Lebanon; there was no noticeable attempt to question or reconsider the concept of the "security zone." Despite repeated salvos of Katyusha rockets onto the northern Galilee and the failure of operations "Accountability" and "Grapes of Wrath," the IDF and the security establishment remained unshaken in their adherence to the concept of the "security zone," which seemed to have struck roots as a permanent fact, hardly reviewed either at the level of the General Staff or by military commentators in the media.[51] A number of reasons may explain the Israeli public's disregard of the matter:

1. A relatively small number (up to 1,200) of Israeli soldiers served in the "security zone" itself (in addition to about 900 soldiers in the South Lebanon Liaison Unit) with a relatively low level of casualties (an average of twenty a year, which seemed to be tolerable).
2. Military service in South Lebanon fulfilled the expectation of Israeli combat soldiers for action and was seen as more prestigious and legitimate than policing assignments in the Occupied Territories.[52]

3. The military units employed in South Lebanon were purely regular, unlike those in the Occupied Territories, enabling relative isolation and
   distance from the public.[53]
4. Finally, the IDF managed to impose a curtain of secrecy on media coverage of the "security zone," preventing visits of reporters and minimizing information to the public. Supplementing the "communication fog"
   was the language used by the Israeli written and electronic media and of
   the term *saboteurs* (*mehablim*) when reporting on any act of violence or
   terror against Israel or the "security zone," regardless of the nationality,
   let alone the motives, of the perpetrators.

The issue of South Lebanon returned abruptly to the Israeli public
discourse following the crash on February 4, 1997, of two helicopters over
northern Galilee, which claimed the lives of 73 soldiers on their way to
the "security zone." Shortly before this disaster, the soaring number of
Israeli casualties in Lebanon and the restrictions on Israel's freedom of
action by the April 1996 understandings of Operation "Grapes of Wrath"
brought Minister of Domestic Security Avigdor Kahalani to state that
the IDF soldiers in Lebanon were "sitting ducks" for Hizbullah attacks
and to call for a unilateral withdrawal from Lebanon.[54] The shocking disaster triggered a new debate in the political system, which soon receded,
leaving the impression that Israel had no better realistic options.[55] The
helicopter crash, however, led to the spontaneous grouping of a handful
of mothers of combat soldiers under the name Four Mothers. Within a
few months the group was joined by hundreds of men and women and
assumed the form of an organized protest movement. Henceforth, it
was this movement that kept the issue of the "security zone" high on the
agenda, stimulating an ever-expanding public debate. While the initial
goal was somewhat hesitant, calling on the government to adopt "a new
and creative approach" to save the lives of young Israelis, by early 1998
the movement had adopted a clear stand in favor of complete pullout
from Lebanon.

Most Four Mothers Movement (FMM) senior members were from
the middle class and belonged to the center-left of the Israeli political
spectrum. Among them were bereaved parents and parents of soldiers in
active service, which helped shape their cause as appropriate and facilitated the movement's access to top political echelons. Hence, the movement's leadership insisted on adhering to the consensus on key issues of
national security and symbols. In 1999, the movement refused an invita-

tion from Yesh Gvul—a radical leftist group encouraging, among others, refusal to serve in the Occupied Territories—to take part in the latter's alternative ceremony of lighting torches on the eve of Independence Day, parallel to the central official ceremony attended by the state's civil and military leaders. For the same reasons, the movement refused calls by some activists to escalate the means of action by resorting to violent demonstrations and inciting new IDF recruits to refuse service as long as the IDF remained in Lebanon.[56]

The emergence of FMM and the relatively high level of losses sustained by the IDF in 1997[57] intensified the interest of the Israeli public in the military presence in South Lebanon, including Knesset members, academics, and reserve army officers. In September 1997, MK Yossi Beilin, one of the architects of the Oslo Accord, announced the establishment of the Council for a Peaceful Exit from Lebanon, which included a few MKs, mostly from the Labor and leftist Meretz parties, retired senior officials of the foreign ministry, and university scholars. The Council operated as a lobby, bringing up the "security zone" in academic symposia and working out a detailed plan for an exit from Lebanon with special attention to the defensive needs of Israel's northern settlements and a secure haven for the SLA personnel. The voice of the Council members in the media complemented the activities of the FMM and defused its initial public image as a group of mothers concerned for their kids and "speaking from their womb." In March 1998, the Council was instrumental in attaining a decision in support of a unilateral withdrawal from Lebanon by the "Council for Peace and Security," a prestigious association of retired senior military officers and veterans of foreign and security organizations. This decision legitimized calls by newly retired high-ranking officers in support of a unilateral exit from Lebanon, stating that the "security zone" was essentially a mistaken and harmful concept.[58]

FMM focused on grassroots activities, holding lectures, art and cultural events, happenings along the Lebanese border, and other publicly visible protest activities, and organizing petitions. Yet the most efficient avenue of the movement's activities was a systematic and ever-growing utilization of the media.[59] Leading members of the movement initiated meetings with the media to acquaint them with the movement's objectives and rationale and provide them with written briefings. Many among the presenters of popular radio talk shows empathized with the FMM's effort, especially in response to tragic events that claimed casualties in the "security zone" or northern Galilee. In addition to acting through the media, the movement also initiated ongoing private meetings with top political leaders and public figures, including President Weitzman, PM Netanyahu, Defense Minister Mordechai, and other government members, MKs, the chief rabbis, and mayors. The positive image of the movement connoted by its name helped open doors to decision makers and attracted media coverage.

The participation in these meetings of well-informed retired intelligence officers enabled the movement's delegates to present a professional exposé of the situation in Lebanon and explain their criticism of the current policy on the basis of comprehensive considerations of cost and effectiveness. Soon enough, women in the movement struck a sensitive cord by developing their own version of this discourse, combining rational arguments with rebuke of the military system, questioning the moral basis of employing young soldiers in a hopeless mission of fighting guerrillas, and refusing to accept the argument that this was a reasonable sacrifice for protecting Israel's northern border.[60] Contrary to previous conventions, this argument represented a growing perception among Israelis that, in view of the indefensibility of the "security zone," soldiers deserved no less security than the civilians along the border.[61]

The movement also pointed to Hizbullah's social concerns in addition to its combatant commitments; the fallacy of the linkage between pulling out of the "security zone" and a peace agreement with Syria; the problematic status of the "security zone" from an international normative viewpoint—an Israeli-occupied territory with systematic human rights violations conducted by the SLA[62]—and the strong conviction of freshly retired senior military officers that the defense of Israel's northern settlements could be conducted from the border itself. Spokespersons of FMM underlined that, since the "security zone" could not prevent the Katyusha rockets and Hizbullah had never crossed the border into the Israeli territory, the IDF was effectively protecting the "security zone" and the SLA, not northern Israel.

Remarkably, politicians and public figures repeatedly rolled the ball into the military's court, stating that they would accept the IDF's professional opinion. By and large, senior officials and public figures were poorly informed about the original causes of maintaining the "security zone," let alone its function and role under the current Lebanese and regional conditions, or Hizbullah's identity (Lebanese or Palestinian?) and motivation (implementing Syrian and Iranian orders?). In response to the arguments against the "security zone," the IDF officials were at pains to explain the purpose of the "security zone," except through the worn-out slogan about "defense of northern Galilee." Some pointed to its significance as a watch point on the Hasbani, one of the three tributaries of the Jordan River. Others claimed that it was a shock absorber for Syria's frustration about the continued Israeli occupation of the Golan Heights and a guarantee for maintaining the calm in this area.[63]

Indeed, opponents of a unilateral withdrawal emphasized the inevitable linkage with Syria as the only realistic alternative to the "security zone" because "only Syria" could guarantee the appropriate security arrangements between Lebanon and Israel.[64] This argument effectively admitted that Israel's presence in South Lebanon was to Syria's interest, enabling it to wage guerrilla warfare by proxy without risking costly Israeli retaliations. However, there was fear that denying Syria this advantage might force that country to opt for a strategy much more costly for Israel. This argument, held firmly by the right-wing government of Binyamin Netanyahu, as well as by senior members of the Labor and Meretz parties on the left, increasingly lost ground during Netanyahu's term as PM (May 1996–May 1999), during which no official negotiations were held with Syria, leading former supporters of this line of thought to advocate a unilateral withdrawal from South Lebanon.[65]

Support for unilateral withdrawal from Lebanon was steadily on the rise in public opinion polls: 41 percent in 1997, 44 percent in 1998, and 55 percent in early 1999.[66] The growing disenchantment with the "security zone" triggered an Israeli diplomatic initiative on April 1, 1998, by which Israel would withdraw from Lebanon in an agreement with its government and the latter's commitment to security arrangements along the border based on UN Security Council Resolution 425. Yet the initiative was totally refused by the Lebanese government, which stressed that any arrangement with Israel should be part of a comprehensive peace agreement with both Syria and Lebanon.[67] In late 1998, Netanyahu's government was on the verge of collapse, which precluded crucial decisions on the "security zone." In fact, the cabinet, fully backed by the GS, remained unanimously opposed to any withdrawal without an agreement with the Lebanese government.[68]

In early March 1999, three months before the general elections, prime-ministerial candidate Ehud Barak publicly undertook to "return the boys home" within a year of taking office, with or without a Syrian and Lebanese agreement. Barak's undertaking came a week after a Gallup poll showed that about two-thirds of the Israeli public were dissatisfied with the government's policy in Lebanon, with a substantial part of them favoring withdrawal via an agreement with Syria.[69] Barak's victory in the May 1999 elections, coupled by the SLA withdrawal from Jezzin that month, signaled the countdown to Israel's exit from Lebanon. The withdrawal from Jezzin was a result of the growing losses and crumbling morale of the local SLA militia under Hizbullah's attacks, not of political considerations. Indeed, the SLA commanders and personnel could hardly overlook the meaning of Barak's election as prime minister, and in hindsight it was only a matter of time before this force experienced a total collapse.[70]

Despite Barak's election victory and the appointment of MK Beilin as Minister of Justice, FMM decided to keep the pressure on the PM to make good on his promise to pull the IDF out of Lebanon. This turned out to be necessary in view of Barak's eagerness to renew peace negotiations with Syria as a preferable strategy to reaching a settlement over South Lebanon. Barak's first ten months in office focused on an attempt to bring the Syrians back to the negotiating table, using his commitment to withdrawal from South Lebanon as a stick. This strategy indeed brought Damascus back to negotiations with Israel in December 1999, but was insufficient to make Hafiz al-Asad accept Israel's conditions. It was only after the total collapse of the talks in March 2000 that the Israeli government decided on a unilateral withdrawal from South Lebanon. The decision was openly criticized by the CGS Mofaz, coupled with consistently alarming military intelligence estimates of the results of such a withdrawal: continued attacks by Shiite guerrillas joined by radical Palestinian groups and serious danger to the northern Galilee settlements.[71] As in other cases of such conduct, the PM refrained from taking measures against the CGS, which he later explained as stemming from the latter's incomplete information about the final demarcation of the reinstated international border.[72] In addition, senior military officers leaked to the press their frustration about PM and DM Barak for his avoidance of providing them with any information regarding the target date of the withdrawal or allocating financial resources for defensive infrastructure along the border.[73]

The destructive effect of this deliberate "battle fog" on the preparations for the final withdrawal from Lebanon and the fate of the SLA soon unraveled. Indeed, even at this pre-withdrawal stage, senior IDF officers of the northern command as well as the GS worked toward preserving the SLA and continuing to support it from the Israeli side of the border. According to testimonies of SLA officers, until the very last days before the withdrawal, IDF officers told the SLA personnel that they would stay put and that Israel would continue to back them.[74] This policy was apparently led by Deputy Minister of Defense Ephraim Sneh, an ardent supporter of the "security zone" concept and the SLA, leaving little doubt that it could occur without the PM's knowledge or consent.[75] These contradictory messages left the SLA in limbo: concerned about being abandoned by Israel, fearing for their own lives and their families' well-being, especially under Hizbullah's deliberate intimidation campaign regarding the gloomy future awaiting the SLA, the latter's personnel could hardly continue to fulfill their role as usual and watch the IDF leave the "security zone" in an orderly manner.

By mid-May, growing defection and morale collapse among SLA Shi'i units triggered a domino effect which culminated in the IDF's decision on 23 May for immediate and complete withdrawal from the "security zone." The hasty IDF exit from Lebanon that night together with more than five thousand SLA personnel and their family members was marked by panic and disarray, resembling a flight rather than the organized operation originally scheduled for one month later. The withdrawing forces left behind precious equipment and critical intelligence, all of which fell into the hands of Hizbullah. Indeed, the scenario of a sudden collapse of the SLA was not overlooked by commentators, yet this is precisely what took place.[76] Despite what was perceived by many as a "shameful" withdrawal from Lebanon, the three senior commanders responsible for the Northern command, territorial division, and the "security zone" were promoted to higher positions.

Israel's unilateral withdrawal from South Lebanon came under heavy criticism by analysts and politicians as a serious blow to Israel's deterrence capacity. Especially in view of the al-Aqsa Intifada, critics maintained that the eruption of Palestinian violence represented an attempt to emulate Hizbullah's success and drive Israel out of the Occupied Territories by force. Furthermore, these critics point to Hizbullah's continued effort to attack Israeli positions in the Sheba Farms and occasional shelling of Israel's territory along the Lebanese border as proof of the miscalculated withdrawal from South Lebanon. Although the discussion of these arguments belongs to another essay, two comments are relevant. The first argument ignores, or at least reduces, the Palestinian independent motivation for uprising, even if certain Palestinian leaders indeed linked their uprising to the withdrawal from Lebanon. As to Hizbullah's continued attacks, the argument ignores the fact that Hizbullah has been complying[77] with the international Israeli–Lebanese border and shifted the focus of its military activity to the Golan Heights, and that the total number of Israeli losses since May 2000—mostly due to attacks by Palestinian groups—hardly matched the average number of losses in the years prior to the withdrawal.

Conclusion

Israel's unilateral withdrawal from the "security zone" was a result of pressures from the bottom up on the political–military policymakers, initiated by a small but determined grassroots voluntary group that triggered a broad public debate and challenged the military's concept and rationale. Notwithstanding the role of retired military officers in the process and the adherence to a core national consensus, the campaign for pulling out of Lebanon involved typical character traits of civil society represented by FMM as an essentially feminine group in its concerns, discourse, and employment of the media. Indeed, that civilians could take part in discussing the hitherto monopolized sphere of security clearly demonstrated the blurred boundaries between society and the military in Israel rather than the militarized nature of society.

Unlike the IDF's "security discourse," which typically adhered to established military concepts of military defense as the ultimate response to terrorist threats, the protest discourse questioned the relevance of these concepts, underlining the gap between perceptions and realities about the enemy's identity and motivation. Even more significant was the civil discussion brought up by soldiers' mothers regarding the state's moral responsibility for the safety of their children, demanding that their lives should not be risked in futile missions such as the "security zone." The civil pressure for unilateral withdrawal from South Lebanon was indeed interpreted as an indication of the growing fatigue of the Israeli society of wars and sacrifices.[78] Yet it also signaled a civil drive to check the military's powers on security policymaking. In this context, the growing sense of a deadlocked policy, coupled with the knowledge provided to the public by critics of the "security zone" and their ability to define a clear objective to the politicians, forced the adherents of the concept into the defensive.

The public debate on the "security zone" reflected the nature of the issue at stake as a practical interest, with no symbolic attachment to the area, religious or national—other than the general commitment to the SLA—assuming an almost purely pragmatic, yet more complex nature. Opponents of the concept focused primarily on the cost and effectiveness of the "security zone" by demonstrating its futility in preventing any kind of attacks against Israeli civilians and questioning the convention that the only realistic alternative to the "security zone" was a comprehensive settlement with Syria and Lebanon. The public debate revealed the built-in discrepancies between objectives and performance of the "security zone" and pointed to its being a burden rather than an asset.

Adversely, the failure of repeated attempts during the first two years of the al-Aqsa Intifada by voluntary groups to apply the patterns of protest and discourse on South Lebanon to the Occupied Territories attests to the limits of civil society's capabilities to affect the national security agenda in Israel. Not only had these territories been long settled by Israelis, and perceived by large segments of Israeli Jews as indivisible parts of the Land of Israel, but the deepening sense of insecurity in the face of intense terrorist attacks against civilians in Israel's urban centers also left little room for civil discourse favoring a renewed strategic policy on these territories.

Notes

1. For acknowledgment of the role and impact of the movement, see (former PM) Ehud Barak, *Civil-Military Relations and the Withdrawal from Lebanon,* lecture at the Jaffe Center for Strategic Studies, Tel-Aviv University, March 17, 2003 [Hebrew];

Leora E. Frucht, "The Movement That Shaped the Lebanon Pullout," *Jerusalem Post,* June 8, 2000; Ronen Sebag, "Lebanon: The Intifada's False Promise," *Middle East Quarterly* 9 (2002): 16–17; Gal Luft, "Israel's Security Zone in Lebanon—A Tragedy?" *Middle East Quarterly* 7 (2000): 19.

2. Moshe Lissak and Dan Horowitz, *Trouble in Utopia, the Overburdened Polity of Israel* (Albany, N.Y., 1989), 203–213.

3. Yoram Peri, *The Israeli Military and Israel's Palestinian Policy* (Washington, D.C., 2002), 10–11, 25.

4. As admitted in Lissak and Horowitz, *Trouble in Utopia,* 208; Peri, *The Israeli Military and Israel's Palestinian Policy,* 11–12.

5. Peri, *The Israeli Military and Israel's Palestinian Policy,* 19–20, 25–26; Yoram Peri, *Between Battles and Ballots* (Cambridge, 1984), 145–48; Lissak and Horowitz, *Trouble in Utopia,* 208. For examples of civil-military coalitions, see Raful (Rafael) Eitan, *Soldier's Story: The Life and Times of an Israeli War Hero* (New York, 1991), 194–95, 227–28, 231–32.

6. Amos Perlmutter, *The Military and Politics in Modern Times* (New Haven, Conn., 1977), 267; Lissak and Horowitz, *Trouble in Utopia,* 207; Peri, *The Israeli Military,* 11, 37; Baruch Kimmerling, *The Invention and Decline of Israeliness: State, Society and the Military* (Berkeley, Calif., 2001), 226.

7. Peri, *Between Battles and Ballots,* 8.

8. Peri, *The Israeli Military and Israel's Palestinian Policy,* 22, 52; Lissak and Horowitz, *Trouble in Utopia,* 214–15.

9. Baruch Kimmerling, *The Invention and Decline of Israeliness,* 209. See also his "Militarism in the Israeli Society," *Theory and Criticism* 4 (1993): 123–40 [Hebrew].

10. See, for example, (Brig. Gen. Res.) Shlomo Brom, *Israel and South Lebanon: Prior to an Agreement with Syria* (Tel-Aviv, 1999) [Hebrew].

11. Craig Calhun, "Civil Society and the Public Sphere," *Public Culture* 5.2 (1993): 273–97; Simon Chambers, "A Critical Theory of Civil Society," in Simon Chambers and Will Kymlicka (eds.), *Alternative Conceptions of Civil Society* (Princeton, N.J., 2002), 92–93.

12. Joel S. Migdal, *Through the Lens of Israel: Explorations in State and Society* (Albany, N.Y., 2001), 108.

13. Ilan Talmud and Shaul Mishal, "The Network State: Triangular Relationship in the Middle Eastern Politics," *International Journal of Contemporary Sociology* 32.2 (2002): 178–81.

14. Oz Almog, *The Sabra: A Portrait* (Tel-Aviv, 1997), 357–59 [Hebrew]; Kimmerling, *The Invention and Decline of Israeliness,* 67–73.

15. Lissak and Horowitz, *Trouble in Utopia,* 32–97, define Israeli society as a "multi-cleavage society."

16. Kimmerling, *The Invention and Decline of Israeliness,* 110–12.

17. Migdal, *Through the Lens of Israel,* 116, 119–20.

18. Yael Yishai, *Between Mobilization and Conciliation: Civil Society in Israel* (Tel-Aviv, 2004), 83, 128 [Hebrew]; Migdal, *Through the Lens of Israel,* 117–19.

19. Asher Arian, *Security Threatened: Surveying Israeli Opinion on Peace and War* (Cambridge, 1995), 3, 250; Joel Beinin, "Challenge for Israel's Military," *Merip Reports* 92 (1980): 2–6.

20. Arian, *Security Threatened,* 263.

21. Oren Barak and Gabriel Sheffer, "Israel's Security Network and Its Impact: An Exploration of a New Approach," *International Journal of Middle East Studies* 38 (2006): 235–61.

22. Ofer Shelah, *The Tray and the Silver: Why a Revolution in the IDF Is Needed* (Tel-Aviv, 2003), 102–103 [Hebrew]; Kimmerling, "Militarism in the Israeli Society,"127; Yagil Levy, *Another Army for Israel: Materialistic Militarism in Israel* (Tel-Aviv, 2003), 87–88 [Hebrew].

23. Ilan Suliman and Stuart A. Cohen, "The IDF: From 'the People's Army' to a Professional Army," *Ma'arakhot* 341 (1995): 46–60 [Hebrew]; Stuart A. Cohen, "Changing Societal-Military Relations in Israel: The Operational Implications," *Contemporary Security Policy* 21.3 (2000): 116–38.

24. Cases in point were Kiryat Shmona, Ma'alot, Shamir, Nahariya, Beit She'an, and Rosh Hanikra (1974); Nahariya (1979); and Misgav Am (1980).

25. Beate Hamizrachi, *The Emergence of the South Lebanon Security Belt* (New York, 1988), 63–67.

26. Eitan, *Soldier's Story*, 185–86; Yitzhak Rabin, *Pinkas Sherut* (Tel-Aviv, 1979), 502–503 [Hebrew]; Laura Zittrain-Eisenberg, *My Enemy's Enemy: Lebanon in the Early Zionist Imagination 1900–1948* (Detroit, 1994); and Avi Shlaim, *Iron Wall: Israel and the Arab World* (New York, 2000), 186–217.

27. Rabin, *Pinkas Sherut,* 503; Patrick Seale, *Asad of Syria* (London, 1988), 279–80.

28. Hamizrachi, *The Emergence of the South Lebanon Security Belt,* 130, 143–44.

29. Rabin, *Pinkas Sherut,* 503; Hamizrachi, *The Emergence of the South Lebanon Security Belt,* 107–112; Eitan, *Soldier's Story,* 186–88, 192–93.

30. Eitan, *Soldier's Story,* 200–201; Hamizrachi, *The Emergence of the South Lebanon Security Belt,* 179–81.

31. Efraim Sneh, "South Lebanon Zone, a Model for an Israeli Security Zone," *Ma'arachot* 288 (1983): 2–8 [Hebrew].

32. Ibid., 6, 8; Hamizrachi, *The Emergence of the South Lebanon Security Belt,* 179–81.

33. Yezid Sayigh, *Armed Struggle and the Search for State: The Palestinian National Movement 1949–1993* (Oxford, 1997), 524; Ze'ev Schiff and Ehud Ya'ari, *Israel's Lebanon War* (New York, 1984), 83–84.

34. Arye Naor, *A Government in War* (Tel-Aviv, 1978) [Hebrew]. For the CGS response to postwar incriminations about misleading the government, see Eitan, *Soldier's Story,* 244, 248, 251–61, 256–57, 304.

35. Arian, *Security Threatened,* 75–77.

36. Uri Lubrani, "The Israeli Operative Aspect," in Joseph Alpher (ed.), *Israel's Lebanon Policy: Where To?* (Tel-Aviv, 1984), 39. See also Yitzhak Rabin, "In the Aftermath of the Lebanon War: Israel's Objectives," in Alpher (ed.), *Israel's Lebanon's Policy,* 43–44.

37. Reuven Erlich, "The Security Zone Concept and Its Practical Trial," in Yaacov Bar-Siman-Tov (ed.), *The Security Zone in Lebanon: A Reassessment* (Jerusalem, 1997), 11–12 [Hebrew].

38. See his soul-searching interview, Nahum Barnea, "Lubrani Exits Lebanon," *Yediot Aharonot* (Supplement), June 23, 2000, in which he admits that the concept had been essentially mistaken.

39. Cabinet Communique on the withdrawal from Lebanon, January 14, 1985, http://www.mfa.gov.il/MFA/Foreign%20Relations/Israels%20Foreign%20Relations%20since%201947/1984-1988/36%20Cabinet%20Communique%20on%20the%20Withdrawal%20from%20Leban.

40. Yosef Olmert, "Is a Stable Lebanese Arrangement Possible?" in Alpher (ed.), *Israel's Lebanon's Policy,* 6–7; and Gabriel Ben-Dor, "The PLO's New Military and Political Posture in Lebanon," in Alpher (ed.), *Israel's Lebanon's Policy,* 9–14.

41. Yossi Peled, "The Background of the IDF Presence in the Security Zone," in Bar-Siman-Tov (ed.), *The Security Zone in Lebanon: A Reassessment,* 31–33.

42. Nizar Hamzeh, "Lebanon's Hizbullah: From Islamic Revolution to Parliamentary Accommodation," *Third World Quarterly* 14.2 (1993): 321–37; Augustus R. Norton, "Hizbullah: From Radicalism to Pragmatism," *Middle East Policy* 5.4 (1998): 147–58.

43. See, for example, Luft, "Israel's Security Zone in Lebanon—A Tragedy?" 15–16; Erlich, "The Security Zone Concept and Its Practical Trial," 27.

44. Erlich, "The Security Zone Concept and Its Practical Trial," 22–23. In 1998 and 1999, the toll of IDF soldiers killed in Lebanon was 23 and 13, with 110 and 57 wounded, respectively; IDF Spokesperson's Office.

45. Luft, "Israel's Security Zone in Lebanon—A Tragedy?" 15, maintains that in 1985–2000, some 4,000 Katyusha rockets landed in the Galilee, with seven civilians killed by this weapon.

46. Barnea, "Lubrani Exits Lebanon," *Yediot Aharonot,* June 23, 2000; Itamar Rabinovich, *The Brink of Peace: The Israeli Syrian Negotiations* (Princeton, N.J., 1998), 102–103, 231–33.

47. Erlich, "The Security Zone Concept and Its Practical Trial," 20.

48. Danni Reshef, intelligence officer in South Lebanon until 1998, e-mail circular, January 12, 1999.

49. Rabinovich, *The Brink of Peace,* 102, 156, 226–27, 230; *Ha'aretz,* November 25, 1998, quoting the Head of the Military Intelligence Research Division on the Knesset's Foreign and Security Committee.

50. On Hizbullah's deliberately ambiguous objectives, see also Eitan Azani, "Hizbullah Movement—From Revolution and Pan-Islamism to Pragmatism and Lebanonism," Ph.D. diss., The Hebrew University of Jerusalem, 2005, 317–22 [Hebrew]; Daniel Sobelman, *Ha'aretz,* December 19, 1999, quoting Muhammad Ra'ad, MP and chair of Hizbullah's Political Council. Ra'ad's statement was in line with Syrian FM Farouq al-Shara's speech to the Arab Writers Association's meeting in Damascus, *al-Safir* (Lebanon), February 12, 2000.

51. The issue was discussed by the government in 1986 following a series of defeats sustained by the SLA; see Peled, "The Background," 31–32.

52. Amos Har'el, "The IDF Waits for Barak," *Ha'aretz,* May 20, 1999.

53. Eitan Rabin, "Officers in Golani: We Are Not Geese," *Ha'aretz,* February 11, 1997.

54. *Ha'aretz,* February 7, 1997. See also his previous statement calling for reconsideration of the "security zone" concept, *Jerusalem Post,* September 2, 1996.

55. For a comprehensive analysis of Israel's options, see Yossi Levy and Daniel Mor, "To Withdraw or to Attack—What to Do in Lebanon," *Ma'ariv,* February 10, 1997.

56. Some militant members seceded in early 1999 and established Kav Adom (Red Line), which conducted some illegal demonstrations and collided with the police.

57. In addition to the helicopter crash, in September, five soldiers in the "security zone" died in a fire in their barracks, followed by a failed Israeli seaborne raid of a Hizbullah base near Sidon, which left nine soldiers dead.

58. See, for example, a self-searching interview with Brig.-Gen. (Res.) Giora Inbar, Avihai Beker, "That's It, [We] Must Exit." The scope of this phenomenon led the CGS to prevent testimonies by IDF officers to the Knesset Committee of Security and Foreign Affairs, *Ha'aretz,* April 25, 1999.

59. For details, see Frucht, "The Movement That Shaped the Lebanon Pullout."

60. Danni Rabinovich, "Women in the Security Discourse," *Ha'aretz,* November 30, 1998.

61. Frucht, "The Movement That Shaped the Lebanon Pullout"; Dov Tamari, "The War in Lebanon Reassessed," in Bar-Siman-Tov (ed.), *The Security Zone in Lebanon,* 62.

62. *Human Rights Watch Report* (1999), Date accessed: June 8, 2006, http://www.hrw.org/reports/1999/lebanon/isrlb997-02.htm.

63. Zeev Schiff, "The Exit from South Lebanon Is Linked to an Agreement with Syria," in Bar-Siman-Tov (ed.), *The Security Zone in Lebanon,* 55.

64. Ibid., 53–57.

65. See, for example, (Maj.-Gen. Res.) Shlomo Gazit, "Unilateral Exit," Position Paper, September 15, 1997; (Brig.-Gen. Res.) Ran Peker, "Lebanon, Another Possibility," *Ma'ariv,* January 25, 1998.

66. Asher Arian, *Israeli Public Opinion on Security 2000* (Tel-Aviv, 2000), 24–25.

67. On the initiative and diplomatic efforts, see Barnea, "Lubrani."

68. *Ha'aretz,* November 21 and 25, 1998.

69. Sebag, "Lebanon: The Intifada's False Promise," 16.

70. On the SLA fears of abandonment by Israel, see Amos Har'el, "Abandonment Anxiety," *Ha'aretz,* March 24, 2000.

71. Uzi Benziman, "Confrontations," *Ha'aretz,* October 8, 1999; Ze'ev Ma'oz, "The Military Intelligence and the Withdrawal from Lebanon," *Ha'aretz,* February 21, 2000; Aluf Ben, "The Military Intelligence's Seniors to the Cabinet: The Terrorist Attacks Will Continue," *Ha'aretz,* April 28, 2000. For a detailed review of the pre-pullout estimates, see Daniel Sobelman, *New Rules of the Game: Israel and Hizbullah after the Withdrawal from Lebanon* (Tel-Aviv, 2003), 28–31.

72. Barak, *Civil-Military Relations;* Amir Oren, "The General Staff to Barak: Reserved about a Unilateral Withdrawal," *Ha'aretz,* March 12, 2003.

73. Amos Har'el, "Knowing How to Stay in Lebanon, Not Knowing How to Exit," *Ha'aretz,* November 17, 1999.

74. This was publicly confirmed by Uri Lubrani, Coordinator of the Government's Activities in Lebanon, in a symposium conducted by the Truman Institute, November 2001; see his interview with Barnea, *Yediot Aharonot,* June 23, 2000. See also Niv Hakhlili and Nir Hasson, "The IDF Property," interviews with former SLA officer in Israel, *Kol ha-'Ir* (Jerusalem), March 21, 2003, 48; Antoine Lahad's interview, Smadar Peri, "You Left a Scorched Land," *Yediot Aharonot* (supplement), June 14, 2002.

75. Barnea, "Lubrani Exits Lebanon," *Yediot Aharonot,* June 23, 2000.

76. Amos Har'el, "Lahad: I Will Not Be a Pawn of Israel," *Ha'aretz,* October 13, 1999; Har'el, "Knowing," *Ha'aretz,* November 17, 1999.

77. Until July 12, 2006, when Hizbullah attacked an Israeli military patrol across the border and abducted two soldiers, triggering a massive Israeli operation against Lebanon.

78. Deputy DM Efraim Sneh stated that Israel would leave South Lebanon because the Israeli public had problems standing firm. *Yediot Aharonot,* May 19, 2000.

FOUR

Intractable Conflict
and the Media

YORAM PERI

From a Postwar to a Warring Society

Growing recognition of media influence in society has led scholars of civil–military relations in Israel, as elsewhere, to pay increasing attention to the way the media interacts with the military, war, or "military affairs," as the realm of national security has come to be known.[1] These scholars are mindful of the rapid changes that have affected the media ecology in Israel since the early 1990s: proliferation and diversification of media outlets, the growing ascendancy of profit considerations, globalization, changes in the modes of action and in the professional culture, and more.

Scholars also dwell on the changes that have occurred in the media's approach to military affairs. They note the opening of the military to civilian systems and the media's encroachment on military spheres, which in the past were shielded from civilian eyes, such as elite security organizations, Mossad, the Air Force, and the Israel Security Agency (ISA, or Shabak). Even the previously hush-hush nuclear issue has not escaped this opening. Concurrent with this is the reduced standing of military correspondents, hitherto the main channel through which military–media relations were conducted, and above all the media's ever-increasing criticism of the military.

Broad consensuses over the transformation notwithstanding, scholars are divided between two fundamental approaches to these changes. One school holds that the media enjoyed considerable empowerment in the late 1990s, largely thanks to the easing of restrictions over its freedom of action (seen in the diluted power of military censorship) and the adoption of a critical approach toward the national defense establishment, even so far as slaughtering the sacred cow of security. All of the above serve to demonstrate the extent to which the traditional role of the military has contracted and the mechanisms of civilian control over it have strengthened.[2]

Adherents of this school, however, offer a variety of interpretations for the developments described here. Some ascribe them to the media's structural and functional changes.[3] A broader explanation relates these developments to the general decline in statism—of which the military is the ultimate expression—to the rise of civil society, and to processes of individualization in Israeli society, manifested in the citizens' demand for a larger contribution to determining their fate, including in the national security sphere.[4]

Proponents of the second school argue that although media–security relations have undergone a change, the basic pattern, in fact, remains unchanged. Even though the Israeli media of the 1990s were more diverse than those of the 1950s, more inquisitive, and more suspicious of the political and military establishment, they did not really act as representatives of the citizens vis-à-vis the apparatus of government: "More than the media represent society vis-à-vis the state; they serve the state vis-à-vis the citizens."[5] Since their establishment, the Israeli media have served the Zionist ideology, continue to disseminate the national narrative,[6] and serve as a socialization agent of the military–political elite. At bottom, the media, like institutions of education and other socialization agents, cause their clients to internalize the centrality of the military and of war, accepting them as inevitable and justified, as a natural part of life, and in this way they construct Israeli militarism.[7]

The distinction between these two viewpoints on the specific question of media–security relations reflects the general division between the traditional and radical paradigms in social sciences in general and media studies in particular. However, even among those who do not share the critical approach—whether it is neo-Marxist, poststructuralist, or neocolonialist—there are some who believe that the changes in media–security relations barely touch the surface and do not necessarily suggest a substantive transformation.

Which of the two schools more properly describes the profound process occurring in Israeli society? Do the changes, whose existence nobody denies, really reflect a fundamental transformation, or are they just superficial changes that in fact conceal more sophisticated systems of supervision and control that are used to restrict, restrain, and supervise the media, as in the past? A case in point is the increasing use of gag orders by the courts in the present decade, as well as the Attorney General's invocation of clause 113 of the 1977 penal law, dealing with "severe espionage." Might it not be argued that these legalisms are intended to make up for the relaxation of military control, and serve as an "alternative censorship"?[8]

By way of addressing this question, two distinctions ought to be drawn. First, the past two decades need not be regarded as a single time period. Rather, one should view them as two separate phases. Second, we need a more elaborate conceptualization of patterns of civil control of the security sphere, distinguishing between two types of supervision: instrumental control and fundamental control. Nicos Poulanzas's concept of "relative autonomy"[9] can be very helpful here. Let us begin with the first point.

The New Security Discourse at the Beginning of the Twenty-first Century

The summer of 2000 heralded a dramatic change in Israeli society. The collapse of the Camp David summit, followed by the outbreak of the second Intifada, marked the end of a decade which had seen the rising expectation that a hundred years of Israeli–Palestinian conflict might come to an end. Israeli society had regarded the peace process, or the Oslo process, as the beginning of a new era. Terminology of conflict resolution dominated the public discourse. The military leadership talked in earnest of a postwar era and the creation of a peacetime army; sociologists used American concepts of a post-military society, that is, a society marked by a decline in the centrality of the military and of the military ethos. Uri Ben-Eliezer defined this as "devaluation of the nation in uniform model."[10]

It is also possible to explain the changes from the opposite direction, namely, to claim that it was the decline in militarism—resulting from globalization and the interests of the dominant groups in the new economics—that led the parties to seek an end to the conflict. Whatever the case may be, the peace process undermined the national security ethos and brought about the beginning of demilitarization, to quote Yagil Levy.[11]

An article I wrote at that time,[12] reflecting views widely held in the second half of the 1990s, laid out the political and ideological discourse that prevailed within the elites in the forefront of the peace talks; at first with PM Rabin and, after a short interruption, with PM Barak.[13] It was not by coincidence that upon Barak's assumption of power, Chief of the General Staff (CGS) Shaul Mofaz publicly vowed to be Israel's first peacetime CGS.[14]

This euphoria was shattered in the second half of 2000, with the failure of the Camp David talks and the outbreak of the second Intifada. Israel's eighth war revived the national security discourse in a new version. First, the concept of limited conflict, or Low Intensity Warfare (LIC), was adopted; this was a radical change from the IDF's classic military doctrine. Then, when it became clear in the third year of the Intifada that Palestinian resistance could not be stamped out by military means, a new conceptual framework developed, whereby Israeli society is fated to be a "warring society."

This concept, the brainchild of CGS Moshe Ya'alon, means that the conflict is intractable. Israel is destined, at least in this generation and perhaps the next, to live by the sword. Ya'alon defined the Intifada as nothing less than a "continuation of the War of Independence (of 1948)" or "war for our home." Peace was again seen as an illusion and the belief that there was "no partner," nobody to talk to, was reinstated.[15] The Intifada dealt a severe blow to the "peace camp."

The relations between media and national security in Israel after 2000, therefore, cannot be couched in terms of the preceding decade. During the 1990s new media ecology had sprung up, along with a weakening of the government apparatus and a decline in militarism; an atmosphere of conflict resolution developed. In stark contrast to this, the first decade of the twenty-first century was marked by support of, and solidarity with, the state apparatus in the face of a military struggle, which was set forth in existential terms of life and death. The ethno-national view again rose to the fore, in a post-territorial version (a version which elevates ethnic cohesion above control over territories) and the warring society concept was adopted.

Nations at war tend to look askance at dissent. Quite a few peacetime liberties, including ones that are constitutionally enshrined, are no longer taken for granted and are offered little protection by the courts. War, after all, requires warriors to display perseverance and discipline, not to question their superiors. This view—expressed by Supreme Court Justice Oliver Wendell Holmes in the case of Schenck v. United States (1919)—resurfaced as the War on Terror was gathering momentum, even before and certainly after American's invasion of Iraq.[16] Indeed, freedom of expression, freedom of the press, and the public's right to know have always been the first victims when a democracy engages in war—all the more so in a war that is not waged thousands of miles away across the ocean, but very close to home, in the cafés and shopping centers of the capital.

It is hardly surprising that when confronted with a choice between security needs and freedom of expression, a high percentage of Israelis always preferred the former.[17] In 1995, 41 percent of Israelis agreed with this general statement: "The slightest threat to the security of the state is enough to justify serious restriction of democracy."[18] In another survey, a representative sample of Israeli society was asked whether freedom of expression in the media contributes to or endangers national security; 38.8 percent thought it contributed to security, while 61.2 percent thought the opposite. It is "security considerations" that account for the high rate of respondents (46.4 percent) who thought that freedom of expression in Israel was excessive, while only 7.1 percent thought there was too little of it. (A narrow plurality, 46.5 percent, thought the amount of freedom was sufficient.)[19]

There is little wonder that this pattern was repeated in 2001, within months of the outbreak of the new Intifada, with 74 percent of the public favoring greater self-restraint on the part of journalists at a time of national crisis and greater consideration for the perceived national interest. A mere 23 percent supported the notion that journalists should base their reporting on professional considerations. Approximately two-thirds of the public felt that the media should accept restraints and defer any criticism of the government; only one-third thought that they should continue to criticize the government even in times of crisis.[20]

Two years later, and still at the height of the Intifada, 73 percent of the respondents in a national sample replied that democracy could not exist without free media. By the same token, however, approximately half of the respondents felt the Israeli media had too much freedom; 70 percent favored the notion that the media should refrain from reporting "incidents" in the Palestinian territories that might be detrimental to Israel's reputation overseas, suggesting that freedom of the press was secondary to a matter of public relations.[21]

The Media as an Agent of Socialization for Conflict

Helped by the public's willingness to concede certain freedoms, the media, a most significant socialization agent in contemporary society, helped journalists in their task as manufacturer of meaning and consent in a society that exists in a prolonged war. In the past, sociologists dwelt at length on the role the media played in helping Israelis adjust to the realities of the conflict. They devoted little attention, however, to the media's promotion of the national security ethos and their elevation of the military culture to the fore of Israel's collective consciousness.

During the early days of the state, the press was largely mobilized and was expected to do its share in furthering national goals as defined by the political–military elite. Even later, when the deferential media changed their style and became critical and confrontational, they continued with political socialization of the masses, this time perhaps less consciously, not always openly, but more subtly. Before seeking an explanation, we should take a look at their mode of operation.

The Exclusivity of the IDF as the Main Source on National Security Matters

Unlike other social fields, information in the realm of national security is held as a virtual monopoly. In education, economy, sports, and culture, journalists enjoy access to a variety of sources, but when it comes to national security, the sources of information are few and access to them is controlled. Changes in media ecology notwithstanding, the national security establishment has managed to keep the lid on the free flow of information.

To this end, as discussed in other scholarly works, the defense establishment curtailed reporters' direct access to inside sources, forcing them to clear all contacts with the army's press office, stipulating that publication is conditional on prior arrangements such as clearance, censorship, or the presence of an officer at a journalist's meeting with a military source.[22] All of these enable the military to manipulate information related to national security, but there are also less obvious arrangements, such as leaking information to the Israeli media in the context of psychological warfare. One particularly interesting arrangement involves the accreditation of military correspondents.

The military correspondent is the only reporter whose assignment requires an official acquiescence of the agency he would cover. No editor would concede such a veto, say, to the minister of education or transport. Yet, not until the mid-1990s had a single editor opposed such a veto when national defense was concerned. The common argument editors proved reluctant to challenge was that, given the likelihood of a military correspondent encountering state secrets, he or she required security clearance. While not an unreasonable notion, the IDF could still be tempted to exercise the veto in a way not so much related to considerations of security, but as a means to deflect critical reporters and newspapers.

Despite the liberalization in the coverage of military affairs, the IDF still retains the ability to decide arbitrarily what topics journalists are not permitted to cover. It was only in 2005 that senior officers in the northern command revealed how they had conducted the war in southern Lebanon throughout the 1990s, without allowing reporters to enter the area to see what was really going on there. The IDF used draftees for combat duty and avoided calling up reserve soldiers in order to shield the Lebanon theater from the civilian population at large. For the same purpose, it prevented close coverage of events in southern Lebanon and manipulated the media without journalists being aware of it.[23]

The Military as a Source of Information on the Arab World

The media are the Israelis' main agent of meaning with regard to the Arab world. What are their sources of information on this world, and who shapes their perception of issues that are so important to the existence of the Israelis? For many years, the IDF was the chief source of information for Israeli journalists. In the early decades of the state, the availability of information on the Arab states was limited and slow, while the IDF provided the Israeli press with files of information from the Arabic media, compiled by its intelligence-gathering agency. Even after 1967 and the revolution in the media and telecommunications—opening of the skies, proliferation of channels, penetration of the Internet, and so forth—intelligence officers continued to serve as interpreters of the Arab world. Sometimes contact with them was especially smooth because the correspondents on Arab affairs were themselves former members of the intelligence community.

This was most salient with regard to Palestinian society. Despite the ongoing interaction in the occupied territories, the bulk of information flowing to the Israeli public has come from military sources. Senior reporter Danny Rubinstein, an old hand of the Palestinian beat, remarked, "there's a vast intelligence network, which provides information on what transpires in Palestinian society—no one can match it."[24]

Whereas the logic of a steady relationship between the IDF and military correspondents is self-evident, the close contacts the IDF maintains with reporters who cover Arab affairs raise an eyebrow. Is the military indeed best qualified to brief the media on nonmilitary aspects of life there, well beyond its jurisdiction? Few have questioned these close ties, even during the 1990s, when it became possible for the Israeli media to establish direct contacts with Arabs. Yet, although Israel had embassies in Egypt and Jordan, and Israeli correspondents could move freely there, no Israeli media organization has ever had a bureau in Cairo or Amman.

Not only the correspondents on Arab affairs, but also senior analysts in the print and broadcast media rely on evaluations and interpretations provided by the CGS and his deputy and various generals, first and foremost among them the head of military intelligence. Their evaluations relate not only to the Arab world, but also to Israel's foreign policy and to the international scene in general. Members of the public are offered little direct information from Arab sources, Arabic media outlets, or even to reports and analyses by foreign reporters stationed in Arab capitals. All in all, the information that comes their way is often processed by Israeli "analysts of Arab affairs," as they are regularly referred to, who closely rely on the military and many of whom were graduates of the security services.

Pack Journalism

Widespread journalistic practices in Israel serve to accentuate the formative influence the military exercises in shaping common views of the conflict, whether in a regional context or in a global sense. Those practices have to do with pack journalism that is so characteristic of the Israeli media. The close camaraderie among journalists who cover military matters, politics, or Arab affairs generates peer pressure for harmonization and coordination of the news output produced in various media outlets. While seemingly inconsistent with a reporter's natural impulse to beat the competition, there is a concurrent inclination to tread on safe ground, thereby reducing the risk of error and deflecting criticism from one's editor or colleagues. This eases the burden on a journalist operating in conditions of uncertainty.[25]

In a small society, where the pressures for uniformity and conformity are strong, such group thinking is liable to have disastrous results. This happened with the national security "conception" that led to the Yom Kippur War of 1973. The same happened in southern Lebanon, where for many years the IDF vehemently opposed withdrawal from the so-called "security zone," arguing that this would impede its ability to defend the towns and villages in northern Israel. When the IDF was finally ordered to withdraw, in 2000, it emerged that the security situation actually improved and the number of casualties dropped dramatically.

Journalists in Uniform

Like most other civilians, journalists are subject to military reserve call-up; quite a few end up serving in the military press office. In the past, the numbers used to be even higher. Serving as PR officers for the military is bound to influence the journalists' attitudes to security matters when they take off their uniform and return to their work in their respective news organizations. One manifestation of that was evident in 1991 in a television debate about the role of the media during the first Gulf War, when *Ma'ariv* editor Ido Dissenchik declared: "I am first of all an Israeli and an IDF reserve officer, and only then a newspaper editor."

In previous wars writers and intellectuals were also drafted by the military press handlers. Their wartime experiences in the Six-Day War, for instance, not only affected the way they covered the battles but also shaped their political outlook on issues that emerged as a result of this war. Many of them were carried away by the historic reunion with the beloved motherland, swept up in the national pathos, and became ardent supporters of political attitudes which would in time cause them embarrassment.[26]

Old Boys' Network

The IDF's influence on the Israeli media stems from the fact that it serves as the major training college for journalists. For many years, Army Radio, *Galei Zahal,* was the largest and most productive school of journalism in Israel, followed closely by the IDF journal, *Ba-Machaneh.* Dozens of journalists, editors, and anchors as well as producers, who reached the peak of the Israeli media in all the news organizations, had done their military service in IDF media organizations. After their mandatory service, many fulfilled their reserve duty in the same units, keeping up their professional and social contacts, and thus the old boys' network continued to influence them over the years. Added to this are people who went through the socialization process in military media organizations and became key figures in the worlds of culture and politics.[27]

Methods of Influence

The security establishment and the military use various mechanisms to induce the media to promote the security ethos. The media, on their side, also use more subtle methods in addition to direct indoctrination. Below are a few of the most effective ones.

CONCEALMENT

Israeli journalists are in the confidence of members of the administration much more than their counterparts in other open societies, but there was always a gap between what they knew and what they wrote. Following the first works by Dina Goren and Moshe Negbi, various scholars took up this issue and brought as evidence the matter of the Editors Committee. In exchange for becoming privy to state secrets, the daily newspaper editors undertook not to publish them, thus compromising freedom of the press.[28] This evidence, however, is less impressive because the Editors Committee had already lost its standing and influence back in the 1980s. In contrast, other mechanisms, some less familiar and overt, have left their mark. Paramount among them is the fact that frequently a journalist would *choose* not to release information he or she had acquired on matters related to foreign policy and national defense. Here are two typical examples:

Immediately after the Six-Day War, Defense Minister (DM) Moshe Dayan famously proclaimed that Israel was "awaiting a phone call" from King Hussein of Jordan if the monarch were indeed interested in reclaiming lost territories in exchange for peace. Should he do so, Dayan assured the world, he would encounter a positive response in Jerusalem. The Israeli press went on reproducing this quote time and again as if the king had really been keeping silent, but in fact they were concealing the truth.

King Hussein did not remain silent. He did make the proverbial phone call. Be it in person or by proxy, he engaged Israeli officials in serious talks and expressed willingness to sign a peace accord in exchange for Israel's withdrawal from the occupied territories. It was Israel that failed to pick up the receiver. On June 19, 1967, the cabinet voted for withdrawal from the territories captured from Egypt and Syria in exchange for a peace treaty. Conspicuous in its absence from this formula was the West Bank that King Hussein was so eager to regain. By accepting Dayan's theatrics as genuine, the media helped foster the false notion of an intransigent king, undeserving of Israeli trust or generosity.

The media also concealed the extent to which the military involved itself in *political* decisions, offering advice and exhortations on matters that are only partly related to defense. The following cases would attest to it. One is that of Rehavam Zeevi, then assistant to the chief of the Operations Division, and later Central Command General Officer Commanding (GOC) and Knesset Member, who, on August 7, 1967, addressed a question raised in the General Staff over Israel's territorial aims. Israel's purpose, he asserted, "was not to seek peace, but to dictate order." He went on to explain:

> I am afraid of peace. I think that from the point of view of the Jewish and Israeli nation, peace in the next ten years would entail many hazards. I had spoken about this even before I saw Jews entering the West Bank, but with our demographic structure today half of the Israelis are "second class Israelis" possessing a Levantine background. If we can travel to Beirut for a vacation, it involves great danger. We need indeed to get there, but not to dictate peace but to force a resolution . . . to break the enemy's ability to defeat us.[29]

Ten years later, when peace talks began with Egypt, DM Ezer Weizman asked CGS Motta Gur to sketch a peace map for Israel. Gur refused, although he was given an explicit order by the minister, replying: "I will not draw such a map, and I recommend that you do not draw any map of peace borders. We must not present a map of peace borders to the American Secretary of State who asked for it, and we must not present it at the Geneva Conference." What was the CGS's explanation? There is no need to present a peace map because we don't need peace at all now. "The aim of the state of Israel, and of world Zionism, was and will be to gather most of the Jewish nation in Israel. For this purpose we must go on building an infrastructure of settlement, industry, government, and military in all the areas that we consider vital for the fulfillment of Zionism. The better we build this infrastructure, the more the final borders will be firmly established and accepted by all the parties to the conflict, by agreement or by force."[30]

The CGS also had another argument against peace. In a discussion with the DM on December 17th, he said: "So long as the war and the tension go on there is a social melting pot in Israel. The moment it stops the melting pot will disappear. In my opinion the melting pot will come to a premature end if there is peace now. We can build much more and only later reach a final resolution concerning the borders and the relations between us and the Arabs."[31] Gur's attitude was known to the journalists who were close to him, but it didn't occur to them to share this knowledge with their readers. Instead, they went on repeating the conception that the IDF was not involved in politics, and also that it was the Arabs who were not interested in reaching a settlement, so Israel had no partner for negotiations.

A comparative analysis of the coverage of the first Intifada by Israeli television and by international television networks illustrates the fact that the Israeli TV avoided showing basic information on what was happening in the territories. From time to time, material on IDF actions, the various government authorities, or the settlers was published in official reports (e.g., the Karp Report in the 1980s, the Sasson Report at the beginning of the present decade) or in books,[32] but these were exceptional cases. Documentaries (such as one showing what happens at checkpoints) do not reach the national media channels but only niche channels (such as channel 8) or alternative outlets (e.g., cinematheques). When they are aired on the national media, as happened with Haim Yavin's TV series on the settlers (2005), the Israeli audience reacts with surprise and shock despite the fact that anyone who seeks information can easily get it through alternative channels.

SILENCING

Even worse than concealment is the action of deliberately silencing voices that come from other, subversive, "undesirable" sources. Following the collapse of the Oslo process and the outbreak of the Intifada, in the 1990s many right-wing speakers alleged media suppression of information and attitudes inimical to the process. They asserted that the Israeli public would not have been so surprised at the failure of the Camp David summit and the outbreak of the Intifada if the attitudes of those who opposed the agreement—attitudes concerning corruption in the Palestinian Authority or the continued incitement against Israel—had been made known.

With hindsight, senior journalists have acknowledged the truth of this criticism, just as today they acknowledge the tendency to apply this mechanism in other matters. This issue was raised publicly when, in 2005, one of Israel's senior journalists, Amnon Abramovich, argued that his colleagues should be lenient on then PM Ariel Sharon, who was implicated in a major corruption scandal. The reason, Abramovich suggested, was Sharon's disengagement policy, which journalists favored. The allegations triggered a public controversy; a journalist had publicly called upon others to use the silencing method. In most cases, the silencing policy is not exposed, and is often implemented unconsciously.

WORD LAUNDERING

A mechanism no less effective than concealment and silencing is word laundering. What I refer to is not the age-old philosophical quandary concerning the ability of words to express the things themselves, to signify the signified, but rather the more mundane issue of an Israeli media practice to misrepresent national security–ated news by resorting to a refined, diluted, and emasculated language with the effect of voiding it of meaning. This is evident primarily in media coverage of events in the Palestinian territories.

The killing of a Palestinian by IDF soldiers is softened by the use of such terms as "the man found his death." When the one killed or injured is a child under the age of twelve, he is described as "young." Demolition of houses and uprooting of trees in order to extend the IDF's field of vision is described as "stripping." In other cases, the choice of words may be made unconsciously, but it helps to establish the only truth that is acceptable from the viewpoint of the national security establishment.

Many years after 1967—still under the Labor-led government—it was impossible to use the word *Palestine* in publications. When a journalist wrote "the Palestinian mayor," the text was rewritten as "the Arab mayor." During the period of the Likud government, denial of the Palestinian nation's existence was given legal expression through prohibitions of all contacts with PLO members. At the journalistic level this was expressed by the prohibition on interviewing Palestinian leaders. "Not long ago," said one journalist, "I saw a large orchard being uprooted near Beit Hanun [in the Gaza Strip]. This is how I heard it described by the IDF spokesman: 'The IDF removed shrubbery that served as a hiding place for terrorists.' Removed shrubbery! This is simply a linguistic corruption, it is a corruption of the mind."[33]

Sometimes word laundering was imposed by the political leadership. One example was PM Menachem Begin's instruction to state radio and television, as soon as he assumed power in 1977, to substitute the ideologically loaded "Judea and Samaria" for the "West Bank" in describing the largest Palestinian enclave under Israeli control. Similarly, the Gaza strip was unstripped and was recast as "the Gaza *region*," a clear implication it was no longer a land locked between the sea and Israel but rather an integral part of Israel. Begin's nuances were reciprocated years later by Yitzhak Rabin. As soon as he became prime minister in 1992, he switched back to "the territories," a common, neutral post-1967 reference. That was the first indication, however subtle, of a pending policy change. In most cases, word laundering was used by editors and journalists who knowingly adopted concepts and speech patterns that were prevalent in the IDF and the other security services.

The Role of the Media in Limited Conflict

The operational nature of Israel's response to the second Intifada, which assumed the form of counter-insurgency warfare, served to exacerbate traditional tensions between the needs of a free press and the perceived needs of national security.[34] In this kind of limited conflict, also known as a fourth-generation war, the trademarks of conventional wars are blurred: it is not a war between armies, and the belligerents, at least on one side, are civilians. There is no distinction between the front and the rear. The fighters mingle in the civilian population and deliberately attack it. It is an ongoing war of attrition with no apparent winners. Its aims are not to conquer territory or destroy enemy formations but to wear down the antagonists' resolve. The demarcation lines between the political and military echelons are blurred, with the civilian echelon going as far as involving itself in micromanagement of the military (as happened in the United States) or the reverse, a situation in which the military gains strength at the expense of the political leadership (as happened in Israel).[35]

Wars tend to challenge democratic liberties and make their defense ever more difficult, but the blurring of boundaries that characterizes limited conflict increases these difficulties yet more. Since it is a struggle against clandestine terrorist organizations, intelligence plays a crucial part in the war, and since the battle is waged to change the minds of the adversary's civil society, it is a war between narratives. For this reason, the U.S. Senate so willingly adopted the Patriot Act, which has curtailed some civil rights. Similar policies were adopted in other democracies, such as Britain and Australia, who were American allies in the invasion of Iraq.

Particularly detrimental to free speech and free press is the IDF's openly proclaimed goal of remolding the state of mind of the Palestinian civilian society. An author of Israel's new security doctrine, CGS Ya'alon, stated openly that the IDF was waging a struggle to "embed in Palestinian consciousness" the realization that the price of insurgency is so high that continued violence is no longer worth pursuing. There are, however, two sides to this coin. Reshaping an adversary's consciousness requires "the media [not only] to fire psychological bullets" at the enemy. It is as vital to influence the entire "theater of conflict," that is to say, to shape perceptions of civilian society in Israel proper: to deepen its belief in its rightness and to secure domestic accord. Discord and excessive disagreements on the home front are likely to erode unity from within and send a signal of weakness to the enemy.[36]

In and of itself, the utilization of mechanisms of representation, socialization, and propaganda during wartime is hardly a groundbreaking notion. New here, however, is the IDF's quest for full partnership in the process of shaping civilian consciousness, a role hitherto assigned to civilians. In pursuit of its newly claimed role in the battle for minds, the IDF has now restructured its public relations work, expanded the Spokesperson's Unit, and redefined its tasks and mode of operation. For the first time ever, the IDF is now placing considerations of publicity and image-making on a par with other elements of operational planning. The supportive media appeared unperturbed by the role they were assigned in reporting the Intifada, and carried it out in the belief that displays of patriotism were necessary.

Discussion: Instrumental Control and Fundamental Control

In the first decade of the twenty-first century, the media stood firmly by the government. With the aim of broadening the national consensus, the media set off to propagate the Israeli national narrative and minimize the effect of that of the Palestinians. Other meaning-making systems rallied to help the IDF win the battle for the people's minds. Just as the Hebrew University cancelled courses on Palestinian society when the second Intifada broke out, "because the time is not appropriate," newspaper editors refrained from carrying Hebrew translations of articles by Palestinian writers.[37]

Media outlets, however, did not stop airing opinions critical of the IDF. Once the level of terrorist attacks declined in the course of the Intifada's third year, there was a marked increase in the number of articles questioning the military's mode of operation, its conduct in the Palestinian territories, its decision making, and the actions of individual army units. In the latter category, media reports alleged the abuse of corpses by soldiers and the excessive use of lethal force against Palestinian children.

The apparent contradiction between rallying around the flag on the one hand, and criticizing the military to the extent of damaging the flag on the other, may in fact not be a contradiction at all. By way of solving the quandary, we need to distinguish instrumental control from fundamental control. Under the former, the media play the role of loyal insiders whose criticism is intended to reinforce the prevailing order, not to challenge it. Under the latter, the media position themselves as outsiders willing to question not merely failed practices but the very policy assumptions that made those failures possible in the first place. It is the difference between a facilitator of the national security doctrine and a detractor. The former uses considerations of effectiveness while the latter examines the basic assumptions of the security doctrine, such as self-reliance, self-defense, and perception of the just war.

Media scholars, such as Daniel Hallin and Lance W. Bennett, who addressed the media's criticism during wartime conceived of the indexing model. They argued that when media systems assume a critical attitude, the degree of freedom that they allow themselves reflects the range of opinions existing among decision makers, and in all events they will not deviate from the range of dominant ideologies.[38]

This explanation lowers the evaluation of the media's autonomy in polyarchic regimes. A comparison of journalists with intellectuals as agents of meaning may be helpful, as both take part in the struggle to determine meaning within a field of alternative meanings. In the Western liberal tradition, the intellectual is supposed to be a person who questions the nature of the social and political order, and does this out of moral commitment to the truth. An intellectual's standing derives largely from the perception of selflessness, which is to say that he or she is expected to be entirely disengaged from the power players, subject to the intellectual's skepticism and criticism. His or her only commitments are to the values of justice and integrity, which form the basis for the social and collective being, and to provide a true account of reality.[39] In this respect, the intellectual's role resembles that of a biblical prophet, the one who speaks truth to power, but for the caveat that few public intellectuals nowadays claim a divine mandate.

The journalist's mission has two aspects, one prophetic and the other social. The prophetic mandates a relentless quest for the truth, to be upheld under all circumstances irrespective of the consequences. The social entails a service to the collective as represented by the supreme political authority, the state. As such, journalists have a socializing, educational, and mobilizing role. They act in the service of the sovereign or the ruler, and their purpose is to promote social solidarity and support the existing order—indeed, to manufacture consent. This second aspect is more evident, particularly in social movements struggling for national independence, in the early stages of nation-building or state-building, or when external or internal forces threaten the existence of the collective.

After World War I, Europe abandoned its expectation that the intellectuals would fulfill their role. Julian Benda, in his classic book *The Betrayal of the Intellectuals*,[40] showed how intellectuals had surrendered their autonomous status and availed their services to a brutal racist or nationalist authority. When this eager subservience to a cause other than the truth recurred with even greater intensity under fascism (with Heidegger, who rallied behind the Nazi regime, and French intellectuals, who offered support to the Vichy government), the standing of intellectuals in the realm of righteous expectations suffered a devastating, possibly fatal blow. A far more skeptical evaluation has come to dominate public perceptions, that which had viewed intellectuals all along as agents for the powers that be. If this is the case, is there no difference between intellectuals in totalitarian regimes, where they serve as full agents, and those functioning in polyarchic systems, where they appear to have a certain degree of autonomy?

Poulanzas addressed this question, suggesting that we distinguish between autonomy and partial autonomy.[41] He argued that even national institutions, including ideological state institutions, might retain a certain degree of independence or autonomy in their actions. This autonomy is granted to them by a ruling class bent on enhancing its legitimacy by fostering the illusion of freedom.

Without accepting Poulanzas's theory in its entirety—for example, his class approach—we can adopt the concept of partial autonomy, and identify the conditions in which the autonomy of agents of meaning, such as intellectuals or journalists, will be strengthened or weakened. Evidently, a threat to the existence of the collective or to its internal solidarity will serve to restrict their autonomy. Poulanzas's notion of relative autonomy is useful in explaining the nature of Israel's transition from the twentieth to the twenty-first century.

Toward the end of the twentieth century, when the sense of physical security in Israel grew stronger, the formerly hegemonic uniform ideology lost its monopoly and alternative narratives reappeared. The hegemonic ideology retained power within the community of agents of meaning, but could no longer claim unfettered predominance. This state of affairs permitted the media a broader range of interpretations. In addition, alternative opinions critical of Israel's security ethos, Zionist creed, and Ashkenazi dominance finally emerged from the fringe of society to claim a more central role.

One reflection of this is apparent in the public school system. There, history textbooks became the subject of vigorous criticism, whereas until the 1990s, the official national narrative resided all by itself. Since then, alternative narratives, hitherto unheard of, vie for recognition. A case in point is the suggestion that the 1948 war no longer be referred to only as a war of "liberation" or "independence," but also be recognized by its Palestinian designation, *Al-Nakba,* or disaster.[42]

So is the case of the media: in a departure from the past, they give expression to civil society and to individuals, yet their autonomy is relative, their civil control instrumental, not fundamental. Content analysis of news, essays, and articles on military affairs reveals plenty of rebukes and chidings, but by and large they are directed at the perceived failure to carry out the policies rather than at the policies themselves. The media would elaborate on the extent to which mishaps and deficiencies undermined stated goals; it would study conscripts' service conditions, officers' normative conduct, treatment of women in the military, and even the normative behavior toward Palestinians. The most outstanding example is that of Carmela Menashe, national radio military correspondent, who has become something of an informal IDF ombudsman.

In contrast, there is an almost total absence of fundamental control—criticism of the place of the military in Israeli society, the basic assumptions of the security ethos, the guiding principles of the national security doctrine, the nature of national security decisions, or the weapon systems policy. The public discourse regarding the defense budget reflects this lack of fundamental control. Though the occasional voice would be raised in support of budget cuts, at no time has the call been made for a thorough budget overhaul, one that would necessitate a moratorium on all entitlements, indeed a zero-based budget to be drafted from scratch rather than from the expense level of the previous year. With practically everything laid on the table, fundamental questions, hitherto absent, would be posed regarding the very nature of national security and the definition of security needs. Actual answers would have to be provided if an entirely new budget were to be submitted.

In conditions of relative autonomy, instrumental control examines the effectiveness of the existing system, while fundamental control asks questions about the character of the social and political order, the nature of the defense arrangements, the basic assumptions underlying the security concept, the basic principles of militarism, the possibilities of reaching a diplomatic solution to the conflict, and the use of force in foreign policy.

Fundamental criticism would first address the primary problem of Israeli society since 1967—the ongoing occupation. The Intifada, which broke out in 2000, bolstered Israel's military–political elite in its basic assumption that the conflict with the Palestinians was existential rather than territorial, and as a result, the elite has failed to see the link between continued occupation and perpetuation of the conflict. The Hamas victory in the 2006 Palestinian elections rendered even more credence to the "existential" assumption in that it made it possible for its proponents to depict the Israeli–Palestinian conflict as one that began some sixty years ago and has raged practically uninterrupted ever since. In Ya'alon's words, this is "the war for our home," or "the continuation of the War of Independence." Even those who dismiss the Palestinian narrative might still acknowledge that the conflict is being conducted in two dimensions, and in fact two battles are taking place simultaneously. One is the Palestinian struggle against the very presence of a "Zionist entity" in the midst of the Muslim Arab space. In this battle, the Palestinians do not shy away from acts of terrorism. The other battle is that which the Palestinians wage in pursuit of national liberation and for self-determination, goals whose attainment is not irreconcilable with coexistence alongside Israel. Two dimensions are also evident in Israeli thinking and practices. One is that in which Israel is conducting counter-insurgency warfare against organizations that resort to terror. The other dimension is the one in which Israel is fighting a colonial war designed to expand its territorial control and ensure that any future agreement will leave in its possession the greatest portion of territory west of the River Jordan.

The Palestinian struggle against Israel's existence has little international legitimacy, which is why the Palestinians make an enormous effort to describe their struggle as a war solely intended to extricate themselves from the yoke of Israeli occupation. Equally, there is no international legitimacy for Israel's war of territorial expansion, which is why Israel chooses to portray the war as self-defense against a terrorist onslaught bent on destroying it.

Since the outbreak of the Intifada, the Israeli media have joined in the effort to describe the war as having only one face, a struggle for national survival, "the battle for our home." For this reason, footage showing the colonial aspect of Israel's presence in the territories rarely hits the television screen. TV reporters do not show the behavior of the settlers, the actions of the army, or the suffering of the Palestinians. That is why techniques of concealment, silencing, distortion, and word laundering are being used. Anyone defying the restrictions and attempting to shed light on the real situation in the territories is seen as damaging the national narrative and undermining national resolve and strength. They are regarded as unpatriotic.

One example of this is Israel's self-perception as a hapless victim at the receiving end of the conflict, while the Palestinians are the instigators and the aggressors, the incorrigible enemies of an otherwise perfectly acceptable status quo. To the extent that Israel engages in violent activity, it is but a response to unprovoked Palestinian violence. The Palestinians, on the other hand, view the status quo as an unacceptable perpetuation of aggression that Israel originally unleashed. They merely respond to Israel's unlawful seizure of and continued presence on their land. We are not concerned here with historical verdicts on right and wrong, but rather with how the media construct the narrative. I would argue that the Israeli media present the Israeli side almost exclusively, while ignoring, concealing, silencing, and denying the other narrative.

A study of the very term *occupation* could help us navigate through the intricacies of the struggle over the narrative. Noteworthy is the absence of the term *occupation* from the political vocabulary. Not until the late 1990s had the term been invoked by mainstream media outlets, and even then it was used only by some representatives of the Israeli left. The hegemonic concept was dominant in major media outlets—three television channels, two radio stations, and two mass circulation tabloid newspapers. Few reporters or commentators dared employ the term *occupation*. The other approach found an outlet mainly in alternative channels, local papers, certain small political journals, and Internet sites.

Criticism voiced on the national channels was purely instrumental, not fundamental, and the existence of instrumental criticism actually reinforced the legitimacy of the national media, because in an era of critical media the total absence of criticism would have damaged the status of the media in the public eye.

From this point of view, the case of *Ha'aretz* is worthy of close scrutiny. Israel's newspaper of record was the only mainstream media outlet that persisted in carrying fundamental control throughout the period of the Intifada. It was the only paper that assigned a staff correspondent to cover the conflict from within the Palestinian territories (first stationed in Gaza and later in Ramallah); it has run a regular editorial page column by a senior writer focused on the Palestinian viewpoint; and it has offered a stage for a profound dissent, bitter at times, from the dominant security-centered approach.

The contention that *Ha'aretz*'s coverage of the Intifada did not differ all that much from the rest of the media[43] is simply not borne out in that it ignores the iconoclastic role this paper sometimes played in defying the hegemonic national security ethos, at times alienating the elite readership to which it caters. *Ha'aretz* has earned a place in the annals of the Israeli media as the one that provided a platform for dissenting voices and served as a tool of fundamental supervision in the matter of national security.[44] Little wonder that the paper reaped harsh criticism both from the political class and its own subscribers. In the first years of the Intifada, *Ha'aretz* lost a few thousand readers (a significant number given that its overall daily circulation is well below 100,000) and even some of its writers, who disagreed strongly with the paper's "unpatriotic" inclinations.

Ha'aretz's case is fascinating because it was the opposite of what might have been expected. One might have expected a publisher, stung by declining circulation and lost revenue, to pressure his editors to come to terms with the *Zeitgeist* and toe the line. In actuality, *Ha'aretz's* publisher not only strongly approved of the critical line but in fact overruled senior editors who sought to moderate the paper's contrarian tone and bring its editorial positions closer to those of the government and the defense establishment.

This internal debate in *Ha'aretz* appears to cast some doubt over the applicability of political–economic theories in the media. If radical media scholars were to be believed, and the conduct of the media could be understood in pure economic terms, the publisher would have been expected to hold his economic interests well above political or moral principles. In the case of *Ha'aretz,* quite the opposite was true. *Ha'aretz* notwithstanding, free speech in wartime Israel was subjected to voluntary self-rationing. Rationed freedom is of course vastly superior to no freedom at all, yet rationed freedom deserves little idealization.

Notes

1. Udi Lebel, *Security and Communication: The Dynamics of the Interrelationship* (Beer-Sheva, 2005) [Hebrew].

2. Stuart A. Cohen, "The IDF's Over-dependence? Change in the Relations between the Civil and Military Echelons in Israel," *Studies in Middle Eastern Security* 64 (2006): 1–24 [Hebrew].

3. Hillel Nossak and Yehiel Limor, "Military and Media in the Twenty-first Century: Toward a New Model of Relations," in Udi Lebel, *Security and Communication,* 69–100 [Hebrew].

4. Yoram Peri, "The Changed Security Discourse in the Israeli Media," in Daniel Bar-Tal, Dan Jacobson, and Aharon Kleiman (eds.), *Security Concerns: Insights from the Israeli Experience* (Stamford, Conn., and London, 1998), 215–40.

5. Gad Barzilai, "State, Society and National Security, Mass Media and Wars," in Moshe Lissak and Baruch Keni-Paz (eds.), *Israel Facing the Year 2000* (Jerusalem, 1996) [Hebrew].

6. Daniel Dor, *Intifada Hits the Headlines: How the Israeli Press Misreported the Second Palestinian Uprising* (Bloomington, Ind., 2004).

7. Haggit Gur (ed.), *The Militarization of Education* (Tel-Aviv, 2005), 9–14 [Hebrew].

8. Moshe Negbi, "The Rise and Fall of Security Censorship in Israel," in Udi Lebel, *Security and Communication: The Dynamics of the Interrelationship* (Beer-Sheva, 2005) [Hebrew].

9. Nicos Poulanzas, "The Problem of the Capitalist State," *New Left Review* 10.4 (1969): 761–80.

10. Uri Ben-Eliezer, "Civil Society and Military Society in Israel: Neo-militarism and Anti-militarism in the Post-hegemonic Era," in Majid Al-Haj and Uri Ben Eliezer, *In the Name of Security* (Haifa, 2004) [Hebrew].

11. Yagil Levy, *The Other Army of Israel* (Tel-Aviv, 2003) [Hebrew].

12. Peri, "The Changed Security Discourse."

13. For a detailed analysis of these two viewpoints, using retro metro concepts, see Yoram Peri, *Brothers at War: Rabin's Assassination and the Cultural War in Israel* (Tel-Aviv, 2005) [Hebrew].

14. Yoram Peri, *Generals in the Cabinet Room: How the Military Shapes Israel's Policy* (Washington, D.C., 2006).

15. Yehezkel Rahamim (ed.), *No One to Talk to—A Critical View of Politics-Media Relations* (Tel-Aviv, 2005) [Hebrew].

16. Schenck *v.* United States, at: http://caselaw.lp.findlaw.com/scripts/getcase.pl?court=US&vol=249&invol=47.

17. Asher Arian, *Security Threatened: Surveying Israeli Opinion on Peace and War* (Tel-Aviv, 1999), 228–29 [Hebrew].

18. Yochanan Peres and Ephraim Yaar-Yuchtman, *Between Consent and Dissent: Democracy and Peace in the Israeli Mind* (Jerusalem, 1998), 238 [Hebrew].

19. Ephraim Ya'ar, "Who Is Afraid of a Free Press?" *Israeli Democracy* (Winter 1990): 19. In another study conducted in the same year, the public was also asked a specific question concerning the publication of articles or photographs showing IDF soldiers abusing Palestinians in the territories. The respondents were asked: "Do you think that publication of such things should be forbidden because they damage Israel's image, or that they should be published because that is how to fight against this phenomenon?" Here, too, there was a similar distribution of answers: one-third of those queried (34 percent) thought the articles and photographs should be published, while two-thirds (63 percent) opposed their publication. Figures are from a survey by the Dahaf Institute, which examines attitudes on issues that may involve conflicts of interest between security needs and democratic values; February 1990, unpublished.

20. Martin Sherman and Shabtai Shavit, "Media and National Security: The Role of the Israeli Press in the Eyes of the Public," in Udi Lebel, *Security and Communication: The Dynamics of the Interrelationship* (Beer-Sheva, 2005) [Hebrew].

21. "Measure of Public Trust in the Media," Report 1, Herzog Institute, May 2004.

22. Zeev Schiff, "Information in the Grip of Security," in Benjamin Neuberger and Elan Ben-Ami (eds.), *Democracy and National Security in Israel* (Tel-Aviv, 1996), 484–90 [Hebrew].

23. Moshe Tamir, *War without a Sign* (Tel-Aviv, 2005) [Hebrew].

24. For the interview with Danny Rubinstein, see http://www.keshev.org.il/Site/FullNews.asp?NewsID-110&CategoryID=24, January 2006.

25. Gaye Tuchman, "Making News by Doing Work: Routinizing the Unexpected," *American Journal of Sociology* 79 (1973): 110–31.

26. Michael Keren, *The Pen and the Sword* (Tel-Aviv, 1991) [Hebrew].

27. A partial list of these journalists includes Erez Tal, Avri Gilad, Allon ben David, Geulah Even, Yaron Dekel, Tal Berman, Yaakov Eilon, Yonit Levy, Udi Segal, Elana Dayan, Gil Tamari, Alon Shalev, Rafi Man, Chilik Sarid, Arieh Golan, and David Gilboa. Some examples of the second group are Nahman Shay, Ron Ben Yishai, Yitzhak Livni, former minister Yosef Paritsky, Knesset Member Inbal Gavrieli, and Shinui party head Ron Levental. On the security network, see Oren Barak and Gabriel Sheffer, "Israel's 'Security Network' and Its Impact: An Explanation of a New Approach," *International Journal of Middle East Studies* 38 (2006): 235–61.

28. Dina Goren, *Mass Communication* (Tel-Aviv, 1975) [Hebrew]; Moshe Negbi, *Paper Tiger* (Tel-Aviv, 1985) [Hebrew].

29. Amir Oren, "Halutz's Second Blow," *Ha'aretz,* March 17, 2006.

30. Mordechai Gur, *Chief of Staff* (Tel-Aviv, 1998), 349 [Hebrew].

31. Ibid., 352.

32. Idith Zertal and Akiva Eldar, *Lords of the Land* (Tel-Aviv, 2005) [Hebrew].

33. Rubinstein, January 2006.

34. Haggai Golan and Shaul Shay, *Low Intensity Conflict* (Tel-Aviv, 2004) [Hebrew].

35. Kobi Michael, "The End of Deterministic Distinction," in Golan and Shay, *Low Intensity Conflict,* 201–238.

36. Shmuel Nir, "The Nature of the Low Intensity Conflict," in Golan and Shay, *Low Intensity Conflict.*

37. Danny Rubinstein, *Ha'aretz,* May 2, 2006.

38. S. L. Althaus, J. A. Edy, R. M. Entman, and P. Phalen, "Revising the Indexing Hypothesis: Officials, Media, and the Libya Crisis," *Political Communications* 13.4 (1996): 437–54.

39. Rivka Feldhai, "The Betrayal of the Intellectuals," in Hanna Herzog and Kinneret Lahad, *Knowledge and Silence: On Mechanism of Denial and Repression in Israeli Society* (Jerusalem, 2006), 162–67.

40. Julian Benda, *The Betrayal of the Intellectuals* (New York, [1928] 1955).

41. Poulanzas, "The Problem of the Capitalist State," 761–80.

42. Gur, *The Militarization of Education,* 163. Similarly evolved are national rituals performed in public schools, as anthropologist Edna Lomsky-Feder demonstrates in "From a Heroic Ceremony to a Mourning Rite: Different Voices on Remembrance Day Ceremonies in Schools," in Haggit Gur, *The Militarization of Education* (Tel-Aviv, 2005), 276–99 [Hebrew].

43. Daniel Dor, *Newspapers under the Influence* (Tel-Aviv, 2001) [Hebrew].

44. This fact stands in contrast to the hegemonic status of the paper in other social and economic spheres. It was only with the change of editors in 2005 that the paper became slightly more open to other (religious) culture groups, other (residents of peripheral areas) social strata, and other economic attitudes (opponents of neoliberalism).

FIVE

Tensions between Military Service and Jewish Orthodoxy in Israel: Implications Imagined and Real

STUART A. COHEN

Of the several recent transformations in the sociological profile of the Israel Defense Forces (IDF), arguably the most conspicuous is the growth in the number of male troops in field formations who adhere to Jewish Orthodox practice and now wear a *kippah serugah* (knitted skullcap). Signs of that development, although evident for some time, have of late become especially obtrusive. Analysis of the distribution of IDF fatalities during the second Intifada indicates that the overall number of *kippot serugot* in infantry units may be roughly twice their proportion in Israel's Jewish male population as a whole. Informal surveys of the cadre of petty officers (second lieutenant through captain) suggest that in those ranks the discrepancies in representation may be even higher. Graduates of the religious state educational network, it seems, have altogether appropriated the mantle of extraordinary commitment to combat military service that once belonged to products of the secular kibbutz system.[1]

This chapter discusses some of the implications of that situation for societal–military relations in Israel. Its point of departure is that the *kippah serugah* constitutes a (male) symbol of affiliation; it serves as a widely recognized mark of attachment to what is termed the "national-religious" (alternatively "religious-Zionist") community. Admittedly, those designations beg serious questions: How "national"? In what way "religious"? They are also misleading, since they imply that the sectors thus defined are far more homogeneous than is in fact so.[2] *Kippot serugot* come in several sizes, colors, and patterns, each favored by a different shade of the national-religious rainbow. Nevertheless, they remain generic badges of affiliation. A *kippah serugah* proclaims its wearer's commitment to a way of life that—broadly speaking—seeks to harmonize religion with Zionism, and that is therefore distinct from that of both the ultra-Orthodox (*haredim*) on the one hand, and secularists on the other. The *kippah* also declares fidelity to teachings that, to one degree or another, endow military service in the IDF with transcendent meanings.[3]

That is precisely why the prominence of national-religious soldiers amongst the IDF's combat complement sometimes generates undisguised dismay. Alarmists warn that members of the national-religious community who have attained senior ranks (and, at the latest count, over a dozen brigadier-generals in field formations now wear a *kippah serugah,* as do four members of the General Staff) might be in a position to impose a religiously dictated straitjacket on the conduct of Israel's entire security policy.[4] More sophisticated, but only slightly less ominous, is the argument that even the *suspicion* that so many troops and their officers might subordinate their professional military commitments to their ideological/religious preferences could confuse the chain of command and thereby spread dissension throughout the Force. At root, runs this argument, there will always exist a fear that the obedience of national-religious servicemen—of all ranks—to military commands will ultimately be dependent on their perception that the military institution's corporate behavior conforms to the religious Zionist understanding of security. Should the two ever collide, troops wearing a *kippah serugah* might refuse to obey orders or, in extreme circumstances, even rebel.[5]

The possibility that they could do so en bloc seems to be enhanced by the web of institutional networks through which many of the national-religious youth in Israel pass. Besides a popular youth movement (B'nei Akivah), the range includes a countrywide system of gender-segregated and residential national-religious high schools (*yeshivot tichoniyot* for boys and *ulpanot* for girls). Still more influential, it seems, are the post–high school frameworks that, with the sanction of the IDF, permit national-religious youth, females as well as males, to combine their military service with advanced theological studies. One such framework comprises the *yeshivot hesder* (arrangement academies), which offer a five-year program that allows students to intersperse their studies with an abbreviated conscript term, during much of which they serve in their own segregated companies. The other consists of the *mekhinot toraniyot kedam tzevaiyot* (pre-military Torah colleges) whose students undergo a year of spiritual and physical "fortification" prior to enlistment.[6] Both frameworks are suspected of fostering a system of dual control, which compels the IDF command to share authority with the *hesder* and *mekhinah* rabbis to whom, as we shall demonstrate below, national-religious troops frequently turn for guidance, even while on active service. This situation raises several questions: Can those rabbis be trusted to resist the temptation to exercise—or threaten to exercise—their influence? Should they consider a military order to transgress a religious commandment, would they not feel obliged to instruct their pupils to express conscientious objection? In addition, would not the very publication of such an edict dissuade national-religious troops from remaining obedient to the conventional military chain of command?

Such fears have been intermittently expressed ever since a reservist who had graduated from one of the most prestigious *yeshivot hesder* assassinated Prime Minister Yitzhak Rabin in November 1995. But they reached a crescendo a decade later, in the spring of 2005, when the IDF prepared to implement the disengagement from the Gaza Strip and northern Samaria, in accordance with the program that PM Ariel Sharon had announced in December 2003 and which, after considerable public debate, the Knesset eventually sanctioned by sixty-seven votes to forty-five in October 2004.

Far from putting an end to public controversy, the Knesset decision merely stimulated an even more intensive furor. Attention now shifted from the legitimacy/illegitimacy of the measures used by Sharon to bulldoze his program through the parliamentary process to the steps that might be taken in order to sabotage its implementation. In this context, particular significance was attached to reports that several rabbis in the national-religious community were calling on those of their disciples who served in the IDF to refuse whatever orders they might receive to participate in disengagement operations. Led by Rabbi Abraham Shapira, an octogenarian former chief rabbi of Israel and longtime principal of one of the most prestigious academies (Yeshivat Merkaz Harav Kook)—and indeed virtually a cult figure in religious Zionist circles—this group buttressed its exhortations with supposedly impeccable theological reasoning. The establishment of Jewish settlements up and down the country, and not least in the regions so miraculously "liberated" in June 1967, had constituted an act of religious significance (*mitzvah*), making the settlers partners in the fulfillment of God's design. It followed that participation in the dismantlement of such settlements would signify a sinful absence of confidence in the Almighty's support. In Rabbi Shapira's phrase, "Heaven would never forgive" those who obeyed orders to evict settlers from their homes.[7]

Throughout subsequent months, speculation that significant numbers of *kippot serugot*—reservists, regulars, and conscripts alike—might declare their conscientious objection to disengagement attained obsessive proportions. The opposition to military disobedience voiced by senior nonrabbinic (and ex-military) figures in the national-religious world did nothing to quell anxieties,[8] principally because the influence of the rabbis was in this case deemed to be more relevant. What instructions were graduates of the *yeshivot hesder* and *mekhinot* receiving from their spiritual mentors in those institutions? How many would be likely to be thus persuaded to act in accordance with Rabbi Shapira's ruling (or dissuaded from doing so)? In the absence of precise data, various figures were bandied about. From time to time, opponents of disengagement claimed to have persuaded "tens of thousands" of reservists to add their signatures to proclamations of intent-to-refuse service.[9] Even supposedly hardheaded observers warned that feelings among national-religious troops were running high, especially since many were personally acquainted with—and related to—the settlers whom they would confront. On the morning that the disengagement operation commenced, the military correspondent of one of the country's most popular newspapers pronounced that the possibility of widespread conscientious objection had brought the IDF face-to-face with "an existential test."[10]

In the event, such projections turned out to be widely off the mark. Testifying orally to the Knesset's Foreign Affairs and Security Committee in September 2005, a month after completing disengagement, the CGS, Lt.-Gen. Dan Halutz, stated that just sixty-three soldiers had been placed on trial for refusing orders during the operation (fifty conscripts—twenty-four of whom served in the framework of the *yeshivot hesder*, five petty officers, three other ranks in professional service, and five reservists).[11] Possibly, these figures do not tell the entire story. Earlier,

Ba-Machaneh, the IDF weekly, had reported an additional one hundred cases, including those in which male and female troops, a handful of whom were junior officers, either declared their intent to disobey military orders or refused to take part in some of the preliminary standoffs between the IDF and the settlers.[12] Arguably, allowances also have to be made for troops who came to private "understandings" with their immediate commanding officers, and hence managed to detach themselves from units directly engaged in disengagement.[13] Even so, the overall picture remains clear. En masse, the *kippot serugot* neither rebelled nor shirked their duties.

The remainder of this chapter seeks to account for that outcome. I begin by presenting its two most obviously apparent causes: first, the measures taken by the IDF to minimize the possible incidence of conscientious objection; and second, the moderating effect exercised by divisions of opinion within the national-religious community's spiritual leadership over Rabbi Shapira's call for military disobedience. Thereafter, however, I draw attention to a third circumstance, whose influence seems to have been even more decisive. Specifically, the chapter will analyze evidence indicating that, contrary to most public perceptions, settlement dismantlement was not the sole source of anxiety to most national-religious troops. If anything, as an issue likely to generate their dissent, it was subordinate to other concerns. Failure to note that dimension of the subject, it will here be argued, not only inhibits an appropriate understanding of what occurred in the summer of 2005. More seriously, it also misrepresents the true nature of the elusive relationship between national-religious troops and the IDF, a relationship whose theoretical implications extend far beyond the confines of this particular segment of Israeli society.

The Steps Taken by the IDF

From the military–institutional perspective, "disengagement" deserves to be considered an outstanding operational success. The IDF accomplished its mission swiftly, without any serious casualties, and with a minimum of internal turbulence.[14]

What makes the ultimate result especially remarkable is the fact that it was by no means assured. After all, the Force had few reserves of relevant experience on which to draw for this type of operation. The only valid precedent was the evacuation in 1982 of the settlements that Israel had established in Sinai after 1967 and whose dismantlement constituted part of the Israeli–Egyptian peace treaty signed by PM Begin and President Sadat in 1979. The parallel was hardly precise. By the spring of 1982, most Sinai settlers had voluntarily left the region, and the IDF was only called upon to evacuate the township of Yamit, which then housed just a few hundred permanent residents (compared to almost 8,000 who remained in the Gaza Strip and northern Samaria in the summer of 2005). Besides, other than by a small faction of right-wing ideologues, Sinai had not been invested with the sanctity attached to the "historic" Land of Israel; in return for its evacuation, Israel had attained a peace agreement with the largest and most powerful of its neighbors; and the decision to withdraw (unlike disengagement) had been sanctioned by a clear majority of the Jewish citizenry.[15] Besides, the Yamit experience had taken place long ago: before the settlement enterprise had taken deep root in the national consciousness and—most sensitive of all—before the settlers slated for eviction had paid a blood-price for their residence in the area.[16] For all these reasons, the IDF clearly needed to invest extraordinary resources in preparing its personnel for the delicate challenges that disengagement would undoubtedly present.

That is precisely what was done. Despite his barely disguised suspicion that disengagement was a misguided policy, the CGS (Lt.-General Moshe Ya'alon) insisted on meticulous preparations for the operation, ultimately code-named *yad le-achim* (a hand [stretched out] to brothers). Moreover, the general staff outline which, although not formally approved by the DM until February 2005, was to all intents and purposes ready as early as August 2004, made the parameters of IDF activity absolutely clear. Until complete, *yad le-achim* would take precedence over every other scheduled IDF mission. Fully 15,000 troops, male and female, were assigned to the task, and hence released from regular training exercises and courses of instruction.[17] At the same time, however, disengagement was to be viewed as a constabulary mission. This designation not only mandated full cooperation with the police force, but—above all—the adoption of an appropriate attitude toward the settlers. During disengagement, they were to be dealt with "firmly but with sensitivity."

Hence, the soldiers most likely to come into contact with settlers were not to carry any weapons during the entire operation[18] and would be supplied with special training on maintaining the prescribed "rules of the game."

Ultimately, much of the latter burden devolved on the IDF's education branch and on psychologists serving in the ground forces command and in the behavioral sciences department.[19] Together, these units prepared several "kits" for use by the immediate commanders of the forces assigned to the operation. Consisting of videotapes, two CDs, and eleven printed pamphlets on various aspects of the operation (free speech, the settlements, relations between the IDF and media), these were distributed throughout the early summer, and thereafter supplemented by several day-long seminars. With the approach of D-Day (set for August 14, 2005, corresponding to the morrow of the fast of the 9th of Av in the Jewish calendar, commemorating the destruction of the second Temple in 70 CE) preparations moved into higher gear. The troops massed in the temporary military base near the Gaza Strip, especially constructed for the purposes of disengagement, received what to the rank and file seemed like an unending stream of talks from IDF psychologists, sociologists, and senior commanders—all designed to inculcate the message that the settlers were by no means to be considered an "enemy," and that the disengagement mission was as much a test of the individual soldier's civility as of his or her loyalty to the government whose orders they were carrying out.

Notwithstanding all this activity, there still remained the delicate issue of the *kippot serugot*. How could the IDF minimize the number of national-religious troops who might disobey orders to participate in the operation? Ultimately, two courses of action were adopted. On the one hand, senior commanders unambiguously warned that conscientious objectors would be heavily punished.[20] At the same time, however, some concessions were made to national-religious sensibilities. Thus, the Golani [infantry] Brigade, in which the concentration of *kippot serugot* was known to be particularly high, was kept outside the "first circle" of troops assigned to eviction duties. Likewise, soldiers whose immediate families lived in settlements due to be dismantled were told that they could, if they so wished, ask to be excused from duties. Perhaps most subtly of all, all troops and policemen were instructed to wear caps throughout the operation (ostensibly to protect them from the sun, but also in order to deny settlers the opportunity of easily identifying, and attempting to influence, the *kippot serugot* among the personnel concerned).

Noticeable by its absence from this matrix of activity was the IDF chief rabbinate, the military institution officially responsible for the maintenance of religious life in the IDF and, by extension, for ensuring the well-being of the Orthodox soldiers. Specifically, the rabbinate neither sought, nor was it assigned, anything other than a marginal role in the containment of tendencies toward conscientious objection among national-religious troops. In part, that circumstance merely reflects the lowly status of the IDF rabbinate, which the *kippot serugot*, especially, have long ceased to regard as a source of authority.[21] It also owed much to the personal dilemma faced by Brigadier-General Yisrael Weiss, the IDF senior chaplain. Himself one of Rabbi Shapira's former students, Rabbi Weiss simply could not bring himself to issue anything other than a lukewarm statement of opposition to conscientious objection, which carried little conviction. During the disengagement operation itself, Rabbi Weiss and his staff kept a deliberately low profile—well away from the main areas of military activity.[22]

More important than the causes of the military rabbinate's irrelevance are its consequences. With the senior IDF chaplain patently incapable of providing national-religious soldiers with coherent guidance, that task devolved on civilian religious authorities, whose institutional commitment to the IDF was less blatant. This situation further augmented the influence likely to be exerted on the behavior of the *kippot serugot* by the views expressed in the wider circle of the national-religious rabbinate.

The Intra-Rabbinic Debate

Whereas the IDF (with the marginal exception of its rabbinate) thus presented an unambiguous position with respect to conscientious objection, attitudes within the national-religious community were far less monolithic. This was not unexpected. *Religious Zionism*, it bears repeating, is very much an umbrella term that encompasses an assortment of lifestyles and forms of worship. Beneath the surface of shared values, there have long lurked deep divisions of attitudes and priorities among both the *kippot serugot* and their spiritual mentors—not least where the notion of "the Greater Land of Israel" is concerned.[23]

Given that background, there was nothing surprising in the fact that the intra-rabbinic debate on the conduct expected of national-religious troops assigned to disengagement duties was particularly intense. Within days of Rabbi Shapira's call to troops to disobey orders, fifty-seven rabbis—including two principals of *yeshivot hesder*—signed a manifesto supporting his exhortation. The ink on that document was barely dry before a further eighty rabbis—again, the roster included heads of (other) *hesder* academies and some *mekhinot*—published a counter-manifesto, adopting precisely the opposite position. There followed a round of intense exchanges between the two camps, which although invariably couched in the lingua franca of traditional intra-rabbinic disputation, occasionally violated the norms of scholastic cordiality.

A tangled web of individual allegiances compounded the complexity of the situation thus created. The principals of some institutions owed ties of personal loyalty to Rabbi Shapira, with roots in a distant teacher–disciple relationship. Others were, for similar reasons, inclined to defer to the opinions of Rabbi Tzvi Tau, the charismatic head of the prestigious Har Ha-Mor yeshivah in Jerusalem who long declined to come out openly on conscientious objection one way or the other.[24] In yet a third category, the issue split single institutions right down the middle. Thus, in Birkat Mosheh, the large *hesder yeshivah* situated in the West Bank town of Ma'aleh Adumim, conscientious objection was advocated by the principal (Rabbi Nachum Rabinovitch) but vigorously opposed by one of the senior members of his faculty, Rabbi Chaim Sabato.

Much of the intra-rabbinic debate on the *tactics* to be adopted vis-à-vis disengagement was conducted behind closed doors.[25] Where the *principle* of conscientious objection was concerned, however, discussion was public and exerted an impact that extended beyond the confines of the academies. Indeed, echoes of the debate resounded in both the websites and newspapers that specifically cater to a national-religious audience, and especially in the popular pamphlets that various groups distribute in large numbers each Sabbath eve to synagogues up and down the country. Thus it was that "the Expulsion" (*ha-gerush*), as disengagement was commonly termed by its opponents, became an even more divisive issue among this sector of the population than it was elsewhere in the country.

As both sides to the national-religious debate on disengagement appreciated, the arguments that they each adduced in the spring and summer of 2005 were not novel. In intellectual terms, the lines of battle had essentially been drawn as early as the dismantlement of Yamit in 1982, and had been reiterated with considerable passion in 1993, in the wake of the news that Israeli and Palestinian representatives had reached agreement at Oslo.[26] On both occasions, those who advocated refusal to obey orders based their arguments on the belief that the Jewish people possess an exclusive, God-given, and irrevocable right to possession of the entire Land of Israel, over which it is forbidden to relinquish sovereignty—no matter what the cost in blood and treasure. Those teachings were frequently buttressed, moreover, by the time-honored rabbinic contention that the relationship between human and divine authorities is anyway akin to that of a slave to his master. Hence, when government orders conflict with God's commandments, only the latter are to be obeyed. Harnessed together, these two positions led to one conclusion: the IDF's true mission is to act as the instrument of God's will and to facilitate the realization of His plan. Once its actions contradict that role, however, military orders necessarily become devoid of all authority. Indeed, they have to be disobeyed.

Ever since the mid-1980s, at the latest, opponents of conscientious objection had likewise appealed to the bar of hallowed texts and their traditional interpretations. The keystones of their theses, however, were entirely different. Even though many declared themselves personally opposed to PM Sharon's program (which, besides all else, many considered to be an act of political betrayal on his part), they regarded the theological rights and wrongs of disengagement per se to be a subsidiary issue. In advocating a review of the arguments advanced by proponents of national-religious conscientious objection, opponents of that course cited two alternative considerations, the importance of which they believed to surpass even the preservation of Jewish control over the Holy Land.

One is the altogether overriding value that rabbinic Jewish traditions have always placed on the preservation of human life (*pikuach nefesh*). The authors of the call to military disobedience adduced this principle as one reason for objecting to any territorial compromise, on the grounds that concessions on Israel's part would merely encourage the country's enemies to seek further gains, if necessary by force, and hence ultimately cause further bloodshed.[27] Opponents of that opinion, by contrast, argued that matters were far more complex—so much so that they doubted whether rabbis are empowered to make any unilateral judgment one way or the other. Rather, in this case they have to allow the country's political and military authorities to come to their own conclusions with respect to the relative costs and gains of a withdrawal from the territories. Indeed, rabbis must relate to politicians and generals in the same way that they have for centuries related to, for instance, medical authorities: as lay experts to whose professional advice rabbis conventionally defer when the observation of a specific commandment (such as abstinence from food on a mandatory fast day) raises issues of life and death. Since no one could guarantee that disengagement would not, as promised by its advocates, save some lives, no one possessed the halakhic right to prevent the implementation of that program.[28]

A second consideration adduced by rabbinic opponents of Rabbi Shapira's call to national-religious troops to refuse orders to participate in disengagement operations carried more community-centered overtones. Drawing on a distinguished tradition of teachings that preached the importance of preserving Jewish unity, opponents of conscientious objection invested the concept of mutual responsibility with a meta-eschatological meaning. From that perspective, they argued, adherence to Rabbi Shapira's pronouncement could only play havoc with the hallowed notion of national Jewish solidarity. Precisely because of the numerical prominence of national-religious troops in the IDF, their conscientious objection would necessarily impair the cohesion of Israel's military and thus irrevocably damage this, the most obtrusive symbol of the miraculous renewal of Jewish sovereignty. In the last analysis, therefore, what was most disturbing about Rabbi Shapira's pronouncement was the apparent irresponsibility with which it related to the possible consequences of its very implementation. In the words of one (nonrabbinic) summary of this argument: "Bad though disengagement is from a national-religious perspective, to refuse orders would be even worse."[29]

The Contexts of the Debate

No single circumstance can adequately explain why, in the event, the overwhelming majority of *kippot serugot,* of all ranks, found the arguments in favor of participation in the disengagement operation to be more persuasive than Rabbi Shapira's warning that Heaven would never forgive them for doing so. In part, of course, that result may simply have reflected "institutional conformity"—the inherent tendency of all soldiers in uniform to obey military commands, especially when the vast majority of the comrades-in-arms with whom they serve are prepared to do so.[30] In this case allowances must also be made for other possible causes. One might be sheer intellectual conviction; the troops may have found the theses adduced against conscientious objection to be, on their merits, more persuasive than those in its favor. Another could be the sociology of the debate. Although the two rival rabbinical camps were numerically almost equal, in terms of the personalities involved they were far less evenly matched. Certainly, Rabbi Shapira's name carried considerable authority in the national-religious community. So, too, did those of rabbis Elyakim Levanon, principal of the *yeshivat hesder* located in the settlement of Alon Moreh, and of Eliezer Melamed, of the settlement of Bet-El, who were two of the most articulate and persistent advocates of conscientious objection.[31] The vast majority of figures in this camp, however, tended to be somewhat obscure; they were known only to the small coterie of their immediate circles. Principally, this is because the *yeshivot* of which they were principals were invariably small—and in any case not usually of the sort whose pupils performed any military service at all.

Many rabbinical opponents of conscientious objection were of an entirely different type. Several were principals of some of the largest *yeshivot hesder* and *mekhinot,* and hence enjoyed close relationships with substantial bodies of pupil-soldiers. Some had also established an independent following among even larger numbers of conscripts, of both sexes, by virtue of their extensive writings on issues of concern to national-religious youngsters. This was certainly so in the cases of rabbis Shlomo Aviner and Yuval Sherlow, heads of *yeshivot hesder* in Jerusalem and Petach-Tikvah, respectively, who had been two of the most adamant opponents of conscientious objection from the very start. Both men had long contributed regularly, and prolifically, to popular works of homiletics and halakhic literature.[32] Theirs were therefore virtually household names in the national-religious circles most likely to be interested in rabbinic opinion on whether to refuse military orders.

To these considerations must be added, finally and, it seems, most decisively, the religious context of the debate. Even in the months leading up to the implementation of the disengagement program, the theological rights and wrongs of the dismantlement of settlements was not the sole subject of concern to the *kippot serugot*. Even as a potential cause for disobedience to military orders, the internal discourse conducted by this community was clearly overshadowed by other issues. Herein, it is proposed, lies a supplementary, and far subtler, explanation for what occurred in the summer of 2005. National-religious soldiers did not obey orders solely because they had been conditioned to do so (by the IDF) and/or convinced to do so (by many of their own rabbis). Their behavior also owed much to the fact that, for many of them, disengagement *at that stage* touched only peripherally on the topics that they considered to be most salient as far as relations between themselves and the military were concerned.

Evidence for that contention initially surfaced in random interviews that I conducted with national-religious conscripts and junior officers in the months before and after the implementation of disengagement. The impressions thus formed, however, were substantiated by sources that provide additional authentic glimpses into the state of mind of young adults in the national-religious community. Of these, undoubtedly the most informative are the collections of epistolary exchanges that take place between rabbis and those individuals who turn to them for advice and/or instruction on a matter of relevance to their conduct as religiously observant Jews. Known in the traditional Jewish literature as *shutim*—an acronym for *she'elot u-teshuvot*, literally "questions and answers," otherwise translated as "responsa"—this form of communication draws on a tradition that stretches back for more than a millennium and a half, and whose value as a source for an understanding of Jewish life has long been apparent to social historians.[33] The working hypothesis of the present chapter is that contemporary responsa serve a similar purpose. Orthodox Jews, and most particularly young Orthodox Jews in Israel who serve in the IDF, have by no means released themselves from dependence on rabbinical guidance.[34] If anything, the adaptations that have taken place in the responsa genre have merely intensified that dependence and extended it to new spheres.

Two such adaptations are especially relevant in the present context. The first is the appearance of responsa specifically devoted to matters of relevance to military life. This is a sphere of human activity with which Jews had virtually no contact throughout their Diaspora history, and which is consequently rarely even mentioned in the vast corpus of letters between rabbis and their correspondents that records every other conceivable topic of Jewish concern between medieval and modern times. Clearly, however, universal conscription, together with the prevalence of Israel's resort to military force as an instrument of policy, has wrought a change of revolutionary proportions. Ever since 1948, responsa—indeed, entire volumes of responsa—specifically dedicated to military issues have become an increasingly prominent item on the Orthodox Jewish bookshelf.[35] Their authorship has added to their appeal. Most contemporary responsa on military matters are written by rabbis who have personally served in the IDF, often in field formations and sometimes at fairly senior ranks. Not incidentally, many also function as principals or senior faculty members in one or another of the *yeshivot hesder* and *mekhinot,* in which capacity they come into virtual daily contact with the successive cohorts of *kippot serugot* to whom they act as spiritual guides.

A second relevant feature of the contemporary responsa literature is its new format. Although (as noted above) many of today's exchanges between rabbis and their correspondents on military matters, as on others, are published in the traditional format of books, an increasing number are being posted on one of the several websites that specifically offer "ask-the-rabbi" types of portals.[36] In addition, most of the *yeshivot hesder* publish (and sometimes post on the Web too) weekly or bimonthly newsletters, several of which also contain records of the issues with which student-soldiers on active service have recently corresponded with their teachers.[37] The importance of these developments lies in their influence on the style and availability of the queries and responses. Electronic modes of communication lend themselves to a much more abbreviated and accessible style of writing than was considered de rigueur in the traditional responsa, which were customarily encrypted in highly technical and prolix rabbinic prose. In addition, e-mails allow for anonymity, speedy response, and almost instantaneous distribution to a virtually infinite audience.

A comprehensive analysis of what the contemporary responsa literature can (and cannot) reveal about the state of mind of the *kippot serugot* in contemporary Israel lies beyond the scope of this chapter. Moreover, limitations of space dictate that no more than telegraphic note can be taken of the numerous methodological difficulties that arguably restrict the usefulness of this source as a research tool (to what extent do the participants in the published epistolary exchanges constitute a representative sample of national-religious opinion? How can observers weigh the differences in editorial approach and style of the various available websites? Is it possible to ascertain the degree to which the website managers and/or the rabbis who are their respondents might have censored the questions posted, or otherwise influenced the timing and frequency of their appearance?). Even so, however, when collated with allied sources, the responsa literature does seem to place in proportion the types of issues that seem to be of most pressing concern to the contemporary generation of *kippot serugot*. In so doing, it also provides a means of gauging the extent of the inner turmoil generated among them by the disengagement program and its implementation in the summer of 2005.

Rabbi Shapira's call for Orthodox troops to pronounce themselves conscientious objectors over disengagement clearly struck several sensitive cords. This is apparent from the sharp rise in the number of appeals for rabbinic guidance with respect to conscientious objection that were thereafter posted on the Internet, principally by young men and women who identified themselves as soldiers on active duty—and in one particularly interesting case from the wife of a battalion commander.[38] Even so, it is clear that even in this period disengagement was not the sole—and certainly not the principal—topic of concern to the *kippot serugot*. Most of their inquiries continued to focus on the conventional span of ritual and personal issues. More significant still, even within the specific category of responsa dedicated to matters relating to the IDF, disengagement and its consequences did not constitute the most obtrusive topic of interest to the *kippot serugot*. Statistical analysis shows that they were far more troubled by a wide range of other issues: the relative merits of military service vis-à-vis Torah study, Sabbath observance while on duty, interpersonal relations with secular troops, and gender relations in military units.[39]

This list is instructive, principally because it reveals a basic continuity in the principal topics of concern to national-religious troops. Of all the items in the roster, only gender relations (to be discussed below) constitute a novel topic of halakhic inquiry. All the others have been staple items on the agenda of military-centered responsa ever since 1948. This finding dovetails with the conclusions of previous research, which had indicated that at the root of the dilemmas confronting national-religious troops in the IDF lies an existential tension between "the scroll" (i.e., religious obligations) and "the sword" (military service), which runs far deeper than the surface friction generated by debates over the integrity of the greater Land of Israel. How to maintain Sabbath observance in a military environment, for instance, had been a primary bone of contention long before the issue of "the territories" arose. Moreover, and as the voluminous literature devoted to adapting the dos and don'ts of the Orthodox Sabbath code to service life amply demonstrates, the subject has remained at the very top of the national-religious serviceman's agenda ever since.[40]

Only marginally less persistent, likewise, are the dilemmas confronting national-religious young people (girls as well as boys) who, on the eve of their enlistment, have to choose between a full term of conscript service or registration in one of the programs whose timetable combines military duty with Torah study. Especially frustrating is the feeling that, even after decades of experiment, neither of these choices deserves to be judged entirely successful. The young religious recruit will still be likely to experience the shock generated by sudden close contact with conscripts from an entirely different—secular—background. The evidence provided by the responsa indicates that it is still true to say that:

> Quite apart from experiencing the alarm to which every conscript is submitted on entering the military framework, the religious soldier is estranged and struck dumb by the comportment of his secular comrades. Even their everyday speech contains phrases and terms which his own mouth, accustomed to prayer, is unable to utter and which his ears, attuned to words of wisdom, refuse to absorb.[41]

By comparison, how to react to disengagement seems to constitute a relatively minor problem.

That impression of priorities is confirmed when attention is turned to those responsa that concern gender relations in the military. This is a relatively new topic of inquiry, which shot to prominence in the late 1990s, when the IDF began integrating female soldiers into combat units. Because the new assignments place men and women in unavoidably close proximity (for instance within the confines of a single tank or armed personnel carrier [APC]), they necessarily offend the sensibilities of religious soldiers, who have been educated to observe traditional Judaism's stringent laws of "modesty" (*tzeniyut*) that restrict gender relationships, especially prior to marriage. After some hard bargaining, the principals of the *yeshivot hesder* and *mekhinot* managed to come to an "arrangement" with the IDF High Command, according to which troops in those frameworks were to have the option of serving in gender-segregated units.[42] As the responsa indicate, however, several areas of contention remained:

> I am currently in a military course for medics. The "modesty" problems in this course are terrible—all the instructors are girls, as are many of the other participants. . . . The instructors demonstrate many of the exercises on themselves, and in the process uncover their bodies. When they ask the participants to do likewise, the result is an endless torrent of rude remarks. . . . In rest periods, too, it is hard to avoid licentiousness. The girls walk around immodestly everywhere, so that even the way to the synagogue is replete with forbidden sights. We are just a few religious troops here—and although we have tried to speak to everyone we can— instructors, officers etc.—nothing seems to help.[43]

No less significant than the frequency of such appeals for assistance and guidance are the tone and substance of the rabbinical responses that they generated. By any gauge these are distinctive. On other issues, including as we have seen on disengagement, the responses reveal various hues of opinion. With respect to gender issues, by contrast, they are uniformly emphatic. Jewish law (*halakhah*) can no more sanction concessions to the traditional regulations governing intergender modesty than it can tolerate unnecessary, and unauthorized, infringements of Sabbath observance.[44] This is made plain in the published response evoked by the plea for assistance quoted above. The authority (Rabbi

Ratzon Arusi)—although generally opposed to conscientious objection, not least with respect to disengagement—was in this case adamant that an exception had to be made:

> If matters are indeed as you describe, it is forbidden for you to be in that course. . . . Should all the authorities refuse to deal with the matter then you will have to disobey orders, and go to prison.

The unambiguous and consistent nature of such statements seems to have sent the troops concerned a clear message, which served to delineate the borders of their right to refuse to obey military orders. From the halakhic point of view, only with respect to Sabbath observance and gender issues was the legitimacy of conscientious objection absolutely firm. Where other issues of contention were concerned, all such claims rested on somewhat shakier ground.

Implications

At one level, the conclusions of this chapter seem self-evident. The absence of any large-scale incidence of conscientious objection on the part of national-religious troops during the summer of 2005 put to rest many of the fears that their prominence in IDF combat units had once generated. Ultimately, this segment of the force complement did not prioritize the preservation of "the Greater Land of Israel." The same is true of all but a minority of the persons whose advice the *kippot serugot* most often seek—the rabbis who teach in *yeshivot hesder* and *mekhinot,* and who (also) reply to questions posed on the Internet. When pragmatic push came to doctrinal shove, they, too, largely decried conscientious objection.

Nevertheless, the evidence presented in this paper also cautions against placing too sanguine an interpretation on what transpired in the summer of 2005. Closer scrutiny suggests that those who warned of the possibly fissiparous implications of the prominence of *kippot serugot* in IDF combat units were not altogether erroneous; their mistake was to look for the wrong symptoms. A less simplistic analysis of the available data indicates that a significant proportion of the national-religious complement does indeed consider its military service in the IDF to be conditional on its convergence with Jewish law. The roots of that attitude have far less to do with a religious and ideological commitment to the settlement enterprise per se than is often supposed. Far more substantive, rather, is their determination (a determination that is deliberately and unanimously fueled by their rabbinic mentors) to preserve and enhance those elements of their lifestyles to which they attach intrinsic religious value.

From that perspective, settlements possess essentially talismanic importance. They certainly signify a religious value, but by no means constitute the sum total of the *kippah serugot*'s interests. Like many of their rabbis, religiously observant soldiers, female as well as male, are by and large more troubled by other concerns: How can they best reconcile the need to perform military service with the religious duty to devote their time to the study of the sacred texts? How can they avoid unnecessarily desecrating the Sabbath? How can they harmonize military life with the observance of traditional laws of "modesty"? Perhaps most encompassing of all—how can they best preserve their distinctive identities in a military environment? These are issues on which no compromise is at all possible.

Of the several implications of these findings, two appear to be especially noteworthy. First, and at their most restricted level, they serve to underscore the strength of the impulse to segregation that characterizes the service patterns of many *kippot serugot*. Far from being universally committed to exerting an influence on the entire IDF, significant numbers are principally concerned with minimizing as far as possible the impact of military norms on their own introspective world. That is why increasing numbers of the national-religious conscript segment now elect to perform their military service in the more sequestered structure of the *nachal haredi*;[45] that is why they reacted so strongly in 2005–2006 to hints that the IDF might shut down segregated *hesder* companies; and that is why they may yet be receptive to post-2005 calls for them to "disengage" from other keystones of secular society too.[46]

The second set of implications of the findings of this paper is broader, and casts light on relations between the IDF and its service complement as a whole. Recent research has altogether begun to question the validity of the conventional assumption that militaries justify their reputations as useful agents of social engineering. If anything, quite the opposite has often been the case.[47] Not least is this so with respect to the IDF.

As numerous studies have pointed out, the multiple communities of which Israeli society is composed do not evince any single (let alone hegemonic) attitude toward military service. Different segments exhibit varying levels of propensity to enlistment in the IDF; they also harbor different expectations of the benefits and costs that, as citizen-soldiers, they are likely to receive as a result of the military experience.[48] Edna Lomsky-Feder and Eyal Ben-Ari claim that the IDF has increasingly found it necessary to take account of that situation. Consequently, although still officially committed to the notion of a unified "people's army," it has been compelled to "manage" the diversity of its intake. It does so, they claim, by "handling each group according to policies and on the basis of practices that are unique to it."[49]

A study of the events of the summer of 2005, while ostensibly indicating the successes of that strategy, also points to its potential limitations. As we have seen, the IDF cannot claim exclusive credit for moderating inclinations among the *kippot serugot* to opt for conscientious objection where disengagement was concerned. Equally significant, if not more so, was the influence exerted by rabbinical opponents of military disobedience in this case. Hence, there exists no guarantee that the military formula adopted vis-à-vis this segment of its complement in 2005 will likewise work in the future. On the contrary, the evidence contained in the responsa, especially, indicates that the IDF, in its corporate capacity, has still to come to grips with the roots of the concerns that most of the *kippot serugot* find more troubling: their fears that the military environment impinges upon the values that give most salient expression to their group identity.

Should other segments of the population harbor anything like the same sentiments (Lomsky-Feder and Ben-Ari speak specifically of immigrants, women, and non-Jewish minorities), the IDF will be compelled to reconsider some of the fundamental premises upon which its personnel policies have hitherto been built. Instead of functioning as a pro-active "melting pot," it will be reduced to the far more passive status of an arena within which adherents to different Israeli identities seek to give expression to their individuality. Whether the IDF can fulfill that role without impairing its own corporate character as a unified fighting force deserves to be considered one of the most compelling of the issues on the agenda of societal–military relations in Israel in the years to come.

Acknowledgments

This research was supported by the Israel Science Foundation (grant no. 157/04).

Notes

1. Yagil Levy, *A Different Army for Israel: Materialistic Militarism in Israel* (Tel-Aviv, 2003) [Hebrew] and "The War of the Peripheries: The Social Map of IDF Fatalities in the El-Aktzah Intifada," *Theory and Criticism* 27 (2005): 39–67 [Hebrew]. For the kibbutzim, see Yarden Ben-Tzur, "Staying in the Kibbutz," *Ba-Machaneh* 17 (2005): 27–29 [Hebrew].

2. The heterogeneity of the national-religious community is now a convention of sociological analysis. Still a useful map to the variations is Yair Sheleg, *The New Religious Jews: Recent Developments among Observant Jews in Israel* (Jerusalem, 2000) [Hebrew]. See also Asher Cohen, "The Knitted Kippah and What Is Beneath It: Plural Identities in Religious Zionism," *Akdamot* 15 (Autumn 2005): 9–30 [Hebrew].

3. For the intellectual background, see Gideon Shimoni, *The Zionist Ideology* (Hanover, N.H., 1995), 127–64, and Ehud Sprinzak, *The Ascendance of Israel's Radical Right* (New York, Oxford, 1991), 30–35.

4. Uri Ben-Eliezer, "Is a Military Coup Possible in Israel? Israel and French-Algeria in Comparative Historical-Sociological Perspective," *Theory and Society* 27 (1998): 311–49, and "Do Generals Rule Israel?" in Hanna Herzog (ed.), *A Society Mirrored* (Tel-Aviv, 2000), 235–69 [Hebrew].

5. Professor Asa Kasher, interview in *Ha'aretz* weekend supplement, January 23, 1997, 16.

6. For a thorough and incisive study of these frameworks and their several variants, see Elisheva Rossman-Stollman, "Religion and the Military as Greedy Frameworks: Religious Zionism and the IDF," Ph.D. diss., Bar-Ilan University, 2005. The number of *yeshivot hesder* rose from just one in 1964 to thirty-four in 2004, and of *mekhinot* from one in 1988 to thirteen today. While most of these frameworks cater to males, there now also exist three *hesder* institutions for women. The first female *mekhinah* was opened in 2006. Rossman-Stollman estimates that each year more than two thousand students enroll in one or another of these frameworks, graduates of which now constitute some 40 percent of the annual cohorts of all national-religious conscripts in the IDF.

7. Interview with R. Shapira in *Ba-Sheva* (Hebrew-language right-wing religious daily), October 15, 2004, 1.

8. For example, by Brig.-Gen. (res.) Effie Eitam, chairman of the National Religious Party, reported in *Ha-Tzofeh* [Hebrew daily; organ of the National-Religious party], January 7, 2005, 1; and by Yisrael Harel (former chairman of the Settlers' Council), *Ha'aretz,* January 6, 2005, B1.

9. Claims to that effect were regularly made in leaflets issued by some anti-disengagement pressure groups. For a sample see: http://www.seruv.co.il. Com-

pare, however, the more balanced prognosis in Yehuda Ben-Meir, "The Disengagement: An Ideological Crisis" (March 2005), at http://www.inss.org.il/publications.php?cat=21&incat=&read=72.

10. Amir Rappaport, *Ma'ariv,* August 14, 2005, 7.

11. *Ha'aretz,* September 8, 2005, A12.

12. *Ba-Machaneh,* August 23, 2005, 1.

13. This was the retrospective claim of several correspondents to *Ba-Sheva;* see, for example, September 15, 2005, 3.

14. For a particularly laudatory assessment, interesting because it comes from a commentator often critical of the IDF, see Ofer Shelach, "The Israel Surprise Force," *Ma'ariv,* weekend supplement, August 26, 2005, 12–15 [Hebrew]. For assessments of the minimal psychological damage suffered by troops (and least of all by women soldiers), see Amos Harel in *Ha'aretz,* October 6, 2005, A3.

15. For a comparison of the two situations, see Nurit Kliot, *Decision-Making on Settlement Evacuation in Israel, Compensation and Resettlement: Sinai 1982 vs. Gaza Region and North Samaria 2005* (Jerusalem, 2005) [Hebrew].

16. According to IDF statistics, some 57 percent of all Palestinian attacks on Israeli targets between September 2000 and July 2004 were directed at Jewish settlements and settlers in the Gaza Strip. http://www1.IDF.il/SIP_STORAGE/DOVER/files/5/21835.doc.

17. IDF deployments for this operation are detailed in the Logistics Branch website. http://www1.idf.il/atal/site/templates/controller.asp?lang=he&fid=47360. For a retrospective assessment of the impact exerted on potential conscientious objectors by the massive show of force, see Rabbi Shemuel Eliyahu at http://www.moriya.org.il/shut/indexid.asp?id=29278.

18. I have been unable to find any confirmation for the reports in the foreign press that troops received orders to open fire on settlers who forcibly resisted evacuation—and were prepared to do so if necessary; for example, July 24, 2005, http://www.times-online.co.uk/tol/news/world/article547393.ece. As published in *Ha'aretz,* July 12, 2005, A1, the guidelines to troops explicitly forbade fire other than in clearly life-threatening situations.

19. What follows has benefited greatly from informal conversations with members of the IDF's Behavioral Science Unit and with individual IDF troops who were on service during the disengagement operation.

20. Lt.-Gen. Dan Halutz, who succeeded Ya'alon as CGS on June 1, 2005, was especially adamant. See, for example, the letter that he addressed to all commanders on this subject on July 12, 2005, in http://www1.idf.il/DOVER/site/mainpage.asp?sl=EN&id=7&docid=42312.EN. *Ba-Machaneh,* the IDF weekly, reported on July 8, 2005, p. 1, that senior officers had received special advice from the Judge Advocates office on how to pass quick sentence on COs, punishment for which included twenty-one days of imprisonment and banishment from the unit.

21. For comments on this situation, see Rabbi Nerya Gutel—himself a reservist who holds senior rank in the IDF rabbinate, "The Loud Silence of the IDF Rabbinate," *Meimad* [a journal of the left-wing national-religious movement of the same name] (Summer 1992): 8–10 [Hebrew].

22. Weiss later issued an apologia for his behavior, which did little to restore his reputation. See Yedidya Meir and Sivan Rahav-Meir, *Days of Disengagement* (Tel-

Aviv, 2005), 39–60 [Hebrew]. Early in 2006, COS Chalutz announced that Weiss was to be retired from his post.

23. As has long been noted, such divisions are also apparent within the network of the *yeshivot hesder*. See Eliezer Don-Yehiya, "The Book and the Sword: The Nationalist Yeshivot and Political Radicalism in Israel," in M. E. Marty and R. S. Appleby (eds.), *Accounting for Fundamentalisms* (Chicago, 1994), 264–301.

24. Rabbi Tau's position was thought to be especially important, since he was a former teacher of rabbis Eli Sedan and Rafi Peretz, the principals of two of the largest of the *mekhinot,* at Eli and Atzmonah, respectively.

25. For a rare account of one such discussion (attended by all the *mekhinot* heads), see the recollections in an address delivered to his students by Rabbi Eli Sedan, entitled *Our Loyalty to the Torah and the Army* (Spring 2005), esp. 36, 37, 53, 54 [Hebrew].

26. For what follows, see Arye Naor, *The Greater Land of Israel: Belief and Policy* (Haifa, 2001) [Hebrew], describing this debate in considerable detail.

27. Arye Naor, "The Security Argument in the Territorial Debate in Israel: Rhetoric and Policy," *Israel Studies* 4.1 (1999): 150–77, shows how this argument—with its emphasis on personal security—ultimately provided a halakhic justification for Rabin's assassination. The same arguments were occasionally used in some rabbinic statements with reference to disengagement. See, for example, Rabbi Avigdor Nebentzal, Rabbi of the Old City of Jerusalem, quoted in *Ha'aretz,* July 1, 2004, A9.

28. In many respects, this argument had been authoritatively presented long before military disobedience became an issue. For an English-language version, see Rabbi Ovadiah Yosef, Sephardi Chief Rabbi of Israel, "Ceding territory of the Land of Israel in order to save lives," *Crossroads* 3 (1990): 11–28. In 2005, Rabbi Aaron Lichtenstein, principal of the Har-Etzion yeshivah, also dwelt at some length on this consideration, which he listed as the second of his main arguments in his densely argued plea, "Not to Disobey Orders," *Ha'aretz,* July 19, 2005, B3–4 [Hebrew].

29. Maj.-Gen. (res.) Ya'akov Amidror, cited in *Ha'aretz,* January 27, 2005, A4. The same view was articulated at considerably greater length by, among others: Rabbi Shlomo Aviner, *Be-ahavah u-ve-emunah* (Hebrew weekly) 429 (October 2004) 12; R. Yuval Sherlow, *Ha'aretz,* September 26, 2004, B1; Rabbi Aaron Lichtenstein, n. 29 supra, and two letters by the latter (dated September 2005) available at: http://www.etzion.org.il/hitnatkut/hitnatkut.htm.

For counterarguments see, for example, Rabbi Zalman Melamed, "Opposition to the Evacuation of Settlements," *Ba-Yom Ha-Shevi'i,* October 26, 2004, A3 [Hebrew]; and Rabbi Yehudah Hankin, "Obedience to a [Military] Order that Contravenes the Torah. Pt. 2," *Ha-Tzofeh,* August 5, 2005, B3; and the response by Rabbi Yoel Bin-Nun, ibid., August 12, 2005, B3.

30. William D. Henderson, *Cohesion: The Human Element in Combat* (Washington, D.C., 1985).

31. R. Eliezer Melamed published his views regularly in both the right-wing newspaper *Ba-Sheva* and on the *yeshivah* website. See, for example, his talk "The Command to Settle the Land of Israel" in http://www.yeshiva.org.il/midrash/shiur.asp?id=1018&q=/. On R. Levanon (head of the *yeshivat hesder* at Alon Moreh), see http://www.ynet.co.il, 20.4.05.

32. Besides contributing regularly to two of the most widely read of the weekly pamphlets distributed to synagogues throughout the country (*Ma'ayanei Ha-Yeshuah*

in the case of Rabbi Aviner and *Shabbaton* in the case of Rabbi Sherlow), both have published several books of responsa (on which, see below) that illustrate the span of the audience with whom they are in contact. See Shlomo Aviner, *Shut Tzniyut* [responsa on matters of modesty] (Bet-Al, 1999) [Hebrew]; *Me-Hayyil le-Hayyil* [responsa on military matters], 2 vols. (Jerusalem, 1999) [Hebrew]; *Al Diglo* [responsa on public affairs] (Jerusalem, 2000) [Hebrew]; and Yuval Sherlow, *Reshut Ha-Rabim* [responsa on public affairs] (Petach-Tikva, 2002) [Hebrew]; *Reshut Ha-Yachid* [responsa on personal matters] (Petach Tikva, 2003) [Hebrew]; *Reshut Ha-Tzibbur* [responsa on public affairs] (Petach Tikva, 2005) [Hebrew].

33. For the history of this genre, see "Responsa," *Encyclopedia Judaica* (Jerusalem, 1971), 14, cols. 83–95. For particularly sophisticated examples of its use, see Jacob Katz, "The Rule of Halakhah in Traditional Jewish Society: Theory and Praxis," in Jacob Katz, *Divine Law in Human Hands: Case Studies in Halakhic Flexibility* (Jerusalem, 1998), 171–90.

34. See Menachem Friedman, "Life Tradition and Book Tradition in the Development of Ultra-Orthodox Judaism," in Harvey E. Goldberg (ed.), *Judaism Viewed from Within and from Without: Anthropological Studies* (Albany, N.Y., 1987), 235–56.

35. The prototype of all such works is *Responding to War,* 4 vols. (Jerusalem, 1983–1992) [Hebrew] that summarizes the work and opinions of Rabbi Shlomo Goren, the first and most influential of the IDF's chief chaplains. This work has been succeeded, and in some respects superseded, by: Rabbi Nachum Rabinovitch, *Learned in War* (Ma'aleh Adumim, 1994); Rabbi Avi Rontski, *Like Arrows in the Hands of a Hero,* 3 vols. (Itamar, 1996–2003); Rabbi Eyal Mosheh Krim, *Ties of War,* 4 vols. (Jerusalem, 1999–2004); R. Mishael Rubin, *Those Who Draw the Bow* (Hebron, 1998) [all in Hebrew].

36. The four main sites, all in Hebrew, are: http://www.moreshet.co.il; http://www.kipa.co.il; http://www.moriya.org.il; and http://www.yeshiva.org.il. Each maintains a portal dedicated to responsa, which are catalogued by subject matter. In addition to "army and security," these categories include such topics as ritual issues, blessings, Sabbath observance, personal matters, economics, and medical ethics.

37. With the help of a grant from the Israel Science Foundation, I am presently attempting to collate and catalogue these materials. To the best of my knowledge, they have hitherto been entirely overlooked by researchers in the field.

38. The inquiry also indicates that a high proportion of the husband's troops wore *kippot serugot,* and that the brigade was to be assigned to the disengagement operation. "My husband is very much concerned, especially in view of the confusion on this that is so rife in the religious Zionist sector. What he finds most difficult is [the prospect of] confrontation with those of his troops who will refuse orders. How should he act? What about the rabbinic decisions in this matter? Is Rabbi Shapira's pronouncement definitive? Please help the confused." http://www.moreshet.co.il/shut/shut2.asp?id=47658; posted October 26, 2004.

39. This list was compiled on the basis of an audit of all the available responsa, whether on websites or in the various yeshivah newsletters. For further details, see Stuart A. Cohen, "The Inner World of the Religious Soldier: The Evidence of the Responsa," *Military Psychology* 5 (December 2006): 147–96.

40. See especially pp. 42–45 in Stuart A. Cohen, *The Scroll or the Sword? Dilemmas of Religion and Military Service in Israel* (London, 1997). Sabbath observance, in

its various forms, constitutes by far the largest single item covered in such comprehensive guides of religious law for the soldier, such as Yitzchak Kaufman, *The Army in Halakhah* (Jerusalem, 1994) [Hebrew], and Mosheh Binyamin and Yair Cohen, *Index to Military Halakhot* (Atzmonah, 2000) [Hebrew].

41. Ya'akov Levi and Aaron Furstein, "It's Not Easy to Be a Religious Soldier," *Zera'im* 8 (July 1995): 8–9. These sentiments are echoed (albeit in more restrained language) in the interview that one of the most senior-ranking national-religious officers gave to Amir Rappaport in *Ma'ariv,* on June 5, 2003 ("Religious officers have a harder time . . .") and in the "Open Letter to the Draftee" from rabbis Yuval Sherlow and David Stav, of the Petach Tikvah *Yeshivat Hesder,* published in *Ha-Tzofeh,* July 29, 2005, 3.

42. Conclusions of the IDF committee established to examine the issue, *Ha'aretz,* weekend supplement, July 26, 2002, 38–40.

43. http://www.moreshet.co.il/shut/shut2.asp?id=49689; posted December 26, 2004.

44. The circumstances under which religious troops would have to disobey a military command to desecrate the Sabbath are discussed exhaustively in Eliav Schocheteman, "A Military Order to Desecrate the Sabbath," *Techumin* [a religious annual devoted to contemporary issues], 24 (2004): 373–82 [Hebrew].

45. Ze'ev Drori, *Between Faith and Military Service: The Haredi Nahal Battalion* (Jerusalem, 2005) [Hebrew]. Although originally established as a means of integrating *haredi* males into the military, this unit has increasingly become populated by the more right-wing segments of the national-religious population, categorized as *hardalim.*

46. For warnings of this development, see Rabbi Shlomo Aviner, "I Secede," *Ma'ayanei Ha-Yeshuah* 234 (January 2006): 1 [Hebrew].

47. Ronald R. Krebs, "School for the Nation? How Military Service Does Not Build Nations and How It Might," *International Security* 28 (2004): 85–124.

48. In addition to Levy (n. 1 supra), see also Baruch Kimmerling, *The Invention and Decline of Israeliness: State, Society and the Military* (Berkeley, Calif., 2001); and Adriana Kemp, David Newman, Uri Ram, and Oren Yiftachel (eds.), *Israelis in Conflict: Hegemonies, Identities and Challenges* (Brighton [UK] and Portland, Ore., 2004).

49. Edna Lomsky-Feder and Eyal Ben-Ari, "From 'The People in Uniform' to 'Different Uniforms for the People': Professionalism, Diversity and the Israel Defense Forces," in Joseph Soeters and Jan van der Muelen (eds.), *Managing Diversity in the Armed Forces: Experiences from Nine Countries* (Tilburg, Holland, 1999), 157–86.

SIX

From "Obligatory Militarism" to "Contractual Militarism"— Competing Models of Citizenship

YAGIL LEVY,
EDNA LOMSKY-FEDER, AND NOA HAREL

In the mid-1980s, following the 1973 War and the Lebanon War of 1982, scholars of Israeli society identified a decline in military motivation among Ashkenazi secular youth, mainly pupils from elite, secular high schools[1] and kibbutz youngsters,[2] formerly the military's social "backbone." The Oslo peace process, the 2000 withdrawal from Lebanon, and protest against the mass exemption from military service given to Haredi yeshiva students, all intensified the process toward the end of the 1990s. Although the drop in motivation was somewhat tempered after the outbreak of the al-Aqsa Intifada in September 2000, as controversy began to surround the army's behavior during the Intifada it became clear that the graduates of prestigious high schools had ceased to take their prospective military service for granted.

This trend has been expressed in various ways: a clear, slow, and yet continual decline in the general desire to be recruited; a weakened readiness to be recruited into combat units; fewer volunteers for command courses; a rise in the number of youngsters changing their medical profile so as to avoid combat roles; an escalation in the number of soldiers requesting to serve in rear roles; and a significant increase in the number of people dropping out before or during their service for mental health reasons.[3] An additional phenomenon is that of youngsters from elite high schools exploiting their resources to be assigned to units that do not participate in the Intifada, such as the artillery, anti-aircraft units, and the navy.[4] This enables them to retain the aura of the combat soldier without putting their lives at risk. Positions vacated by the elite groups are gradually being staffed by other groups that had previously been positioned outside the core of the army, and who saw military service as a suitable location for consolidating their identity, attaining mobility, and leaving an ideological mark. These groups include the national-religious, immigrants from the former Soviet Union and Ethiopia, *Mizrachim* (who emigrated from Muslim countries during the state's first years and were relegated to peripheral segments in the labor market), and members of the Druze and Bedouin communities.[5]

This process, defined by then Chief of the General Staff (CGS) Amnon Lipkin-Shahak in a speech on the anniversary of Prime Minister Rabin's assassination as a "motivation crisis," articulates quite explicitly the erosion of the hegemonic military ethos. In the terms of this chapter, this "motivation crisis" embodies a retreat from "obligatory militarism," which sees compulsory military service as an unconditional contribution to the state, and the adoption of "contractual militarism," that is, making service conditional on its meeting the individual's ambitions and interests. In this chapter, by analyzing institutional sites of socialization that affect Ashkenazi secular youth, we shall demonstrate how the shift from obligatory to contractual militarism is taking place. We argue that the Ashkenazi secular group[6] is devoting its resources into shaping such sites so as to redefine its relationship with the state in a way that furthers its interests. Thus, the military ethos has become a text subject to various interpretations that replace the state-driven hegemonic canonization that was dominant until the mid-1980s. We shall examine this claim in two fundamentally different yet central sites of socialization: the first, school memorial ceremonies, and the second, pre-military preparatory frameworks.

Historical Analysis and Theoretical Framework

The starting point for our explanation of the erosion of the hegemonic military ethos—obligatory militarism—is Yagil Levy's historical–structural argument, which aims to contend with the level of militarism in Jewish Israeli society by deploying the concept of "materialist militarism." *Materialist militarism* is the exchange between the ability of social groups to acquire power within, and owing to, military service—that can be converted into valuable social positions in the civilian sphere—and their willingness to legitimize preparations for war and war itself by sacrificing human and material resources and by reinforcing the military effort (as soldiers and the families of soldiers, and as taxpayers). This exchange is defined in terms of *convertibility*, which in this context means the ability to exchange an asset accumulated in the military sphere with a resource or asset in the civilian social sphere.[7]

Convertibility largely rests on the republican concept. Historically speaking, the nation-state was founded on the republican order that established a reciprocal relationship between the state and its citizens, according to which citizens were willing to sacrifice their bodies and wealth in bearing the burden of war and preparations for it in return for civil, social, and political rights granted to them by the state. This exchange laid the foundation for Western democratization and the creation of the welfare state. By definition, therefore, modern military service fulfilled a historical role in defining the boundaries of citizenship by equating it with bearing arms. It is against this background that the army became a historical mechanism of mobility for social groups.[8] In other words, the republican order enhanced the convertibility of one's contribution to the military into a symbolic resource that could be exchanged for social rights. A high level of convertibility, especially in a substantially militaristic society, enables the bidirectional replication of the military and civilian social hierarchies.[9]

Based on an exchange of resources in return for military sacrifice, the republican order was thus a veiled arrangement between the state and leading groups of its citizens. This arrangement did not require ongoing negotiation, in particular because it had a universalistic character, at least at the declarative and formal level, in that it posited a uniform set of criteria for military service based on universal, and not attributive, criteria for recruitment and promotion. Accordingly, this arrangement assured a high level of citizenship—in other words, internalizing the state's authority while also internalizing the reciprocal relations established by the state with its citizens.[10]

An arrangement of this sort was also embedded into Jewish society in Israel. The IDF was organized on the basis of mass compulsory recruitment, which, under the auspices of the ethos of statism (*mamlachtiyut*) tied a Gordian knot between soldiering and citizenship.[11] This order was consolidated and led by the dominant social group of the middle class: secular, Ashkenazi men—the group that founded the army, populated its senior ranks, and was associated with its achievements. The army was purportedly built on egalitarian foundations, although in fact, and as a by-product of its being shaped as a Western and modern army, the Ashkenazi secular group was designated to set the tone in terms of its quality. Peripheral social groups, and in particular the *Mizrachim*, were portrayed as able to quantitatively contribute to the army, but not to shape its qualitative values.[12]

The high convertibility of resources from sphere to sphere ensured that the military hierarchy definitively shaped the social hierarchy. High convertibility rested on the statist, republican military ethos that defined Israeli society's devotion to the military effort as a supreme social value. Military service became a decisive standard by which rights were awarded to individuals and collectives acting in the service of the state. Male Ashkenazi warriors, identified with the military's glorification, thereby succeeded in translating their military dominance into legitimate social dominance, and thus also to preferentially enjoy the fruits of war, such as land, exploiting cheap Palestinian labor, the arms industry, and more. These resources could outweigh the sacrifices this group made. For as long as it advanced its social status, the secular Ashkenazi group was the bearer of militaristic ideology.[13] This is the Israeli version of materialist militarism.

This kind of pattern of exchange is modified when the republican equation is violated, that is, when the dominant social groups come to believe that the security provided by the state is too materially or morally expensive, or that it is disproportional to threats on the state (for example, of the diminishing Cold War), or that the rights the state offers its citizens in return are inadequate. Violation of the republican equation, therefore, is no less than a breach of a structural contract between the state and social agents. This state of affairs enables social agents to accumulate autonomous power, particularly when there is a gap between the cost of maintaining militarism and its utility. Social groups are then motivated to place conditions on their military service—whether political (see the opposition to the Vietnam War in the United States) or monetary, that is, improved payment for their service. It was this pattern of resistance that gradually led most Western states to bring an end to the draft and to move toward a voluntary professional army. At this stage, the pattern of exchange that was internalized as an unquestionable civilian pattern is converted into an exchange that takes the shape of open and even direct bargaining. This is the shift from obligation to contractualism.

Just as the republican order based on materialist militarism in the West was gradually contravened following World War II, a similar process took place in Israel after 1973. Until this juncture, the state successfully balanced the security burden imposed on its citizens and the rewards they were provided with. Until then, significant increases in the cost of security were met by external sources, namely, the war-driven economic growth (since 1948) and foreign aid. These sources even left a considerable surplus for the middle class. After 1973, however, the price that the leading groups among the "security consumers" were prepared to pay for the commodity of security dropped. Unlike previous wars, which had effected an expansion of the Israeli economy, the 1973 war brought with it a financial crisis, which reduced the material rewards that the Ashkenazi secular middle class received for its part in bearing the burden of war. On the other hand, the real cost of the security product actually increased as a result of the outlay on strengthening the military. At the same time, the motivation for sacrifice also declined as a result of the growing materialist, consumerist ethos among the middle class—itself a consequence of the economic fruits of the 1967 war such as the flow of a cheap Palestinian labor force and the growth of the military industry that boosted the Israeli economy.

The weakness demonstrated by the army in the 1973 war was heightened in the Lebanon War (1982–1985) and in the first Intifada (1987–1993)—all of which were politically controversial wars—and contributed to the erosion of its prestige and sharpened the desire of the Ashkenazi secular sector to distance itself from it. Moreover, the change of government in 1977—which saw the ascension of the Likud after fifty years of the Ashkenazi-based Labor Party domination—even further alienated this social group. Economic globalization, which gradually took hold of Israeli society, also eroded the importance of the individual's contribution to the state as the central criterion for the distribution of social goods and the justification for social dominance in favor of individualistic accomplishments.[14] At the same time, groups that do not serve in the army, or whose military contribution is minimal—such as *Haredim,* Palestinian citizens of Israel, and women—made significant gains in promoting their political, social, and civilian rights that were no longer dependent on the test of military service. Military service even became a factor that impeded members of the Ashkenazi secular class from exploiting their initial advantage in a competitive labor market. By the same token, the vertical military hierarchy no longer provided the professional, value-based socialization that could be germane for an economy characterized by the emergence of flat-hierarchy, high-tech organizations. In short, the state demanded a higher payment for reduced returns.

Violation of the social exchange equation eroded the republican ethos, which had constructed a social hierarchy based on the differential allocation of civic rights according to the perception of various groups' contributions to the national project, mostly through the military.[15] The republican ethos was challenged by both the liberal discourse and the ethno-national discourse, which gives center stage to the individual's Jewish ethnic belonging, and not his civic contribution. These two alternative discourses weakened the relationship whereby the acquisition of civil status is conditional on military service, thus eroding the social value of military service, with consequences for groups' motivation to serve. As in other societies, upsetting the republican equation gave rise to patterns of bargaining between individuals and groups on the one hand, and the state on the other, negotiations that took place via the army. We shall now review some of the dimensions of this bargaining.

> *Personal bargaining:* Soldiers have begun to negotiate with the army in person or via their families or other networks. These negotiations can determine the individual's role in the army, the conditions under which he serves, restrictions on his service and military function, and even the very fact of his serving at all. The strengthening of liberal values and their partial infiltration into modes of action among governmental systems have empowered the individual's standpoint and put him in a stronger negotiating position, sometimes with the assistance of the legal system, while the penetration of the media into the army impedes it from efficiently imposing internal discipline. The individual's ability to shorten or cancel his service due to apparent "mental health" conditions, and the weight the army gives to personal preferences with regard to one's role in the army are but two of the expressions of this bargaining. Youngsters make their considerations based on the package of incentives that the army offers them, and their

expectations for self-fulfillment as compared to alternative, extra-military routes (mostly employment or study). Only a reasonable match between the individual's expectations, originating from his private sphere, and what the army has to offer will be incentive enough for the youngster to agree to a demanding, or at least full, military service.[16]

Military parenting: This can be seen in the increasing and quite open involvement of parents, mostly from the Ashkenazi secular stratum (later followed by other groups as well) in affairs of the army. Parents, among them bereaved parents, even get involved in matters such as training accidents, operational accidents, the political justification of missions, and service conditions in the army. They do not restrict themselves to expressions of anger or pain, but rather issue penetrative criticism that directly or indirectly strikes at the root of professional practices in the army. The combination of a lack of faith in the military, mostly since the war in Lebanon, along with a culture of consumerist privatization, in which parents can be perceived as customers who paid society with the lives of their sons and who are now demanding payment in the form of compensation, an explanation, or a change in patterns of behavior, has ensured that the parents, acting as social–political entrepreneurs, attracted the attention of the public.[17]

The political selection of missions: This can be seen in the strengthening of the phenomenon of types of both overt and selective, and "gray" conscientious objection, and the appearance of political movements that ideologically endorse it.[18] Because of the particularly strong grip of this phenomenon among reservists, the army limits their use in politically contentious missions. It is against this background that pressure has been mounting to recognize national service as an alternative to compulsory military service.

Economic bargaining: This includes making missions conditional on economic remuneration—for instance, the "revolts" among reservists (such as pilots) due to a lack of insurance coverage, and consumerist-style associations of reserve soldiers demanding easier conditions or a redistribution of the burden, and appropriate financial compensation for their service. Such ad hoc organizations bear the threat—be it overt or latent—that the recruits' profile of motivation is stipulated by the army's response to their demands.[19]

The power of the historical–structural explanation lies in its proposing a mechanism—the dynamics of convertibility—that explains dynamic changes in the level of militarism in Jewish Israeli society. However, inherent in this explanation is the weakness in tracing the processes as they are reflected in bargaining patterns to social structures and cultural discourses. Indeed, this level of analysis lays out the rules of the game, but conceals the field of play, the actors, and the very game itself. In other words, the linkage between structure and behavior is missing.

Therefore, we want to move on from the structural explanation so that we might trace the way in which structural changes simultaneously influence agents and are constructed by them. Structural analysis assists us in identifying the changing interests of the dominant group and how they are translated into a pattern of bargaining with the state. However, an analysis that is focused on agents' behavior is required to examine the subjects' social action within the structural boundaries, and to understand how they perform the changing interests that stem from the structure, which they in turn transform. A structural analysis presents the environmental conditions that create a structural opportunity for the development of collective action,[20] yet one must still study how agents' behavior is shaped within and shapes those structural circumstances.

To this end, we focus on sites of socialization that from the outset were designated to construct and preserve the canonic military ethos, and we ask how these locales are recruited so as to impart a different ethos. More specifically, we argue that the retreat of the Ashkenazi secular stratum from obligatory militarism in favor of contractual militarism takes place in and is supported by (with varying degrees of intentionality) different sites of socialization in both formal and informal educational frameworks. We test this argument through two central yet differing sites of socialization: the first, annual memorial ceremonies in schools, which are meant to establish social solidarity and commitment to the value of military service via the memory of fallen soldiers; and the second, pre-military frameworks (private and public) with a more instrumental characteristic, which try to equip youth shortly before their recruitment with quasi-military skills, knowledge, and motivation.

Sites of Socialization in the Service of the Dominant Groups

SCHOOL MEMORIAL CEREMONIES—
CHALLENGING THE WARRIOR ETHOS

The ceremonies conducted on Memorial Day for the Fallen of Israel's Wars are one of the main cultural sites that constitute Israeli national identity and commitment to the military ethos.[21] Accordingly, the Israeli education system made it mandatory for all schools to hold a memorial ceremony and instituted the model of a canonic ceremony, characterized by military practices, the ethos of self-sacrifice, and the de-personification of mourning.[22] However, we understand the ceremony as a symbolic site that is not only open to the state but also to civil groups who exploit it in an effort to advance their political and social agendas.[23] Thus, school memorial ceremonies should be examined as potential locales for struggles over national interpretation, and schools should be seen as a social arena where the state and civil society encounter each other. Accordingly, we maintain that the dominant groups make use of the school memorial ceremony to question the republican definition of citizenship and to examine their traditional relationship with the military ethos.

Analysis of the school ceremonial field[24] discloses a deep commitment to the Israeli Jewish nation. Indeed, most ceremonies maintain a structural core congruent with the canonic ceremony: the flag, the fire motif, the national anthem, the Yizkor prayer, and a pageant-like atmosphere. One could argue, following Don Handelman, that the meta-structure of the memorial ceremony as a formal state ceremony still exists.[25] Yet, at the same time, one cannot ignore the emergence of ceremonial variations and new meanings around this core: some echo the canonic ceremony and voice formal state memory (mostly in mainstream schools, particularly grammar and high schools identified with marginal groups), some appropriate the canonic ceremony to demarcate group identity and struggles over domination (national-religious identity), and others challenge the canon in order to advance a competing ideology.[26]

Attempts at challenging the canon are particularly notable in magnet schools and established high schools, both of which are associated with traditionally hegemonic groups in Israeli society—the educated, secular, and Ashkenazi middle classes. At first glance this is surprising, as these groups are most closely tied to the masculine warrior ethos that stands at the center of the canonic ceremony, an ethos that still defines what is considered a meaningful contribution to the collective and dictates the social hierarchy in Israeli society.[27] We argue that their very affinity with that ethos, for so long the central source of their power, is now that which gives those groups the social legitimacy to oppose it and speak in a different voice.[28] This point is very clearly seen in the more established and elitist high schools, which "boast" large numbers of fallen soldiers among their graduates, a result of their pupils' numerical overrepresentation in combat units due to the strong linkage between military service, masculinity, and social status in Israeli society.[29] The dominant groups exploit their historical monopoly over the warrior ethos in order to redefine it in accordance with their changing interests. This monopoly provides them with the legitimacy to retreat from heroism and an ethos of sacrifice and to introduce a new ceremonial model based on personal mourning and an ethos of victimhood. This can be described in terms of four central practices:

(a) *Minimization of national symbols and heroic messages.* Canonic poetry is replaced by more intimate and less heroic texts, and militaristic practices identified with the disciplined masculine body are diluted, making room for alternative practices, especially dance, associated with the expressive female body.[30]

(b) *Personification of the fallen.* Whereas the canonic ceremony tends to ignore the personal story behind each name,[31] these schools focus on it, with the result that the personal story gains prominence over the national narrative in the shaping of the ceremony. A variety of methods are used to present these personal stories; for instance, parents reminisce about their sons, or pictures of the fallen are shown accompanied by text, videotapes, or poems they left behind.

(c) *The centrality of mourning.* Compared to the canonic ceremony, in which memory governs mourning, we are now witnessing a tendency for mourning itself to become the heart of the event. The bereaved seem to have rejected the expectation to suffer in silence and instead express their pain and anger out loud. Alongside the grief, we also hear a rapidly increasing number of voices of protest that refuse to accept war as inevitable, and demand that peace be made. These voices adopt the global antiwar discourse to which the dominant groups are attentive and reflect the overall change in the bereavement discourse.[32]

(d) *A mnemonic community develops around the fallen and the mourners.* The ceremony defines the boundaries of the remembering and mourning group, and emphasizes that remembering the fallen is one of the most important elements defining the school community. The definition of the school as a mnemonic community is clearly expressed by the attendance of former pupils at the ceremony, which thus becomes a sort of annual school reunion, uniting its participants in memory. The school becomes the site of a yearly "pilgrimage" for its graduates, whose community of memory is first and foremost that of the school, and not the people of Israel. Consequently, the ceremony takes its leave from the national pantheon, and the community of memory creates a mythology based on "local heroes," who are actually represented as victims of war and not as heroes at all. The fallen graduates are socially constructed as a symbolic resource that defines the school's mnemonic community. Moreover, the number of fallen is a yardstick against which school prestige is measured, and the memorial ceremony is a central event that constructs its institutional identity (hence, school websites often display a list of the fallen as well as photos of the memorial ceremony).

To conclude, challenging the canonic ceremony with a competing model that constructs the ceremony as a mourning ritual serves the dominant groups in various ways. First, they use the memory of the fallen to change the nature of their relationship with the state. Leaning on the legitimization of the warrior ethos, they put the individual and his needs at the center, instead of his contribution to the collective. Second, the focus on mourning in the memorial ceremonies is an effective way of creating solidarity in the face of a lack of consensus.[33] At the same time, it reestablishes the social hierarchy (that prevails in a society whose strength comes from war and the warrior ethos) that distinguishes between those who have paid a price and those who have not, a distinction that still serves the dominant groups. Third, the amplification of the ethos of victimhood is part of a larger social discourse about war, which, since the 1970s, has increasingly engaged with its traumatic consequences rather than its heroic features.[34] This social discourse is largely headed by dominant groups in Israeli society, identified since the 1970s with individualistic trends characteristic of Western global culture. Therefore, school memorial ceremonies are a mechanism that preserves Israeli nationalism, though in a different way. Led by society's dominant groups, Israeli nationalism is shifting its center of gravity from the warrior ethos to an ethos of suffering and victimhood,[35] from a nationalism based on obligatory militarism to one associated more with its contractual version. We can see this trend even more explicitly by observing pre-military preparatory frameworks.

Preparation for the Military—How to Bargain over Military Service

Following the "motivation crisis" of the mid-1990s as outlined above, the obligation to serve in the military was no longer taken for granted,[36] and in 1999 preparation for the military was designated by the Ministry of Education as obligatory within the formal curriculum of the higher grades in high school. The trend for privatization in education is also evident here, as private preparatory frameworks evolved alongside those provided by the public system. The various frameworks, public and private, offer a wide range of activities. As with memorial rituals, our point of departure here is that in preparing for the military, members of the Ashkenazi secular stratum mobilize the various frameworks in order to bolster their new motivational agenda, namely, a retreat from an unconditional commitment to the traditional military ethos in favor of a conditional commitment to serving in the military.

We shall investigate this proposition by observing a case study—preparation for the military among high school pupils in a well-established urban settlement near Tel-Aviv.[37]

Two things are common to pupils talking about their future military service: first, they present its significance primarily in terms of self-fulfillment and highlight their potential personal development,[38] regardless of whether they interpret their service as a source of enrichment and growth or as an obstacle and hindrance. Second, not even one of the observed pupils expressed a willingness to serve in combat units that are perceived as lackluster and nonexclusive (such as regular infantry units or the armored corps) and are identified with other social groups. To choose a select combat unit is to choose the proper "social club." The social differentiation between units is very clear, and pupils wish to serve in select and elitist combat units that enjoy social prestige. The alternative is to perform noncombative duties—to be what is known as a *jobnik*. These duties largely fall beyond the combat ethos, but provide their bearers with more time for leisure, the possibility for social prestige (such as serving at the army's radio station), good company (intelligence units), and sometimes even occupational mobility (such as working with computers or in other technology-intensive positions). The pupils present their willingness to serve in the military as conditional, its essence lying in the common Israeli expression "*sayeret* or *nayeret*," literally translated as "commando or paperwork." Even those imbued with motivation to serve represent their motivation as conditional: if they are not admitted to the select combat units they wish to join, they prefer a noncombat position, even if it lacks prestige.

Changes in the military's social structure reflect these preferences: the upper-middle-class secular Ashkenazis are making their presence more strongly felt in hi-tech warfare systems and relatively sophisticated ancillary or organizational roles, while ordinary combat units are being increasingly populated with soldiers from peripheral and semi-peripheral segments of society. Thus the choice between *sayeret* or *nayeret* is no longer quite so clear-cut, and some of the "paperwork" jobs represent a new military ethos based on sophisticated technological and managerial jobs.

This conditional motivation results in those aiming for "commando" status to put more effort into achieving their aims by preparing for the military in private preparatory courses after school hours. The majority of pupils, however—those who want "commando" as well as those who prefer "paperwork"—take part in various state-monitored preparatory programs that are organized through their schools.

In order to better understand this conditional motivation, we shall examine two frameworks that prepare youngsters for the army: the Gadna (the Hebrew acronym for "youth regiments") activity, which is part of school-based civic education, and an informal private course. In the following analysis we relate only to male pupils.

The Gadna is a military framework aimed at strengthening pupils' motivation to serve in the army and preparing them for military life. The activity is for seventeen-year-old boys and girls and lasts for five days under conditions that replicate those of a closed military base. During the week, an attempt is made to simulate basic training, so that the pupils encounter the meaning of the military experience. This includes being cut off from home and civilian life; military discipline; a structured daily routine and time pressure; uniforms and military activities such as field subsistence, treks, and shooting practice; and educational activities such as learning about Israel's wars.

From the outset, the pupils we observed arrived with the goal of being provocative toward military authority. This attitude was fueled by the fact that the military model on which the Gadna is based is that of the ordinary combat soldier (and not that of the elite fighter or noncombat soldier).[39] In other words, the military experience proffered during the week is founded on service models that are mostly perceived as irrelevant to the participants' aspirations. As a result, the pupils resisted the activities and ridiculed and showed disrespect to their instructors as military models. The staff also found it difficult to truly cut the pupils off from civilian life, as parents (and even teachers) phoned the participants during the week, even though this was against the rules.

Hence, given the lack of cooperation from the pupils on the one hand, and being unable to employ real and effective sanctions or punishments on the other, it was difficult for the staff to construct a balance of power with the pupils that would in any way reflect relationships characteristic of military life. The activity was quickly reduced to instructors' attempts to deploy military discipline for its own sake. This discipline was enacted for no apparent reason, arbitrarily and ritually without any purposeful end. The military rules and procedures that the staff tried to enforce were quickly seen by the pupils as ridiculous, failed attempts at controlling their time and bodies.

Accordingly, in contradiction to the Gadna week's goal of bringing pupils closer to the military experience and reinforcing their attitudes to military duty as a civil contribution to the state, the week of activity becomes an arena where they practice their distancing from the republican perception of citizenship and demonstrate their retreat from the military ethos. In practice, the Gadna week prepares them for "paperwork." Those who do possess the ambition for meaningful military duty by being fighters in select units, who want to increase their chances to be accepted to such units, will seek private ways for preparing themselves, such as the course offered by Yair.

Unlike the Gadna week, the ideology guiding Yair's preparation course matches the pupils' expectations, and focuses on the individual and his ambitions. The main goal is to prepare the participants for combat duty in select units.

Most of the participants in this private and expensive course are boys in the eleventh and twelfth grades.[40] The course coordinator and its central figure is Yair, formerly a fighter in a select unit. The course lasts for one year, with two or even three weekly meetings that focus on fitness, simulations of admission trials to select units, and special activities (such as hiking and running). The course also includes activities for body maintenance, correct diets, and prevention of training accidents. Other sessions aim to improve the participants' knowledge of military history; motivational talks are given about the military and military duty.

The course uses two central processes to prepare its participants for the military. The first is the formation of a military ethos appropriate for members of the Ashkenazi secular stratum, one that we call the "new soldier" ethos. The prime value of this ethos is professionalism, which displaces national ethos such as contribution and sacrifice. It emphasizes the use of scientific knowledge in preparing the body for strain through practices such as correct nutrition, monitored physical training, massage, and the proper treatment of injuries. As opposed to the *tsabar* (the Zionist ideal type of the Israeli) who does not nurture his body and views its maintenance as a type of indulgence, or even as unmasculine,[41] the new soldier cares for his body and fosters it.

The management of emotion is also a cardinal component of the new soldier ethos. During the course, pupils learn how to withstand mental pressure and cope with desperation and mental exhaustion. There is an unequivocal requirement to withstand discipline and the demands of the system while demonstrating emotional control. However, this does not imply suppressing one's emotions. Indeed, a significant part of disciplining emotions is in fact their externalization, but under the supervision and direction of Yair.

Another central value that has been codified into the new soldier ethos is personal ambition, focused on the individual and not the collective. Yair does not ignore national values and obligations toward the state, and he addresses the history of Israel's wars, but these are clearly secondary issues. The main theme to get across is that being recruited to a select unit primarily means performing a service for oneself, something that should be seen as an index of one's abilities and an expression of one's achievements. This ambitiousness involves a demand for personal excellence. Recruitment to a select unit is first and foremost perceived in terms of self-fulfillment, and not as a social requirement or as complying with social needs. Therefore, those who choose not to be combat soldiers are not judged, nor is any anger directed at them.

The second process in Yair's preparation course is the accruing of social capital. This social capital ensures efficient use of social ties and information as the pupils strive to realize their goals. The pupils perceive participation in the course as membership in a unique and prestigious club, an image that is constructed and encouraged by Yair himself. Moreover, a community of graduates has developed around the course. The development of such a community is important, mostly because it creates a social network of informal relationships, which helps in meeting the course's main aim—admittance to select units. Participation in the course, therefore, becomes social capital that increases its graduates' chances of being admitted to the units in which they want to serve.

To summarize, the culture of pre-military preparatory frameworks substantiates the educated, secular stratum's shifting attitudes to military duty, and expresses their ambivalent attitude toward the traditional fighter ethos. Analysis of the various preparatory frameworks shows this to take place in a number of ways: firstly, pupils use the preparatory frameworks to express their objection to the traditional military ethos, which is based on the value of contributing to the collective. Secondly, they attempt to maintain their position of power in the military arena by promoting an alternative military ethos that competes with the traditional fighter ethos—one that is built on liberal economic principles (professionalism, excellence, competitiveness) and that focuses on the individual's interests and needs. Finally, they attempt to formulate a contractual relationship with the military, the essence of which is making the nature of their military duty conditional on their ability to bargain with the army.

Discussion and Conclusions

Against the background of the retreat of the hegemonic military ethos as embodied in statist militarism, sites of socialization have been reproducing and constructing a new military ethos, as we have seen in memorial ceremonies and pre-military preparatory frameworks. The new ethos expresses itself in the gradual transformation of the relationship between the Ashkenazi secular individual and the army from obligatory to contractual terms; from a relationship based on a moral commitment to the collective to one that places the needs of the individual at the center and rests on conditions and bargaining.

A central mechanism that links agents' behavior with the structural outcome—in this instance the retreat from militarism, or a change in its form—can be found in sites of socialization that are formally managed by the state. These arenas are changing their patterns of behavior as a result of being caught in a two-way "pincer movement": given feelings of unease concerning the compensation offered by the state for their military sacrifice, the subjects of socialization are demanding alternative content to their socialization, both directly and via their families. That is, there is a growing expectation that agencies of socialization should reflect the changes in the structure of interests among their subjects. At the same time, these sites are becoming more autonomous: the retreat of the welfare state is making the state education system more independent, enabling it to develop an affinity with pupils and their parents, whom it increasingly sees as its customers. The subjugation of state mechanisms to the market is advantageous for the established groups—in this case the Ashkenazi secular group, largely based in the middle and upper-middle classes—who can convert their purchasing power into the ability to shape the content of these sites of socialization.[42]

These sites of socialization are doing two things at once: they are reproducing the centrality of the military ethos while simultaneously acting to empower the young recruit by giving him tools with which to bargain with the army over the conditions of his service and the values that it embodies. Accordingly, memorial ceremonies enhance an individualistic and critical orientation and provide it with legitimacy based in the context of the discourse (mourning) and its bearers (the dominant groups that wish to justify their status via recourse to their former military sacrifices); meanwhile, the "commando"-oriented preparatory course strengthens values of self-realization and a new masculine ethos based on professionalism, rationality, achievement, and nurturing the body and soul; finally, the Gadna preparatory framework quite clearly displays to the youngsters their bargaining power with the army when their expectations to be prepared for (what they see as) the right kind of service are not met.

Observing these sites of socialization, we can clearly see that the commitment to military service among younger members of the traditionally dominant groups is not taken for granted, and that they condition their military service on their personal/class agendas. In terms of the military ethos, we are witness to a shift from "obligatory militarism" to "contractual militarism." Military service remains a formal obligation, but it has lost its quality of totality, which in the past made it an obligation unconditional on individuals' preferences. At the same time, a pattern of contractual relationships has begun to develop. This shift in orientation quite clearly reflects a change in the institution of citizenship in Israel—at least among the Ashkenazi secular middle class—

from republican citizenship to a form that has diluted its republican foundations with liberal ones,[43] or, in other words, one that supports processes that place personal utility and a redefinition of citizen–state relations at the top of the pyramid. A pattern of citizenship is thus developing that wishes to detach one's civil status from one's contribution to the army.

In a circular movement, this shift in the pattern of exchange between the state and its citizens, a shift that the leading groups promoted as their military resources were eroded, plays a part in shaping the sites of socialization under discussion, which in turn reshape the exchange of relations between the state and its citizens. Thus, to a large extent, the modes of bargaining presented above—individual and group bargaining, military parenting, political selectiveness, and economic bargaining—reflect the sites of socialization. These sites empower the agents and imbue them with the skills and values of bargaining; these are reflected in the public sphere, where they further legitimize the changes taking place in the sites of socialization. Furthermore, these very modes of bargaining serve as sites of socialization for those influenced by them, whether in the family, the army, a political movement, or elsewhere.

These modes of bargaining are most notable in the Ashkenazi secular stratum of the middle class, the historical backbone of the army and the group that shaped the canonic military ethos. Their bargaining reflects the way in which youngsters are socialized to develop values and skills that allow them to conduct a different kind of relationship with the army. The social, structural change feeds off changes in the sites of socialization while at the same time feeding into them, thus gradually consolidating a new model of relations with the state, at least among the Ashkenazi secular group.

The erosion of the canonical military ethos is thus discovered exactly where we would least expect it. After all, these are sites in which the historically canonical ethos was forged by the group that was also recompensed for bearing it. What we are witnessing, therefore, is the contravention of obligatory militarism at its very birthplace, which as a result makes it legitimate for other groups to see the military ethos as a flexible text with multiple interpretations that can be deployed in the construction of a range of identities, and no longer as a collection of binding state directives.[44]

For the groups we have been discussing, the utility of military service is measured against the utility of civilian spheres (work, studying, leisure, etc.) in the light of available exchangeable resources, and this comparison shapes the level of motivation to serve. In contrast, other groups perceive the army as a more significant sphere in which to construct new routes of mobility and legitimately attain various civil rights, as well as trying to prove that they too are capable of the elite groups' achievements in combat. This is quite often a direct challenge to Ashkenazi secular dominance. At the same time, they strive to construct their own distinct combatant identity by utilizing sites such as the military in which the communal "common good" is constructed.

Thus, the army has become a locale for the construction of distinct identities for soldiers from social groups located outside the historical Ashkenazi secular core.[45] These groups are also developing contractual patterns of exchange with the army, though not necessarily in the same way as their predecessors. The most notable of these groups is the national-religious (recognizable by their knitted skullcaps). A striking example was the way some of them, with the mediation of their rabbis, made their military service conditional on the army taking no part in the Disengagement Plan in the summer of 2005. However, the knitted skullcap group differs from secular groups in two ways: first, they were bargaining as a distinct group with unique characteristics and did not enter into individual or sectorial–professional negotiations (as the representatives of reservists did, for instance); second, their bargaining would seem to be driven by ideology, and not utilitarian interests.

The relationship between the phenomena is obvious: the retreat of the Ashkenazi secular stratum from the army strengthens the motivation of peripheral and semi-peripheral groups to build their hold on the military. However, the erosion of the canonic military ethos and the strengthening of cultural diversity give these groups an incentive not to settle for participation in the army for its own sake, but rather to make it conditional on the improvement of their status, primarily in the civil political sphere. These groups have taken on board the old, republican model that tied military participation to social remuneration and have projected it onto their own status, while the erosion of the canonic ethos enables them to discuss these exchange relations increasingly overtly. This is another by-product of contractual militarism, but in a different form from that characteristic of Ashkenazi secular youth. As a result, the army is gradually becoming an arena for multicultural distributive struggles, especially as long as it recruits on a voluntary, professional, and selective basis.[46]

The question of whether Israeli militarism is on the decline or, alternatively, is being reshaped remains unanswered. On the one hand, the shift from obligatory to contractual militarism represents a retreat. The militaristic state is not as total as it once was. The leading group no longer perceives military service as a social resource and has reduced its support for the army. The temperance of the Arab–Israeli conflict up until 2000, and, to a certain extent, the Disengagement Plan, testify to the erosion of the state's ability to recruit support for the war effort. On the other hand, perhaps the military ethos has been preserved, but in a different form, with the leading group trying to maintain its hold on the army by matching the military ethos to its needs. An open question indeed.

Acknowledgments

We are grateful to Eyal Ben-Ari and the members of the workshop "An Army that has a State" at Van Leer Jerusalem Institute for their helpful comments.

Notes

1. Ofra Mayseless, "Attitudes toward Military Service among Israeli Youth," in Daniella Ashkenazy (ed.), *The Military in the Service of Society and Democracy* (Westport, Conn., 1992), 32–35.

2. Danny Zamir, "The Kibbutz-Born Soldiers and the Military Service," *Ma'arachot* 312–13 (1988): 18–20 [Hebrew].

3. Stella Korin-Liber, "An Interview with the IDF Head of the Personnel Directorate," *Globes,* November 7, 1999 [Hebrew]; Neomi Levitzky, "The IDF Closed Its Eyes," *Yediot Ahronot:* The Yom Kippur Supplement, September 22, 1996, 19–21 [Hebrew]; Baruch Nevo and Yael Shor, *The Contract between the IDF and Israeli Society: Compulsory Service* (Jerusalem, 2002), 9–35 [Hebrew].

4. Sari Makover-Blikov, "Why Should I Fight?" *Ma'ariv* Supplement, February 11, 2005, 22–26 [Hebrew].

5. For an indication, see Yagil Levy, "The War of the Peripheries: A Social Mapping of IDF Casualties in the Al-Aqsa Intifada," *Social Identities* 12.3 (2006): 309–324; Amir Rappaport, "The New People Army," *Ma'ariv,* Independence Day Supplement, April 26, 2005, 26–38 [Hebrew].

6. The secular Ashkenazis are joined by the upwardly mobile *Mizrachim*, who adopted a pattern of motivation similar to that of the secular Ashkenazis, whose social status is similar.

7. Yagil Levy, "Militarizing Inequality: A Conceptual Framework," *Theory and Society* 27.6 (1998): 873–904; *The Other Army of Israel—Materialist Militarism in Israel* (Tel-Aviv, 2003) [Hebrew].

8. James Burk, "Citizenship Status and Military Service: The Quest for Inclusion by Minorities and Conscientious Objectors," *Armed Forces & Society* 21.4 (1995): 503–29; Charles Tilly, "Democracy Is a Lake," in Charles Tilly, *Roads from Past to Future* (Oxford, 1997).

9. Levy, *The Other Army of Israel,* 56–81.

10. Anthony Giddens, *The Nation-State and Violence* (Cambridge, 1985).

11. Gershon Shafir and Yoav Peled, *Being Israeli: The Dynamic of Multiple Citizenship* (Cambridge, 2002).

12. Sammy Smooha, "Ethnicity and the Military in Israel: Theses for Discussion and Research," *Medina, Mimshal Viyahsim Benleumiyim* 22 (1984): 5–32 [Hebrew].

13. Uri Ben-Eliezer, *The Making of Israeli Militarism* (Bloomington, Ind., 1998).

14. Uri Ram, *The Globalization of Israel: McWorld in Tel-Aviv, Jihad in Jerusalem* (Tel-Aviv, 2005), 27–95 [Hebrew].

15. Shafir and Peled, *Being Israeli,* 213–307.

16. For example, see Tsippy Gon-Gross, *The Family Joins the Army* (Jerusalem, 2003) [Hebrew]; Korin-Liber, "An Interview," in Nevo and Shor, *The Contract between the IDF and Israeli Society,* 9–35.

17. Uri Ben-Eliezer, "The Civil Society and the Military Society in Israel," *Palestine-Israel Journal of Politics, Economics, and Culture* 12.1 (2005): 49–55; Gideon Doron and Udi Lebel, "Penetrating the Shields of Institutional Immunity: The Political Dynamic of Bereavement in Israel," *Mediterranean Politics* 9.2 (2004): 201–220; Hanna Herzog, "Family-Military Relations in Israel as a Genderizing Social Mechanism," *Armed Forces & Society* 31.1 (2004): 5–30; Hila Levi, "Care Package Packers: Motherhood vs. Army in the Israeli Culture," master's thesis, The Hebrew University of Jerusalem, 2001 [Hebrew].

18. Sara Helman, "War and Resistance: Israeli Civil Militarism and Its Emergent Crisis," *Constellations* 6.3 (1999): 391–410.

19. Levy, *The Other Army of Israel,* 253–55; Edna Lomsky-Feder, Nir Gazit, and Eyal Ben-Ari, "Notes on the Study of Military Reserves: Between the Military and Civilian Spheres," in Kristina Spohr-Readman (ed.), *Building Sustainable and Effective Military Capabilities: A Systematic Comparison of Professional and Conscript Forces* (Amsterdam, 2004), 64–78.

20. Sidney Tarrow, *Power in Movement: Social Movements, Collective Action and Politics* (New York, 1994), 62.

21. Maoz Azaryahu, *State Cults* (Sde-Boker, 1995) [Hebrew].

22. Avner Ben-Amos, "Rituals and Celebrations of Patriotic People in the Israeli Society," in Avner Ben-Amos and Daniel Bar-Tal (eds.), *Patriotism: Homeland Love* (Tel-Aviv, 2004), 275–315 [Hebrew]; Avner Ben-Amos and Ilana Bet-El, "Holy Day and Memorial Day," *Israel Studies* 4.1 (1999): 258–84; Meira Weiss, "Bereavement, Commemoration and Collective Identity in Contemporary Israeli Society," *Anthropological Quarterly* 70.2 (1997): 91–100.

23. Christopher Bjork, "Reconstructing Rituals: Expressions of Autonomy and Resistance in Sino-Indonesian Schools," *Anthropology and Educational Quarterly* 33.4 (2002): 465–91; David Kertzer, *Ritual, Politics, and Power* (New Haven, Conn., and London, 1988).

24. Fifty-three descriptions of memorial ceremonies (elicited from semi-structured observations) were collected over the period 1994–2003. The observed ceremonies were staged at schools that belong to the Jewish sector of the state education system (comprising about 60 percent of the Israeli student population, as Arab and Jewish ultra-Orthodox schools were not included): twenty-four elementary and junior high schools, and twenty-nine high schools. Of these schools, eight came from the national-religious sector while the others were from the secular sector. The variety of sources is intended to reflect the diversity of the Israeli educational system: vocational and academic schools, day schools, boarding schools, and so on. The focus is on twelve ceremonies that were held in various high schools that serve the dominant group. The analysis discusses these ceremonies in comparison to the other ceremonies.

25. Don Handelman, *Models and Mirrors: Towards an Anthropology of Public Events* (Cambridge, 1990).

26. Edna Lomsky-Feder, "The Memorial Ceremony in Israeli Schools: Between State and Civil Society," *British Journal of Sociology of Education* 25.3 (2004): 291–305.

27. Yagil Levy, *The Other Army of Israel*, 56–81.

28. Sara Helman, "From Soldiering and Motherhood to Citizenship: A Study of Four Israeli Peace Protest Movements," *Social Politics* 1.2 (1999): 292–314; Edna Lomsky-Feder, "Life Stories, War and Veterans: On the Social Distribution of Memories," *Ethos* 32.1 (2004): 1–28.

29. Edna Lomsky-Feder and Eyal Ben-Ari, "From 'The People in Uniform' to 'Different Uniforms for the People': Professionalism, Diversity and the Israeli Defence Forces," in Joseph Soeters and Jan van der Meulen (eds.), *Managing Diversity in the Armed Forces: Experiences from Nine Countries* (Tilburg, Holland, 1999), 157–86.

30. Edna Lomsky-Feder, "The Bounded Female Voice in Memorial Ceremonies," *Qualitative Sociology* 28.3 (2005): 293–314.

31. Ben-Amos and Bet-El, "Holy Day and Memorial Day," 258–84.

32. Udi Lebel and Natti Ronel, "Parental Discourse and Activism as a Response to Bereavement of Fallen Sons and Civilian Terrorist Victims," *Journal of Loss and Trauma* 10.4 (2005): 385–405.

33. Vered Vinitzky-Serossi, "Commemorating Narratives of Violence: The Yitzhak Rabin Memorial Day in Israeli Schools," *Qualitative Sociology* 24.2 (2001): 245–68.

34. Yoram Bilu and Eliezer Witztum, "War-Related Loss and Suffering in Israeli Society: An Historical Perspective," *Israel Studies* 5.2 (2000): 1–31; Edna Lomsky-Feder and Eyal Ben Ari, "Trauma, Therapy and Responsibility: Psychology and War in Contemporary Israel," in Mobika Boeck, Aparna Rao, and Michael Bolling (eds.), *The Practice of War* (Munich, 2007); Rubik Rosental, *Is Bereavement Dead?* (Jerusalem, 2001) [Hebrew].

35. Yael Zerubavel, "Combat, Sacrificial, and Sacrifice: Changes in the Ideologies of Patriotism's Sacrificial in Israel," in Avner Ben-Amos and Daniel Bar-Tal (eds.), *Patriotism: Homeland Love* (Tel-Aviv, 2004) [Hebrew].

36. Moshe Israelashvili and Orit Taubman, "Adolescent Preparation for Military Service: A Preliminary Evaluation," *Megamot* 38 (1997): 408–20 [Hebrew].

37. The material was gathered through participant observation in Yair's course and at the Gadna week (youth regiment activity), as well as interviews with participants in each of the activities. See Noa Harel, "Playing Military: The Culture of Preparation for the Army in a Private Course and in the Gadna," master's thesis, The Hebrew University of Jerusalem, 2000) [Hebrew]. In the case of Yair's course, interviews (personal and group) were held with graduates of previous sessions.

38. Mayseless, "Attitudes toward Military Service," 32–35.

39. Limor Even-Ari, "The Program of Preparation of 11th & 12th Grade School Pupils for Military Service and Its Implementation at School Level," master's thesis, The Hebrew University of Jerusalem, 2004) [Hebrew].

40. Every term has a number of girls; this is not included in this chapter.

41. Oz Almog, *The Sabra: A Profile* (Tel-Aviv, 1997) [Hebrew].

42. Mimi Ajzenstadt and Zeev Rosenhek, "Privatisation and New Modes of State Intervention: The Long-Term Care Programme in Israel," *Journal of Social Policy* 29.2 (2000): 247–62; Geoff Whitty, *Making Sense of Education Policy* (London, 2002).

43. Ram, *The Globalization of Israel,* 27–95; Shafir and Peled, *Being Israeli,* 213–307.

44. Uri Ben-Eliezer, "Civil Society in Israeli Society: Politics and Identity in New Social Movements," *Israeli Sociology* 2.1 (1999): 51–98 [Hebrew].

45. See Stuart A. Cohen, "Towards a New Portrait of a (New) Israeli Soldier," *Israel Affairs* 3 (1997): 77–117; Yohai Hakak, "From the Army of God to the Israeli Armed Forces: An Interaction between Two Cultural Models," in Inger Marie Okkenhaug and Ingvild Flaskerud (eds.), *Gender, Religion and Change in the Middle East: Two Hundred Years of History* (Oxford, 2005), 29–45; Lomsky-Feder and Ben-Ari, "From 'The People in Uniform'," 157–86; Edna Lomsky-Feder and Tamar Rapoport, "Juggling Models of Masculinity: Russian-Jewish Immigrants in the Israeli Army," *Sociological Inquiry* 73.1 (2003): 114–37; Orna Sasson-Levy, "Military, Masculinity and Citizenship: Tensions and Contradictions in the Experience of Blue-Collar Soldiers," *Identities: Global Studies in Culture and Power* 10.3 (2003): 319–45.

46. Yagil Levy, "Israel's Rough Draft," *Foreign Policy* 142 (2004): 84–86.

SEVEN

Shadow Lands: The Use
of Land Resources for
Security Needs in Israel

AMIRAM OREN

From time to time in recent years, the media in Israel have reported on security infrastructures. These reports refer to such topics as "IDF Deployment and Readiness along the Lebanese Border," "The Separation Fence," "Evacuation of Camps in Urban Centers," "Civilian Activity on Training Grounds," "Environmental Damage Caused by Military Camps and Installations," and "IDF Deployment along a New Defense Line Opposite the Gaza Strip after the Disengagement." All these news articles comprise but a small fraction of the broader topic that has yet to be related to properly—the use of the state's and the public's land resources for security needs.

The security sector,[1] especially through the IDF, holds on to more than one-third of the territory of the State of Israel within the Green Line, and it influences, to various degrees and ways, more than half of the territory of the state, as well as dictating to a large extent the uses of air space and extensive portions of sea space. Up to now, this fact and its implications have gained very little attention. Academic-research discussion or planning and professional clarification or public debate have hardly raised any issues dealing with the relationship between security, on the one hand, and the resources of real estate and state territories, geographical space, environmental quality, and the image of the landscape, on the other. The purpose of this chapter is to clarify why discussion and research on the extensive use of land resources for security reasons have been placed on the back burner and to offer a new agenda for this topic.

Discussion Framework and Background

Security uses of land are part of military power. The exploitation of the best real estate, state lands, and land and sea space is intended to ensure the utmost utilization of the military and other security forces' operational ability. They are part of the response to the security challenge facing the state. In other words, they derive from a concept of security that responds to threat—the possible political and military ways of acting, the use of force and military strength, the favorable military doctrine, and the principles of building and organizing a force. Military doctrine includes an operational concept for activating a force, which constitutes the basis for determining the abilities required of the military. It generally distinguishes between two situations in which the army finds itself: first, an army that operates during a time of tranquility and whose task is to deter an enemy, warn of its intentions, undertake ongoing security activity, prepare for battle, and be on daily alert; second, an army that operates during wartime and whose tasks are defense, offense, subduing the other side, and protecting the home front.

The elements of the demand for land derived from these abilities will enable the army to function and to fulfill its objectives. The roots of the demand also pass through the building of a military force for action on the battlefield. In all these, additional components of resource demands for land are present, among them the arrangement of the forces—its size, structure, and the functional and spatial organization of the command over its fighting and professional arms.[2]

The areas that serve security purposes appear in two forms: a direct form, in which the bodies of the security sector are consumers of land in the broad sense of the term—real estate, territory, and space, which also includes air and sea space; and an indirect form, of civilian land that serves security needs in one or another form and to different degrees. Therefore, land uses for security purposes are lands and territory owned by the security sector and civilian land that the security sector purchases, leases, or grabs, depending on the particular event, and holds on to and uses for ad hoc purposes, as well as land and civilian infrastructure, whose objectives it directs; it even participates in the costs of setting up this infrastructure so that it will serve it in the future. Security land uses are not an end in itself, but one input in the gamut of security strength components, such as personnel, capital, and technology.[3]

The theoretical framework and background for discussion of the subject of this chapter are derived from the research field called "the geography of security." At the end of the 1980s, British geographers defined this field as a secondary field of political geography and as being concerned with the political aspects of security and strategic space.[4] As for Israel, the scope should be enlarged to see the broad frame that includes subjects from a number of disciplines: geography and spatial physical planning topics, on the one hand, and security and the military and military–civilian area relations, on the other hand. These topics may be examined separately or combined from two points of view. The first is "The Land—The Security Arena"; in other words, the physical and settlement geography of the state and its neighbors is a factor (though not the only one) that affects security. A definition that is a little different from this point of view is "the geography of the land as one of the security elements." The other viewpoint is the obverse of the first one: "Security—A Territorial Arena"; in other words, a translation of security needs into terms of physical foundations and land, which in itself is a geographic phenomenon that has implications for the image of the space, for environmental quality, and for the look of the landscape.

Two basic assumptions stem from these viewpoints and reflect the Israeli reality of the combination of security and sovereign territory. The assumption derived from the first viewpoint was that territory is an important component in Israel's concept of security. From the initial days of the state and in light of the situation in which it is placed, the term *security* was comprehended as protecting the very existence of the political entity, defending the lives of its residents, and preserving sovereign and other territory under Israeli rule.[5] Therefore, territory is the end-all and be-all of security—the space that must be protected. The land is also an input for realizing security. Ground resources and space are meant for camps and installation, for infrastructure, and for undertaking security actions.

Another assumption, derived from the second point of view, concerns the territorial mix between security and civilian uses of the land, which is manifested in the popular Israeli proverb "All the land is a military front." The area of the State of Israel is relatively small, but its population profile and physical face present a densely populated, widely diverse country. Civilian needs for land are for building and development purposes, but also for preserving nature and landscape values; these are combined with security needs that are scattered throughout the country. In Israel, it is difficult to point to a region or place where there is no territorial "contact" between security consideration and civilian interests.

Military Deployment and Its Implications

GENERAL

The subject of the geographical implications of military deployment has been discussed in the military geography literature. This field was defined in the 1960s as "implementing principles and geographic knowledge for solving military problems."[6] Our discussion includes the study of geographical conditions that affect military strength[7] or military systems at all levels—strategic, operative, tactical,[8] as well as the geographical aspects and military space during wartime and in times of peace.[9]

Until the early 1990s, research on the combined area of security and territory hardly dealt with issues of the interface between military and civilian areas. At that time, with the global geopolitical changes following the break-up of the Soviet Union, attention started to be given, too, to the civilian–military combination. Researchers began to examine the geographical–spatial significance and implications stemming from these substantive changes and what derived from them: reduced security and military infrastructure.[10]

An examination of the content of the publications of academic research centers in Israel that deal with security and strategic studies shows that they did not specialize in topics having to do with the combination of security and geography, not to speak of any discussion of military deployment and its implications. This was also true of university departments of geography. Surveys of the development of the geography profession in Israel[11] show that despite the centrality of the subject of security in Israel and its many territorial contexts, there was no research area defined as the geography of security, except for that at the University of Haifa. There are those who have related to the geostrategic aspect—Israel's geographical location, its boundaries, its form, size, and population as components in the national security equation[12]—or to the geopolitical aspect: the geographical aspect in security discourse.[13]

START OF ACADEMIC DISCUSSION

The first time the subject of military deployment and its implications came up for academic discussion and planning clarification was in the aftermath of the signing of the peace agreement with Egypt. At the end of the 1970s, in light of the IDF evacuation of Sinai and the reduction in territory controlled by Israel, a fear was created that the Negev would be too narrow to contain both military and civilian needs. The thinking was that the IDF deployment in the Negev would be a "death blow" for civilian development programs. By contrast, the prevailing opinion was that the IDF deployment there would constitute a window of opportunity and a lever for its development. Several works were written on the subject from a desire to examine the possible future reciprocal spatial relations that would be created in the Negev with the massive redeployment by the IDF. Among them, a program was proposed for Negev development that related to the new deployment in the region.[14] After the IDF left Sinai and deployed in the Negev, two articles were published examining whether a conflict existed between the consumers of the civilian sector and the ground uses of the IDF on this strip of land.[15]

In the mid-1980s, an initial academic attempt was made, one that had no follow-up, to deal with the issue of Israel's military landscape. The aim of that paper, written by Arnon Soffer and Julian Minghi,[16] was to classify the components of the security landscape at the different levels of national, regional, and local space, and to examine their geographical dispersion and suggest the extent of their influence on national physical planning. Several years later, Amiram Derman[17] presented criteria for defining military strategic space. In his opinion, in addition to strategic depth, the vital space that enabled fighting with minimal casualties in the rear, there are three other components for assessing the vital nature of military strategic space. The first is the space that is meant to contribute to military readiness: training areas, experimental areas, storage areas; the second is the space that is intended for alert and warning: intelligence installations and control and command–communication installations; the third is the space for battle maneuvers themselves, to achieve tactical abilities and prevent harm to the rear. In this framework, a series of components were presented that could be used to create military strength, as were measures for evaluating these components.

These two facts could constitute the beginning of methodological discussion of the territorial needs of security in general and of the army specifically. However, as could have been expected, works on the subject were not written for many years.

In 2003, work on a doctoral dissertation was completed that analyzed, from a geographical–historical viewpoint, the development of the array of uses of land that the IDF demanded and the reciprocal relations between it and the civilian sector on the subject of physical planning and the allotment of real estate in the initial years of the state, from its establishment until the Sinai Campaign of 1956. This period of the War of Independence and its aftermath in the early 1950s was one that established and shaped the spatial geographical area of the state, and in the course of this period the settlement program was formulated and security land uses regulated. In this period, the framework was set for the territorial interface between the IDF, society, and space in the State of Israel.[18]

In 2005, a monograph was published with the goal of clarifying the concepts, terms, and methodologies relating to security land uses and to examine the implications stemming from them.[19] Also published was an article that presented the goals and aims of security land uses, the norms for creating a security land-use map for Israel, and ways of classifying them.[20] These publications shed light on security land uses as a geographical–spatial issue in which much was hidden about what was known.

THE BUDS OF PROFESSIONAL DISCOURSE

National physical planning was and still is a topic of many works; however, its connections with the military system have not merited research. The lack of treatment of the subject has also led to a lack of studies on conflicts between civilian and security land uses, a topic that will now be elaborated.

In the first half of the 1990s, following intensified civilian development and reverberations of the peace steps with the Palestinians and with Syria, the idea arose that in the wake of the possible evacuation of the Golan Heights and significant parts of the territories under civilian administration in Judea, Samaria, and Gaza, the IDF would need to redeploy in areas within the Green Line. It was only natural that a request was made for an extensive study to be conducted that would deal with this issue, especially its implications. This expectation was only partially realized. In 1995–1996, in the context of preparing the planning project— "Israel in the 2000s"—civilian planning bodies examined for the first time, and comprehensively, the IDF's spatial physical planning policy. This work was not empirical, but a qualitative and conceptual analysis that focused principally on analyzing the variables influencing policy goals and strategies for realizing them. The product of this research was a policy paper that recommended the outlines for IDF deployment in the far term, two and a half decades in the future.[21]

The importance of the document is twofold: it was the first of its kind, and it provided a theoretical presentation of some of the civilian planning issues emanating from an IDF deployment. It is interesting that, despite the fact that the work was commissioned by the Ministry of Defense and the IDF in the framework of their participation in the planning project, they did not discuss its contents after the report's presentation. Since the document was not prepared by the security sector, it was not approved as a binding document. With its completion and even several years later, it was related to as a "cognitive exercise" and nothing more. Furthermore, only several copies of the work were circulated, mainly to parties in the security sector. The public did not get to look into it, and naturally it remained confidential, so it was not possible to develop further research in the field.

During those same years and afterward, the IDF prepared an annual infrastructure and deployment master plan that included information about the future of army camps and installations. Like most military plans, the details were not made public; but what was derived from it served IDF and Ministry of Defense representatives in the various discussions with regional planning authorities. The general lines of the program were presented in 2000 by the then head of the Planning Division, Gen. Shlomo Yanai, in a lecture at a symposium sponsored by the KKL-JNF (Keren Kayemeth LeIsrael–Jewish National Fund) Institute for Land Uses. This was the first and only public reference to the IDF's deployment policy and the way it would carry out changes in the future.[22] One can also find references of one sort or another to the program—if they exist at all—in protocols of the National Council for Planning.[23]

Part of the program included a master plan for training areas. The methodology for carrying it out was also presented to civilian parties to whom the program pertained. In its framework and as a basis for its preparation, a mapping was prepared of the civilian needs for which potential conflict with the IDF over space might arise.[24] This document could have served as an opening for the start of research on the subject; however, it, too, was not widely circulated. A number of years prior to it an article had been published that examined the legal aspects of determining training areas in accordance with defense regulations (during an emergency) for closing off areas.[25]

At the close of the 1990s, a staff officer of the IDF Planning Division published two articles in the journal of the JNF Institute for the Study of Land Policy and Land Uses on subjects relating to infrastructure and deployment. The first article, whose subject was environmental quality, presented the reciprocal relations and conflicts between the army and environment and the way of ameliorating them.[26] The second article dealt with the evacuation of camps from the urban centers, describing the process and progress since the government's decision on the matter in 1993.[27] This article and the state comptroller's report on the subject, which will be presented below, are two references to a subject that comes into public consciousness from time to time. In fact, the process of evacuating camps is undertaken at a snail's pace. One still cannot point to any large number of camps that have been evacuated, despite the many announcements and proclamations about doing so.

Since the end of the 1980s, the state comptroller has delved into the subjects of infrastructure and deployment in the context of his critique of the security sector. His 1987 report discussed the scope of training areas, along with the intensity of the use of these lands and interference with civilian development.[28] In the 1993 report, the dispute between the IDF and the Israel Lands Administration with regard to paying a user's fee for firing ranges was raised.[29] Other subjects that elicited criticism were setting building limits on the civilian environment close to army munitions storage facilities;[30] the beginning of the slow evacuation of IDF camps from urban centers, a move stemming from the government's

1993 decision on the matter;[31] the scope of the spread of mined and suspected mined areas throughout the country and its implications;[32] and
the worrisome situation of environmental pollution and the handling of
subjects of environmental interest by the IDF.[33] All in all, though, interest in the findings of the state comptroller and his comments on these
subjects did not last long. In the best case, there was a discussion at the
Knesset's State Auditing Committee, but without media reverberation.
Critique of these subjects never developed into any public or professional
debate, nor was there any academic research.

In 2005, media interest began to pick up on the subject of the scope
of the use of land resources for security needs in Israel. The subject was
presented on the radio on five occasions. The printed press also related
it twice.[34] Thus, it may be said that media attention to the subject, as an
expression of public interest, was very poor.

In 2005, too, an unsuccessful attempt was made to show professionals examples of physical planning in the security sector. The association
of planners in Israel, in cooperation with the infrastructure and deployment section in the Planning Division, initiated a tour of the Haifa and
Lower Galilee region. The intention was to present the following subjects
in the course of the tour: the IDF's multiyear program for redeployment
of army camps, evacuation of camps from urban areas, and the significance of these moves. This was a welcome initiative by means of which a
window could have been opened to the physical planning of the security
sector; following that, dialogue and professional discussion could take
place. However, it was not to be. At the last minute, the army canceled
this initiative.

The subject of security land uses also came up at three conferences.
One, a university symposium on Environmental Quality held at the University of Haifa in June 2005, presented the effects of the Israeli security
sector on natural resources and the environment. However, the presentation, though innovative, relied on the aforementioned state comptroller's report. The second conference that was open to the public at large
took place in November 2005 at the Sde-Boker academic center and was
devoted to the subject of "The IDF in the Negev: Settlement and Environmental Implications—Past, Present, and Future." A senior officer
from the General Staff's planning division presented the principles of
IDF deployment policy and sketched out redeployment in the Negev. The

importance of this conference was both in its being held at all and in its shedding new light on the subject. Time will tell whether this conference will have a follow-up. The third conference was presented by the Israeli Planners Association, one of whose professional sessions was devoted to security and spatial physical planning. These three gatherings constitute the initial professional debate on the subject and provide an indication of the future.

The Territorial Kingdom of the Security Sector

As presented at the outset, the security sector holds and influences in various ways and to different degrees more than half of the sovereign territory of the state, not including areas of the military government on the West Bank. According to statistics of the Planning and Deployment Branch of the IDF General Staff's Planning Division, which appears in the State Comptroller's Report 55A of 2005,[35] 46 percent of the lands of the state are security territory, consisting of 30 percent for training areas, 4 percent IDF camps and installations, 1 percent Ministry of Defense installations, and 11 percent off-limit areas that the security system imposes because of its activities in installations or areas adjoining them, including areas where low-flying air force planes and helicopters are permitted. IDF statistics do not reflect the whole picture of the scope of the rate of land uses. Even in the 54 percent of the state territory that the IDF presents as civilian, there is security affinity and use. To a large extent, it also dictates the uses of air space and extensive sections of sea space.

The use of land resources for purposes of security is a large-scale spatial–geographical phenomenon both in absolute terms and in relation to the size of the state, with implications for many areas: the land regime, image of the cities and the rural settlement configuration of one sort or another, transportation, communication, energy infrastructure development possibilities, mining and quarrying opportunities, the maintenance of environmental quality and nature preserves, the face of the landscape, and so on.

Territorial control and the influence of the security sector are enabled by laws that give the system broad freedom of action. In contrast to the civilian sector, the security sector has exceptional and sweeping status in the Planning and Building Law, which permits it to erect security installations almost without approval by the relevant civilian agencies. The security sector does not act on the basis of any outlined plan or a crystallized worldview of planning and construction, but in response to its territorial needs and the statutory protection of these needs. This causes its representatives on planning boards to air the broadest opinions, and at times every representative acts according to his or her own opinion. Furthermore, even when the security sector formulates a certain stand, it is subject to change under the pressure of close political parties. Through its representatives in planning institutions, it is also involved in various ways in civilian physical planning at the national, district, and local levels. Security sector representatives use their power in planning institutions and in many cases bring about changes in plans from a fear, baseless at times, that they will affect or interfere with security installations.

In addition, the security sector has a sweeping exemption in many laws dealing with preserving environmental quality. This, despite the fact that IDF activities and installations and the defense industries have a real potential to harm the environment and pollute the air, sea, ground, and nature through solid and liquid waste, sewage, dangerous materials, noise, and radiation. In effect, there are defects, some of them basic, that point to a worrisome picture in relation to the IDF's and the Ministry of Defense's handling of the subject of environmental quality.

The security sector uses defense regulations (for emergencies) to close off areas, particularly for training and experimental purposes, effectively expropriating them from their owners. According to those same regulations, it also closes off sea lanes.

Even from a real estate aspect, the security sector has many advantages relative to any civilian party. It administers its real estate with completely different tools from any others in the state. The allocation of land for its needs is undertaken through an exclusive channel, the special Allocation Committee for Security Needs, which operates in the framework of the Israel Lands Administration. The areas that serve minefields in no-man's land were never allotted to it. The security sector does not pay the Israel Lands Administration rent for lands used for training areas.

The security sector, jointly with the Finance Ministry and the Israel Lands Administration, conducts negotiations for vacating camps in cities, and it demands high sums for the alternative construction. Its behavior is similar to that of a real estate trader who owns many properties. However, it is worth mentioning that these are not its private assets, but, rather, are those of the state that it obtained for its needs and that it must return with the conclusion of their use. That does not happen; its terms for returning them are payment for their economic value.

In an emergency, it has an appropriate legal basis for seizing lands for an ad hoc purpose. Furthermore, the cloak of secrecy under which the security sector operates is exploited to avoid payments of property tax that it should pay for part of hundreds of military camps and facilities that are located in the jurisdictional territory of scores of local authorities.

It could thus be concluded that, from a territorial aspect, consequently, the security sector acts as an "independent system" operating alongside the civilian sector and at times even separate from it, and this has much influence on it in the area of physical–spatial planning, construction and lands, environmental quality, and more. Academic and professional occupation with the subject of security land uses is important in order to study its effect on the civilian sector in these areas. However, it turns out that there is a paucity of such studies. This fact is surprising, if not amazing, in light of the fact that land in Israel is at a premium and that the shortage has grown over time and intensified in the past two decades.

Questions about Dealing with the Subject

Subjects related to the use of land resources for security needs and the developments stemming from this use provide leeway for a wide range of academic research, professional discussion, and public clarification that has yet to be exhausted. One can point to several reasons, some or all of which can constitute the explanation for the paucity of preoccupation with the subject.

ABSENCE OF KNOWLEDGE, LACK OF AWARENESS, AND CIVILIAN DISINTEREST

The simple response to the aforementioned can be the fact that most of the civilian sector is not familiar with the phenomenon, does not know its dimensions, and is unaware of the power and extensive influence of the use of land resources for security needs.

For the public at large, which is not knowledgeable or interested in professional issues of physical–spatial planning, land economics, the infrastructure array, and environmental quality, the extensive use of land resources for security needs serves a real need and is not considered special or unusual. It may be assumed that the public relies on the planning committees to do their work faithfully, keeping the good of the public before their eyes. Therefore, from the public's viewpoint, there is no reason not to make available to the army what it requests.

Issues concerning the relationship between security, on the one hand, and land resources and state territories, geographical space, environmental quality, and the image of the landscape, on the other hand, rarely interest the politicians who deal with matters of security and think that there are subjects of far more importance to discuss.

Another explanation for this disinterest is the claim that in reality there is no problem with security land uses and that they do not interfere with physical–spatial planning or the national land economy; according to this premise, the civilian sector can allot land, and there is especially no need for discussion. Even if there are many security land uses, it is argued that civilian life is conducted as usual, without breakdowns. Proof of this is that one-third of the state's area is training grounds, a significant percentage of which the army opens on holidays (Sukkot, Pesach, and Hanukka) and temporarily ceases training to allow trips and hikes through these grounds. There is also an unwritten agreement, which is legally improper, that people can take trips through them undisturbed on Saturdays, since training exercises are not held on the Sabbath.

Another explanation is that in the public's consciousness, security land uses are a self-understood phenomenon, and not the sort in need of explanation. There are those who would say that a large proportion of the land that the army uses has no civilian demand at all and no alternative use; therefore, why is it wrong that it is at its disposal? The Israeli public, in particular those experts on the subject, are already used to the fact that the Israeli security sector is a large land consumer, not subject to appeal. A conceptual fixation is what prevents other reasoning and does not allow the raising of questions about the broad scope of security land uses. According to this outlook, questions are perceived as extraneous and perhaps even argumentative, so there is no need for opinions on the subject.

Still another argument justifying non-preoccupation with the subject is that security land uses and the manner in which they are managed by the security sector do not constitute a geographical problem—spatial or planning. Even if it did, discussion and presenting solutions are not priority matters. On the agenda of physical planning, land management, and national infrastructure are other, weightier issues on which discussion has concluded, but about which a decision has yet to be made. Therefore, the research effort must be concentrated on them, and professional discussion must be exhausted. It is more than enough to deal with these issues. According to this approach, dealing with them probably does not leave enough energy or desire to handle secondary topics, about which there is apparent agreement.

Despite the fact that these subjects are awaiting debate, public preoccupation with the topic of the use of land resources for security purposes is perceived by many as a Pandora's box: there is no one who will agree or dare to risk opening it. The nonhandling of the subject and avoidance of extraneous questions about the use of land resources for security purposes in Israel stem from an apparently broad public consensus about security and the sanctity of security. The existence of an objective threat to the territorial space of Israel necessitates an appropriate response that will draw in its wake the need for the security sector, which is entrusted with this response, to be strengthened and to use many chunks of Israeli space.

CONSIDERATIONS OF THE SECURITY SECTOR

From an academic point of view, another approach may be presented, according to which the security sector has institutional interests. Thus another explanation can be that because of bureaucratic and systems considerations, the security sector obviates discussion of the subject and does not rejoice at public debate over alternatives between security and civilian land uses. This explanation, the source of which is bureaucratic politics, does not negate in advance the possibility of the manipulation of the actors in the political arena or of those in the civilian–security sector. In other words, this approach holds that security considerations, whose importance strengthens the security sector, are meant to serve its standing and seniority. This may be demonstrated by the annual dispute that without fail goes on between the Ministry of Defense and the IDF, on one side, and the Treasury Ministry, on the other, over the size of the security budget. Every year, as a set ritual at the time of the budget discussions, those in senior positions would reveal to the public at large the threats that still face the state, and this is done to create favorable public opinion for their budgetary demands.

This approach, which views, in the existence of structural interests, the central reason or another reason for the lack of research activity on this issue, subliminally posits the existence of an agreement on uniform concepts: objective threat and objective response. Maybe the security sector as a rule is professional and acts without considerations of favoritism. Opposite it are civilian interests that are perceived as legitimate—the desire to develop infrastructure, to preserve environmental quality, and so on. Explanations of manipulation assume the existence of concepts common to the party that conducts it and to the party for whom it is being done. Thus, the lack of interest in the subject stems from an absence of any desire to throw down a challenge to the dominant standing of the security sector in general and to the territorial aspect in particular.

The explanation for the absence of academic research and professional discourse is possibly simpler. It is impossible to work on a subject for which there are no readily available and current information, suitable empirical data, and relevant initial documentation. Until now, except for the general IDF data presented in this article, the Ministry of Defense and the IDF, arguing the secrecy of security information—what in the past was called field security—did not publish detailed information about areas and lands in its possession, uses or limitations on the use, and on civilian activity. The unwillingness to present specific data publicly may be understood and perhaps even accepted. However, it is not clear why unclassified data that would enable receiving a clearer picture of the scope of the security sectors' land holdings (for instance, the size of the camps inside or close to urban areas) and in particular the implications of this phenomenon are hidden. There is no logical reason why data on the use of land resources for security purposes cannot be presented to the public, just as the size of the security budget and general data about it are made public.

In the context of available information, two things should be noted: certain parties that are not counted with the security sector, the Israel Lands Administration and the district zoning committees, have data. Apparently they prevent the publication of information in accordance with the guidelines of the security sector or on account of self-censorship, because what is involved here is the soul of the state: security. It is possible that the security sector or civilian parties have no detailed data at all; therefore, there is nothing to present. On second thought, however, this assumption is unacceptable. Apparently there is a reason for the nonpublication of the data: information that is not made public is a kind of power, and who wants to relinquish power?

THE BUREAUCRATIC APPROACH

One may discuss the use of land resources for security purposes from another academic viewpoint, and offer another explanation for the absence of research in the area. The intention here is the approach that holds that reality is not objective and should be examined in the light of the changing system of concepts. According to this approach, concepts of the Israeli geographical security discourse are a product of the Israeli society—which gives prime standing to security. Therefore, against the background of the feeling of a threat (which itself is the fruit of cultural construction), the entire space is "security space," for good or for bad. This approach is not partner to the discourse but only points to the affinity between any group of concepts and the culture from which it arose. Therefore, according to this approach, there is no place at all for discussing the question of the appropriation of space by the security sector, and thus the absence of research on the topic.

Up to this point, possible reasons have been presented to explain why no academic research or public discussion has taken place on the special territorial standing of the security sector. Any reason can be apt, and the very asking of questions does not mean casting aspersions on the security sector or intending to harm it by leveling criticism. The questions are worthy of being asked and are to be examined in a manner that is impartial and to the point.

The Challenge to Research, Discussion, and Clarification

The discussion of the use of land resources for security needs deals in the main with the geographical–spatial aspect. Discussion and research, however, need not concentrate only on an analysis of the phenomenon itself, but also on an explanation of its sources and implications and the need to exist in the broad context of the security status in Israel. It can also be compared with other countries.

The array of security land uses reflects the broad network of considerations, opportunities, limitations, and constraints. Its formation, since the early days of the state, stems from the multitude of parties and events, in particular the security and political circumstances that cannot be foreseen (at least most of them), as well as economic, technological, social, and other circumstances. Those who research security have not voiced any opinion on the subject of land as a resource and element of military strength. By contrast, even the geographers who have investigated the creation of the settlement map of the State of Israel have avoided security land uses as a component and input to Israeli space. The crystallization of those uses over the years was not a result of orderly planning; rather, they developed and expanded in parallel with the development of regional land uses: settlements of one kind or another, the road and track network, the array of national infrastructure, recreation sites, nature preserves, and so on. In order to complement the great amount of knowledge that has accumulated about the creation of the civilian settlement map, there is room to research how the array of security land uses with which we are all familiar was shaped and how it developed.

Discussion of the development of the use of land resources for security needs in the context of time necessitates relating to another aspect. This is an examination of the central weight that the time dimension has in decisions pertaining to the allocation of resources for security needs, both because security activity deals with assuring strength and survival over time and because of the great importance of preserving options for an effective future use of the limited land resources.

In addition to the security uses of land as a special phenomenon in itself, it also arouses interest in anything to do with the interface with the civilian sector. The point of departure for discussion and debate is the statement that the extensive use of land resources for security needs is not only a territorial–geographical phenomenon, in light of the fact that it is affected by security interests and processes and reflects a security reality, but it also creates a spatial reality that impacts, as well, on the civilian sector.

In Israel, the different security land uses integrate with civilian uses and create a mosaic of coexistence in a civilian–military mix in which these not-simple constraints live side by side. Space will not be monolithic and will include islands and enclaves of military infrastructure of a kind like the civilian infrastructure adjoining it. Development of civilian space will be derived from systems planning for optimal exploitation of the area, setting a settlement hierarchy, putting together a balanced transportation system for known and forecasted needs, constructing various infrastructure systems, and marking "green lungs." The military system that shares the same cell area will behave otherwise, for its goals are different. In contrast, its needs are connected to the civilian space. The military system will ask that the national infrastructures service it; national transportation systems will be suitable and available.

Despite the fact that security land uses are part of the space, in general it is found that there are territorial conflicts and, at times, identical interests between them and civilian land uses. With the latter, conflicts of interests exist between those who represent development considerations and "the Greens," environmentalists who seek to freeze development in order to preserve nature and environmental quality. The existence of military installations in settled areas prevents proper civilian construction and preserves open areas, something that is supported by the Greens. Therefore, there is room for investigating the degree of strength and influence of the security sector on the face of the state; that is, on the geographical space, on the quality of the environment and the quality of life, and on the image of the landscape.

Another subject that should be clarified and delved into in more depth is the way in which the security sector administers and implements its land and space needs. The assumptions that necessitate investigation and analysis are that in Israel two separate special systems are interconnected—one civilian, known and familiar, the other, security, on which information is sparse and unclear—and that the security sector is possibly that which dictates the special priorities and influences the civilian system, although by the same measure (or perhaps somewhat less) it is influenced by it.

An examination of the creation of a map of security land uses, whether spontaneously or ordered, needs to be crafted not only in the military and political context. Discussion must be broader and be a reflection of the triangle by means of which one can read the patterns of interrelationships of the military and civilian areas in Israel. The three vertices of this triangle are security as a state interest with the purpose of defending the country, whose land resources are the means of realizing this objective; space, which is created and managed for civilian and military needs; and society, which seeks to maintain a regular way of life under conditions of protracted, unceasing, political, and military struggle.

In this context, several subjects should be added for in-depth clarification: a comparison of the way a security budget is set and achieved and the way district and territorial needs are set; and supervision and civilian control of the demands of the security sector for land. Are there tools or a system of balances that that are required to weight the needs of the security sector? Or is its stand perhaps generally found to be first or unfortunately first among equals? Here it is possible to expand and examine the absence of the subject of IDF land uses in political–social discussion concerned with who in fact is authorized to determine land uses in Israel. Other considerations are the arrangements between the security sector and the civilian sector and, within the security sector, those who guarantee efficient use of land resources and the space of the state for various purposes and an evaluation of the economic cost that the Israeli economy pays for the security sector to hold on to real estate.

The response to the research challenge needs to be in light of the expansion of research and discussion in recent years in reciprocal relations between the army and society in Israel, part of which is conducted from a critical viewpoint.

The phenomenon of the use of land resources for security purposes demonstrates the dominance of the security sector as one of the operational arms of the state, which has its own system of concepts and clear interests. There is need to clarify territorial conduct that is intended to preserve its power through legislative and other tools that enable it to act almost without limits. Perhaps the security sector should be seen not only as a server that carries out and realizes the territorial needs of security but also as an actor in one space among many, a party producing subjectively defined needs. The security sector is also part of the political and social system, whose actions have geographical–spatial implications. The question, then, is who profits and who loses by its actions?

Understanding the creation of security land uses and the objectives for which they are meant is not enough. One cannot leave unanswered the charge that they take place in contradiction to or as a substitute for civilian land uses. Here there is also room for the question about whether the expression *civilian land uses* contains the concealed assumption that the citizens of the state are only the Jewish population or whether it also includes the Arab minority. Alternatively, whether land uses for security purposes are a means of excluding and controlling this minority, toward which the government's attitude was and perhaps still is ambivalent: the Arabs of Israel are citizens of the state; however, some, if not all, are perceived by many Jews as enemy.

This subject can be dealt with from another viewpoint, that of the critical approach, which holds that it is insufficient to ask only questions about "security space," which is part of the physical space that is perceived by decision makers, with the backing of the public at large, as an important—vital—response to the feeling of threat. This approach necessitates expanding the security canvas and the relationship between it and space. From the postmodern geography field, which deals with the issue of factors that shape the space,[36] there is the question of what is the space and who defines it. A third question is what is the epistemological connection—that is, the way in which decisions are made with regard to reality—between security and space? In other words, what is the security–geographical discourse in Israel? How is the concept of security space understood? What interests does this concept serve? Is the view of all the space as security space an objective need? Alternatively, is the view of all the space as security space created in order to intensify the fear of the threat and to plant anxiety within the broad public so that it will give blind trust to what is called the military professionals, those who are perceived as an elite acting without discrimination, whose considerations are completely objective? In sum, the questions are: How is space perceived as vital for security? How does a certain elite mobilize space for security needs?

Conclusion

Research and discussion of the subject of the use of land resources for security needs and its implications should be conducted along a broad front, and should include all topics and points of view. It should be on five planes, which may be dealt with separately or jointly, so that they are complementary. First is the *conceptual and methodological plane:* this will develop a system of concepts and a method of discussing the subject. The *empirical plane:* this will add knowledge to that which already exists on three central topics: a) the narrative—the process of the creation of the territorial dimension of security in terms of time and place, b) the procedures according to which the security sector operates and its interface with the civilian system, and c) the practical aspect—the implications and significance (political, economic, social, and ecological) stemming from the territorial dominance of security. There is also a *theoretical plane,* in the framework of which issues can be examined, such as security as a factor in creating space, security as a means of spatial control and realizing the territoriality of the state in land areas that for its part are peripheral regions, or a general discussion held about militarism and space and the geographical hegemony of security and state–military–space relations. The *comparative plane* offers a comparison with other places around the world—presenting similar pointed examples of the use of land resources for security needs and "confrontations" with civilian parties and considerations, and an examination of the question about whether the whole of the Israeli case is special or whether parallels can be found in other locations in the world. The *area of policy recommendation:* this emanates from the fields of research and discussion and in essence offers proposals for directions of thinking about changing the patterns of the interface between the security sector and the civilian system in everything connected with the planning and use of the land resources of the state.

Currently, there are skeptical voices with regard to the sanctity of security in Israel. In many circles in the Israeli public, the security sector is no longer perceived as a sacred cow that cannot be touched. In light of this, and because of the fact that Israeli space is becoming more and more crowded, its activity in space and its land uses do not need to be taken for granted. Now, with the undermining of the seniority status of security in Israel, when there is a growing body of research that is free from the dominant Zionist discourse, the curtain can be raised little by little in order to delve into questions that have to do with the combination of military, land, and space in Israel—questions that are important and that pertain to every citizen of the state.

Notes

1. For our purposes, the security sector includes the IDF, Ministry of Defense, Border Patrol, the security services, and the government defense industries.

2. Amiram Oren, "Security Land Uses in Israel—Needs and Implications" (Haifa, 2005) [Hebrew].

3. Amiram Oren and Rafi Regev, "A Land in Khaki—Land Uses for Security Needs in Israel," *Karka* 60 (2005): 96–117 [Hebrew].

4. Michael Bateman and Raymond Reily (eds.), *The Geography of Defence* (London and Sydney, 1987).

5. The term *territory* in the perception of security also relates to that under state rule since the Six-Day War—i.e., the territories of the military occupation and the territories of the Palestinian Authority. However, discussion in the context of this chapter will not include them because these territories are not defined as territories of the State of Israel.

6. Albert H. Jackman, "The Nature of Military Geography," *Professional Geographer* 14 (1962): 7–12.

7. Louis C. Peltier and G. Etzel Pearcy, *Military Geography* (New York, 1966).

8. John M. Collins, *Military Geography for Professionals and the Public* (Washington, D.C., 1998).

9. Patrick O'Sullivan and Jesse W. Miller, Jr., *The Geography of Warfare* (London & Canberra, 1983); Eugen J. Palka and Francis A. Galgano (eds.), *The Scope of Military Geography: Across the Spectrum from Peacetime to War* (New York, 2001); Palka and Galgano (eds.), *Military Geography: from Peace to War* (New York, 2005).

10. Martin Coulson, "The Geography of Defense—Developing Themes of Study," *GeoJournal* 36.4 (1995): 371–82; Ewan Anderson (ed.), "Military Geography—The Changing Role of the Military," *GeoJournal* 34.2 (1994); Ewan Anderson (ed.), "The Military Environment," *GeoJournal* 37.2 (1995).

11. Yehuda Gradus and Shaul Krakover (eds.), *Israeli Scholars' Publications in Human Geography and Development Studies* (Beer-Sheva, 2000); Yoram Bar-Gal, "On the 'Tribal Elders,' the 'Continuers,' and the 'Newcomers' in Israeli Geography," *Horizons in Geography* 51 (1999): 7–39 [Hebrew].

12. Arnon Soffer, "Geography and National Security," in Zvi Ofer and Avi Kover (eds.), *Quality and Quantity* (Tel-Aviv, 1985), 321–30 [Hebrew]; Arnon Soffer, *Israel, Demographics 2000-2020—Dangers and Opportunities* (Haifa, 2001).

13. David Newman, "The Geopolitics of Peacemaking in Israel-Palestine," *Political Geography* 21.5 (2002): 629–46.

14. Avraham Wachman and Rafi Lerman, "A Program for Development of the Negev, Deployment and Infrastructure," Interim Report No. 1 (1979) [Hebrew].

15. Amiram Derman, "Is There a Conflict between Civilian Planning and Military Planning in the Negev?" in *Man and Desert,* Abstracts of Lectures at the Geographical Society Conference, 1992, Beer-Sheva, 46–48 [Hebrew]; Amiram Derman, "The Negev after the Sinai Evacuation—Space for IDF Deployment or Space for Civilian Development?" *Nofim* 17 (1983): 55–70 [Hebrew].

16. A. Soffer and J. Minghi, "Israel's Security Landscapes: The Impact of Military Considerations on Land Uses," *The Professional Geographer* 38 (1986): 28–41.

17. In the 1980s, Derman served as senior staff officer in the General Staff's Planning Division.

18. Amiram Oren, "Army and Space—IDF Land Uses from the War of Independence to the Sinai Campaign (1948–1956)," Ph.D. diss., University of Haifa, 2003 [Hebrew].

19. Oren, "Security Land Uses in Israel."

20. Oren and Regev, "A Land in Khaki."

21. Erez Swerdlov and Amiram Derman served, until just a few years prior to the planning project, as senior staff officers in the General Staff's Planning Division.

22. Shlomo Yannai, "The IDF's Land Policy," *Karka* 50 (2000): 32–42 [Hebrew].

23. The officer who served as head of the Infrastructure and Deployment branch in the Planning Division of the General Staff during those years testified this to me.

24. Shmuel Shilo et al., "Survey of Trends in Civilian Development: Development, Building, and Preserving Nature and Landscape Values" (private publication, 1998) [Hebrew].

25. Daphna Barak-Erez, "Firing Areas and Training areas—The Legal Aspect," *Mishpat U'Ttzava* 11–12 (1992): 153–72 [Hebrew].

26. Ram Gal, "Activity in the IDF in Regard to Environmental Quality," *Ecologiya U'sviva* 5 (1999): 244–50 [Hebrew].

27. Ram Gal, "Evacuation of IDF Camps from Urban Areas," *Karka* 48 (2000): 30–45 [Hebrew].

28. *State Comptroller's Annual Report* 37 (1986): 1096–1107 [Hebrew].

29. *State Comptroller's Annual Report* 44 (1993): 1079–88 [Hebrew].

30. *State Comptroller's Annual Reports* 38 (1987): 1090–92, 1096–1107; 40 (1989): 764–65; 43 (1992): 801–804 [Hebrew].

31. *State Comptroller's Annual Report* 46 (1995): 813–15 [Hebrew].

32. *State Comptroller's Annual Report* 50A (1999): 93–101 [Hebrew].

33. *State Comptroller's Annual Report* 55A (2004): 75–113 [Hebrew].

34. One article was published in *Ha'aretz* on October 10, 2005: Amir Oren, "A Substitute for the West Bank Gush Emunim"; the other article was published in *Ma'ariv* on December 14, 2005: Amir Rappaport, "Israel, a Military Area."

35. *State Comptroller's Annual Report* 55A (2004): 78 [Hebrew].

36. Edward W. Soja, *Postmodern Geographies: The Reassertion of Space in Critical Social Theory* (London, New York, 1989).

EIGHT

"The Battle over Our Homes": Reconstructing/Deconstructing Sovereign Practices around Israel's Separation Barrier on the West Bank

YUVAL FEINSTEIN AND URI BEN-ELIEZER

In June 2002, the Israeli government decided to construct a barrier that would separate Israel from the Occupied Territories in the West Bank. The decision followed massive pressure by the Israeli public that had been subjected to nonstop suicide bombing attacks by Palestinians during the Second Intifada. Soon, however, it became clear that such a massive and ambitious project embodies various purposes that go beyond the security issue. What were these purposes, and were they realized? A "security fence," as the Israeli authorities called it, or a "wall" according to its opponents, generated controversies and conflicts not only with the Palestinians but within the Israeli society as well. What were these conflicts about, and what influence did they have on reality?

In order to answer these questions, one should trace the events that preceded the construction of the barrier. In 1993–1994, the Israelis and Palestinians signed various agreements that were regarded as a breakthrough in their relations and a crucial step toward a lasting solution to the Israeli–Palestinian conflict. In October 2000, however, the al-Aqsa Intifada flared up. The two sides, which just a few years earlier had shaken hands and started to plan their future together, became involved in a long and brutal war in the course of which the barrier was constructed.

Besides giving the formal explanation for the barrier—namely, a necessary means to protect Israeli civilians from terrorist attacks—this paper will present it as part of a more ambitious Israeli project that was meant to be realized through war. Not a conventional war, but war of a new kind, whose nonformal purpose was to reconstruct Israel's sovereignty and national identity in time of turmoil and crisis. By presenting the barrier in this manner, and in describing the way it became a locus of conflicts within Israeli society, we see this chapter as part of the debate concerning the allocation of power, the character of nation-states, and the status of sovereignty in the so-called late, reflexive modernization period, or simply, the era of globalization.[1]

Statehood Sovereignty, National Identity, and New Wars

At the end of the twentieth century, many believed that the time of a strong state leaning heavily upon its sovereignty had gone. Certainly, the comprehensive and totalistic meaning of the principle of statehood sovereignty, which is the right to rule and the obligation to obey, was facing a change. The downfall of the Iron Curtain, the unification of Europe, the creation of international financial markets, the privatization of the economy, the appearance of big corporations, the new waves of immigration, the new international laws, the global culture which put the individual and his or her rights at the center, and the growing importance of nonstate actors, not to say the phenomenon of global terrorism, are all examples of direct and indirect challenges to the old Westphalian notion of statehood sovereignty, which seemed to be eroded by both local and global actors.[2]

Nevertheless, some scholars argued firmly that sovereignty still organizes and frames political relations within the nation-state as well as between states. Kalevi Holsti,[3] for example, claimed that "the only way sovereignty can be lost today is either by formal conquest and annexation or by voluntary amalgamation of a polity into a larger political unit." Concurrently, others said that globalization does not reduce state sovereignty, but the other way around; the nation-states are in fact the principal agents of globalization itself.[4]

Can we reach a decision whose claim is more plausible in describing current reality? The long realist and neorealist tradition in International Relations tended to see sovereignty as a constant, and minimized the concept to relations between states. The more sociological perspective, the so-called social constructivist, which emerged within International Relations in the last decade or two, regards sovereignty as a social construct, "a product of the actions of powerful agents and the resistance to those actions by others."[5] Such perspective seems to us the preferable method for empirically analyzing sovereignty, as it takes into consideration groups and organizations other than states, which may be involved in the constructing/deconstructing processes of sovereignty. Moreover, unlike neorealism that minimized sovereignty to states' narrowed interests of accumulating power and increasing security in an anarchic world, social constructivism highlights the importance of values, norms, and ideals, which are embedded within any process of reconstruction/deconstruction sovereignty.[6]

As a variable that draws up the boundaries between those who belong ("the insiders") and who do not belong ("the outsiders") to the political community, sovereignty is inseparable from national identity, as giving both meaning and significance to a political community. Thus, struggles over sovereignty are mostly struggles over national identity and vice versa, which are more crucial and effective in times of uncertainty and change.[7]

Unlike the neorealist well-known idea according to which "external" conflicts minimize "internal" strife and society is highly integrated in the face of the enemy, internal struggles over sovereignty and collective identity are nowadays quite often related to actual or potential wars.[8] In some cases, questions around sovereignty and national identity are brought to wars, and in others they are part of the war itself, its spirit, course, strategies, and tactics. Those who see the connection between these components characterize some of the recent wars as "new wars."

These new wars are different from the former conventional wars in many respects. They are no longer wars between states headed by standing armies only; instead, they express the transformations that have occurred in the world at large, from politics which is characterized by naked power and narrowed interests to one which embodies other elements, such as culture, norms, emotions, sentiments, and identity. Moreover, the new wars are regarded as wars that can serve as a political means to reconstruct/deconstruct identity and sovereignty.[9]

The Israeli situation does match fairly well these definitions. For many years, Israel was a nation-in-arms, having a centralized strong state, a mass army, and a highly mobilized society ready for war.[10] The decline of this model, which started at the beginning of the 1980s, reached its peak in the 1990s. The end of the Cold War, the influence of globalization, the neoliberal economy, and the emergence of a new civil society, after long years of a blurring distinction between state and society, led not only to a relative decline in the Israeli state's authority and legitimacy, but also to the emergence of new cultural perspectives connected with a reflexive modernist orientation. The carriers of this new outlook, new social movements, new associations, and various NGOs, busied themselves with an unprecedented number of existential debates and conflicts around post-material issues, identities, and various lifestyles, together with attempts to influence the contested boundaries of reality.[11]

Many of these conflicts touched upon questions of national identity ("What is Israeliness?") and sovereignty ("Who is entitled to rule over Israel, how, and where?"). These questions became crucial in 1993 with the Oslo Agreement, which was signed both by Israel and the PLO. For many Israelis the agreement symbolized a promise, for others a threat. Soon, around the accord, internal contradictions sprang up in Israel, gradually organizing around the line of two separate "societies": one "civil," the other "militaristic."[12] Each society was heterogeneous, a composition of various groups, organizations, and opinions about reality. Nevertheless, the dividing line between the two societies became much clearer during the 1990s: the civil society carried liberal and civic values, emphasized human rights issues, and combined with ideas concerning the importance of making peace through compromises and concessions to the Palestinians. Even ideas about the "New Middle East," which would create a sort of economic integration, could be heard within this society. Conversely, the militaristic society was less homogeneous and combined two sets of values: secular Israelis who stressed the importance of security measures and believed that only military means would solve the Israeli–Palestinian conflict, and religious circles, who believe in the sacredness of Great, undivided Israel, and the need to use military means in order to hold up that idea.[13]

These controversies related to questions of sovereignty. As against Israel being a small, secular, civil, and democratic state open to its region and to the entire globe, the militaristic society's main purpose was to close Israel to outside influence, to preserve most of the territories, and to continue with Israel's wars, which for some of them are holy wars guided by a supreme, sovereign, mighty God, who governs all.[14]

In the second half of the 1990s, with the "help" of terrorist attacks against Israeli civilians, it seemed that the militaristic and religious society gained much influence within Israel. Neither the appointment of the Labor party leader, PM Ehud Barak, nor the return to talks with the Palestinians in 2000 changed that situation. The talks failed, a second Intifada erupted, and Barak very soon lost his post to Sharon, the new elected prime minister, who promised an iron hand against the Palestinian upheaval.[15]

As a typical representative of the militaristic society in Israel, Sharon expressed for many years his clear opposition to the idea that the territories could be divided into two states, and that the Israeli–Palestinian conflict could be solved through a policy of compromise and concessions.[16] PM Sharon did not waste much time trying to realize his ideas. At first, he objected to the idea of a separation barrier; however, as terrorist attacks continued and public opinion went against him, Sharon gradually changed his mind and construction started. In the following, we will examine the construction of the barrier and the struggles within Israel that arose around it. We will concentrate on the Anti-Wall Movement, a coalition of various small groups that objected to the barrier. In order to grasp the specific framing of the barrier's objectors, we gathered ethnographical materials and did some fieldwork. These allow us to show how the construction of the barrier and part of the objections to it were diverted to struggles over reconstruction/deconstruction of sovereignty and national identity.

The following discussion has two parts. While the first describes the barrier as part of the new war methods which reconstructed statehood sovereignty and national identity in times of crisis, the second depicts the practices of direct resistance to the barrier that subsequently appeared within Israel, and the way the nation-state dealt with them.

The Separation Barrier as a Method of a New War

The Second Intifada was partly the result of the failure of the statesmen—Clinton, Arafat, and Barak—to reach an agreement. Some may claim that it was Arafat who constantly refused to accept the proposals put forward by Barak and Clinton. Without minimizing the role of Arafat and without ignoring the simple fact that the Palestinians chose the road of violence, it can be said that the war was used by the Israeli militaristic and religious society as a means to realize their basic assumptions concerning the need to use harsh military methods against the Palestinians ("Let the IDF Win" was their slogan) which would express Israel's mastery in the region and avoid any possibility of dividing the land between the two nations.

Such solid definition of sovereignty, which clearly was fueled by the Palestinians' struggle and attacks on Israeli civilians, was carried not only by the settlers in the occupied Palestinian territories, but also by the army and its Chiefs of the General Staff (CGSs), first Shaul Mofaz, then Moshe Ya'alon, and, since May 2001, by PM Sharon and his government as well.[17]

As in many other areas of the world that witnessed new wars, be they the former Yugoslavia, Chechnya, Somalia, or Afghanistan and Iraq, ethnonational groups, paramilitary units, and even fully fledged armies struggled in an attempt to consolidate identity, to determine new cultural boundaries, and to impose new rules of sovereignty. This relatively new phenomenon of identity politics and sovereignty politics, which stamp the character of the new war, can be contrasted with the politics of ideas which, according to Mary Kaldor,[18] was more typical of modern times. The latter, concerned about innovative projects that entail a promise for all, has an integrative effect and is inclusive in its character. In contrast, identity politics and sovereignty politics tend to mobilize people around forms of labeling, such as ethnic, racial, or religious. This latter form is exclusive in its character, and tends to create unity (of the in-group) through the construction of unbridgeable differences with the others (the out-group). In the new wars, practices expressing cruelty and uncompromising hatred can serve as "just the thing" to clearly delineate this line of "us" versus "them."

When the Palestinian violence started, the supreme command of the IDF immediately became one of the main supporters of reconstructing Israel's sovereignty by using strict punitive measures against the Palestinians. The IDF's involvement in reconstructing sovereignty was clear not only by its peculiar military operations but also even by the public declarations of its generals.[19] For example, in an interview in 2002, the

CGS, Shaul Mofaz, said, "We have defeated militarily the Palestinians, but we have not succeeded in defeating their mind. Their aims have not changed. . . . They are interested in driving Israel into the sea."[20] Such statements reflected an attempt to dictate a reality on the basis of generalized categories that are typical of national identity and sovereignty politics: the Palestinians wish to drive Israel into the sea; not some of the Palestinians, not their military organs, not Hamas, for example, but all of them.[21]

Through such discursive practices, accompanied by harsh military means, the Israeli chiefs of command put themselves in one camp only, that of the Israeli militaristic society. They were associated not with those Israelis who considered the Intifada a struggle of Palestinians against a long-lasting occupation, but with those who saw it as a total war and a terrorist campaign that expressed a kind of Huntingtonian clash of civilizations.

Practically, the politics of identity and sovereignty led the Israeli leadership and army into a war not only against the armed Palestinians who were involved in fighting against Israel, but against civilians as well. How does an army fight civilians? The practices of the new war give numerous examples: arbitrary arrests, humiliations, collective punishment, and destruction of infrastructures, demolishing of houses, untargeted massive shootings, as well as "targeted assassinations," which killed many innocent people.[22] Were these methods of war at all effective? Could they wear out a whole society? Could they bring victory in the battlefield? Without entering into another domain, that of military strategies and tactics and their efficiency, noticeably these military practices reconstructed Israel's sovereignty and served as a means to force a separation between "us" and "them." In this way, the cultural, ethnonational perspective on reality was translated into military strategy and tactics, and the Separation Barrier was another means that was used for the same purpose.

In order to understand that, one should bear in mind not only that during the 1990s Israel was exposed to terrorist attacks by Palestinians who objected to the Oslo Agreement or reacted to its nonapplicability, but that the attacks created antagonism and strife among the Israelis, which was mainly directed toward the Israeli leadership. During the Second Intifada, as the death toll was heavy, the feeling that the government could not rule due to the terrorist attacks became widespread.[23] As early as the first months of the Second Intifada, time and again, members of the Knesset, public figures, and journalists complained to the Israeli government about not protecting its civilians from the attacks: "And what should we say today to our children and civilians in the streets?" asked one member of the Knesset. "Is it possible that a sovereign state with such a strong army—one that we constantly boast about—cannot provide security for its citizens? And cannot prevent panic among members of the public?"[24]

In face of the ongoing terrorist attacks, most Israelis supported Sharon and the IDF's idea of using strict measures against the Palestinians. In those first years of the Intifada, it seemed that even the differences between the two societies, the civil and the militaristic, disappeared. The "Security Fence," the government promised, would reduce the terrorist attacks to almost nil.[25]

The separation barrier consists, for the most part, of a network of fences with trenches designed to stop vehicles. Five percent of its length is composed of walls, and there are occasional gates and roadblocks. The barrier, almost 800 km in its planned length, was gradually erected.[26] It symbolizes a mighty, prodigious, and menacing power of the occupier, expressed by the barrier itself in the watchtowers, the warning signs, the armed soldiers, and a wall that is eight meters high (twice the height of the Berlin Wall).

Mastery and sovereignty were presented not only through the façade of the barrier but through the process of its edifice as well. Sovereignty practices usurped land and resources, and created separation and hierarchy. "Security needs" was the means through which the process was legitimized. Trying to set new borders through the barrier that would include as many as settlers as possible, the Israeli authorities decided not to build the barrier along the Green Line (the 1967 border)—a step that could create approval even by the Palestinians, but at a certain distance from it along a route that they had designed. The plan also contained "fingers" that are supposed to penetrate deeply into Palestinian territory in places where there are clusters of settlements. In this way, they would not only annex Israeli settlements, but would "cantonize" the Palestinian territories as well, and would prevent a possible Palestinian state. In some places this "slithering snake," twice as long as the pre-1967 borders, was situated at quite a distance from the Green Line and was adjusted according to the location of the settlements, allowing settlers the possibility of grabbing more land around the Palestinian villages.[27] One had to be naïve to think that the barrier was a temporary military obstacle—as the authorities claimed—and not an attempt to set permanent political borders unilaterally and by that to reconstruct Israel's sovereignty.

At first, more than 20 percent of the occupied territories were to be annexed by the barrier course. Then, following the appeal of inhabitants from both the Jewish town of Mevasseret Zion and the Palestinian village of Beit Surik, the Israeli Supreme Court decided that not only security but human rights as well must be taken into consideration by the government. As its verdict became a precedent, the confiscation was reduced to only 9–10 percent of the territories.[28] Still, the Israeli authorities built the "Jerusalem Wrap," which has resulted in tens of thousands of Palestinians remaining on the western side of the barrier, dislocated from their nation and territories.[29]

The motive of sovereignty that delineated the "us" versus "them" line was as well concretized through the method of collective punishments that were embedded within the barrier's route: what can a farmer who has to get to his land through a gate in the barrier do, not knowing that on the same day there is a Jewish holiday and the gate will not be opened? There are children who must go to school in the morning: what will they do if they are late by a few minutes and the gate is already closed? A woman who wants to buy some milk for her child will have to be at the gate exactly at eight o'clock in the morning in order to pass through, but will only be able to return home at four o'clock in the afternoon, when the gate is reopened. In addition, if an ailing person needs medical attention at night, who will open the gate for him? In such ways, thousands of Palestinians have been enclosed in huge prisons, with every gate, every line of people, every police officer, soldier, or guard becoming the emblem of Israel's supremacy and sovereignty.[30]

As though the idea was to mark the distinction between "us" and "them," the barrier had a substantially different meaning for the Palestinians and for the settlers in the West Bank who remained within the east side of the barrier. For the Palestinians, the barrier, with its gates and roadblocks, was a means of isolation, separation, humiliation, and discrimination. It was not once but many times that Palestinians were stopped in roadblocks and stayed there for hours. Sometimes, it was due to orders from above; in other cases, as a result of an arbitrary decision of eighteen- or nineteen-year-old soldiers, who were tired and bored by their task, and could not always forgo the opportunity to exercise their power over people who are sometimes forced to flatter, bribe, laugh, cry, or do anything, provided they will be allowed to pass.

These are the cultural ways in which identity-certainties and practices of sovereignty are asserted in new wars. At the same time, and at the same roadblock, armed settlers have gone across, driving at excessive speeds, waving to the soldiers, without stopping at all. They were still the masters of the land. For them, the barrier and the roadblock were no obstacle, but rather a reconfirmation of their ethnonational superiority and a bridge connecting them with Israel.

Were we in the typical modern era, in which states did more or less as they pleased unless they had to confront other states, the barrier venture could be accomplished without much interference. In the late, reflexive modernity, however, the project which was built within the Palestinian territory and violated international law was accompanied by resistance. Mostly, the objection within Israel was to the barrier's route; the legal procedure was the way to deal with that in court, and sovereignty was barely the issue.[31] One network of groups, however, expressed in its struggle a clear antisovereign perspective. It came from the Anti-Wall Movement and their demonstrations, which often escalated into clashes with the Israeli security forces. We are dealing here with small movements that were active all through the Intifada, such as Taayush,[32] Gush Shalom,[33] Machsom Watch,[34] together with newer groups such as Anarchists against the Wall[35] that collaborated with global protest movements, such as the International Solidarity Movement.[36] In the following pages we will shed light on this protest campaign and look at its relevance to questions of sovereignty and national identity.

The Anti-Wall Movement

As in most social movements, the activists of the Anti-Wall Movement differ in their social characteristics and in the motivations that brought them to the scene. Only in the demonstrations themselves, through collaboration with the Palestinian farmers, and through confrontations with the Israeli security forces did they develop a common framework. In 2005–2006, most protest activities took place every Friday noon near the village of Bil'in. Almost always, the protest activity led to violent clashes. Formally, the Israeli security forces were there to prevent any interference with the work on, or attempts to sabotage, the barrier. Interestingly, these clashes happened on Fridays, when there was no work on the barrier, at sites where the construction work had not yet started. Indeed, the soldiers and police presence were symbolic: they represented, even by their presence alone, Israel's sovereignty.

The resistance of the Anti-Wall Movement to the ambitious Israeli project appeared in a peculiar frame. First used by Erving Goffman,[37] the term *frame* refers to "schemata of interpretation" that enable individuals "to locate, perceive, identify and label" occurrences within their life space and the world at large.[38] These human interpretations of social situations are actively built up through their involvement in the situations. In this way, collective actions are seen as part of the politics of signification, which highlight certain aspects of an issue and not others. Typically, these frames include the identification and definition of a social "problem," its causes—or the answer to the question, "Who should be blamed?," the desired solution to the "problem," and the preferable way to achieve it.[39]

The protestors' declared objective was embodied by slogans such as "Stop the Wall."[40] However, their outgrowing frame was more ambitious: to challenge the hegemonic Israeli discourse on sovereignty, which disguised occupation and legitimized the construction of the barrier in terms of "security needs," and the right of a state to protect its citizens.

The reconstruction practices of sovereignty around the separation barrier were aimed at creating and enhancing the cultural and political lines that divide Israelis and Palestinians. The demonstrators were busy doing quite the opposite. In this regard, we discern the pattern of cooperation that arose between three social categories of demonstrators: Israeli Jews, Palestinians, and international activists. This version of cooperation deconstructed sovereignty by both physical and symbolic means; it put into question the two divisional lines of sovereignty: the national division of "us" versus "them," and the state division between the "internal" territorial unity, and the "external" "world of states."

Bearing in mind the cultural meaning of the barrier, the Israeli and Palestinian activists made tremendous efforts to develop close and egalitarian relationships between them. Such efforts can be observed in the minute details of their cooperation: first, unlike many other meetings between Israeli Jews and Palestinians, no exotic and romantic "oriental" hospitality manners were displayed by the host Palestinian villagers in the demonstrations. Second, Israeli and Palestinian activists communicated with each other by speaking both Hebrew and Arabic. One may claim that this detail is trivial; however, it is a remarkable finding, considering the fact that most Israeli Jews do not speak Arabic, and the rest are reluctant to use the language unless they are involved, as soldiers or as soldiers on reserve duty, in a clear indication of occupiers against the occupied.

The blurring of the distinction between Israelis and Palestinians in the Anti-Wall Movement was intentional, but noninstrumental. As one of the activists said: "It is not only political relations, it is also friendship . . . I do not think about the demonstration, but about Aa'id, Majid, and Abdullah. For me it became trivial . . . we are reaching a village and everybody can say hello and everybody speaks [with us]."[41]

This method of deconstructed sovereignty exposed a post-national element of unity and egalitarianism standing in direct opposition to Israel's collective identity of the past. It was seen again and again in the demonstrations, where Israelis, Palestinians, and international activists did everything as one: together they marched dressed in symbolic costumes, together they planted olive trees, symbolically replacing the uprooted ones, and together they wrestled with the soldiers. Quite often, when a Palestinian or an international demonstrator was arrested, the Israeli activist tried to be arrested too, in order to make it hard for the Israeli security forces to carry out severe methods of punishment toward the non-Israeli. "The importance of the demonstrations," said Jonathan Polak, the informal leader of the Anarchists Against the Wall, "is in their contribution to the transformation of the occupation to be ungovernable."[42]

Frequently, these methods of deconstructing sovereignty happened to be efficient. More than once, senior IDF officers have used the Israeli media to convey their frustration at the "operational difficulties" caused by the presence of Israeli citizens in demonstrations along the barrier route.[43] Indeed, an army of occupation which by itself is a symbol of sovereignty, no less than a carrier of sovereign practices that are executed through military operations creating the distinction between "friends" and "foes," was looking for means to deemphasize the impact of the demonstrations. Sometimes, as a means to avoid criticism and publicity, which could magnify the effect of the Anti-Wall Movement's deconstructed sovereignty, the IDF sent a minimum number of soldiers, who were warned not to use live ammunition. When it did not help, on other occasions, the military headquarters chose the opposite tactics, sending more units, and ordering them to use additional measures.

These sovereignty effects sometimes had horrendous results, bringing the death of a few Palestinian demonstrators, mainly in the first period of the resistance.[44] In another event, a young Israeli man, Gil Naamati, was shot by soldiers when he and his "anarchist" friends firmly shook one of the barrier's gates near the village of Masha.[45] From an ethnonational perspective, this case of a young Israeli Jew who had just finished his three years of military service received much more publicity in Israel than hundreds of cases of wounded Palestinians. From the numerous videos that captured the scene, it was clear that, while using their guns, the soldiers had not been put at any risk. Moreover, the soldiers knew that many of the demonstrators standing in front of them were Israeli Jews. Still they shot. Was it just a mistake, a result of weariness and fatigue? Was it also just coincidental that the officer in charge, the one who ordered the shooting, was a settler? Alternatively, could it have been a military sign and a warning to those willing to desecrate Israel's sovereignty, in this case, by shaking one of the barrier's locked gates? As if to verify that hypothesis, CGS, "while considering the facts," decided afterward not to raise accusations against the shooters. On the other hand, the police considered accusing Naamati, who was wounded by two gunshots, for breaking the military rules by his attempt "to destroy" the barrier.[46]

The activists of the Anti-Wall Movement not only tried to blur the "us" versus "them" division, but they also tried to deconstruct another sovereign, modern distinction, that of so-called "internal affairs," against so-called "foreign affairs." The blurring of that distinction was made by the Anti-Wall Movement's tendency to involve global activists in their demonstrations. This mode of global–local action, completely inappropriate to the Westphalian code of "a world of states," became popular in many protest events around the world in the late-modern era. As in many other cases, it served as a practice of deconstruction of sovereignty.[47]

Through the actions of global activists, the struggle was exported all over the world. The global participants could speak English or French fluently while being interviewed. Returning to their countries, they participated in information campaigns, bringing testimonies from primary sources. In one case, the activists produced an international petition to support the struggle of the people of Bil'in.[48] All these actions enabled the Anti-Wall Movement to catch the attention of various audiences around the world which, at least potentially, could put some pressure on the Israeli government.[49] No less important was the symbolic meaning of blurring the distinction between the local and the global that emerged from the global activists' participations in the demonstration. As one of the Palestinian activists said, "against an army which represents one citizenship, stand people who represent many international citizenships."[50]

Deconstructing sovereignty was, furthermore, the way in which the Anti-Wall Movement often used cosmopolitan themes to justify the struggle; they would, for example, present the issue of the barrier in human rights terms. Using this issue, the activists deliberately borrowed a supranational theme taken from the cultural "toolbox" of the global peace movements. Again, various symbolic practices clearly expressed it: the global activists in Bil'in often led with the rhythmic shouts: "Hey, Hey, Soldier, Hey, How Many Kids Did You Kill Today?" This well-known slogan, originally used by American antiwar activists during the Vietnam War, has been adopted by many peace movements around the world in various cases; at the moment it is being used to oppose the U.S. occupation in Iraq.[51] On certain occasions, activists in Bil'in have chosen to carry large pictures of Mahatma Gandhi, Rosa Parks, and Martin Luther King; they have even used King's famous "I have a dream" slogan of liberation to confer a universal character upon their struggle over the barrier.

Thus, in a manner typical of the spirit of reflexive modernization, and almost without any precedent in Israel's past, Israeli protestors tended to cooperate both with Palestinians from the Occupied Territories and with international activists. They did all they could so that their protest would be effective. However, when it comes to sovereignty, nation-states can be quite obsessive.[52] Time after time, Israel's security forces oppressed the demonstrators by shooting rubber bullets, tear gas, using cudgels, and by carrying out arrests and trials. Although they may have received better treatment than the Palestinians, many of the Israeli demonstrators were arrested, and their names were put into the police criminal records, something that has future consequences, especially in the job market.[53] As for the global activists, the state made vast efforts to prevent their presence at demonstration scenes. When these efforts failed, they were deported.[54]

Practically, the IDF used various methods to reconstruct Israel's sovereignty at the scene. In this regard, it was striking to notice how important it was for the soldiers to manifest their control in the demonstration arenas. Despite the fact that demonstrators usually recognized the strength of the security forces and therefore neither tried to destroy the barrier nor to stop the work, the security forces insisted on playing small "sovereignty games" with them. For example, they would define narrow borders to the demonstration area, usually by placing a barbed wire fence on the ground where the demonstrators were standing and by declaring that the wire fence is the final line and whoever crossed it would be arrested. Such an act sent a sharp message of sovereignty, not by the physical means itself, but mainly by the presentation of the ability of the state to set rules in the territory.

Besides the violent practices, reconstructed sovereignty was made mainly through cultural means. This included processes of counter-framing,[55] based on distributing the knowledge that the barrier is a legitimate means of a sovereign state aiming at protecting its civilians, "a battle over our home" as the Second Intifada was generally framed in the Israeli discourse. While ignoring the other interests embedded within the barrier, mainly those of the settlers, and by making the route of the barrier a nonissue, the state authorities presented the protestors as eccentrics, oddballs, "leftists," and traitors. A typical example was the report that appeared in an Israeli newspaper, following one of the antibarrier demonstrations in Bil'in: "It is time to state the plain fact"—the columnist wrote—"demonstrations against the separation barrier are neoterrorism . . . everybody who fights the IDF is a traitor. Those whose choice is to embrace the Palestinians at a price of endangering IDF soldiers shall not wear human rights as a feather in their cap. One who wishes to fight for [his] opinions, should do it inside his home and not with the enemy."[56]

This example illustrates why it was difficult for the Anti-Wall Movement, whose framework did not resonate with the Israeli dominant discourse and its pivotal national-security motives, to mobilize the Israeli public against the IDF's methods of collective punishment. However, this augmented another obstacle; more than once, the Anti-Wall activists, instead of basing their protests on purely humanistic arguments, preferred to be identified with the Palestinian National Movement. In this way, and in complete contradiction to their contention, their resistance was not a post-national, but a purely national, one. To a certain degree, the activists had fallen without noticing into "the trap" of the national discourse, illustrating that even among those who regard themselves as post-nationalists, nationalism still plays a central role as a basis for political claims.

The Israeli activists themselves defined the resistance to "the wall" as a "Palestinian battle."[57] Indeed, most of the participants in the demonstrations were Palestinians, the locations of the demonstrations were almost exclusively in occupied Palestine, and the modes of action were mostly subjected to decisions made by the local popular leadership of the Palestinian village and the representatives of the Palestinian National Authority. Symbolically, the national aspect of the struggle was conveyed in many ways in the demonstrations: the most observable symbol was the Palestinian national flag, and many slogans were national-religious, calling to "Free al-Aqsa" or for "More Shaheeds [martyrs]."[58]

The use of the Palestinian national discourse by Israeli and international activists may be attributed to a well-known problem for many activists who are active in human rights and peace campaigns all over the world: often they act in a way that deemphasizes their neutrality, by making others believe that they support one side only. Human rights and peace activists may be very honest in their humanistic aspirations; in the context of a national or ethnic conflict this may be realized in efforts to protect the rights of those who are considered "the underdogs," people from the inferior group. However, by avoiding dealing also with the plight of people of other groups (typically the stronger group in a social conflict), they create an "aesthetic blight"[59] that makes their cosmopolitan ideology less credible, especially in the eyes of members of the superior group.

Indeed, the identification of Israeli and international activists with Palestinian suffering has resulted in a partial adoption of the Palestinian national discourse. As a result, most Israelis have not seen the protestors as human rights adherents, not even as peace activists, but as firm supporters of Palestinian nationality and the Palestinian struggle against Israel. Generally, the human rights discourse has hardly succeeded in penetrating the Israeli public debate over the separation barrier. After being exposed to terrorist attacks, most Israelis became completely blind to the Palestinian misery.[60] Any idea about Palestinians being victims of human rights abuses was completely neglected through the reconstructed sovereign practices of "us" versus "them."

For these reasons, the protestors of the Anti-Wall Movement never succeeded in obtaining substantial support within Israel for their activities, and the works on the Separation Barrier, which were carried out at full speed, sometimes with five hundred bulldozers working day and night, were almost never slowed down by the demonstrations. It was only with some appeals to the Israeli Supreme Court—the Beit-Surik appeal was the famous one—that some signs of a change appeared. These changes, however, did not undermine Israel's sovereignty, as they were based on the principle of "proportionality," which enabled the state to continue using security argumentation as a means of reconstructing sovereignty.[61]

To sum up, Israel's Separation Barrier was not only a means to protect civilians from terrorist attacks. It signified, as well, an attempt by the state authorities to reconstruct sovereignty in a time of crisis and change. This attempt was made not only through the barrier itself but also through the discriminatory methods that accompanied the barrier's construction and its route. As presented in this chapter, substantial resistance to the barrier came from a network of groups and associations, including the Anti-Wall Movement that, in its style of organization and collective action, resembled many late-modern movements; on various issues these delegitimize authority and deconstruct sovereignty around the world. However, the inability of the Anti-Wall Movement to attract a large audience within Israel and to pose a substantial objection to the barrier project has been explained in this chapter through the state authorities' and security forces' ability to reconstruct state sovereignty, while neutralizing the deconstructing practices of sovereignty carried out by their objectors.

In the post–Cold War world, in which ethnic and national conflicts are arising again, it seems that Israel's style of separation on the West Bank is an indication that although deconstructing sovereignty is a political force that should not be ignored today, reconstructing sovereignty by state agencies, using various discursive and nondiscursive practices based upon the argument of "security needs" and "the battle over our homes," is still more effective and influential.

Notes

1. On the concept of late–reflexive modern era, see Ulrich Beck, Wolfgang Bonss, Christoph Lau, "The Theory of Reflexive Modernization," *Theory, Culture and Society* 20.2 (2003): 1–33.

2. James Anderson, Chris Brook, Allan Cochrane (eds.), *A Global World? Reordering Political Space* (Oxford, 1995), 76–85.

3. Kalevi Holsti, *Taming the Sovereigns* (Cambridge, 2004), 137.

4. Clyde Barrow, "The Return of the State: Globalization, State Theory, and the New Imperialism," *New Political Science* 27.2 (2005): 123–45.

5. Thomas J. Biersteker and Cynthia Weber (eds.), *State Sovereignty as Social Construct* (Cambridge, 1996).

6. John Gerard Ruggie, *Constructing the World Polity* (London, 1998).

7. See Rob B. J. Walker and Saul H. Mendlovitz, *Contending Sovereignty* (Boulder, Colo., 1990); and Roxanne L. Doty, "Sovereignty and the Nation: Constructing the Boundaries of National Identity," in Thomas J. Biersteker and Cynthia Weber (eds.), *State Sovereignty as Social Construct* (Cambridge, 1996).

8. Edward Rice, *Wars of the Third Kind: Conflict in Underdeveloped Countries* (Berkeley, Calif., 1988).

9. Kalevi Holsti, *The State, War, and the State of War* (Cambridge, 1996); Mary Kaldor, *New and Old Wars* (Stanford, Calif., 1999). On Israel's reconstruction of sovereignty and national identity during the al-Aqsa Intifada at large, see Uri Ben-Eliezer, *Old Conflict, New War: Israel's Identity Politics and Sovereignty in the Al-Aqsa Intifada* (forthcoming).

10. Uri Ben-Eliezer, *The Making of Israeli Militarism* (Bloomington, Ind., 1998).

11. Baruch Kimmerling, *The Invention and Decline of Israeliness* (Berkeley, Calif., 2001); Gershon Shafir and Yoav Peled, *Being Israeli: The Dynamics of Multiple Citizenship* (New York, 2002); Uri Ben-Eliezer, "New Associations or New Politics? The Significance of Israeli-style Post-materialism," *Hagar, International Social Science Review* 4.1 (2003): 5–34; Uri Ram, *The Globalization of Israel* (Tel-Aviv, 2004) [Hebrew].

12. The term *militarism* is defined here as an institutional tendency to solve political problems (on the national level) with military means. See Ben-Eliezer, *The Making of Israeli Militarism,* 7–10.

13. Uri Ben-Eliezer, "The New Social Sources for Both Peace and War in Postmodern Israel," *Israel Studies Forum* 18 (2003): 7–41.

14. Kimmerling, *Politicide: Ariel Sharon's War against the Palestinians* (New York, 2003); Akiva Eldar and Idith Zartal, *Lords of the Land* (Tel-Aviv, 2004) [Hebrew].

15. Danny Rubinstein, Robert Malley, Hussein Agha, and Ehud Barak, *Rashomon Camp David* (Tel-Aviv, 2004) [Hebrew].

16. Amos Harel and Avi Isacharoff, *The Seventh War* (Tel-Aviv, 2004), 107–35 [Hebrew].

17. On the changes within the IDF's high-ranking officers, which made them closer to the militaristic and religious society, see Ben-Eliezer, "Postmodern Armies and the Question of Peace and War: The I.D.F. in the New Times," *International Journal of Middle East Studies* 36.1 (2004): 49–70. On the political influence of the IDF, see Oren Barak and Gabriel Sheffer, "Israel's 'Security Network' and Its Impact: An Exploration of a New Approach," *International Journal of Middle East Studies* 38.2 (2006): 235–61.

18. Mary Kaldor, *New and Old Wars*.

19. Traditionally, the involvement of any army in politics has been examined through two major channels: either the army as an interest group, trying to realize or to preserve its vested interests and privileges through participation in politics; or the possibility of a military coup, usually in times of turmoil and in weak states where the authorities lack legitimacy, and the political culture is open to the possibility of military coups and military regimes. The cultural involvement of any army in politics, meaning its influence on norms, identities, ways of life, perspectives toward reality in general, and in questions of peace or war in particular have never been fully and comprehensively examined.

20. Dan Shilon interview with CGS Shaul Mofaz, *Ma'ariv,* January 4, 2002 [Hebrew].

21. Ben-Eliezer, *Old Conflict, New War.*

22. According to B'tselem—the Israeli Information Center for Human Rights in the Occupied Territories—the number of Palestinian deaths in "target assassinations" in the five years of the Second Intifada was 359; approximately one-third of these deaths were passersby (123)—people who were not the targets of the assassinations. During this period, the total number of Palestinian deaths was 3,413, 29 percent of whom were killed while fighting, and 54 percent killed while not fighting (for the remaining 17 percent, it is unknown whether they were killed while fighting). See www.btselem.org/English/Statistics/Casualties.asp; the Palestinian Red Crescent reports 4,000 Palestinian deaths and 30,000 wounded in the five years of the Second Intifada. See http://www.palestinercs.org/crisistables/table_of_figures.htm.

23. According to the IDF, the number of Israeli casualties during the five years of the Second Intifada was 1,084 dead, nearly 8,000 wounded; 70 percent of the dead and wounded were civilians. See www1.idf.il/SIP_STORAGE/DOVER/files/7/21827.doc.

24. Mordechai Mishani, *Knesset Protocol,* July 18, 2001.

25. The number of Israeli casualties was drastically reduced from 2005 on. However, it is not clear whether it is the result of the barrier's construction. In 2005–2006, most of the barrier was not yet built, and within the segments that were built, huge breaches remained, mainly within the "fingers," which annexed large portions of territories and were "waiting" for U.S. approval. Moreover, there can be many reasons for the decline in the Israeli death toll: the death of Arafat and the moderation of his

successor, Abu Mazen; the February 2005 meeting between Sharon and Abu Mazen in Sharm el Sheikh; the decision of the Palestinian armed organizations to agree on a cease-fire (*a-tahadia*) on March 17, 2005; and effective military measures used by the IDF during the Intifada.

26. There are various estimations about the length of the barrier. See Amos Harel, "The IDF: 42% Is Completed, At Least One More Year to Finish the Construction," *Ha'aretz*, May 27, 2006 [Hebrew].

27. B'tselem and Bimkom, *Under the Guise of Security: Routing the Separation Barrier* (Jerusalem, 2005) [Hebrew].

28. See the statistics page of the separation barrier on the B'tselem website: www. Btselem.org/english/Separation_Barrier/Statistics.asp.

29. "The Humanitarian Impact of the West Bank Barrier on Palestinian Communities," UN, March 2005. http://www.humanitarianinfo.org/opt/docs/UN/OCHA /OCHABarRprt05_Full.pdf.

30. See, for example, Human Rights Watch (HRW), February 2004, "Israel's 'Separation Barrier' in the Occupied West Bank: Human Rights and International Humanitarian Law Consequences," http://hrw.org/english/docs/2004/02/20/isrlpa7581.htm. See also: Office for the Coordination of Humanitarian Affairs (OCAH), February 2005, "Preliminary Analysis: The Humanitarian Implications of the February 2005 Projected West Bank Barrier route": www.humanitarianinfo.org/opt/docs/UN/OCHA/Barrier Projections_Feb05_En.pdf#search=%22Preliminary%20Analysis%3A%20The%20 Humanitarian%20Implications%20of%20the%20February%202005%20Projected%20 West%20Bank%20Barrier%20route%22.

31. We are not dealing here with the NGOs that chose to confront the state through appeals to the courts, and thus refrained from deconstructing sovereignty.

32. *Taayush* (the Arabic word for coexistence) is a grassroots movement of Arab and Jewish Citizens of Israel. The movement was founded at the end of 2000 "to break down the walls of racism and segregation by constructing a true Arab–Jewish partnership." The movement acts mainly to present solidarity with the Palestinian people, to end the occupation in the Palestinian territories, and to achieve full civil equality for all Israeli citizens. www.taayush.org

33. Gush Shalom, "the Peace Bloc," presents itself as "the hard core of the Israeli peace movement." Founded in 1993 by Uri Avnery (former journalist, MK, and one of the most prominent activists holding Israeli radical left-wing opinions), its main goal is "to influence Israeli public opinion and [to] lead toward peace and conciliation with the Palestinian people," especially by establishing a Palestinian state in all the occupied territories including East Jerusalem as its capital. http://gush-shalom.org /english/intro.html.

34. Machsom Watch is a movement of women for human rights. Founded in January 2001, this movement focuses on monitoring and reporting abuses of the human rights of Palestinian people by soldiers and policemen at the IDF checkpoints. www.machsomwatch.org

35. Anarchists against the Wall (AATW) is a group of Israeli activists; it was founded in late 2002 to support popular Palestinian resistance to the separation barrier. Activists in the AATW are involved in direct actions such as dismantling parts of the separation barrier; they also form the hard core of Israeli participants in Palestinian demonstrations against the barrier. www.squat.net/antiwall/main.htm.

36. The International Solidarity Movement (ISM) is a Palestinian-led movement committed to resisting the Israeli occupation of Palestinian land, using nonviolent, direct action methods and principles. Founded in August 2001, the ISM's activities aim to encourage and coordinate the participation of international individuals and groups in the Palestinian popular resistance. www.palsolidarity.org.

37. Erving Goffman, *Frame Analysis: An Essay on the Organization of Experience* (Boston, 1974) 1–10.

38. David A. Snow, E. Burke Rochford, Jr., Steven K. Worden, and Robert D. Benford, "Frame Alignment Processes, Micro-Mobilization and Movement Participation," *American Sociological Review* 51 (1986): 456–81, 464.

39. David A. Snow and Robert D. Benford, "Master Frames and Cycles of Protest," in Aldon D. Morris and Carol M. Mueller (eds.), *Frontiers in Social Movements Theory* (New Haven, Conn., 1992), 133–55; and Robert D. Benford and David A. Snow, "Framing Processes and Social Movements: An Overview and Assessment," *Annual Review of Sociology* 26 (2000): 611–39.

40. "Stop The Wall," the website of "The Grassroots Palestinian Campaign": www.stopthewall.org.

41. Interview with Einat Podjarni by one of the authors, January 31, 2006.

42. Interview with Jonathan Polak by one of the authors, January 31, 2006.

43. Meron Rappoport, "Without Shaheeds," *Ha'aretz*, June 9, 2005.

44. Amos Harel and Arnon Reguler, "Palestinians: The IDF Used Live Ammunition against the Protestors; The Security Forces: There was a Shooting of Live Ammunition into the Air," *Ha'aretz,* February 2, 2004.

45. Eitan Rabin, Itai Asher, Uri Yablonka, and Uri Binder, "Why Did They Shoot Me?" *Ma'ariv,* December 28, 2003.

46. Amir Rappoport, "The State Will Claim Compensation from Gil Naamati," *Ma'ariv,* January 11, 2004.

47. Margaret E. Keck and Kathryn Sikkink, *Activists beyond Borders: Advocacy Networks in International Politics* (Ithaca, N.Y., 1998).

48. See www.petitiononline.com/Bilin/petition.html.

49. For details on the worldwide activism against the separation barrier, see "Stop The Wall," the website of the Grassroots Palestinian Campaign: http://stopthewall.org.

50. Demonstration in Berlin, May 26, 2005.

51. Activists in the Antiwar Movement used to march and shout: "Hey, Hey, LBJ [U.S. President, Lyndon B. Johnson], How Many Kids Did You Kill Today?" Recently, during a demonstration against the U.S. military presence in Iraq, which took place in Blackburn, England, peace activists shouted at visiting U.S. Secretary of State Condoleezza Rice: "Hey, Hey, Condi, Hey, How Many Kids Did You Kill Today?" See the reports of Glenn Kessler, "Rice Concedes Likelihood of Thousands of Iraq 'Tactical Errors'," *Washington Post* and *The Independent,* April 1, 2006; Ann Penketh and Ian Herbert, "It's Grim up North, if You're the U.S. Secretary of State," *The Independent,* April 1, 2006.

52. Adriana Kemp and Uri Ben-Eliezer, "Dramatizing Sovereignty: The Construction of Territorial Dispute on the Israeli-Egyptian Border at Taba," *Political Geography* 19.3 (2000): 318–44.

53. During the Second Intifada, some Israeli activists against the state's policy in the territories were detained in the airport, and a thorough search was made of their

baggage. No reason was given for these actions, and the activists were later released without charge. From an interview with Jonathan Polak by one of the authors, January 29, 2006.

54. According to the ISM Coordinator in the occupied territories (telephone interview with Neta Golan by one of the authors, July 14, 2005). More than one hundred global activists, who took part in or intended to participate in activities against the barrier or the occupation, were deported from Israel and the occupied territories by the Israeli authorities. Testimonies of several activists who were interrogated by the Israeli border control, some of whom were even deported, can be found on the ISM's website: www.palsolidarity.org.

55. Benford and Snow, "Framing Processes and Social Movements," 617.

56. Roi Sharon, "They Are Not Anarchists," *Ma'ariv,* July 17, 2005.

57. This definition was repeated in almost every interview and conversation we had with activists.

58. "Free al-Aqsa" is a slogan that refers to the Palestinian name of the Second Intifada, which is Intifadat al-Aqsa. This name means a battle over al-Aqsa, an extremely sacred Muslim mosque located on the Temple Mount in Jerusalem (this mount is also the most sacred place for Judaism). The Second Intifada erupted immediately after a provocative visit to the mount by Ariel Sharon, at that time head of the Israeli parliamentary opposition, on September 28, 2000. Al-Aqsa thus became one of the symbols of the Palestinian struggle. The Arabic word *shaheed* (originally a Muslim religious term, literally meaning "witness") is currently used for glorification of the Palestinian dead in the Israeli–Palestinian conflicts, who are considered as martyrs in a holy war (jihad). In Israeli society, this term is identified with the Palestinian suicide bombers of the Second Intifada; it is therefore important to clarify that this slogan, "More Shaheeds," was used by Palestinians and not by Israeli activists. However, this clarification does not reduce the importance of the fact that the framework of the demonstrations against the barrier became integrated, to a large extent, with the framework of the Palestinian national struggle for independence.

59. David Kennedy, "The International Human Rights Movement: Part of the Problem?" in Robert McCorquodale (ed.), *Human Rights* (Hanover, N.H., 2003), 581–603, 584.

60. In February 2004, for instance, two-thirds of the Jewish citizens of Israel thought that Israel should not include Palestinian suffering in its considerations in the issue of the route of the barrier. See Efraim Yaar and Tamar Herman, "The Peace Index—February 2004," *Ha'aretz,* March 9, 2004.

61. Supreme Court of Justice, 2056/04: Beit Sourik Village Council *v.* The Government of Israel; Ilil Shahar and Amir Buchbut, "Sharon Ordered: Learn the Verdict and Come Back with Plans for the Route of the Fence," *Ma'ariv,* July 2, 2004.

NINE

The Debate over the
Defense Budget in Israel

ZALMAN F. SHIFFER

Israel is a small country whose very existence has been repeatedly challenged by its neighbors. To confront these threats, it has invested large quantities of human and material resources in the development of a strong army—the IDF. Over the years, the country has achieved peace with two of its neighbors, but the security problem has not disappeared and its many facets continue to affect Israeli society in many ways.

This chapter deals with one important aspect of the security problem —the domestic debate regarding the allocation of budgetary resources to the defense sector.[1] Part 1 offers a characterization of the defense expenditures—their definitions, their importance in absolute and relative terms, and their development over time. Part 2 presents the major players involved in the debate over the defense budget, and parts 3 and 4 review the major arguments and disagreements regarding the resources allocated to defense and the defense budget management. Part 5 deals with the development of the debate in recent years and part 6 offers some concluding remarks.

Defense Expenditures in Israel

There are essentially three major definitions of defense expenditures in Israel:[2]

> *The Defense Budget.* This refers to the cash outlays of the Ministry of Defense (MOD) out of the central government's budget. As such, it does not include defense expenditures of other ministries and government

agencies or nongovernmental bodies, unless they are financed out of MOD transfers. On the other hand, it includes expenditures that do not directly finance the production of defense, at least in its narrow sense.

Defense Consumption. This is a National Accounting concept, calculated by Israel's Central Bureau of Statistics (CBS) according to the international System of National Accounting (SNA). It refers to defense expenditures on an accrual basis, allocates expenditures among different ministries accord-ing to their purpose, rather than their administrative affiliation, and re-places pension transfers paid for *past* services by the imputed cost of *future* pension payments to active personnel.

The Total Cost of Defense. This is a broader concept calculated by the CBS on the basis of the recommendation of a government committee charged with estimating the full cost of defense to the Israeli economy.[3] It is not calculated in other countries (and therefore cannot be compared internationally). Its major additions to the Defense Consumption concept are the imputation of the full economic opportunity cost of the manda-tory regular and reserve military personnel and the inclusion of defense shelter construction in the civilian sector. The imputed alternative cost of the use of land by the defense sector is not included because of practical difficulties.

ISRAEL'S DEFENSE EXPENDITURES IN
A COMPARATIVE PERSPECTIVE

Out of the three aggregates discussed above, only defense consumption has been calculated and published consistently for many years. It has reached some 46 billion shekels or about 8 percent of GDP and 23 per-cent of total government expenditures in 2005. After deduction of the U.S. defense transfers, which are available only for defense spending, the defense burden on the domestic economy is about 6 percent.

In spite of the differences in definition, the defense budget and the defense consumption aggregates are roughly equal. The Gross Defense Budget presented by the treasury in October 2005 for 2006 was also 46 billion shekels. The Total Cost of Defense is generally around 25 percent higher than Defense Consumption and could amount to some 57 billion shekels, namely about 10 percent of GDP.

In absolute terms, the 2004 Israeli defense budget, at around $10 billion, was the twelfth highest in the world, similar to that of Canada, Turkey, and Australia, and about one-fourth that of the United King-dom, France, or Japan.[4] In the regional scene, the Israeli defense budget was similar to that of the combined dollar value of the published defense budgets of the four countries with which it shares borders—Egypt, Lebanon, Syria, and Jordan, and about half that of Saudi Arabia. Note, however, that in adjusted purchasing power terms, which correct the comparisons for differences in dollar prices, Israel's relative ranking is considerably lower when compared to less-developed countries in the Middle East and elsewhere (since its dollar prices are relatively high).[5]

Turning to the comparison of defense expenditures as a share of GDP, we find that the Israeli allocation of resources to defense is very high relative to that of other countries. Thus, in 2003, most Western countries spent about 2–3 percent of their GDP on defense, compared to 9 percent for Israel. The Israeli Defense–GDP ratio was also high in comparison with that of highly populated Middle Eastern countries such as Egypt, Iran, and Turkey (each of which spent between 3 and 6 percent of their GDP on defense). On the other hand, Saudi Arabia and some smaller Middle Eastern countries, including Jordan and Syria, devote higher proportions of their GDP to defense.

THE HISTORICAL RECORD

Israeli defense expenditures increased dramatically between the mid-1960s and the mid-1970s as a cumulative result of the 1967 Six-Day War, the IDF deployment in the Occupied Territories, the 1968–1970 War of Attrition, the development of an arms race with Egypt and Syria, large investments in fortifications on the Suez Canal front, the 1973 Yom Kippur War, and a massive postwar military buildup. By 1975, real defense expenditures were five times higher than ten years earlier and their share of the GDP had increased from 10 to 32 percent (!).

Thereafter, real defense expenditures decreased gradually by some 20 percent and their share of GDP fell to around 9 percent in the late 1990s. This reduction was instrumental in the stabilization of the Israeli economy, enabling it to reduce the government and current account deficits and to channel larger amounts to transfer payments and consumption.

The al-Aqsa Intifada brought a 16 percent increase in defense expenditures between 2000 and 2002. These expenditures were reduced by about 11 percent in 2003–2004 as the intensity of the conflict dwindled, but rose again in 2005 on the background of the defense fence construction and Israel's disengagement from Gaza. By that time, defense expenditures were still 8 percent higher than in 2000.

The Participants in the Debate

The debate over the defense budget in Israel is carried out at different levels and forums by the following major groups:

1. *The Army.* The IDF is a very strong participant in the debate. It enjoys a high degree of prestige and a strong position in Israel; it is extremely well informed and invests considerable resources in its staff work. It operates a system of long-term planning, and presents its case efficiently. Due to the quality of its staff work and its information advantage, it often dominates the discussions in different governmental forums. It is important to note, however, that the potential dangers of this situation are mitigated by the fact that the Israeli army considers itself a part of Israeli society and accepts the supremacy of the civilian authorities.

2. *The Ministry of Defense.* In principle, the Ministry of Defense is supposed to represent and enforce the views and authority of the civilian authorities vis-à-vis the army. In practice, however, it is often directed by ex-military officers and generally tends to accept and advance the positions of the army. It is considered a strong ministry in view of the importance of its subject matter and the generally high political profile of its ministers. Within the defense establishment, however, it is viewed as a relatively weaker party compared to the military and relies to a large extent on military staff work.

3. *The Ministry of Finance (the "Treasury" or the MOF).* The ministry of finance is the principal challenger of the defense establishment in the debate over the defense budget. It derives its strength from its control over the government budget and some other important government functions. Some of Israel's ministers of finance have enjoyed powerful status in the government, even if this post is not as important as in some other democracies on the way to the PM's office.

4. *The Prime Minister and the Cabinet.* The cabinet, under the generally strong leadership of the prime minister, acts as the board of directors of the government and is responsible for its major policy decisions. Unfortunately, it does not employ a strong professional advisory staff to assist in the performance of its responsibilities. Neither do the cabinet members have enough time to study the issues thoroughly. In matters of national

security, the decisions are often left to the discretion of the PM, who may have a strong security background, but is also overloaded by the multiple demands for his attention.

In 1999, the government decided to set up a National Security Council (NSC) which was supposed to act as the staff unit of the government on national security matters, and prepare the material for cabinet meetings on these issues. Unfortunately, the council has not been able to carry out these functions effectively, to a large extent apparently due to the objection of the ministries, which were concerned about their potential loss of influence and the reluctance of the cabinet and the prime ministers to overrule this opposition.

5. *The Knesset.* The Knesset has traditionally dealt with security questions and the defense budget mainly through two committees: the Foreign Affairs and Defense Committee (FADC) and the Defense Budget Committee, which includes members of both the Finance Committee and the FADC. Members of the two committees have repeatedly complained that they do not get access to sufficient information. In addition, they have almost no staff to help them digest and understand the complicated defense reports.

6. *The Domestic Defense Industries (and other suppliers to the IDF).* The Israeli Defense Industries are modern, sophisticated industries with an important share in the country's industrial sector production, employment, and exports. They are naturally interested in increasing their sales to the IDF, both because of the direct income involved and because of the favorable effect of domestic sales on their export markets. Since exports are considered necessary to ensure the profitability of these industries and their ability to develop efficient products for the IDF, there is a mutual interest in increasing the budgetary allocations to acquisitions from the defense industries. Consequently, the directors of these industries (who are generally well connected) and other domestic suppliers to the IDF lobby strongly in favor of higher domestic defense budgets and larger conversions of U.S. grants into shekels for domestic purchases.[6]

7. *The Public and the Media.* The general public's access to information concerning defense matters is limited. It seems that in recent years more information has become available through the Freedom of Information Act and some investigative journalists, who are often quite knowledgeable, but are also constrained by secrecy requirements and by their dependence on their sources of information.

The major "fights" over the defense budget are waged between the military and the MOD on one side and the budgetary division of the MOF on the other side. The annual budget preparation process is characterized by a series of confrontations between two groups of highly motivated professionals.

The officials of the MOF see themselves as representatives of the taxpayers, alternative budgetary uses, and the macroeconomic stability cause. Their staff is small and, while they are very knowledgeable about budgetary matters, they cannot and do not pretend to be experts on military issues. By and large they tend to adopt an *input approach*—concentrating on the overall level of budgetary allowance and letting the MOD decide on its allocation.

The MOD/IDF representatives are probably well aware of the wider economic and social aspects of budgetary decisions, but tend to concentrate on their area of responsibility. Their basic approach is one of *outputs,* rather than of inputs—determining the needs and deriving from them the military power and budget required.

The debate between these two parties often heats up as the budget determination process reaches its focal points. Both sides do not shy away from exerting pressures on the decision makers, mobilizing the media to their cause and using partisan arguments. Thus, the treasury sometime blames defense circles for issuing exaggerated and unnecessarily alarming statements, and they retaliate by describing some of the treasury claims as petty and unprofessional.

In spite of these frictions, there is also a considerable degree of cooperation between the two parties. In particular, the treasury is often willing to spread payments for efficiency-promoting adjustments over time. The MOD also enjoys immunity from the same detailed intervention of the MOF in the articles of other ministries' budgets.

The Debate over Defense Needs and the Optimal Size of the Defense Budget

The debate about defense expenditures is conducted in budgetary terms, but it reflects major differences of opinion about the optimal allocation of the nation's economic resources between the provision of defense and civilian goods and services.[7] Basically, one can look at the issue in terms of the choice of the optimal combination of the costs of security and of insecurity. Given the country's geopolitical situation, it is exposed to certain threats that imply costs in terms of life and injury risks on the one hand and productive capacity on the other; this is the cost of insecurity. The allocation of resources to defense reduces these costs, but it also reduces the resources available for civilian ends; this is the cost of security. The decision maker has to weigh the relative importance of these two costs to determine the optimal allocation of resources to the defense sector.

More specifically, the debate focuses on the following major issues:

1. *The Cost of Insecurity—the Nature and Significance of the Threats.* These include the existing and potential capabilities of different parties— both active and would-be enemies and third parties, their intentions, and the importance of the damages they can inflict (or prevent). The damages involved include both direct human suffering and material destruction and indirect effects on production, employment, international trade, investment, and the like.

2. *Potential Responses, Their Effectiveness, and Their Adaptability.* These responses include both means and strategies—the size and structure of the military power in terms of hardware, personnel, and human capital and their application according to different military doctrines.

The effectiveness of the responses obviously depends on the nature of the threats and, as this changes over time, requires flexibility and adaptability of the responses. The specific mix of responses will depend on the evaluation of the probability of different threats, the available resources, and the *time constants* required for the development, purchase, and introduction of changes in the nature and structure of military power.

3. *Interactions between Threats and Responses.* A basic question is whether security threats should be regarded as exogenous "States of Nature" or as moves in an interactive game between the home country and other parties. This question relates both to general geopolitical positions and to actions undertaken in the defense domain, such as defense spending decisions.

Regarding the latter, there are essentially two competing views on the nature of the arms race interactive game: *the escalation model,* according to which increased defense expenditures by one party trigger increased expenditures by its opponent, thereby creating a destabilizing spiral; and *the "Star Wars" model,* which predicts that, beyond a certain point, a credible player who is able and willing to invest the necessary resources can break his rival's ability or willingness to reach a certain power balance and bring him to a unilateral spending reduction.

In the past, Israel has been engaged in escalating arm races with its Arab neighbors. There are, however, differing views about the present situation. Some observers argue that Israel is in a favorable military position vis-à-vis these countries, and that given their financial problems, they will gladly follow Israel in a mutual reduction of military spending. Other observers, however, believe that some of Israel's potential opponents, who have given up their ambition to beat Israel in the arms race, may react to a reduction in military spending by a renewed effort to gain a relative advantage against Israel.

4. *The Cost of Defense.* From an economic point of view, the cost of defense is the foregone cost of diverting economic resources from civilian to defense uses. This cost may manifest itself in a variety of ways both within and outside the budget.

Budgetary costs may take the form of reduced government allocations to health, education, administration, infrastructure, and transfer payments, or alternatively may lead to increased taxation or increased public indebtedness, which imply higher future taxes. The latter may also have adverse effects on the country's productive capacity and future growth. Nonbudgetary costs include unpaid or underpaid resources employed by or for the defense sector, and different negative externalities, such as environmental damages.

One important issue in the evaluation of the cost of defense is the appropriate treatment of foreign (mainly U.S.) unilateral defense transfers to Israel. Spokespersons of the defense establishment argue that these transfers should be deducted from the cost of defense since they cannot be used for other ends, especially since the United States is committed to Israel's security, but not necessarily to its standards of living, and since most of the U.S. defense aid is earmarked for acquisitions from American industry. Critics of this position maintain that even if certain sources of income are earmarked for predetermined uses, money is still fungible because the addition of earmarked sources for one use can be neutralized by the transfer of "unmarked" funds to other uses. In addition, there is a certain degree of substitution between military and nonmilitary aid to Israel (for example, through the willingness of the U.S. government to provide credit guarantees for Israel). Moreover, it is also argued that U.S. defense aid to Israel imposes certain constraints on Israel's political and commercial choices.

5. *Externalities or the Spillovers of Defense Activity on Civilian Economic Activity.* On the macroeconomic level, it is often argued that defense demands play an important role in increasing aggregate demand and in accelerating economic activity. This effect is relevant only in situations of demand-restricted economic activity, and should be applied with caution and due attention to possible crowding out of other activities. In addition, the possible benefits of such a move should be compared to those of boosting aggregate demand by other means.

On the microeconomic level, defense sector demands affect civilian production potential through the mix of these demands, the imposition of higher standards, and the creation of professional cadres. Thus, military demands have apparently contributed considerably to the development of hi-tech industries in Israel, and, in particular, to the rapidly growing Information Communication Technology (ICT) sector.

In principle, it could have been possible to attain similar progress through the encouragement of nondefense industries and investments. Unfortunately, it seems that the government's ability to advance civilian goals had lagged behind that of its ability to advance military goals. While this implies that the productive contribution of the defense sector may indeed be important, it also sadly points to another, less tangible effect of the important role played by the defense sector in Israel, namely its influence on the performance of the civilian public sector (see below).

The Debate over the Structure and Preparation of the Defense Budget

We now turn from the wider questions of the determination of the size and composition of defense expenditures to more specific questions relating to the status and modus operandi of the defense budget.

THE BALANCE OF POWER AND RESPONSIBILITY IN THE DEFENSE BUDGETING PROCESS

Given the democratic ethos of the Israeli society and the democratic structure of the country's political institutions, it is generally agreed that the IDF should report to the MOD, the MOD and the MOF to the cabinet, and the government to the Knesset.

In practice, however, the defense establishment (and the IDF in particular) enjoys a strong edge in the defense budget preparation process due to its information advantage and the meager resources that other players are able or willing to devote to redress this imbalance (see above). The MOF is the only participant to challenge the MOD's dominance—on the basis of its budgetary power, but not on the basis of expertise in the subject. The cabinet makes its decisions on the basis of limited information and assessments provided mainly by the military; the Knesset is still a marginal actor in the process. This unsatisfactory state of affairs has been repeatedly deplored, but, as we will see, attempts to reform it have led so far only to modest advances.[8]

THE DIVISION OF LABOR BETWEEN THE DEFENSE AND OTHER BUDGETS

The defense budget includes allocations for some activities that are not strictly part of the country's defense, while at the same time, some important defense activities are budgeted in other ministries. Thus, for example, the IDF has been engaged over the years in education and immigration absorption tasks, civilian rescue operations, land cultivation, and, recently, police operations such as the forced evacuation of Israeli settlers from the Gaza Strip. On the other hand, the Ministry of Interior Security is in charge of the border guards—police units that carry out semi-military defense activities. The blurring of the division of labor between civilian and defense authorities represents not only the possibility of an improper mixture of considerations between the two branches of government, but could also lead to inefficiencies in the allocation of resources to defense at large.

THE IMPOSITION OF EFFICIENCY INCENTIVES

Decision makers of different kinds generally tend to optimize their behavior in terms of the constraints to which they are subject. Therefore, if they are confronted with prices that do not reflect the true cost of resources (by either understatement or overstatement of the cost) to society, they will tend to use them in a socially wasteful way. This has been the case to a large extent with the use of resources by the military in the past and to a lesser extent in the present. Thus, until the beginning of the 1990s, the IDF was paying reserve soldiers called to duty only a small part of the value of their foregone civilian earnings; when this changed, the army cut its reliance on reservists dramatically.

The army still has no incentive for efficiently using the service of the compulsory draft soldiers and of the land under its control, for both of which it is paying less than market value. It is hoped that the wasteful use of draft soldiers will be partly reduced in the future due to the application of the recommendation of a public committee which suggested that the army pay a higher price for the last months of compulsory service.[9] As for the use of land, the Ministry of Finance is trying, together with the Administration of Israel Lands and other public agencies, to create incentives for the army's migration from expensive lands.

In principle, the army should have no objection to the imposition of correct prices, or other efficiency-augmenting measures (such as outsourcing of noncore activities) provided that its budget is adjusted accordingly. It is, however, sometimes less than fully enthusiastic about adopting such measures, possibly because of its concern that it will not be fully compensated or because of the material and cultural costs involved in applying the necessary behavioral adjustments.

ANNUAL VERSUS MULTIANNUAL BUDGETS

Many of the MOD projects are long-term development and power-building projects that may lose much of their value if discontinued. Consequently, the MOD has repeatedly been asking for multiannual budgets to support its multiannual plans.

The problem with this apparently plausible suggestion is that the commitment of funds in advance to a certain end reduces the degrees of freedom of the treasury and its ability to adjust the budget to unexpected developments in needs or resources. Consequently, it diverts the costs of such adjustments to other clients of the budget (or sources of revenue), thereby potentially increasing the overall adjustment costs. The problem is most likely aggravated by the implied assumption of the MOD that the treasury will, in any case, bear the burden of adjustment to unexpected increases in defense needs.

The MOD spokespersons have suggested on some occasions that indexation of the defense budget to the GDP could reduce the risks of multiannual funding of defense expenditures. Note, however, that this argument meets only the problem of uncertainty in resources, but not in needs.

The MOF opposes the idea of indexing the defense budget to the GDP on the additional grounds that it introduces an automatic upward trend in defense expenditures, while the optimal level of defense expenditures does not depend on the availability of resources. This last argument is, however, theoretically ill-founded to the extent that additional defense expenditures increase the sense of security of the population and that such security is a normal good, namely one that people want to enjoy more as their income increases.

Avi Ben-Bassat and Momi Dahan[10] argue that "hard" multiannual budgeting is not applied in any other country and that "soft" indicative multiannual budgeting can be useful in checking the ex ante feasibility of long-term plans, but cannot and should not be interpreted as pre-commitment. They add that soft three-year budgeting has been applied in Israel and, in their opinion, was found useless. In addition, they point out that the treasury allows the MOD to undertake future commitment at the average value of 71 percent of its budget, as against an average of 31 percent for the whole budget (see also the State Comptroller on this issue below).

PENSIONS AND REHABILITATION PAYMENTS

The defense budget includes pensions for army veterans and rehabilitation expenses for people injured in fighting operations and from terrorist activities. While these are obviously related to security, they are not part of the current defense decision making. In other words, a relatively important part of the defense budget does not reflect the cost of the production of current and future security, but includes transfers for past service and suffering. At the same time, the budget in the past did not include allowances for future pension payments and for expected future rehabilitation payments that are derived from current military decisions.

This problematic presentation will apparently be partially corrected as a result of the planned transition to pensions based on accumulated deductions by the personnel and the employer. This will however, not apply to formerly accumulated pension claims and, as a result, the phasing out of the former type of payments from the defense budget will take several decades under the existing budget accounting conventions.

THE ARMY STANDARD OF LIVING AND OTHER "LUXURIES"

According to some critics, the living standards of career military personnel are higher than the one needed to attract that personnel—implying that they will be willing to serve for a more modest remuneration and that they enjoy an unnecessary "rent." In particular, it is often claimed that nonfighting personnel should be compensated on a basis similar to that of other public employees. One important example that has often been quoted in this context is the early retirement age, which allows personnel to develop a second career at a relatively young age, with a relatively high pension. While this arrangement seems justified on the basis of both equity and efficiency for field personnel, it may not be optimal to lose the investment in the human capital of defense staff and technical personnel in their middle age.[11]

Spokespersons of the defense establishment have repeatedly rejected this criticism or at least have argued that it is exaggerated, warning that an erosion of the standard of living of military personnel will lower their motivation and bring about a dangerous deterioration in the quality of career army cadres.

The Evolution of the Debate in the Present Era

INCREASING DIFFERENCES

During most of the 1990s, the defense budget remained more or less constant in real terms while its share of the GDP decreased, due to the rapid growth of the latter. The confrontations between the treasury and the MOF continued, but the differences between their short-term budget positions were relatively modest.

The question of the allocation of resources to defense received renewed importance with the outbreak of the violent Israeli–Palestinian confrontation at the end of 2000 (the al-Aqsa Intifada). The outburst of the hostilities and, in particular, the suicide terrorist attacks against Israel inflicted high costs in terms of lives lost and injuries to the civilian Israeli population. They also imposed a high economic cost on the economy.[12] These events clearly demonstrated the cost of insecurity, apparently strengthening the case for higher defense spending.

This was, however, not the unique insight to be gained from these years' dismal experience, for Israel suffered not only from an attack on its security, but also was brought very close to a financial crisis, barely escaping it to find itself in a social crisis. These two last developments were related to the burden of high government spending that, on the background of a lower ability to raise taxes, threatened to increase the budget deficit to alarming levels. To avoid the destabilizing effects of such a development, the government reduced its transfer payments to the needy population, thereby augmenting their suffering and increasing the incidence of poverty. As time passed, the security situation improved and the economy gradually recovered, but the hard feelings concerning the social developments by and large continued, turning the social issue into one of the major issues of the 2006 national elections (see below). Thus, the events of the Second Intifada years also demonstrated some of the hazards of high government spending and of increased defense outlays in particular.

While the immediate need to increase defense spending between 2000 and 2002 was accepted without much discussion, the conflicting lessons gained from the Intifada expressed themselves in a huge wedge between the positions of the MOF and of the defense establishment during the 2003 budget deliberations. These deliberations were conducted after the accomplishment of the April 2002 "Defense Wall" military operation, which was considered the turning point of the military confrontation and was followed by a gradual decrease in the intensity of fighting and a reduction in the number of Israeli casualties.

The difference between the original claims of the MOD and the treasury proposals for the 2003 budget, according to press records of the time, reached some 9 billion NIS—about a fifth of the defense budget and a quarter of the domestic outlays of this budget. While the treasury felt that the time was right for a massive reallocation from defense to civilian objectives, the MOD considered the treasury proposals as irresponsible, not only because of their different views of the defense needs, but also because of the high short-term rigidity of many of the defense programs. The implication of this rigidity claim was that in order to achieve a given budgetary saving in the short run, it would be necessary to discontinue abruptly, and at high costs, many activities that could be preserved under a similar budget reduction spread over several years.

The differences between the two sides were finally brought to the prime minister, who imposed a sizable budget cut on the MOD, although not as high as requested by the treasury. The same ordeal was repeated with some variations a year later during the 2004 budget preparation (with the difference that this time the treasury side was able to argue that threats of an attack on Israel from the east had diminished considerably as a result of the American invasion of Iraq).[13]

Following these decisions, the army reported that it had to apply painful reductions in its expenditures, dismantle part of its power, and discharge more than 5,000 officers and other career personnel.

THE ISRAEL DEMOCRACY INSTITUTE MEETING

The importance of the issues at hand, the intensity and bitterness of the confrontation, and the general frustration over the shallowness of the discussions brought about a desire to improve the process by which decisions concerning the budget were made.

This mood found strong expression in a September 2003 meeting of the Israel Democracy Institute that brought together top IDF officers, MOF and other government officials, academicians, businessmen, journalists, and others.[14] The major theme of the meeting was not determination of the "optimal" level of defense expenditures, but the establishment of mechanisms that would bring about a more thorough, cooperative, and transparent analysis of the issues by the parties involved, and the presentation of alternatives and their implications to the decision makers.

One of the products of this meeting was a proposal submitted by an interdisciplinary group of academicians and experts.[15] This document suggested the establishment of two mechanisms aimed at improving the defense budget preparation process:

1. The establishment of a well-defined cooperative defense budget preparation process, based on directives of the prime minister and aiming to provide the cabinet with a clear presentation of the alternatives and their implications, with a specification of the time schedule of the various stages of preparation, the participants in each stage, and the products required. The NSC was to play a central role in this process as the staff unit of the PM.
2. The establishment of several working groups charged with development of the knowledge base required to develop and improve the analytical tools and other instruments required for a deeper understanding of the basic issues involved and the implications of different courses of action. These groups were supposed to deal with questions concerning Israel's

national security doctrine and construction of the defense budget, and develop mutually agreed databases and a friendly and transparent glossary for the common use of the army, the MOD, the MOF, and the decision makers.

THE STATE COMPTROLLER'S REPORT

The next few years witnessed some secondary progress. The differences between the initial positions of the MOF and MOD were reduced (as was apparently also the intensity of the confrontation between these two partners). Some advances were also made on the organizational side, including the nomination of an MOF representative as chief accountant of the MOD;[16] the NSC was given some role in the defense budget preparation process, and in August 2004 the PM directed the MOD to prepare a multiannual plan for the defense budget with the cooperation of the MOF and the NSC.

In spite of these changes, the improvement was apparently marginal, as can be seen from the critical evaluation of the defense budget preparation process published by the State Comptroller (2005).[17] In this detailed document, which referred mainly to the 2003–2005 period, the comptroller stated, inter alia, that:

a) In spite of its complexity, the defense budget preparation process is not regulated in the MOF by a clear and systematic procedural framework. The MOF does not practice an orderly documentation process and does not invite the MOD to participate in the determination of the defense budget framework.

b) The Budget Division of the MOF does not operate comprehensive staff work to support the decision-making process, including analysis of the full economic and budgetary implications of changes in the defense budget, their operational military implications, their applicability, and the time span needed to execute them. In addition, the Budget Division of the MOF does not use an appropriate database for the analysis of the implications of its proposals.

c) The IDF Planning Division and the MOD Budgetary Division do not investigate the economic implications of changes in their working plans and do not compare them to alternative adjustments. This deprives the decision makers of very valuable information.

d) In addition to the preparation of the defense budget and its submission for Knesset approval, the MOF and MOD reach understandings regarding different supplements to the defense budget, subject to the approval of the PM. These understandings have, on some occasions, created a situation in which the cabinet decided on defense budget reductions, while, at the same time, supplementary funding was extended.[18]

e) In the preparation of the defense budget proposal, the MOF does not take into account the MOD income-dependent expenses that are conditional on the mobilization of resources by the MOD (for example, by the sale of discarded equipment).

f) The MOF does not monitor and adequately control the creation of multiannual obligations for future transactions by the MOD, in spite of their influence on future budgetary degrees of freedom (see above).

g) The MOF has not established formal requirements for current reporting by the MOD; as a consequence, its control over the defense sector is limited and its ability to contribute to a more efficient use of resources is undermined.

h) The deliberations over the defense budget with the PM's participation are dominated by the analyses and data provided by the MOD. The MOF is not able to check these data and analyses and, as nobody else has the authority to do so, there is an overreliance on the material provided by the defense sector.

i) The government does not present updated multiannual budgetary plans to the Knesset and the MOF does not transmit to the MOD its multiannual planning for the defense budget.[19]

j) The PM conducted two parallel sets of budgetary deliberations, a formal one leading to the discussion and ratification of the budget by the Knesset, and the other dealing with the de facto defense expenditures, including the different supplements. This state of affairs undermined parliamentary control and confronted the other ministries with the need to readjust to lower allocations than provided for in the ordinary budgeting process.

k) Finally, the comptroller concluded that the prime minister's office, including the National Security Council, has no meaningful role in the staff work preceding the prime minister's decisions regarding the defense budget framework.

THE ISSUE OF PARLIAMENTARY CONTROL

While most of the comptroller's criticisms related to mismanagement and inefficiencies within the government, his comments regarding the lack of transparency in the presentation of the defense budget to the Knesset deserve special attention since they raise the very basic democratic issue of legislative power over the executive branch. Since the actual size of the defense budget is made public knowledge anyway with a year delay, and since the supplements do not change dramatically its order of magnitude,[20] the ex ante partial disclosure even to the confidential FADC and Defense Budget Committees may reflect administrative convenience and disregard toward the Knesset, rather than genuine security imperatives. This belated reporting is apparently only one demonstration of the reluctance of the executive to sharing information with the Knesset.

In May 2005, the Chairman of the Knesset FADC, MK Yuval Steinitz, stated that the Joint Finance-FADC Defense Budget Committee does not function properly since it could not go into the details of the defense budget.[21] He also referred to the recommendation of a public committee charged with investigating the means for increasing parliamentary control over the defense budget. This latter committee (headed by MK Amnon Rubinstein) suggested that responsibility for the endorsement of the defense budget be transferred from the specialized defense budget committee to the finance committee, which is in charge of the general state budget, but that the detailed allocation of the defense budget be left to a confidential subcommittee of the FADC. Another recommendation of the Rubinstein Committee was that state and defense sector employees would have to testify before the FADC when invited and present any requested document (unless it was extremely sensitive).[22]

RECENT POLITICAL DEVELOPMENTS

While there was little progress in the reform of the *process* of preparing the defense budget, the general public debate over the *size* of the defense budget has intensified. This trend was apparently related to the combination of two factors:

a) From one side there was a general feeling that Israel's security situation has improved as a result of the reduction in the number of murderous terrorist attacks against Israel and the continuous U.S. military presence in Iraq. The effect of these developments seems to have overshadowed that of some negative developments, such as the Qassam rocket launches against Israel from the Gaza Strip, the progress of the Iranian nuclear effort, and the victory of the extreme anti-Israel Hamas party in the Palestinian Authority general elections.

b) On the other side, there was growing concern and frustration about the increasing incidence of poverty and shortcomings of the welfare, health, and education systems.

Against these background factors, the media and different politicians increasingly pointed to apparent inefficiencies and waste in the defense sector and called for a change in the public agenda and the reallocation of funds from defense to social budgets.[23] As the 2006 elections approached, it turned out that many of the political parties were in favor of reducing the defense budgets.[24]

Following the March 2006 general elections, a new government was formed. In his victory speech, which was later considered as laying the ground for the new government agenda, Ehud Olmert referred to the need for more social compassion and for investing more resources into education. He did not specify, however, whether the required funding would come from the defense budget, as urged by many, or from other sources.

One of the most interesting features of the new government subsequently presented to the Knesset was that neither Prime Minister Olmert, nor Defense Minister Amir Peretz had significant military experience and that neither of them was identified with the defense lobby. Moreover, the new defense minister was known as a strong supporter of increased social spending.

In April 2006, Dan Meridor, a former finance and justice minister and one of the best civilian experts on security matters, submitted a secret report on the Defense and Security Doctrine of Israel. According to the press, the Meridor report stated that Israeli governments do not carry a full and serious staff in security matters and recommended that the NSC become the central staff unit of the cabinet. Regarding the defense budget, the report recommended that its present magnitude be preserved, with a small reduction, but that at the same time, a five-year defense budget be introduced, on the assumption of continuous GDP growth.[25]

Following the establishment of the new government, the PM announced that he would relocate the National Security Council from its out-of-center location into the prime minister's office in Jerusalem and turn it into cabinet-level political-security staff.[26]

In July 2006 Israel was drawn into an armed conflict with Hizbullah in the north of the country. This conflict—"The Second Lebanon War"—revealed some major problems in the preparation and equipping of military troops and the civil anti-missile defense and in the conduct of the war. To many critics, the Second Lebanon War demonstrated both the risks of an overconfident military leadership and of an inexperienced civilian leadership. Frustration over the results of the war led to public demands for better control of the defense sector and to the establishment of an inquiry committee to investigate the war. This committee, headed by Eliyahu Winograd, published two highly critical reports.[27]

As Israel found itself once again in armed conflict in December 2008 against Hamas in the Gaza Strip, there was a general feeling that many of the Winograd Committee's recommendations had been successfully adopted.

THE BRODET REPORT

Following the Second Lebanon war, the government decided to allocate an important addition of 8.2 billion NIS to the defense budget. At the same time, the budgetary performance of the Defense Ministry was also criticized severely.

Following this criticism, in November 2006 the government nominated a high-profile committee, chaired by David Brodet, to investigate the defense budget. It was asked to submit recommendations about the optimal size and composition of this budget, and to refer to a wide range of issues concerning the budgeting process and the allocation of resources to the defense sector.

The Brodet Committee Report concluded that the IDF and the security sector were trapped in a multidimensional crisis—budgetary, managerial, organizational, cultural, and strategic.[28] According to the committee, this crisis originated in a series of conflicts, such as the tensions between the building of a strong conventional army and low intensity antiterrorist activities, disproportionate numbers of noncombatant troops, high current outlays versus inadequate long-term investments, and a highly developed air force versus neglected ground forces. Against this grave and wide crisis, the committee recommended the application of an overall recovery program.

The specific recommendations included the following:

1. The preparation of an overall strategic plan for the army.
2. The application of a five-year defense budget framework for all defense outlays, backed with an indicative planning horizon for five additional years.
3. Explicit budgeting of reserve funds for unexpected developments.
4. A specific numerical ten-year defense budget path, allowing for some real increase at a rate lower than that of economic growth, thus bringing about a gradual reduction in the share of defense in GDP and in government expenditures.
5. The application of a large-scale efficiency-promoting program, as a major source of financing the increased security outlays.
6. Defining minimal levels of allocations to key "anchor" activities, such as acquisitions, R&D, training, and preparedness.
7. The creation of an intergovernmental forum to advise the IDF chief of staff and the defense minister on budgetary and economic issues and to monitor the implementation of the government budgetary decisions.
8. The determination of a well-defined and transparent yearly budgetary preparation process.

In addition, the report dealt with questions of manpower, pensions and rehabilitation, organizational changes, and the upgrading of the NSC position.

Three aspects of the Brodet Report should be emphasized:

a) In the choice between rules and discretion, the report favored the more rigid approach of a multiyearly budget path. This was apparently based on the assumption that the demand for defense behaves in a regular and predictable way, with relatively small variations most of the time, an assumption that may prove problematic in view of the increased frequency of medium-scale outbursts of violence in the present era.
b) The committee made an attempt to reconcile the top-down (input) approach of the treasury with the bottom-up (output) approach of the defense sector. However, it had to admit that its recommended budget path did not provide an answer to some important demands of the security sector, which were left to later consideration.
c) The imposition of minimal levels of "anchored" outlays reflected a disbelief in the security sector's ability to allocate resources in an optimal way, possibly due to concerns about its professional judgment, preferences, or ability to resist pressures.

The Brodet Report received considerable attention due to the general public's malaise about the defense sector conduct and performance, the authors' standing, and the large scope of its discussion. However, both the treasury and the defense circles were critical about some of its diagnoses and recommendations. It remains to be seen what its long-term impact will be.

Conclusion

This chapter was not intended to discuss the optimal size of the defense budget in Israel or to pass judgment on its composition. Its purpose was to present the major considerations and dilemmas about the allocation of economic resources to defense and the defense budget structure, and to survey the publicly available evidence about the process leading to its determination.

We believe that we have established that there are some severe and potentially dangerous shortcomings in this process. These can be summarized by the statement that neither the cabinet nor the specialized Knesset committees have adequate access to a real-time clear and well-balanced integrative presentation of the major security issues, the possible alternative courses of action, and their implications. As a result, the input of the civilian decision makers to some of the most important issues relating to the security and well-being of Israeli citizens as well as their future is poor and inadequate, and the control of the legislative authority over the executive loses much of its meaning.

To deal with this problem it is necessary that:

a) The defense establishment and the IDF in particular make the necessary effort to present relevant information in a clear and accessible form to the civilian authorities.
b) The civilian authorities realize that they are avoiding their responsibility by leaving the formulation of the problems, the alternatives, and the choice of action to defense professionals by default.
c) The civilian authorities, including the treasury, the cabinet, and the Knesset, invest the resources necessary for building high-quality independent analytical capacities able to challenge military professionals in both security and economic domains.

More is involved here than the mere improvement of the security and budgetary decision processes and of parliamentary control of the executive: we are too often confronted with situations in which the civilian sector in Israel is considered incompetent or unwilling to accept responsibility and the military or the veteran military are called to the rescue. This is a grave system failure that prevents Israel from fully achieving its potential, reduces incentives for professionalism and excellence in the civilian sector, and prevents Israel from fully developing its civil society and achieving a proper balance and division of labor between the different parts of society.

Acknowledgments

I would like to thank Oren Barak, Yaakov Lifshitz, Yakir Plessner, Gabriel Sheffer, and Imri Tov for their helpful comments and advice.

Notes

1. For more detailed and more thoroughly documented discussions of many of the issues presented here, see Yaakov Lifshitz, *Defense Economics: The General Theory and the Israeli Case* (Jerusalem, 2000) [Hebrew]; and Imri Tov, *The Price of Defense Power, the Economy of Defense: The Case of Israel* (Jerusalem, 1998) [Hebrew]. See also Yehuda Ben-Meir, *National Security Decision-making: The Israeli Case* (Tel-Aviv, 1986) [Hebrew] for a very interesting historical perspective on the national security decision-making process.

2. Shmuel Ben-Zvi, "The Expenditure and Cost of Defense in Israel," in Imri Tov, *Defense and the National Economy in Israel: Challenges and Responses in the Defense Production Policy,* Tel-Aviv University, Memorandum, 62 (2002): 38–44 [Hebrew].

3. Leora Meridor (Chairperson), The Committee for the Investigation of the Cost of Defense in Israel: Concluding Report (1995) [Hebrew].

4. International data are based on Stockholm International Peace Research Institute (SIPRI), *SIPRI Yearbook 2005* (Oxford, 2005).

5. Exact relative purchasing power price data for defense outlays are not available.

6. The bulk of the U.S. defense grants to Israel are earmarked for purchases from U.S. manufacturers.

7. On these issues, see also Imri Tov, "The Defense Budget Debate, Yet Once More," *Strategic Assessment* 8(3) (2005): 1–10 [Hebrew].

8. See Avi Ben-Bassat and Momi Dahan, "The Balance of Power in the Budget Process," prepared for The Israeli Democracy Institute Annual Economic Conference "Caesarea XIII" (Jerusalem, 2005) [Hebrew], for a discussion of the same issue in a wider context. For a presentation of the MOF position on some of the issues discussed, see The Ministry of Finance, *The Principals of the State Budget* (Jerusalem, various years) [Hebrew].

9. Avi Ben-Bassat (Chairman), Report of the Committee for the Investigation of the Shortening of IDF Obligatory Service (2006) [Hebrew].

10. Ben-Bassat and Dahan, "The Balance of Power in the Budget Process."

11. The early retirement package may provide incentives for moving from the defense to the civilian sector, even for staff who are more efficient in the first sector.

12. For interesting discussions of the different economic and other effects of terrorist actions, see Zvi Eckstein and Daniel Tsiddon, "Macroeconomic Consequences of Terror: Theory and the Case of Israel," *Journal of Monetary Economics* 51 (2004): 971–1002; and Gary S. Becker and Yona Rubinstein, "Fear and the Response to Terrorism: An Economic Analysis" (2004) [mimeo]. See also the Israel Democracy Institute, "The Economy and Security," *The Annual Economic Meeting, Caesarea X* (Jerusalem, 2002) [Hebrew] and the *Bank of Israel Annual Reports,* 2002 and 2003.

13. For a more detailed record of the defense budget determination process in this particular period, see Oren Barak and Gabriel Sheffer, "Israel's 'Security Network' and Its Impact: An Exploration of a New Approach," *International Journal of Middle East Studies* 38.2 (2006): 235–61.

14. Baruch Nevo and Yael Shur-Shmueli, *The Israel Defense Forces and the National Economy of Israel* (Jerusalem, 2004) [Hebrew].

15. This document was prepared by Daniel Efrati, Arie Melnik, Baruch Nevo, Dan Peled, and Zalman Shiffer. See Nevo and Shur-Shmueli, *The Israel Defense Forces and the National Economy of Israel,* 45–50.

16. The DM also made some organizational changes, such as setting up a Strategic Planning Division, with the intention of strengthening the civilian part of the MOD relative to the IDF. It is not clear whether this reshuffling was also designed with the intention of increasing the relative importance of civilian versus military considerations in decision making.

17. "The Process of Determination of the Defense Budget Framework," in *The State Comptroller's Report 56A* (2005): 5–32 [Hebrew].

18. Note that these additions and changes are not hidden. They are reported ex post and included in the CBS reporting of defense consumption.

19. The PM asked the MOD, the MOF, and the NSC to prepare a proposal for a multiannual defense budget plan.

20. According to data presented in the State Comptroller Report (note 17 supra) the updated defense budget expenditures exceeded the original allocations by 10–13 percent each year between 1999 and 2004. Some part of this difference probably reflects nominal adjustments to price and exchange rate changes, rather than real adjustments.

21. Yuval Steinitz, "The Knesset and the Supervision of the Defense Complex and the Army," in Gabriel Sheffer, *An Army That Has a State: A New Look at the Place of "Security" and the Defense Complex in Israel* (Jerusalem, 2007).

22. Ibid., and *Ha'aretz,* December 29, 2004.

23. Yanai Cohen and Shuki Sadeh, "The Hidden Treasure," *Kol Hair,* October 21, 2005, 50–57, for a journalist's critical investigation of several military projects.

24. Uzi Dayan, the leader of a small new party, and a former Deputy IDF CGS and head of the NSC, called for a 10 percent or 4.5 billion shekel (about $1 billion) reduction in the defense budget. (*The Marker,* October 29, 2005).

25. *Ha'aretz,* April 24, 2006.

26. It was reported that the National Security Adviser would be subordinate to the PM's chief of staff. This could unfavorably affect the degree of the NSC's independence in its advisory capacity and its impact on the budget preparation process.

27. Eliyahu Winograd (Chairman), *The 2006 Lebanon War Events Examination Committee, Interim Report* (2007); and Eliyahu Winograd (Chairman), *The 2006 Lebanon War Events Examination Committee, Final Report* (2008) http://www.vaadatwino.org.il/reports.html [Hebrew].

28. David Brodet (Chairman) *Report of the Defense Budget Examination Committee* (2007), http://www.nsc.gov.il/NSCWeb/Docs?Brodet.pdf (accessed on February 1, 2007).

TEN

Civilian Control over the Army in Israel and France

SAMY COHEN

The problem of civilian control over the armed forces is of major concern in all democracies. It is even of more concern in those countries that have a large army or are engaged in a protracted international conflict. This is particularly the case, or was the case, in countries such as the United States, Britain, France, and Israel. What is meant by "civilian control"? What sort of concerns does it refer to? It usually involves worrying about the excessive influence the army might gain over legitimately elected civil authorities who are not in a position to exercise their prerogatives knowledgeably. Lacking military skill, they might only exercise titular power, rubber-stamping proposals without being able to check the information provided by military officers. Is this the case in Israel? A vast literature has been devoted to Israeli civil–military relations.[1]

Some authors have insisted heavily on the dangers of excessive military power, specifically mentioning not only the risk of "praetorianism," of a "military coup,"[2] but also the "militarization" of Israeli society.[3] Ofer Shelah writes of a "silent putsch."[4] He refers to the significant place the army occupies in Israeli society, its ascendancy over civilian leaders, and the latter's inability to counterbalance their influence. Other analysts have even wondered if the attempted putsch perpetrated by four French generals in April 1961 in Algiers against General de Gaulle might not happen in Israel.[5] Undoubtedly, the French precedent holds considerable fascination for researchers. Other authors, such as Stuart Cohen and Yoram Peri, have presented dissimilar but less radical theses. Cohen mentions an "over-subordination" of the army to political authority, while Peri writes of a "political–military partnership, a pattern that arose due to the prolonged conflict with the Palestinians and the Arab states."[6]

This chapter focuses on the decision to use force in the course of external military operations.[7] It compares France, mainly at the time of the Fifth Republic, and Israel, which teaches us a lot about the capacity of civilian control over the army. Furthermore, it provides a useful instrument in understanding and better assessing the characteristics of the Israeli case. The two countries have in common a number of characteristics: they are considered "medium-sized powers"; have large armies; experienced, or continue to experience, repeated wars; and have been embroiled in the problem of conquest and colonization (as well as decolonization) of a territory.[8]

Civil–Military Relations in France from the Third Republic to the "Nuclear Monarchy"

Relations between political authorities and the army were for a long time governed by a basic, unwritten rule: the army did not get involved in politics. In exchange, the government did not interfere with the running of military affairs except through military budget allocations. This was particularly true from the 1920s on. This unwritten pact in fact granted the military a large influence over foreign and defense policy. Intimidated by the uniform and little versed in military affairs, political leaders, with few exceptions—Georges Clemenceau was one of them—willingly left all decisions regarding defense issues up to military officers. Before the Parliamentary Investigation Commission on the events in France from 1933 to 1945, Albert Sarrault, prime minister at the time the Rhineland was occupied, admitted to the backing down of political authorities, to their "absolute, timidity-bound faith in the military."[9] When German troops invaded the demilitarized zone on the left bank of the Rhine in March 1936, Chief of Staff General Maurice Gamelin was reluctant to take military action and had no trouble imposing his view on Sarrault and Foreign Affairs Minister Pierre-Etienne Flandin, both in favor of a military response. Sarraut and Flandin rallied to the military view with no real attempt to put pressure on the armed forces to request further information or put the issue to debate. From Clemenceau to de Gaulle, virtually no head of government fully exercised his prerogatives "without feeling that any military chief is in some way taboo," as Sarraut admitted.[10]

The Fourth Republic (1946–1958) only partially remedied this weakness with the authorities' shirking of their responsibilities. Defeat obliterated the blind trust that political leaders and the nation had placed in the army. The wars in Indochina and Algeria were waged contrary to the precepts of Carl von Clausewitz's theory, which subordinates the military viewpoint to the political viewpoint that "it is policy that has created war. Policy is the guiding intelligence and war only the instrument, not vice versa." Clausewitz believed that the cabinet and not professional soldiers should determine "the main lines of action" in a war, because only the cabinet has intimate knowledge of the political situation that the military leader, a mere specialist, cannot possess.[11] Heads of governments only demonstrated occasional interest in them, preferring to devote their time to resolving political and financial problems and delegating their powers to national defense ministers without sufficient authority to impose their point of view on the other members of the cabinet.

However, never had statesmen gone so far in abandoning their prerogatives as during the Algerian war. The "military power" that took hold at the end of the Fourth Republic was largely the consequence of political resignation. The army had broad responsibilities, reestablishing order and reconquering the Muslim population by psychological means.[12]

From that point on, disappointed by the political establishment, which had failed in its duty in Indochina and had robbed soldiers of military victory in Suez in 1956, the army began to escape all political control, making successful pacification its personal affair, engaging itself so wholeheartedly in the battle that it became a formidable task for the civilian authorities to regain control of the situation. The principles of obedience and subordination were publicly scoffed at with no reaction from the political authorities. They took a back seat to the commitment the army set for itself—the political reconquest of Algeria.

Discredited and divided, the civilian authorities let things ride. At the first hints of abandonment in May 1958, the army had no qualms about putting pressure on political authorities to keep the French flag flying in Algeria. On May 13, the army openly challenged the political leadership and proclaimed its determination to see de Gaulle, the sole person capable in its eyes of opposing French withdrawal from Algeria, return to power. Unhappy with the turn taken by de Gaulle's policy as of 1960 with his speech on self-determination and contacts made with the FLN, a segment of the army in Algeria decided to take control of Algeria and took the oath that "There is no independent Algeria and there never will be."

The Fifth Republic brought a major turnabout in relations between political authorities and military officers. The political order overrode the military order, thereby confirming the triumph of Clausewitz's theory. The head of State became the de facto commander-in-chief of the armed forces that he always should have been. The generals, with the help of the Algerian affair, had voluntarily encroached on political turf. With de Gaulle and the Fifth Republic, political authorities encroached on the sphere of military command. They assumed responsibility for the main policy guidelines without necessarily seeking the advice of military officers who were relegated to auxiliaries, perhaps not always cooperative ones, but in general subject to political authority.

Generals of the Fifth Republic can still try to manipulate information, at times underestimating it, at other times presenting certain specific options as unfeasible, and some do not deprive themselves of doing so. Nevertheless, in areas where presidents feel they have personal responsibilities, they have not hesitated to acquire the necessary knowledge. The military establishment is confronted with political authorities who are no longer satisfied to listen passively and respectfully to the staff officers. Presidents study dossiers regarding matters for which they feel responsible, demanding further details when information is lacking, and they have not hesitated to refute or dispute the viability of the findings provided. The military leader's word has lost its sacred aura. The army has to convince. It can no longer peremptorily declare what is desirable and feasible. The military no longer intimidates; it is intimidated. What's more, nuclear weapons gave the nation's leader sole power to squeeze the nuclear trigger and consequently that of assuming global responsibilities in questions of both diplomacy and defense as well as in crisis management, whether or not nuclear escalation was involved.[13] France is a "nuclear monarchy."[14]

The Political Weight of the Israeli Generals

What model most closely fits the IDF? Of all the armies in democratic countries, the IDF has one of the greatest potentials for influence. It enjoys extraordinary popularity among the population, not only due to the protracted state of war, but also because it is perceived as the last bastion against destruction of the state and because it represents the "army of the whole nation." This notion, deeply rooted in Israeli minds from the very first decades of the state's existence, has eroded in recent years,[15] but still remains fairly strong.

Generals are respected figures who are destined for promotion to high government positions when they return to civilian life, even if more frequently they are contested by a segment of civil society, thus detracting from their virtually "untouchable" status. Their popularity among the public remains globally higher than many politicians who are often discredited due to mediocrity. The army represents a corps whose members are still perceived as more disinterested, loyal, and devoted than political leaders. A dispute between PM Binyamin Netanyahu and the Chief of the General Staff (CGS) Amnon Lipkin-Shahak, a notable case in 1996,[16] or in 2001 between Defense Minister (DM) Binyamin Ben-Eliezer and the CGS Shaul Mofaz is unlikely to lead to the eviction of the latter.[17] A person of that stature is not dismissed in the midst of a war without taking the risk of initiating a political crisis among public opinion and without opposition leaders seeking to instrumentalize the situation.

In France, the army exists on the fringes of civil society and has not acquired as strong an influence over national politics, and has not managed to impose its values. Its influence on foreign policy is minimal. The armed forces do not aspire to extending their influence beyond strictly military questions, and rarely do generals seek to play a role in the country's general policy. The arms industry has not increased in size as in the United States and especially the former USSR, where the leaders of the military-industrial complex occupied senior positions in the party ranks.

Unlike in the French Fifth Republic, Israeli generals play a major role in public debates and openly express their viewpoint even when it differs from the prime minister's. The chiefs of staff are able to criticize government decisions without being reprimanded. It is difficult to sack a CGS. The position carries considerable political influence regardless of the personal qualities of the incumbent. The army high command often expresses its opinion on subjects that lie outside of its field, such as diplomatic issues, without running the risk of reprimand. In February 2006, Yair Naveh, CGS of the Home Front Command, made derogatory remarks about the king of Jordan's chances for political survival, thus damaging the Israeli government's position, without being severely reprimanded. Dan Halutz, the CGS, merely issued a warning to all generals, asking them to "demonstrate caution and sensitivity." In France's Fifth Republic, this sort of behavior is inconceivable, and the few audacious generals who dared to criticize the government were dismissed.[18] The army is the "big mute." The collapse of the Algiers putsch brought the army to heel, and it now expresses itself cautiously and in closed forums. In France the presidential function has become to a certain degree hallowed. The president is commander-in-chief of the armed forces, and no military leader would dare challenge his authority or openly oppose him.

In Israel, the army has a virtual monopoly on strategic thinking. Any strategic evaluation made by the head of Aman, the Israeli military intelligence, carries considerable weight in the public debate, without this influence being systematic or always decisive. The head of Aman is considered to be the "national evaluator"[19] who publicly defines the nature of the threats facing the state of Israel in the coming years and determines its strategic priorities. His ascendancy over public debate is considerable, despite the huge failure of this department in the Yom Kippur War, when Aman did not properly read the signs of the Egyptian and Syrian armies' impending offensive. Several of these directors have finished their careers as CGS.

In France, apart from a few generals on the fringes of the army high command, there have been no great strategists among the chiefs of staff. The army has left this activity to diplomats at the foreign affairs ministry who have acquired competence on strategic issues recognized even by the army, and benefit from the advice of experts at the Department of Strategic Affairs, headed by a senior civil servant at the defense ministry. The major geostrategy speeches are the prerogative of the president, sometimes the prime minister, or the defense minister. To counterbalance the IDF, no major civilian nexus seems to have emerged to play a role similar to that of the civil authorities in France.

The instruments for counter-expertise in Israel are weaker than in France. Each time a major international crisis arises in which France is involved, as happened during the Gulf War in 1991 and during the Kosovo crisis in 1997, major meetings have brought together senior civil servants and military staff. These forums are usually ad hoc working groups that closely collaborate and then disband when the crisis has passed. Such has not been the case in Israel. Many Israeli authors have lamented the sidelining of the National Security Council created in 1999 under PM Binyamin Netanyahu, prevented by the army from playing its role.[20] It would appear that the prime ministers, too, did not want to see this structure gain too much importance so as to minimize the risk of security leaks and preserve their margin for maneuver. This reticence was not shared by Ehud Olmert, who decided, shortly after becoming prime minister, that the council would no longer be convened in Ramat Hasharon, near Tel-Aviv, but in Jerusalem close to his headquarters—no doubt in order to grant this body increased responsibility. However, this move had no effect on the decision-making process.

The Interdependence between Civil Authorities and the Army

Does this mean that Israeli civil authorities are hostage to the army? Are there safeguards to prevent the military from supplying false information? Ofer Shelah portrays the army as a fairly monolithic corps that presents the government with predetermined positions.[21] The risk of manipulation exists in all democracies, but it should not be exaggerated in Israel's case or in that of France. True, there are generals in Israel, as in France or the United States, who are experts capable of advancing arguments in bad faith, holding back or concealing information, proposing a single option, quashing or supporting options as the case may be, attempting to play on the nerves of inexperienced political leaders in order to secure larger budget allocations, and using even more extensive means to prevent these leaders from making any decision that might run counter to their interests. The system is not always perfectly transparent.

This debate often takes on an emotional quality because whenever the army expresses a need it tends to be considered an act of intolerable pressure. Any request that is granted tends to be seen a concession, a decision "imposed" by the military, a defeat for politics, and an indication of the militarization of society. By nature and by function, the army is necessarily a "pressure group." The existence of interest groups, networks, and alliances that form among the various social groups within the defense ministry to put pressure on political leaders is a characteristic of all developed countries. A vast body of literature in the field of military sociology emphasizes the tendency of the military establishment to protect its sphere of competence from civilian eyes and to preserve its autonomy. Studies also analyze the incapacity of the civil authorities to closely monitor military activity.[22] This does not mean the civil authorities are hostage to the military. There is nothing reprehensible about such pressures and influence in a democracy, as long as they are reined in and framed by political will.

Military corporatism of course exists, but its importance must not be exaggerated. The military may have ideas and sincere convictions about the best way to ensure a country's security. Military staff is capable of understanding the motivations of political authorities and the constraints weighing on them, and can adapt accordingly. They not only haggle over a portion of the budget but also over the very nature of possible conflicts to come. That their function leads them to exaggerate a threat and to request greater means is in the nature of what Samuel Huntington calls "the military mind": since the seriousness of the threat is always difficult to assess, it is better to overestimate than underestimate it.[23] Their interest is to prepare to face a possible crisis in the best of possible conditions, having imagined all possible risks. In the event of failure, they will be the first to be accused. All the armies in the world, democratic or not, strive for a maximization of means.

Not only is the army's possible influence on the civil authorities partly inevitable, but to a certain extent it is not necessarily unhealthy. Not exerting pressure amounts to not doing anything at all, thus condemning the defense system to immobility and eventual obsolescence. A military officer who does not make the armed forces' needs known would be seen as irresponsible. To deny defense experts the right to exert an influence and accept such behavior on behalf of experts in telecommunications, agriculture, or public health is to reject the very idea of a defense force. That there are tensions between political leaders who "try to skimp" and the "spendthrift" military establishment, to use vocabulary de Gaulle might have employed, is only natural.[24] "It might be thought that policy could make demands on war which war could not fulfill; but that hypothesis would challenge the natural and unavoidable assumption that policy knows the instrument it means to use." Clausewitz's axiom remains true.[25]

The interdependency between these two worlds is obvious. Political leaders and military officers form a couple in times of peace as well as in times of crisis. There are no clear frontiers separating the military from the political spheres. De Gaulle himself stated this as self-evident: "What policy can succeed where arms fail? What strategy is valid when the means are lacking to implement it?"[26] The president can short-circuit an ambassador in negotiations. He cannot plan and conduct a war without the help and cooperation of the armed forces chiefs of staff. It is difficult and risky for a president not to listen to objections and trust his own intuition. This interdependency is particularly strong in Israel.

All the accusations leveled at the military refer to the same implicit or explicit postulates and are based on the same negative assumptions: 1) Political authorities are incompetent and unable to impose their viewpoints; 2) Major decisions are made according to a corporatist instead of a strategic rationale, leading to the manufacture of weapons that are as costly as they are useless; and 3) There exist secret networks bound together by the will to preserve their common interests.

Many studies, in particular those of Jerome Slater and Terry Nardin on the notion of the "military-industrial complex," an expression coined by President Eisenhower in his farewell address on January 17, 1961, have shown that these fears were overestimated. I underscore three arguments in their study:

a) The unity and cohesion of the groups targeted is overstated, as is the influence they exercise on foreign policy. The Vietnam War was initiated by politicians and brought to an end under the pressure of public opinion.

b) Advocates of the military-industrial-complex hypothesis ignore the political and ideological factors that brought the United States to its status of a major military power, in particular the ideology of "liberal messianism" that has often legitimated the existence of foreign military intervention.

c) Very often military or industry influence is difficult to prove, and it is hard to find a causal relation between the demands of a given group and the decisions made in an attempt to satisfy these demands.[27]

Civilian Authorities Are Not Hostage to the Army

These same objections can be leveled at the IDF. In all the major decisions to use armed force in Israel, civilian authorities are the dominant actor. Israeli statesmen have never behaved like those of the Third and Fourth Republics. True, their ability to control is not limitless, but they do not have adequately developed means to intrude in the military sphere. The Knesset Foreign Affairs and Security Committee plays a minor role.[28] The military have little respect for MKs, and the equivalent problem can be found in France. University research institutes are hardly involved in the decision-making process and thus find themselves sidelined. Here again, France is in a similar situation. In both countries, the army only acknowledges the legitimate power of the prime minister and, in some cases, the defense minister.

While in France only the head of state, as commander-in-chief of the armed forces, has undisputed authority, the Israeli government is not hostage to its military. The IDF, like the French army, is not a monolithic corps or a restricted caste. It is not unusual to see the various senior military officers speak out on burning topics without coordinating their viewpoints. In major debates on strategy, officials outside the army intervene, such as the director of the General Security Service (GSS) or the Mossad. The prime minister and his defense minister can go into the field and directly question brigade commanders, short-circuiting the military high command. Devoted military personnel are part of politicians' personal staff and are able to diversify their sources of information. As in any democratic army, military officials also think in terms of their career and know that advancement may depend on the loyalty they show toward civilian authorities.

The "Groupthink" syndrome must not be ruled out, either.[29] When an expert is faced with a decision maker having a strong personality, he tends to present options that are likely to be in keeping with the latter's opinions. In asking who is influencing whom, influence is not always one-way, from expert to policymaker. The opposite often exists. Moreover, the army's geostrategic analyses are not always astoundingly innovative. They are often dismally commonplace, or else are a reflection of the prime minister's well-known positions.

None of the great IDF leaders has denied the principle of military subordination to the political sphere. The control of the civil authorities over the army depends more on the importance of political leadership than on the army's conduct. Some prime ministers, such as Levi Eshkol, have had indecisive personalities; others, such as Menachem Begin, who compared his generals to biblical heroes, have shown boundless admiration for the military. When the decision was made to invade Lebanon in 1982, Begin was in fact deceived not by the army but primarily by the defense minister, Ariel Sharon, who gave him inaccurate information about the extent of the IDF's penetration into Lebanese territory. The IDF, of course, did nothing to enlighten Begin. It is difficult to view this case as characterizing the dysfunction of relations between the civilian authorities and the military, in that it was one of the most senior officials in his government who was responsible for deceiving him. Begin's problems stemmed from within the government, not from relations between him and the army.

Most of the time, Israeli prime ministers have imposed their will on decisions involving strategy. None of them has affirmed that "we don't have the right to interfere" in army business, as Sarraut stated with respect to relations between the French government and the army under the Third Republic. None has purely and simply abdicated his powers and handed them over to the military, as was the case in France under the Third and Fourth Republics. In the case of a decision to use armed force, which is the topic at hand, civil authorities have never totally given the military free rein. Many prime ministers had themselves been prominent military officials, including Yitzhak Rabin, Ehud Barak, and Ariel Sharon. Many defense ministers were once generals, such as Moshe Dayan, Binyamin Ben-Eliezer, and Shaul Mofaz. Generals Chaim Bar-Lev, Raphael Eytan, and Mordechai Gur held important government positions. One might think that high-ranking military officers who have gone into politics would behave as army representatives, but they have behaved instead like full-fledged statesmen. Giora Goldberg noted that retired generals who enter senior political posts "are not socially more conservative than political leaders who did not come from the army.... The three prime ministers who made the biggest breakthroughs toward peace and compromise were actually retired generals—Rabin, Barak, and, most recently, Sharon."[30]

The history of Israel is full of examples of disputes between the prime minister or the defense minister and their CGSs that ended to the detriment of the latter. The CGS always ends up submitting. David Ben-Gurion decided to withdraw the army from Sinai in 1956, despite opposition from CGS Moshe Dayan at the time. When Egyptian President Anwar Sadat offered to go to Jerusalem for peace talks with the Israelis, CGS Mordechai Gur and Shlomo Gazit, head of military intelligence, publicly claimed that this visit was merely a "trap." Menachem Begin urged them to get back in line and put a damper on their disagreement. When the Oslo talks started between Israelis and Palestinians, Rabin did not inform the Israeli generals.[31] It was only once the Oslo Accords were signed that the military was reintroduced into the negotiation process with the Palestinians. When CGS Ehud Barak disapproved of these accords, Rabin overrode him, and Barak then loyally implemented Rabin's directives. The decision to withdraw from South Lebanon in 2000 was made by Barak, who had become prime minister. Pressured by troop losses and the erosion of public support symbolized by the "Four Mothers" movement, he acted against the advice of CGS Shaul Mofaz. Despite warnings addressed by the director of Aman military intelligence to Barak at the Camp David summit, claiming that Arafat would not sign the agreement negotiated at this summit, Barak ordered contacts to be pursued with the Palestinian Authority and a unilateral plan for withdrawal to be prepared.[32]

During Ariel Sharon's tenure, CGS Moshe Ya'alon was presented with a fait accompli—Sharon's decision to withdraw from the Gaza Strip. When Ya'alon tried to oppose this policy, he was not only not listened to, but even his request to be kept at his post for another year, as was customary, was turned down by the defense minister, former CGS and future DM Shaul Mofaz. The turn of events created an extremely humiliating precedent for a CGS. In all cases of disagreement, the army submitted and loyally enforced government decisions.

The IDF's influence has never been as all-encompassing as that of the French army. Civilian authorities can reject army proposals or make decisions without first asking for the army's opinion. Moshe Arens, DM from 1983 to 1984 and from 1990 to 1992, stated that he never encountered military resistance that he could not overcome and that the IDF only made decisions when political authorities tried to shirk their responsibilities.[33]

According to Shelah, the decision to eliminate a leader of Hamas, Raad Carmi, in January 2002—thus ending the period of calm that had characterized relations with this movement—was imposed by CGS Mofaz on Sharon, who was powerless to oppose it.[34] This decision, which unleashed bloody reprisals, came after a debate in which DM Ben-Eliezer thought that the disadvantages of this attack would outweigh the advantages. Sharon settled the issue in favor of his CGS, because at the time he shared Mofaz's hard-line positions on the elimination of the main organizers of attacks. That did not make him the military's "puppet," and the proof is that he refused to grant Mofaz permission to eliminate Arafat, despite insistent requests. What is more, in the "targeted killings" policy during the Second Intifada, the GSS became more influential than the IDF. Sharon leaned more on the GSS than on the IDF, which he found "too timorous."[35]

There is frequent mention of the problem of civilian authorities confronted with the "complexity" of military affairs. The "complexity" a civilian leader must face is a real issue, but it is often badly framed. It is less acute in Israel than in other democracies due to the frequent presence of generals in government. Given that the prime minister and defense minister are both civilians, one might conclude that they will never be as knowledgeable as the military experts. From the observation that "the civilian can't know everything," the rather hasty conclusion is drawn that "the civilian knows nothing." Perfectly equal access to knowledge is a problem that obsesses those who cannot manage to put politics in its proper place of responsibility. As with dissuasion of the weak by the strong, the main issue is not parity but sufficiency, and the hardest facet is not acquiring technical knowledge but forging a political viewpoint of the situation. Civilian authorities do not need to "know everything" but must arrive at an overreaching vision that allows them to outline the various constraints: political and economic, diplomatic and military, industrial and technological; and must arbitrate between what is possible and what is desirable, between political risk and strategic advantage. They need to have a clear view of the political and strategic aims to be achieved. The problem in Israel's case is that this has not always been true. For a long time, the incapacity of Israeli statesmen to decide, for instance, on the future of the Occupied Territories often left it up to the military themselves to take public stances of a political nature.[36]

For many analysts, during the Second Intifada the IDF broke free of the political authorities' supervision and imposed its views, stressing the need to win the war and convincing politicians that Arafat did not want to compromise. Yoram Peri writes of "a relative weakening of civilian control over the army" during this period.[37] At the beginning of the Second Intifada, commanders in the field enhanced personal initiatives contrary to the government's policy. Representatives of the Palestinian Authority themselves were stopped at roadblocks that should not have existed in the first place.[38] Checkpoints were set up without a decision by the minister of defense who was also the prime minister. Thus two policies have been implemented: the government's policy that tries to combine security in the Occupied Territories and a decisive breakthrough in the peace negotiations, and the army's policy that is opposed to negotiations, whose primary goal is to restore law and order and its own capacity of dissuasion. For many, these difficulties are proof of the "excessive influence" taken by the IDF in the decision-making process, and the incapacity of the civilian power to impose its rule on the generals. This vision, however, deserves to be qualified.

The problems at that time between Mofaz and Barak's entourage owed more to the incapacity of the prime minister and his prevarications. The Palestinian upheaval put him in a difficult position. He wanted to try to achieve an agreement with Arafat before the February elections, but wanted to show that he would not compromise on security matters. Between these goals, security and peace, Barak, politically weakened and facing a dramatic fall of his popularity, was unable to settle the matter and to find the right balance. As a result he failed to achieve either peace or security. This was a serious failure of political leadership at a crucial moment in the history of the Israeli–Palestinian conflict.

The Lebanese War, or Politics in Search of Legitimacy

Who had the upper hand during the Second Lebanon war in the summer of 2006 that pitted the IDF against Hizbullah—the IDF or the political establishment? This question would never have been raised had not Ehud Olmert and Amir Peretz, the prime minister and the minister of defense, respectively—two men with no appreciable military experience, and who had held office for only two months—acted like amateurs. It has been taken for granted that the two civilian officials were content to merely rubber-stamp the proposals put forward by the general staff without really having studied them, due to their lack of competence and authority.

Two major criticisms were made of them. First, it was stated that they allowed themselves to be manipulated by an army eager to reassert its deterrent capacity, tarnished by the kidnapping of several soldiers,[39] and naïvely confident that large-scale bombing would bring about the desired results. The second criticism, which runs counter to the first, was aimed at their overactive meddling in the conduct of the war. They supposedly kept the IDF from winning by suspending all military operations three days before the UN Security Council's vote on Resolution 1701 that demanded an end to hostilities; and they then gave instructions to relaunch the offensive at a time when it was too late to register a decisive victory, thereby sacrificing "for nothing" the lives of more than thirty soldiers.

The situation, however, was more complex. The politicians did not simply surrender their prerogatives for the benefit of the army. First of all, it was they who decided that Israel would not send in ground troops in the initial stage so as to avoid getting trapped once again in the Lebanese quicksand. Everyone had in mind that the war undertaken in 1982 in order to evict the PLO from Lebanon and assist Bashir Gemayel in establishing a friendly government had resulted in Hizbullah's rise to power and the loss of several hundred Israeli soldiers during the occupation of South Lebanon—an occupation that was to last for eighteen years. Although the PLO was evicted from Beirut, the war was the occasion for Hizbullah to assert itself as a leading military and political force, and one that was hostile to Israel.

The war cabinet set up by Ehud Olmert also demanded and obtained that the military commanders submit all their plans for approval in order to prevent (because of the shadow cast by the First Lebanon War) the army from launching an offensive without first informing the political authorities. When Olmert decided in mid-August 2006 that military operations were to be suspended in order to leave the UN Security Council time to work out a cease-fire agreement, the army, reticent but disciplined, obeyed instructions. Once again, Olmert overrode the advice of several leading members of the general staff and decided to exploit the situation on the ground by renewing the offensive before the cease-fire went into effect.[40] Because there was tremendous pressure from so many generals to do this, it is very doubtful that it can be regarded as the politicians' own decision. The head of the government hoped to reach the Litani River (considered for security reasons as the frontier behind which Hizbullah was to be rolled back), yet there remained little time for the army to fulfill its mission. The offensive was launched in the worst imaginable conditions for the IDF; it lost thirty soldiers in three days without ever succeeding in controlling the area between the Israeli–Lebanese border and the Litani. The prime minister was subsequently taken to task for having given the order for this needlessly dangerous mission. Throughout the conflict, political authorities wielded considerable influence over the course of operations, even if the way the war was waged was far from successful. Contrary to what has been affirmed, the army was not left entirely free to make its own decisions. It is the government and the army together that (mis)handled the war.

It is nonetheless true that there was no open debate before the decision to bomb South Lebanon was taken. The government decided in record time on the strength of the proposals presented by CGS Dan Halutz, who was confident that he could rid Israel of the Hizbullah menace and recover the abducted soldiers by "setting Lebanon back twenty years," as he put it. Halutz's plan was all the more attractive to the politicians in that he counted on bombing raids alone and minimal engagement of ground troops. The problem was that the prime minister and the minister of defense made no serious attempt to evaluate the IDF's capacity to attain these objectives. At no time did the political authorities discuss the consequences that such a war would have on the Israeli population in the north, and they never examined whether the population would be adequately protected from Katyusha rockets fired by Hizbullah. No alternative plan to the air attacks was ever considered. To conclude that this haste can serve as proof of the power of the army vis-à-vis the government is an oversimplification that underestimates the political considerations involved in the decision.

Prime ministers have to take into account their personal image in the public's opinion, especially in a political system that does not allow them to get strong support in the Knesset. The opposition always tries to blame the prime minister "for failing to protect Israel"; that is what the right-wing parties usually do when they are in the opposition. Neither Olmert nor Peretz wanted to take the risk of being accused by the Right of "equivocating when it came to the lives of soldiers or the country's security."

Prestigious generals such as Rabin, Barak, or Sharon had no need to prove their courage or determination when the country was in grave danger. This was not the case for civilians such as Olmert and Peretz. Whether justified or not, in Israel political legitimacy is most often acquired on the battlefield (or by demonstrating exceptional leadership qualities such as those of Ben-Gurion). A reputation as a fearless combatant is a crucial political asset. Israelis have more confidence in men who have demonstrated their bravery on the front lines, and even voters on the left, who say they are in favor of negotiations with the Palestinians, have more trust—when it comes to bringing negotiations to a successful conclusion—in a general with a glorious military background than they do in a civilian. Thus it is that a military leader has more latitude to make concessions, to postpone entry into war, or even to reject such an option. Rabin signed the Oslo Accords despite the opposition of many generals. Sharon decided upon the withdrawal from Gaza despite the hostility of the settlers. Between the years 2000 and 2006, neither Barak nor Sharon agreed to launch a concerted attack against Hizbullah, despite the fact that many in the military pressed them to do so. Yet no one accused these leaders of being "soft."

As for Olmert and Peretz, they had no glorious military exploits to enhance their image in the eyes of their electors. Neither of them could run the risk of being seen as indecisive. They intended to profit from the occasion to appear as genuine war leaders whose determined stance would serve to restore the dissuasive capacity of the army and bring the soldiers home (Shimon Peres acted in a similar manner in 1996 when he unleashed the Grapes of Wrath operation to stop Hizbullah from firing Katyushas into northern Israel). They were won over by the political advantages they counted on earning in the aftermath of the war. The army held out the illusion of an easy victory at a low cost. They lacked political perspicacity, but it is not their weakness vis-à-vis the army that is the reason.

Conclusion

The model of relations between political authority and the army in Israel is without doubt closer to the model of civil–military relations under the Fifth Republic than under the Third and Fourth Republics in France. In both cases, the primacy of civilian power is not called into question. The great freedom of expression used by Israeli generals in no way detracts from the authority of the civilian government to make final decisions. These exchanges respect the legal framework of democracy. All strategic decisions about the use of armed force are made by the government, and in particular by the prime minister. However, there is far from total symbiosis between the two models.

The main difference is that the IDF is invested with the crushing responsibility of ensuring the country's survival. Public opinion finds it normal for generals to speak their minds in public. This situation is not without its disadvantages. It is unhealthy for a general from Aman to define the country's strategic priorities in public or to state how to interpret a threat, as this general, however respectable he may be, does not possess all the facts about domestic and international politics to intervene in such an overreaching and important subject for a nation's future. An error on his part could have serious consequences, as happened during the Yom Kippur war. It is a job that comes under the responsibility of the political authorities.[41] The solution that consists of assigning more civilian experts to key decision-making organizations is certainly well-founded, but it does not guarantee the adoption of policies more conducive to seeking political solutions with the Palestinians. The terms in which civilians who occupy high-level posts in the state hierarchy conceive of strategy are not that different from those of the military.[42] Moreover, the history of Israel—and also that of the United

States and France—provides ample proof of the fact that civilians are not necessarily "doves" and the military systematically "hawks."

The second disadvantage of the Israeli decision-making process is the tendency statesmen have of not wanting to clearly define major political objectives, either because the country is divided over the large questions regarding the future of the Palestinian Territories, or because they prefer not to take risky decisions that might fail. This indecisiveness and the refusal to take decisions regarding subjects as crucial as the future of the Occupied Territories has inevitably produced a situation in which the army, which is held responsible for the maintenance of order, takes initiatives that have far-reaching political consequences (relations with the Palestinian population and the settlers, among others).

The status of the military is less prestigious in France than in Israel, but few military personnel complain about this state of affairs. This situation has two advantages. The first is that in the event that a strategic option fails, it is not the military that will pay the price. Strategy, due to the status of France as a nuclear power, is defined by the head of state. The advantage is that the army's declining influence has paradoxically brought about an increase in the population's sympathy for the armed forces and considerably reduced the prevailing antimilitarism of the past. However, Israel has in the past several years been experiencing protest movements among civilian society: soldiers' mothers, Israeli soldier protest associations, human rights NGOs, and so on. The IDF in a way is suffering the consequences of its widespread influence and the often excessive use of violence in the Occupied Territories.

Notes

1. Among the main authors are Dan Horowitz, "The Israeli Defense Forces: A Civilianized Military in a Partially Militarized Society," in Roman Kolkowitz and Andrzej Korbonski, *Soldiers, Peasants, and Bureaucrats* (Boston, 1982), 77–106; Moshe Lissak, "Paradoxes of the Israeli Civil-Military Relations," *Journal of Strategic Studies* 6 (1983), 6–11; Yoram Peri, *Between Battles and Ballots: Israeli Military in Politics* (Cambridge, 1983); Yehuda Ben Meir, *Civil-Military Relations in Israel* (New York, 1995); Uri Ben-Eliezer, "Civil-Military Relations Paradigm: The Inverse Relation between Militarism and Praetorianism through the Example of Israel," *Comparative Political Studies* 30.3 (1997): 356–74; Stuart Cohen, "Changing Civil-Military Relations in Israel: Towards an Over-subordinate IDF," *Ma'rachot* 403–404 (2005): 8–21 [Hebrew]; Baruch Kimmerling, "Patterns of Militarism in Israel," *Archives Euro-*

péenes de sociologie 34.2 (1993): 196–223; Daniel Maman, Eyal Ben-Ari, and Zeev Rozenhek, *Military, State and Society in Israel* (New Brunswick, N.J., and London, 2001).

2. Zeev Maoz quoted by Cohen, "Changing Civil-Military Relations in Israel," 3.

3. Kimmerling, "Patterns of Military in Israel," 196–223.

4. Ofer Shelah, *The Israeli Army: A Radical Proposal* (Tel-Aviv, 2003) [Hebrew].

5. Uri Ben-Eliezer, "Is a Military Coup Possible in Israel? Israel and French-Algeria in Comparative Historical-Sociological Perspective," *Theory and Society* 27 (1998): 311–49, esp. 312.

6. Cohen, "Changing Civil-Military Relations in Israel," 8–21; Yoram Peri, "The Political-Military Complex: The IDF's Influence over Policy toward the Palestinians since 1987," *Israel Affairs* 11.2 (2005): 324–44.

7. This study is based on personal research conducted in France over many years from interviews with civil and military leaders, which has resulted in a number of publications, including Samy Cohen, "France, Civil-Military Relations and Nuclear Weapons," *Security Studies* 4.1 (1994): 153–79; *La défaite des généraux: le pouvoir politique et l'armée sous la Vᵉ république* (Paris, 1994).

8. Ian Lustick, *Unsettled States, Disputed Lands: Britain and Ireland, France and Algeria, Israel and the West Bank–Gaza* (Ithaca, N.Y., 1993).

9. "Les événements survenus en France de 1933 à 1945: Témoignages et documents recueillis par la Commission d'enquête parlementaire," *PUF* 3 (1947): 671. Quoted by Jean Doise et Maurice Vaïsse in *Politique étrangère de la France: Diplomatie et outil militaire—1871–1991* (Paris, 1992).

10. Ibid., 671.

11. Carl von Clausewitz, *On War* (New York, 1993), 733–34.

12. Raoul Girardet, *La crise militaire française—1945–1962: Aspects sociologiques et idéologiques,* Cahiers de la Fondation nationale des sciences politiques, 123 (Paris, 1964), 188.

13. The subordination of the army to the civilian power was a result of the putsch attempt in Algiers, but the nuclear armaments gave a supplementary reason for de Gaulle to reinforce his legitimacy.

14. Samy Cohen, *La monarchie nucléaire: Les coulisses de la politique étrangère sous la Vᵉ République* (Paris, 1986).

15. Yagil Levy, *The Other Army of Israel: Materialist Militarism in Israel* (Tel-Aviv, 2003) [Hebrew].

16. Binyamin Netanyahu had criticized the army, which was at this stage in favor of applying the Oslo Accords, for lacking firmness in dealings with both Hizbullah and the Palestinians. See Yoram Peri, *Generals in the Cabinet Room: How the Military Shapes Israeli Policy* (Washington, D.C., 2006), 77.

17. Chiefs of staff are not necessarily reappointed for the customary supplementary year.

18. Jean Guisnel, *Les généraux: Enquête sur le pouvoir militaire en France* (Paris, 1990).

19. Shelah, *The Israeli Army,* 69.

20. Ibid., 77–79; Aviezer Yaari, *Civil Control of the IDF* (Tel-Aviv, 2004), 72 [Hebrew].

21. Shelah, *The Israeli Army,* 70.

22. Among others: Samuel P. Huntington, *The Soldier and the State: The Theory and Politics of Civil-Military Relations* (Cambridge, Mass., 1957); Amos Perlmutter, *The Military and Politics in Modern Times* (New Haven, Conn., 1977); Samuel Finer, *The Man on Horseback: The Role of the Military in Politics* (Boulder, Colo., 1988); Peter D. Feaver, "The Civil-Military Problematique: Huntington, Janowitz, and the Question of Civilian Control," *Armed Forces & Society* 23.2 (1996): 149–78.

23. Huntington, *The Soldier and the State,* chap. 3.

24. Charles de Gaulle, *Le fil de l'épée* (Paris, 1973), 135.

25. Von Clausewitz, *On War,* 734.

26. De Gaulle, *Le fil de l'épée,* 126.

27. Jerome Slater and Terry Nardin, "The Concept of the Military-industrial Complex," in Steven Rosen (ed.), *Testing the Theory of the Military-industrial Complex* (Lexington, Mass., 1973).

28. Aviezer Yaari, *Civil Control of the IDF* (Tel-Aviv, 2004), 72 [Hebrew].

29. Irving Janis, *Victims of Groupthink: A Psychological Study of Foreign Policy Decisions and Fiascoes* (Boston, 1972).

30. Giora Goldberg, "The Growing Militarization of the Israeli Political System," *Israel Affairs* 12.3 (2006): 365–75.

31. Peri, "The Political-Military Complex," 329.

32. Ibid., 333.

33. Shelah, *The Israeli Army,* 67.

34. Ibid., 72.

35. Samy Cohen, "The Targeted Killings during the Second Intifada: A Double-Edged Weapon," *Critique Internationale* 41 (2008): 61–80.

36. Shelah, *The Israeli Army,* 67.

37. Peri, "The Political-Military Complex," 342.

38. Amos Harel and Avi Isacharoff, *La septième guerre d'Israël: comment nous avons gagné la guerre contre les Palestiniens et pourquoi nous l'avons perdue* (Paris, 2005), 115.

39. On July 25, 2006, Corporal Gilad Shalit was captured by Palestinian combatants on Israeli territory close to the Gaza Strip. On July 12, Hizbullah kidnapped two soldiers and killed several others, which unleashed the "Second Lebanon War."

40. *Ha'aretz,* September 7, 2006.

41. Peri, *Generals in the Cabinet Room,* 57.

42. Yagil Levy, "A Force to Be Reckoned with," *Ha'aretz,* August 25, 2006.

ELEVEN

The Making of Israel's
Political–Security Culture

AMIR BAR-OR

Complexity is the key feature of civil–military relations in Israel. Many scholars have tried, and will probably continue to try, to comprehend the exact nature of these relations. Given the fact that security still is at the top of the agenda in Israel, several interesting studies have of late joined the list of attempts at fathoming the state's civil–military relations. Among these, one can mention the recent works by Gabriel Sheffer and Oren Barak that suggest analyzing Israel's pattern of civil–military relations in terms of a "security network."[1] Quite differently, Stuart Cohen's work proposes examining a phenomenon that he terms the "inverted turnabout," which occurs in the relationship between the political and military levels.[2] Yoram Peri's monograph deals with the political–military partnership in Israel during the last two decades.[3]

This chapter proposes another approach, analyzing the relationship between Israel's political and military systems in terms of a *political-security culture.* Moshe Lissak first introduced the term "security–political culture" in his discussion of the convergence points between the Israeli Defense Forces (IDF) and Israeli society in the early 1990s.[4] After much consideration, however, I have decided to reverse the order of the words in Lissak's term and to explore the broader ramifications of political-security culture on the supremacy of the political leadership led by David Ben-Gurion, over the military power that the Yishuv developed in the critical period of its evolution to a state.[5]

The starting point for this examination is the adaptation of the term *national security system* coined by Martin Edmonds[6] in reference to the security system of the Yishuv. This system includes two subsystems—one political and the other military. It may seem exaggerated to use the term *political system* in this context since the Yishuv was based on voluntary affiliation, and to view its quasi-military elements, which were still in their initial stages of development, as a "military system." Yet, the scope of the activity of these bodies and the pivotal role that they played in the Yishuv allow us to regard them as its political and military subsystems. Although these subsystems' objectives were, essentially, similar, we may assume that there were differences in their approach to attaining them. There may also have been conflicts related to the political–strategic and military–operational spheres regarding agreed-upon policies, policy-making procedures, and policy implementation.

The proposed course for understanding these phenomena lies, then, in the term political–security culture, which enables us to examine the connection between the terms *political culture* and *security culture.* While the normative rules are generalized worldviews, they are primarily rules and customs "that arrange the mutual relationships between them and the political elites, and between them and ordinary people; [in other words] organizational rules try to apply these rules in practice."[7] It was suggested that the political culture of the Yishuv resembled that of a revolutionary movement that tended to expand its politics and territorial borders and integrate itself into almost every aspect of life.[8] In the case of the Yishuv, politics were imposed upon the developing society, a process that ran counter to the natural development in which the political system emerges from within society. Thus, "the Israeli political culture was shaped by political behavior more than by [general] cultural and social customs."[9]

Regarding the security factor in the political–security culture, the literature recognizes two relevant concepts: military culture and strategic culture. The term *military culture* refers to the army's organizational culture where the army is a unique social institution. This term is common in the literature, and contains many features and gradations. According to Harvey Sicherman,[10] who headed a research project on "The Future of the American Military Culture," in the second half of the 1990s the U.S. army faced a challenge not only to its military culture but also to the American way of war. This was the result of changes that were taking place in that army (such as the integration of minorities, women, and gays) and certain negative phenomena that had been brought to light regarding the conduct of officers.

According to Don M. Snider, the term *military culture* refers to the structure of the military organization and is based on commonly accepted assumptions, norms, values, customs, and traditions that over time have collectively created common expectations among members of the organization. Snider states that the military culture includes positions and behavior patterns that are the cement that transforms an organization into a special source of identity and experience. A stable culture exists when the aggregate of norms and expectations that are shaped by the leadership's inspiration have an effect on the entire organization. Snider holds that a functional approach to this term is needed in a situation where the elements of the military culture stem from the definition of the goal and from the tasks that require society to maintain a modern army. The uniqueness of the "military culture" lies, then, in the fact that these elements emerge from the attempt to deal with the uncertainty of war, the need to enforce fighting patterns based on the nature of society, and the supervision of their results. These factors furnish an explanation and meaning for war.[11]

John Hillen raises additional questions regarding the functioning of the military culture. These relate to the army's main tasks, its legitimacy, and the way military culture reflects the general culture of the society that it serves. Hillen mentions the gap between society and the army, and their respective cultures, and the need to reduce the gap lest it influence the way the army protects society.[12]

Reuven Pedatzur first employed the term *security culture* in the Israeli context. According to Pedatzur, Israel's security culture (*beetachonism,* or security-ism) is an expansion of Israeli culture that was shaped in the late 1940s and early 1950s. Pedatzur felt it necessary to trace the origins of this "security culture" because of its continuing influence on the way Israel deals with its national security. Based on his analysis of the term *security culture,* he found it apt to focus not only on organizational arrangements or a general understanding of the political game, but on the system of norms that characterizes a variety of areas in Israeli society. Thus, he deals not only with the practical features of Israeli security thinking, as developed under Ben-Gurion's inspiration, but also distinguishes between norms, rules of the game, and behavior patterns in Israel's security culture.[13]

Regarding the impact of Israel's political culture on civil–military relations, Baruch Kimmerling posited that one of its main roots was the all-inclusive nature of the Arab–Israeli conflict on the Yishuv. Under these circumstances, "The military force—the army—was reinforced and enhanced as an institution and ethos, and became the center of the Jewish-Israeli cultural experience to the point where a special militaristic culture developed."[14]

Another view of the army's overarching influence on Israeli political culture is offered by Ephraim Ya'ar and Ze'ev Shavit, who claim that the supremacy of political culture in the Yishuv and in Israeli society, and its ability to enforce its authority on the military elite are some of the trademarks of the political culture in the Yishuv and Israeli society (in addition to the military elite's democratic features).[15]

For the purpose of this chapter, the term *political–security culture* refers to the interaction between the political and military systems in shaping a state or a society's security policy. The political–security culture comprises security thinking, institutional and organizational development for policy implementation, working arrangements between the political and military elites, and political supremacy patterns over the military. The greater the number of contact points between the political and military cultures, the greater the need becomes for closer coordination and cooperation. The political–security culture is, in other words, a dynamic environment that changes in conjunction with political, social, economic, security, and technological developments, and in conjunction with the leadership's influence on its operations.

The use of the term *political–security culture* in this chapter is based on the attempt by Gabriel Almond and his colleagues to transform the term *political culture* into an up-to-date operative term by differentiating between three hierarchical levels of analysis: a) the system level, b) the process level, and c) the policy level.[16] To elucidate the complex nature of the political–security culture, I employ this hierarchical structure in the following manner:

> A. *The System Level:* The national security system assesses the political implications emanating from security challenges to the political system

(the state's leadership) and security implications on the military system (the high command). The national security system's ability to deal with these challenges is examined according to its basic assumptions regarding the political world and its norms, beliefs, biases, and values, and according to the role of military power, the threat of its use, and the need to supervise it. In addition, these roles are influenced by historical circumstances and the development of customs, symbols, and behavioral norms at the strategic level;

B. *The Process Level:* This includes expectations, the degree of agreement in the national security system's performance, and the degree of identification with the political and military institutions' functioning. It specifically deals with the balance between security and power social values, the delegation of authority, and secondary systems' areas of responsibility; patterns of decision making and the implementation of mechanisms for conflict resolution; and the organization of relations between the political and military elites.

C. *The Policy Level:* This level includes the national-security leadership's expectations for a policy that provides society with security. It sets forth a political agenda that defines problems and priorities. The issues that are dealt with at this level include defining a war's political goals prior to defining the army's goals; analyzing the army's fighting patterns; building up the military force according to the war's aims and society's resources; applying worldviews, rules of engagement, and patterns of conduct that coordinate relations between the political and military echelons; and controlling the war's results and explaining their ramifications.

An Analysis of Israel's Political–Security Culture

My analysis of Israel's political–security culture in the pre-state period is based on the need to elucidate the role of the security system of the Yishuv, the development of the political institutions' supervisory patterns over the Hagana,[17] and the Hagana's command patterns in the transition from Yishuv to state. Examination of the development of mutual relations between these two elements of the Yishuv's security system during its growth will concentrate on the institutional-organizational, behavioral, and developmental aspects of the two subsystems and their interrelationship, and will attempt to map their borderlines. A demarcation of the two subsystems is vital to a definition of relations in political power and the mechanisms that had to be implemented. Demarcation of the two subsystems also outlines areas of autonomy according to the dynamic circumstances that influenced the two subsystems in their development and the shaping of their mutual relations.

The interrelationship between the political and the military subsystems influenced numerous issues in the junctures between the political and military cultures. In the case of the Yishuv, these junctures were the result of the security perception that developed at the Hagana's senior command level, and the Hagana's political need to operate a military force in an ongoing struggle. They were transitional processes that resulted from changes in the security challenge, and the political system's commitment to determine a formula for balancing diverse values alongside the Yishuv's social needs. This analysis will be based, as stated, on the structure that Almond proposed for the term *political culture*.

ANALYSIS OF THE SYSTEM LEVEL

A study of the Yishuv's structure requires an analysis of patterns of political supervision over the military as they crystallized from the founding of the Hagana in 1920 to the establishment of the IDF in May 1948. The roots of the phenomenon under discussion can be found in Jewish history and the development of the Zionist movement. The nature of political supervision over the Hagana calls for an understanding of the Hagana's place in the history of the Yishuv. Two concepts were at play. The first perceived the Hagana as an organization that was more civilian than military and that was suited solely to the tasks of a particular period. The second concept viewed the Hagana as the rightful heir and reincarnation of an ancient Jewish tradition. In other words, it is necessary to distinguish between the Hagana as a civilian body that assumed the task of defending the Yishuv and as a military body based on the tradition of military force in Jewish history. The Hagana was not a purely military organization but a civilian defense organization that gradually developed its military nature, a process that culminated in Israel's War of Independence.

These two approaches stemmed from different explanations about the Zionist movement's essence in Jewish history. From its inception, Zionism emerged as a pluralistic, ideological movement based on accord and compromise that would enable it to incorporate disparate "ideological trends and opposing political groups: believers and nonbelievers, the politically oriented and pragmatists, socialists and bourgeoisie, liberals, and territorialists."[18] Zionism's various contours and dispositions offered a solution to the Jewish people's survival as a national group in a sovereign state that would be established in Eretz Israel (the Land of Israel) sometime in the future. The Jewish dilemma in the Diaspora would be resolved by the nation's return to Eretz Israel and the renewal of national life in the ancient homeland. The establishment of a political framework, even without sovereignty in the beginning, would serve as a vehicle for alleviating the anomalies of Diaspora life that had created the stigma of enervation. This negative image impaired the Jewish communities' ability to defend themselves from physical violence and struggle for their vital interests.[19] Sovereignty would not only be an answer to Diaspora life, but would also be "the expression of a new [national] feeling . . . [that] restored honor to a people who had suffered humiliation for such a long time."[20]

A significant trend in Zionism "regarded sovereignty and the use of force as necessities resulting from the historical circumstances of the Jewish people in the modern world. Sovereignty was perceived primarily as a basic means of defending the Jews' honor, freedom, and security in the wake of the violence perpetrated against them in their countries of domicile."[21] Sovereignty, then, was the answer to the Zionist movement's debate over the use of force as opposed to traditional Jewish aversion to it.[22] Thus, Zionist ideology demanded for the most part the establishment of a government that would incorporate "a Jewish public reality that maintained itself independently and subsisted on Jewish power and the Jewish people's wielding of it."[23] Zionist ideology offered the Jewish people the tools for regaining Jewish sovereignty.

The need to create conditions for a free and independent existence brought the Zionist enterprise into the struggle for a Jewish state, a struggle that would serve as the locus of Jewish power: "Jewish power is rooted in the soil and labor."[24] These two basic factors would be the future challenges for testing the Yishuv and the Jewish people in the Diaspora.

Ben-Gurion asserted that the Zionist Movement was engaged in national rejuvenation under special circumstances. The Jewish people were not only dealing with its historic fate, but were in an all-out revolt against it. National renewal meant seizing control of Jewish destiny and surmounting numerous debilitating manifestations of Diaspora life: "material, political, spiritual, moral, and intellectual dependency that resulted from living in an alien environment, minority status, lack of homeland, and separation from natural resources such as soil, labor, and economic creativity." Overcoming this dependency and taking control of Jewish fate implied "independence, dissatisfaction with our lifestyle in the Diaspora . . . and exercising our own strength to create the required conditions for a free and independent existence."[25]

Furthermore, the Zionist revolution meant Jewish independence not only in the political, economic, and spiritual sense, but also "independence of the heart, independence of feeling, independence of will . . . independence in daily life, in the executive administration, in foreign affairs, and in the economy. . . . [All this] is taking place and increasing through the conquest of labor, land, language, and culture, [and by the building of] organizational and security tools, a national framework, conditions for creating independent existence, and finally—through the conquest of sovereign independence." The Jewish revolution against historic fate was by its nature "a lengthy, ongoing, perpetual revolution [that will continue] for generations; [it] was not achieved by seizing the government but by the gradual, persistent creation of power; . . . by amassing strength through the conquest of labor, land, culture, organization, unity, and a public framework and [governing] tools; by cumulating strength that endeavors continuously and with concentrated determination to change the fate of the nation."[26]

According to Ben-Gurion, amassing Jewish power in Eretz Israel was a long and complicated process for effecting the desired change in the nation's habits and behavior patterns. The Jewish people's dream of turning the Yishuv into a power center would put an end to the frailty inherent in Diaspora life. This transformation also expressed the Jewish people's ability to gain control over the key events in their lives for the first time in their renewed history by turning Eretz Israel into the central political power of the Zionist movement.[27]

This was true with regard to the exercise of political power for both internal and external purposes. Like the Zionist movement, the Jewish people lacked binding mechanisms. As long as the nation remained in the Diaspora, the creation of power mechanisms for internal and external needs was perceived as the exclusive means for dealing with Jewish weakness. A conceptual change was needed for an appreciation of the inherent ethical value in strength and power. This was where the moral content came in for the goals that strength and power intended to serve.[28] When the bulk of Zionist activity was transferred to Eretz Israel, three basic changes took place in the view of power: there was a greater demand for political and military power, an improvement in the ability to create it, and a pressing need for control over it.

The Arab–Jewish conflict that intensified in the 1930s and 1940s forced Jewish national institutions to secure their authority: "Security matters in this period were the focus of internal struggles in the Yishuv around which debates raged over authority and its dissolution."[29] The problem of civilian supervision over the Hagana can best be understood by examining the organization's role as the Zionist movement's military instrument. Therefore, we shall look at the views, activity, and rhetoric of leading politicians and Hagana figures.

The starting point for this discussion is the Zionist Movement's goal to liberate and revitalize the Jewish people through the conquest of Eretz Israel. According to Moshe Sneh, head of the Hagana's headquarters (1941–1945), this conquest differed from other forms of historical conquests because it avoided the expropriation of another nation's property. "The Zionist conquest . . . has come to create something *ex nihilo* . . . it does not [intend to] dispossess . . . [or] trespass. . . . It is a conquest that may be likened to a genesis. Therefore the Zionist conquest [treads] the path of peace . . . [and] has no need of a military tool."

Rhetoric aside, the reality of the Arab opposition to the return of the Jews to Palestine had to be taken into account. "This opposition has to be overcome; the conquest must be defended peacefully; [Arab] opposition has to be broken without resorting to force; force will have to be used to defend a conquest that does not employ force. From its beginning . . . [the] Zionist conquest has been accompanied by military force. To understand the essence of defense, of the military tool, we must recognize that Zionism cannot be realized by military action . . . but through the creation of Jewish content in Eretz Israel. This must not be achieved by a military act. Zionism . . . can be destroyed by a successful military act that demolishes the Zionist project. . . . This awareness must be internalized. . . . Therefore, the military tool is necessary in order to defend [against] any attempt to destroy the Zionist realization. This [threat] determines the nature of the military tool; it is a defensive tool, and this explains why . . . the organization is called . . . the Hagana [Defense]."[30]

Eliyahu Golomb, one of the founders and first commanders of the Hagana, realized that it had become a Jewish political force that met the challenge of the rival Arab political force seeking to destroy Jewish rights in Eretz Israel. The transformation of the Hagana into a political force called for an understanding of its role and the limitations of its power. The intemperate use of force "for terrorizing the Arabs will cause this power to cease fighting for our rights. There is no place in this country for a Jewish force . . . that enslaves and exploits others. This is not the path to Zionist fulfillment; rather, mass immigration and large-scale settlement are. The Hagana is needed to expedite this process and restrain those who want to obstruct it . . . [and] halt immigration by creating havoc. This is why a Jewish force has been established. Our task is not the conquest of the country [and the expulsion of its Arab] inhabitants with the force we have created . . . [but] the staunch defense [of the country] when necessary. . . . The defense of freedom of settlement, immigration, and development—this is the force's role. It is a force that defends the Jewish people's [right] to come to their country and establish a foothold freely and independently."[31]

Moshe Sharett, who headed the Jewish Agency's Political Department and afterward was Israel's first foreign minister and second prime minister, focused on the political perspective, noting that the expansion of the Yishuv had precipitated a historical clash between the Zionist movement and the Arab Nationalist movement. Under these conditions, "security implied confronting the Arabs' political movement. . . . And with the increase in major violent clashes between us and the [Mandatory] government, the Hagana increasingly assumed a preeminently political nature, since this became a political issue it was a question of political authority, political leadership, and the political leadership of the Jewish people . . . [that] took internal political responsibility for defense. [When] it assumed control of the political authority to direct the Hagana politically, the Yishuv had to face . . . a new test of loyalty . . . and unity. . . . The vast majority of responsible [people] in the

Yishuv overcame their differences . . . and established a country-wide organization that was united and solidified in settlement defense, and accepted the burden of political discipline [issuing] from the national leadership."[32]

Awareness of the importance of authority was not enough; there was also a practical need for it since, as Sharett noted, "the [Hagana] organization is . . . a tool in the hands of the Zionist leadership for the defense of Zionist fulfillment. In other words, the tool must be placed in the hands of civilian leaders so that they can direct [Zionist] fulfillment. If [the Hagana] is to serve the realization [of Zionism] then it has to be in the hands of those who direct the process. . . . The military comes under the authority of the nation in every country. In the defense of the Yishuv—the [Hagana] comes under the command of the World Zionist Organization together with the Yishuv's institutions. . . . National authority is expressed in three areas: 1) the appointment of the head of the High Command and its staff officers . . . 2) directing . . . the [High Command's] operations . . . 3) supervising the High Command . . . its operations and leadership."[33]

Yaacov Dori, the first chief of staff of the Hagana from 1939 until 1946, and later of the IDF, extended the discussion on authority in the military context, focusing on the importance of the underground military organization. He noted as follows: "Supervision and criticism are, in effect, impossible under conditions and circumstances when deviations and unwanted developments are possible. . . . When groups exploit the conditions for goals . . . other than those determined by the highest authority . . . the conditions in an underground are a breeding place for aberrations and malfeasance, and herein lies the importance of a single, united, trusted, stable authority that derives its power from the nation."[34]

ANALYSIS OF THE PROCESS LEVEL

The role of military power in "Zionist fulfillment" was closely connected to the political action, indicating the sensitivity and complexity of the political process in creating the requisite balance between security and social values. While military power played a central role in the attainment of Zionist goals, it was understood that Zionism would not be realized by the Hagana alone, but by creating facts on the ground (according to the "practical Zionists") and political achievements (according to the "political Zionists"). Zionist goals would not be fulfilled if one of these three elements was absent, but only through the correct combination in the right proportion.

For the most sensitive tasks, the political leadership of the Yishuv had to establish national authority on two levels: first, on the external level, requiring political discipline and responsibility on the part of all the political bodies in order to present a united front; second, on the internal level, necessitating strict supervision of the Hagana and the neutralization of the influences of the other paramilitary organizations (the so-called "dissidents") that broke away from the Yishuv's authority.

For the purpose of our discussion, the second level is more important because it relates to civilian supervision over the military. The realization of Zionist goals demanded mechanisms for political operation. However, the system created by the Yishuv and Zionist movement lacked the strength to be implemented. Enforcement was based on "political volunteerism, that is, the willing acceptance of the majority's authority [that became] the criterion for the democratic character of the Zionist political parties which were part of the World Zionist Organization and the Yishuv's institutions."[35] The test came with the election of a political leadership in a broad public vote. The public, which was aware of its responsibility to participate in the election process, readily accepted the national leadership. The preservation of democratic rules of the game was the legitimate source of power that granted the political leadership wide authority for its decisions, but *not* absolute control over all the areas of life for which it was presumably responsible. In security matters, control over military forces was the main criterion for the national leadership's authority. The fact that it managed to gain control over the military High Command is further evidence of the Yishuv's democratic nature.

The Hagana's deference to political authority was an area in which democratic rules of the game had to be strictly maintained. Israel Galili, the last commander of the Hagana, attributed this to the need for a unified high command "based on democracy. . . . Thus, when an order was issued, after much deliberation with the [civilian] institutions . . . a [*Hagana*] member had to obey the order even if it went against his views."[36] In this way the High Command came under the national authority's jurisdiction and acted in its name and authority as the representative of the entire government."[37]

All-inclusiveness was one of the Hagana's basic principles since its inception. Sneh attributed enormous weight to the fact that the Hagana was linked to the entire nation:

> It cannot be both dependent and under the jurisdiction of [only] part of the nation, [it has to come] under the authority of the entire nation. If it were bound to the authority of part [of the nation], or a [particular] political party, then why should it be only this party and not another? One could say that the number of military organizations equals the number of political parties. After all, political parties exist for a reason; they exist because they have certain goals, diverse opinions. . . . When the organization comes under a single authority—then it is a concentration of power; if it is divided, then it is nothing externally. . . . Internal clashes can also lead to civil war. Therefore only one authority is permitted—that of the entire group.

The Hagana's all-inclusiveness was realized not only because it was open to every Jew (unless rejected by its command) but also because it was supposed to defend the overall Zionist effort. This meant that:

> The organization cannot, is forbidden to involve itself in internal matters of the general group . . . [and] is forbidden to use its power for goals not of an all-inclusive nature or where the general group is divided in opinion. The Hagana is not allowed to become involved in and exercise its power in matters the general group is still undecided on. . . . The Hagana cannot be a factor that wields its force in internal, political, partisan, or social conflicts. The Hagana comes under the general authority for the needs of the general public.

Sneh noted two aspects stemming from the Hagana's all-inclusiveness: first, "it was the only legitimate organization allowed to carry arms and engage in military activity . . . with [absolute] authority over its members . . ."; second, its activity had the wide support of the Yishuv. The organization could succeed "only if the entire public is behind us, if we have the strong backing of the public, and all its sectors take part in it. The organization is the spearhead of the fighting public. . . . It does not see itself as different and separate [from the public]; it knows that the masses will follow when the time comes."[38]

However, the leaders of the Yishuv saw things in a different light. Large sections of the public did not support the Hagana; instead, they supported breakaway military organizations (the "dissenters") that employed terrorist tactics against the British. A long and bitter dispute raged between the elected leadership of the Yishuv and the "dissenters," who rejected any form of political direction. It was outrageous, Ben-Gurion stated, that "a gang that purchased a cannon, Tommy Gun, or kilo of dynamite" had the strength to ignore "our questions without conferring with us, without seeking our counsel, without asking our opinion, and [could] determine the nation's response and our position."[39] Sneh, too, regarded these actions as a grave threat to democracy and to the elected institutions which, until now, had been the greatest achievement of the leadership of the Yishuv, along with "national awareness and the viable functioning of independent national life [before] statehood."[40]

The question of authority, or the ability to assert discipline over secondary bodies, played an important role in the building of the political institutions of the Yishuv. This was especially true with reference to the fact that the Yishuv and the Zionist movement lacked a clearly defined territorial base and effective governmental control. According to David Vital, without these tools of power "control of any area, command over military units, and the hold on any form of economic leverage [prevented] the leaders of the [Zionist] Movement . . . from wielding real authority over the rank and file."[41]

Ben-Gurion's appointment to the Jewish Agency Executive in 1933 was an important step in establishing the authority of the political leadership of the Yishuv. His guiding light in directing national affairs enabled him to set up a national authority based on the idea of concentration of power. This was the power that he believed he could use, even if it was not in the form of state authority, for establishing the rudimentary government institutions of the "state-in-the making." The process demanded a large degree of consensus and the creation of common ground in the ideological trends and spectrum of political beliefs. Ben-Gurion's efforts produced the longed-for unity of activity, albeit limited in scope, and allowed institutions of the Yishuv to develop into a multibranched institutional system and political center that increasingly secured its authority.[42]

The broad political consensus in support of a national homeland helped the Yishuv win both support and normative obedience, and exert its authority. However, exercising authority over the Hagana required negotiation and compromise. This ran counter to the way the national institutions effected democratic decisions, because it handed full supervision over the Hagana to a "Parity High Command" beginning in 1931. The agreement meant that the elected institutions ceded majority rule to a parity structure. "In this way . . . the [political] right could attain the right of veto over any decisions it disagreed with."[43]

The parity mechanism is an outstanding example of a system created for regulating the conflict of authority, the allocation of resources, and ideological differences. As Dan Horowitz and Moshe Lissak have observed, it was expressed in public debates about the security apparatus.[44] Despite its obvious limitations, this mechanism was vital in establishing a wide base of consensus for Hagana activity within the voluntary political system of the Yishuv. Considerable political energy was invested in maintaining this fragile mechanism. Its vulnerability became apparent in a series of political crises that erupted once the political leadership gained experience in commanding the military underground. One of the key factors in strengthening the voluntary framework of the Yishuv was the underground status of the Hagana, since joint underground activity served as a restraining factor that prevented the disintegration of the political system of the Yishuv. This system displayed organizational strength and decision-making capability on political issues that enabled it "to maintain the continuity of a political culture and a system of democratic principles."[45]

The limited separation between the political and military levels hampers an adequate examination of the Yishuv's security elite. Hence, at this point it is difficult to assess the occurrence of conflicts between the political and security elites. A comprehensive examination of the Yishuv's elites[46] reveals no direct relations between the security elite and the upper level of the political elite.

ANALYSIS OF THE POLICY-MAKING LEVEL

The Zionist movement applied the national–cultural vision as a driving force for its state-building enterprise. The movement emphasized the need for a new order, the reevaluation of collective terms, and the drafting of master plans for Jewish structures. This vision emphasized the need for Jewish independence in its ancient homeland, and the return to full participation in the family of nations. Zionist ideology also aspired to introduce the Jewish people into modern history as a renewed sovereign nation.[47]

Thus, Ben-Gurion thought that the Zionist policy should focus on the Jewish people as a national unit represented by delegates who would be active in the international arena. Although the status, strength, and ability of the Yishuv differed from those of other nations, the Jewish people were capable of shaping their fate, defending themselves, surviving, laboring, and employing the same resources that other nations had used for attaining these goals. Zionism was thus not based on metaphysical or theological doctrines, but on a practical way of life designed to gain for the Jewish people the same conditions as other nations.[48] Ben-Gurion believed that such a policy could put an end to discrimination against Jews as individuals, as a group, and as a nation. Accordingly, he demanded the free and unhindered right for Jews to immigrate to Eretz Israel. This was his basic understanding of Zionist policy, to whose realization he devoted the lion's share of his energy as a Jewish statesman.[49]

The building of a power base and its use for gaining political objectives were central factors in Ben-Gurion's thinking about security. The notion of "building a power base" refers to issues on the national level such as the use of military power as a tool for attaining political goals. Its rationale relates to the strategic infrastructure that guided Ben-Gurion's political activity.[50] The amassment of power served as a preliminary condition for self-reliance. Independent Jewish power in sufficient quantity and quality on the military level was designed to guarantee endurance, deterrent strength, and the ability to win on the battlefield.[51]

On the political level, the accumulation of power by the Yishuv was intended to create political "facts on the ground" and define and formulate political aims in a way that corresponded to its ability to achieve them. For example, the expansion of Jewish settlements despite the restrictions imposed by the British Mandate was achieved mostly with assistance from overseas Jewish communities. As Ben-Gurion saw it, the size of the Yishuv, despite its limits, was a political factor that had helped shape the borders of the future state after World War I. Ben-Gurion never lost sight of this lesson, which significantly influenced his future political maneuvers. He observed that as the country "developed and its political influence grew, its political weight also increased." The growth of the Zionist enterprise was necessary mainly for ". . . political reasons that, excluding the status of the Jewish people in the Diaspora . . . [should be seen] as a blessing and benefit to us, to the country, and the whole world."[52]

The Yishuv's accelerated pace of expansion increased the Zionist movement's political power base and expanded its political horizon in a way that made possible a change in the rules of the game vis-à-vis both the Mandatory government and the Arabs. An increase in the economic, organizational, moral, quantitative, qualitative, and military strength of the Yishuv was seen as a precondition for preventing an Arab attack in the immediate future. By the same token, only the increase of Jewish power could create an understanding and willingness on the part of the Arabs to reach a state of reconciliation with the large, organized Jewish Yishuv in the long run.[53]

Ben-Gurion concentrated on defining the objectives and tasks that could be attained through war. Each war demanded a different strategy. Strategy was supposed to correspond with the balance of forces during a war, and each crisis had its own rules of engagement. Ben-Gurion defined Zionist policy as a revolutionary process that required continuous adaptation to conditions of time and place until victory was achieved. According to his view of Arab–Jewish relations, strategy more than tactics had to be taken into consideration since policy "is determined by military and strategic thinking."[54]

The need for power and the determination to use it led Ben-Gurion to realize the limitations and advantages likely to stem from its application:

A. "Power is not power if no one knows that it exists."
B. "Power has to work for a goal, not through rhetoric, not in flaming fury, but in a well-reasoned manner just like a machine [operates]."[55]

C. "The use of force . . . sometimes depends on changing circumstances, on reawakened needs, on current situations in domestic and foreign affairs."[56]

D. "There is one mistake that I want to avoid when I speak about power, and this is: regarding its amassment as our main role. . . . The heart and soul of our movement is not based on the might of the arm. . . . Our movement derives its sustenance from the deepest roots of humanism and morality. It would be a distortion of its ethical image . . . if we did not recognize that defending our ideals requires [the accumulation] of power."[57]

Conclusion

The political–security culture during the transition from Yishuv to the State of Israel was a dynamic phenomenon that redefined the Jewish people's past and traditional values while they struggled to establish an independent Jewish state after World War II. It demanded a prolonged political process between institutions involved in the creation of an all-inclusive entity that expressed the collective's uniqueness. This chapter has focused on the special circumstances that characterized the development of relations between the formal political and military institutions in the Yishuv's transition to statehood. It is in this context that the utility of the term that I propose—*political–security culture*—is manifest. This term ought to be seen against the backdrop of the difficulties in theoretical research over the use of the term *political culture* and its derivatives. Incorporation of the term also provides an answer to compartmentalization in the academic treatment of the major elements in Israel's national security issue. According to Horowitz and Lissak, the Israeli alignment toward national security that included strategic-military and social-institutional aspects was dealt with synthetically in research because of the inherent dichotomy in the aforementioned categories due to their disparate agendas and areas of interest.[58]

Discussion of political supremacy over the military sphere during the transition from the Yishuv to the state encourages an examination of the development of the political institutions' supervisory patterns in the military sphere in later periods as well. In particular, comparisons are needed between Israel's wars as historical junctures and watersheds that influenced the shaping of patterns of political supervision over the military.

Notes

1. Oren Barak and Gabriel Sheffer, "Israel's Security Network and Its Impact: An Exploration of a New Approach," *International Journal of Middle East Studies* 38.2 (2006): 235–61.

2. Stuart A. Cohen, *Changing Civil-Military Relations in Israel: Towards an Over Subordinate IDF*, Begin-Sadat Center for Strategic Studies, 64 (Ramat Gan, 2006) [Hebrew].

3. Yoram Peri, *Generals in the Cabinet Room: How the Military Shapes Israeli Policy* (Washington, D.C., 2006).

4. Moshe Lissak, "Civilian Components in the National Security Policy," in Avner Yaniv (ed.), *National Security and Democracy in Israel* (Boulder, Colo., 1992), 55–80.

5. The term *Yishuv* refers to the social–political network established by the Jewish population of Palestine before May 15, 1948.

6. Martin Edmonds, *Armed Services and Societies* (Leicester, 1988).

7. Moshe Lissak, "The Israeli Political Culture: Continuity and Change," in Moshe Stempler (ed.), *People and State: The Israeli Society* (Tel-Aviv, 1989), 116 [Hebrew].

8. Ibid., 119.

9. Itzhak Galnoor, *Steering the Polity: Communication and Politics in Israel* (Los Angeles, 1982).

10. Harvey Sicherman, "Introduction: The Future of American Military Culture," *Orbis* (Winter 1999): 9–10.

11. Don M. Snider, "An Uninformed Debate on Military Culture," *Orbis* (Winter 1999): 11–26.

12. John Hillen, "Must U.S. Military Culture Reform?" *Orbis* (Winter 1999): 43–57.

13. Reuven Pedatzur, "Ben Gurion's Enduring Legacy," in Daniel Bar-Tal, Dan Jacobson, and Aharon Klieman (eds.), *Security Concerns: Insights from the Israeli Experience* (Stamford, Conn., and London, 1988), 139–64.

14. Baruch Kimmerling, "The Sources of the Israeli Political Culture," in Moshe Lissak and Baruch Knei-Paz (eds.), *Israel towards the Year 2000—Society, Politics and Culture* (Jerusalem, 1996), 395–97.

15. Ephraim Ya'ar and Ze'ev Shavit (eds.), *Trends in Israeli Society.* 2 vols. (Tel-Aviv, 2001), 1:87 [Hebrew].

16. Gabriel A. Almond, G. Bringham-Power, Jr., Karre Storm, and Russell J. Dalton, *Comparative Politics Today: A World View* (Toronto, 2000), 50.

17. The *Hagana* was the pre-state national military organization, 1920–1948.

18. Yosef Gorny, "Zionism: From Reassessment to Renewal," *International Problems, Society and State* 30.56 (1991): 26–36; see the quotation on page 29 [Hebrew].

19. Eliezer Schweid, *Between Judaism and Zionism: Essays* (Jerusalem, 1983), 171 [Hebrew].

20. Ehud Luz, *Wrestle at Jabbok River: Power, Morality and Jewish Identity* (Jerusalem, 1999), 61 [Hebrew].

21. Ibid., 219.

22. Anita Shapira, *Land and Power* (Tel-Aviv, 1992), 67 [Hebrew].

23. Natan Rotenstriech, *Examining Zionism Today* (Jerusalem, 1977), 68 [Hebrew].

24. David Ben-Gurion, *Memoirs* (Tel-Aviv, 1976), 2:370 [Hebrew].

25. Ibid.

26. David Ben-Gurion, "On Our Independence and Our Unity," Ben-Gurion Archives [hereafter BGA], Speeches, November 9, 1944.

27. Ibid.

28. Schweid, *Between Judaism and Zionism.*

29. Dan Horowitz and Moshe Lissak, *Origins of the Israeli Polity: Palestine under the Mandate* (Chicago, 1978).

30. Moshe Sneh, "Foundations," 1941, *Hagana* Historical Archives [hereafter HHA], 01151/073.

31. Eliahu Golomb, "The *Hagana* in Jewish History," (n.d.), HHA 080 47/p0034.

32. Moshe Sharett, "Speech," June 22, 1960, HHA 080 146/p00015.

33. Moshe Sneh, "Foundations," 1941, HHA, 01151/073.

34. Ya'acov Dori, "Letter," August 1953, HHA, 080 55/p0002.

35. Yosef Gorny, "The Voluntaristic Zionist System in Trail," in Moshe Lissak (ed.), *The History of the Jewish Community in Eretz Israel Since 1882: The Period of the British Mandate* (Jerusalem, 1995), 2:554 [Hebrew].

36. Israel Galili, "Lecture," 1943, HHA 0018/117.

37. Moshe Sneh, "Foundations," 1941, HHA, 01151/073.

38. Ibid.

39. David Ben-Gurion, *Protocols,* BGA, January 29, 1945.

40. Moshe Sneh, *The End and the Beginning* (Tel-Aviv, 1982), 81–82 [Hebrew].

41. David Vital, *The Zionist Revolution* (Tel-Aviv, 1991), 3:10 [Hebrew].

42. Ephraim Ya'ar and Ze'ev Shavit (eds.), *Trends in Israeli Society* (Tel-Aviv, 2001), 1:38–39 [Hebrew].

43. Israel Galili, "Comments," HHA 080 50/p0015.

44. Dan Horowitz and Moshe Lissak, *Trouble in Utopia: The Overburdened Polity of Israel* (New York, 1989), 222–27.

45. Yosef Gorny, *The Arab Question and the Jewish Problem* (Tel-Aviv, 1985), 554, 581 [Hebrew].

46. Moshe Lissak, *The Elites of the Jewish Community in Palestine* (Tel-Aviv, 1981) [Hebrew].

47. Ya'ar and Shavit, *Trends in Israeli Society,* 1:4 [Hebrew].

48. David Ben-Gurion, *Bama'aracha* (Tel-Aviv, 1948), 3:61–63 [Hebrew].

49. David Ben-Gurion, "Current Zionist Policy," BGA, Articles, October 22, 1942.

50. Amir Bar-Or, "The Zionists' Reluctant Struggle for Power, as the Basis for David Ben-Gurion's Security Thinking," master's thesis, The Hebrew University of Jerusalem, 1989 [Hebrew].

51. Ibid., 88.
52. Ben-Gurion, *Memoirs,* 2:73–74 [Hebrew].
53. Ben-Gurion, BGA, Ben-Gurion Diaries, March 22, 1939.
54. Ben-Gurion, BGA, Ben-Gurion Diaries, December 5, 1936.
55. David Ben-Gurion, *Memoirs* (Tel-Aviv, 1987), 6:236 [Hebrew].
56. Ben-Gurion, BGA, *Protocols,* June 11, 1939.
57. David Ben-Gurion, *Memoirs* (Tel-Aviv, 1976), 4:45 [Hebrew].
58. Horowitz and Lissak, *Trouble in Utopia,* 197–98.

TWELVE

The Discourses of "Psychology" and the "Normalization" of War in Contemporary Israel

EDNA LOMSKY-FEDER AND EYAL BEN-ARI

A former chief psychologist of IDF declares that in Israel, military service is as natural a life-course stage as are pregnancy and birth.[1] A feature magazine article describes how a veteran of the 1973 war discovers and comes to terms with "his" post-traumatic syndrome, and how he is currently involved in litigation for emotional damage.[2] A senior commander of the IDF devotes an op-ed piece to the "organizational climate" of combat units and how their informal activities meet the "needs" of troops.[3] These are just a few typical, if random, examples of how psychological terminology has entered discussions about war and the military in contemporary Israel.

Such common terminology is indicative of how psychology (in its academic and popular guises) has done much to establish understandings of war and military service. In this chapter, we investigate how psychological discourses contribute to the construction of traumatic imagery of war and military service and work to incorporate such ideas into the routines of social life in Israel.

We explore how war and military service are socially "normalized," turned into "natural"—albeit important—parts of society. We examine three discourses: the first, developmental one, focuses on how military service is constructed as a "natural" stage in the progression toward adulthood and manhood; the second, therapeutic, discourse centers on the traumatic influences of war on warriors and (since the first Intifada and the Gulf War) civilians, and thereby blurs the power relations between Israelis and Palestinians; the third, rooted in organizational psychology, deals with the military's effectiveness by likening it to other organizations and thus obscuring its unique character of specializing in the organized use of violence.

Theoretically, our analysis follows the investigations of such critical sociologists as Charles Tilly or Anthony Giddens,[4] who argue that war and the institutions of war-making are integral to the creation of states and the mobilization of social resources. Such scholars have done much to uncover the main social and political mechanisms—recruitment, taxation, or propagation of ideologies of citizenship, for example—by which war has become a routine part of contemporary countries. We take their line of contention but extend it in a different direction: to the social construction of war and military service as "natural" elements in contemporary societies such as Israel.[5] We thus examine the variety of psychological discourses that have entered public discussions and debates to provide the main interpretive frames for understanding national service and the effects of armed conflict.

The background to our analysis is the expansion of psychological discourses that explain and orient behavior in contemporary industrial societies. We follow previous scholars[6] in defining the "psychological" as encompassing the public life of psychological disciplines (in research institutions, intellectual traditions, social policy, and popular culture), as changing visions of the psychological interior (as the soul, the "real" part of selfhood), and as a set of "commonsense" or "folk" models for interpreting social phenomena. Such theorizing about psychological discourse has underscored its development and dissemination as part of global processes.[7] During past decades these discourses have moved from the academic and professional fields to become commonsense knowledge or widely used "folk" models or "lay" theories that people in the industrialized world employ to interpret their lives, which have become mundane. By such terms we refer to the unquestioned knowledge that "everyone knows," to what Clifford Geertz has termed the "of-courseness" of commonsense understandings.[8]

In seeking to examine public discourses, we use an eclectic set of sources for our empirical data: newspaper reports, magazine articles, television programs, academic papers, advertisements, professional handbooks, popular volumes, and primary material (interviews and observations) gleaned from scholarly texts. It is only on the basis of this variety that we can get an idea of the pervasiveness of the psychological discourses we have set out to explore.

Developmental Psychology and the Military:
A "Natural" Way of Growing Up

Nation-states are based on the idea of armies of enthusiastic young men willing to sacrifice their lives for the state.[9] Such ideas endow the experience of war and military service with meaning in terms of maturation and achieving manhood. In Israel this connection seems to be especially strong.[10] The ideal of man-the-warrior is anchored in the central image of the Zionist revolution: the native-born Israeli as the "New Jew,"[11] an answer to the imagery of the weak, effeminate body of the Diaspora Jew that had haunted common perceptions of Jews and Jewish self-perceptions.[12]

These ideals have been challenged in the last two decades.[13] Many groups pose questions on matters previously taken for granted, such as motivation to serve, evasion of military service, or the idea of "man-the-warrior." Acceptance of demands to be a man-soldier is still perceived as a precondition for "full" Israeli membership.[14] Combat service is still seen as superior to other kinds of service, and to a large degree, military service is still accepted as part of the normal and normative life course. This model is expressed in a variety of arenas, such as life stories, advertising,[15] popular songs, novels, movies, and art.

The former IDF chief psychologist expressed the "natural" link between adulthood, manhood, and the military during a conference on the influence of war on Israeli soldiers. "I see a parallel between sex, pregnancy and birth, and wars. In Israel being in the IDF and going through war is natural like becoming pregnant and giving birth in the regular pattern of mature sex life."[16]

Building on his professional authority as a psychologist, the former IDF chief psychologist poses parallels among sex, pregnancy, and birth as the most fundamental processes of life and the "naturalness" of war in the lives of Israeli men. This analogy between war and birth also appears, according to Tsipi Ivry, in the military rhetoric of Israeli gynecologists; she shows how war and the military are the dominant interpretive frames used by these physicians to describe pregnancy and birth.[17] Not only is war introduced into the natural life course, but it also obscures the deep dissimilarity between violence that takes life and the life-giving processes of birth.

In Israel the discourse on war and military service as a "natural" stage in the (especially male) life course is central in routinizing them into individual lives. This process is based on a universalistic model of individual psychological development, according to which life is a sequence of developmental stages characterized by particular psychological profiles and specific developmental tasks.

In this "universal" psycho-developmental model, youth is differentiated from stages coming before and after it and is said to be characterized by emotional turmoil, a "natural" attraction of men to danger and adventure, and a concurrent attraction to ideals and a search for identity.[18] A model developed within the academic discipline of psychology has "migrated" out to society and has become an accepted way to understand the peculiarities of various life stages.

The attributes of youth constantly color the narratives of Jewish–Israeli men about military service and war.[19] They also appear in numerous newspaper articles and media reports published around Memorial Day or anniversaries of wars. In these accounts, military service is described as an arena providing opportunities to actualize desires related to adolescence—intense emotional experiences, adventure, and mockery of death (those very desires that in other social contexts are defined as irresponsible or rebellious behavior). In these contexts, war is described as a special opportunity for risk-taking and testing of boundaries.

According to the universalistic developmental model, adolescence is characterized by a search for meaning and total, uncompromising social participation. Hence, participation in war, according to soldiers' accounts, is often perceived as an expression of commitment to the values of society and loyalty to the state. These expressions often take on a romantic, naïve character that allows no space for critique. An example is an article about an officer, Uri Azulai, who was killed in Lebanon during a skirmish with Hizbullah. In the account, a commander relates a conversation he had with him about death:

> All during my military service I was in dangerous activities and I scraped with death. The role necessitates this. You have to take this into account. Uri looked at me and answered unhesitantly: "I tell my family and my

girlfriend that I will never be hurt, but I know that I may die. I am ready for this, but if it happens, I want to be killed in battle."[20]

The harsh experiences of war in many men's stories are often interpreted by the developmental model as an "identity crisis" within the process of maturation. The fact that a war is interpreted as an identity crisis in becoming an adult and not as a "disaster" or "psychological calamity" softens its impact. Because a crisis of identity is not a deviation or anomaly in adolescence, a crisis brought on by war is thus seen as "normal" and not related to the specific historical context of Israel.[21] This kind of conception is a product of the wider context in which military service is seen as an arena for maturation and, more important, as an arena within which youngsters can face the central developmental tasks of creating individual autonomy, separation from parents, and the crystallization of identity.[22]

These messages are very often transmitted to young people within their families. In a study of fathers of male soldiers serving in the military, Louise Wohllebe found that they regard military service as an important and emotionally powerful life stage.[23] Even when voicing doubts, fathers continue to echo the cultural model of the military as a rite of passage into male society along with a psychological model that stresses military service as important for emotional maturity, crystallizing identity, and building an autonomous personality.

This scenario appears in another study in which Hila Levy interviewed mothers of male soldiers; the mothers describe the separation from their sons as a critical and traumatic event, after which they use different mechanisms to integrate the recruitment of the sons into the routines of family life.[24] When compared to fathers who express loyalty to the military organization, mothers usually express ambivalence and even resistance, which is often explained using psychological concepts.[25] On the one hand, service is represented as maturing ("he is actualizing himself," "it forces him to separate from the parents," or "service molds the identity of my son"). On the other hand, sons are depicted as not yet ready for national service since it distorts their standard or normal psychological development ("the boy is not yet mature," "the separation from home was too traumatic"). They reproduce the idea of military service as an experience that matures individuals and something that "everyone" faces.

This perception of military service is also created outside the family, where messages are explicitly transmitted in graduation ceremonies in Jewish high schools when adults—teachers and parents—talk about the upcoming recruitment of the graduates.[26] Various programs for preparing youngsters for military service (within and outside the educational systems) expose youngsters to ideas centered on maturity, the importance of service, and the army as a place for expressing and achieving personal aims.[27] The developmental discourse of maturation has become a central interpretive frame for the naturalization of military service as part of a key scenario in contemporary Jewish–Israeli society.[28] The "naturalness" of military service in individual life courses has "invaded" the life cycle of countless families.

In 2001, a leaflet placed in our university mailboxes promoted a new review, "The Launching Stage—The Family Coping with the Recruitment of Its Children into the IDF."[29] The blurb included the following explanation:

> The launching stage is that stage in a family's development that begins with the oldest child leaving the home and ends when the youngest child leaves. In Israel, the time of leaving the home is determined arbitrarily by the military. Recruitment is forced and is normative and is not dependent on the personal maturity of the youth or on his choice.

In these examples, the notion is of military service as a stage necessitating certain coping mechanisms on the part of families. In this manner, a "universal" model positing stages of family development is imbued with Israeli peculiarities. The psychologization of the issue further arises out of the contention that if there is a crisis, then there is a need to treat it or care for those undergoing it. This process finds further expression in the fact that its carriers—psychologists, consultants, social workers, and mental health officers—have become increasingly dominant in various stages of recruiting youngsters into the Israeli army. A central agent in organizing pre-army preparation programs in the secular stream of the Ministry of Education is its psychological service, which not only introduced the assumptions of the developmental model into their work but tended also to create programs, curricular material, and advice based on it.

Strong developmental assumptions are also found in and around the management of diverse social groups in the IDF. Nissim Mizrachi, for instance, demonstrates the use of a model based on developmental psychology in the way the army deals with lower-class groups of Middle Eastern origin.[30] This model provides the scientific basis for the diagnosis and classification of emotional and cognitive abilities of soldiers on the basis of ethnic criteria and the institutionalization of an "ethnopsychology" within the military's medical and personnel departments.

Initially, this ethnopsychology underlay military procedures that created a link between psychological and cultural characteristics, on the one hand, and ethnic features, on the other hand. During the 1950s and 1960s, cultural and psychological differences between ethnic groups were defined in essentialist terms as natural. Later this explicit link changed into a "neutral," "objective" discourse that focused on individuals ostensibly disconnected from their social contexts and was supposedly blind to ethnicity. In this manner, however, the newer psychological discourse serves to mask the reproduction of ethnic hierarchies.

This same model is used by members of the middle and middle-high class when opting out of service. Such persons tend to cite an inability to adapt to, or an identity crisis brought about by, military life. Despite the different ways in which the developmental model is used with regard to these two groups, underlying both is a common practice of describing and analyzing differences between soldiers based on individual personalities. Hence, when soldiers negotiate with the military about placement or conditions of service, they usually raise personal-psychological justifications (such as phobias, dependency on families, or personality disorders) and demands are rarely based on cultural differences (religious women are one such exception). These trends are expressed in the 2002 State Comptroller's criticism about the significant rise in the number of soldiers exempt from military service for mental health reasons.

The developmental model forms a key cultural mechanism through which the powerful experiences of war and military service are termed "normal" and even normative. It normalizes war into the life course through stabilizing the experience, toning down the crisis, and anchoring both in models that are a-contextual. Maturation becomes part of the social order and a defined stage in a developmental course that is known, explained, and regulated (among other things through scientific theories). In this way the effects of war can be constructed between the "natural" and the expected (the process of maturation) and the arbitrary and the uncontrolled (the reality of war). Thus, war disrupts maturation while maturation stabilizes war.[31]

Psychotherapy: Pathologizing and Trivializing the Effects of Violence

The second discourse—the therapeutic–traumatic one—has gained force since the 1970s (especially in the wake of the Vietnam War). It contained critical elements focusing on the morality of war,[32] and in Israel it often emphasized private suffering rather than collective mourning.[33] Amia Lieblich's popular *Tin Soldiers on Jerusalem Beach*[34] documented a gestalt group that met after the Yom Kippur War, and exposed the emotional price paid by Israelis living in a reality of constant wars (a reality the dust cover describes as "living with a chronic illness"). Expressions of pain and anguish were a base for protest during Israel's military debacle in Lebanon and the first and second Intifadas.[35] Another side of this discourse is its normalizing variant.

SOCIAL BOUNDARIES, HIERARCHIES, AND TRAUMA

In every war, soldiers undergo hardships and may carry traumatic memories. Social factors, however, decide whether these voices will be heard: traumatic memories result from not only individual experiences but also can only be articulated by people who have received social sanction to do so.

Edna Lomsky-Feder illuminates these dynamics through narratives of veterans of the 1973 war that reflect the absence of social approval to express private traumatic memory.[36] The social imperative voiced was "business as usual," going on with their lives as if the war had not occurred. Her interviewees came to terms with the war, implying proper behavior during battle and not being affected by battle at war's end. This perception reflected a dominant cultural assumption linking one's performance in war and its effect on one's life; that is, by meeting the expectations of the Israeli fighter's ethos, one is not affected by war and is thus considered a real man.

This ethos underlies the complex perception of post-trauma in Israel. Until the 1970s, such reactions were silenced by state authorities, but since then individuals suffering Post-Traumatic Stress Disorder (PTSD) have become more prevalent in the public eye and are treated within and outside the army.[37] Only recently have they been awarded benefits similar to those given the physically wounded (although significant gaps between the groups remain).[38] At times emotionally damaged people are treated in rather hostile terms by MKs[39] and senior IDF commanders.[40] Their difficulties derive from the cultural model linking lack of functioning during war to deficiency in everyday activities. Veterans challenge these attitudes on the basis of their "entitlement" to recall the war as trauma and question its nature. Their right to criticize is seen as legitimate because they fulfilled the ultimate call for personal sacrifice, and because in voicing their pain and critique they do not undermine the fighter's ethos—the hegemonic masculinity. In fact, only men who epitomize the ethos have proven themselves during war and are entitled to be affected by it. They may therefore allow the war to infiltrate their lives but without questioning the social ethos and their self-image as males.

The cultural association between participation in combat and traumatic and critical voice is also expressed in novels, films (*The Sign of Cain* or *Battle Shock*), and the popular press. A magazine featured a combat veteran who is now an artist. His narrative links his traumatic experience in the 1973 war to his artistic output and involvement in left-wing politics. As in many cases of soldiers suffering traumas in Israel's wars,[41] his basis for criticism is the trauma induced by serving as a combat soldier. Accordingly, even if such people disparage war, their license to criticize derives from their combat roles. Soldiers who talk critically about war paradoxically reinforce society's demand to normalize the war. Their memories are linked to the hegemonic ideology via their deep affinity with the fighting ethos.

The intense cultural preoccupation with the experience of warriors (always a minority of soldiers) is part of how war is "naturalized" in Israel. Emotional stories about wars may ironically allow nonparticipants to take war out of their lives because they often lead to the ventilation of emotions, yet rarely examine the implications of being perpetrators or victims of violence. This cathartic function is most evident around Remembrance Day or anniversaries of wars, with newspaper articles and television and radio programs stressing the pain and suffering brought about by war. The intense debates about the price of war taking place during such occasions allow individuals to purify and continue their lives "as usual." The sardonic comments (appearing on television) of a relative of a soldier killed in Lebanon in 2000 sum up this point: "A few viewers [of the television program about the fallen soldier] will cry and wipe the tears away, and five minutes later will change to the sports channel and bring out the snacks [*pitsukhim*]."

EVERYONE TRAUMATIZED

Within the IDF (as in other military establishments) there is vast research literature rooted in psychology and psychiatry examining battle reactions.[42] These concentrate on the therapeutic practices by which soldiers suffering such reactions are returned to active duty,[43] and their orientation is recuperative and restorative (and pertinent to a minority of soldiers).[44]

This discourse in Israel since the Gulf War has been generalized and "civilianized" to apply to all (mainly Jewish) Israelis. An example is a special issue of the journal *Psychologia*,[45] published by the Israeli Association of Psychologists, devoted to the Gulf War of 1991, which presents studies on the war's impact on groups within Israeli society and different treatment methods. The common denominator of almost all the articles is the therapeutic– traumatic approach. The former president and founder of Physicians for Human Rights in Israel stated during the second Intifada, "both national security and personal safety are deteriorating in Israel.[46] This is destabilizing for the Israeli psyche, both at the individual and collective levels." Journalist Yossi Klein Halevi proclaimed that Israel is a "society in shell shock."[47]

A study on the traumatizing of Israeli children during emergency notes: "We live in difficult and confusing times, under the constant threat of crisis and tragedy—and this theme takes on many forms . . . everyone is perforce a victim."[48] The process of gradual traumatization of the whole society became stronger with the eruption of the al-Aqsa Intifada. Convinced that the conflict was affecting the mental health of the city's residents, the director of Jerusalem's psychiatric hospitals suggested setting up communal emergency rooms, a psychiatric ambulance, and new mental health centers in the suburbs.[49] Another case is that of the Israel Trauma Center for Victims of Terror and War (NATAL), whose aim is to furnish support to anyone who has been harmed by a trauma resulting from a national conflict.[50] In effect, the center caters to those suffering the consequences of "the trauma of the Arab–Israeli conflict: terror attacks, bereavement, battle shock, returning POWs, second generation to the trauma, residents of settlements on the line of conflict, parents of combat soldiers and others."[51]

Many more groups define themselves or are defined by others as being traumatized. Galia Plotkin-Amrami shows how the Jewish settler community has mobilized this discourse to bring relief to their distress and to seek empathy from the wider public by constructing the disengagement from Gaza as a national trauma.[52] As James L. Nolan, Jr., suggests, "The therapeutic perspective has spilled into culture more broadly, [and] so has the belief that a growing number of human actions represent diseases or illnesses that need to be healed."[53]

From our perspective, as war is seen to breed ailments, it must be treated through psychological methods. The fact that so many groups are considered "traumatized" banalizes the experience. From being a phenomenon that is unique to certain individuals or groups, trauma has become a concept that characterizes a whole, a public. A further development occurred during the conflict between Israel and Hizbullah in the summer of 2006. Israelis were "bombarded" with media calls for anyone who was suffering trauma to approach any of a plethora of state bodies or NGOs operating around the country.

THE SOLDIER: FROM HEROIC IMAGERY TO THERAPEUTIC DISCOURSE

The culture of bereavement in contemporary Israel has increasingly turned into a psychological–traumatic one. Rather than focusing on soldiers as heroes, memorial ceremonies now concentrate on the bereaved, grieving family. Pictures of victims, weeping soldiers, and stunned or screaming family members accompany such events, and are prominently displayed in the media. War and war-making remain at the center of public attention, not through tales of heroism but through accounts of suffering.[54] The stress on individual vulnerability is related to how soldiers have been infantilized in many discussions about the

IDF. The image of the soldier in public debate is becoming more dependent, more childlike. "Honey, the Soldiers Have Shrunk" warns Doron Rosenblum, a journalist with a biting sense of humor.[55] An array of protective representations of soldiers has recently emerged alongside the ethos of the young hero. Two recent autobiographies[56] depict military service as characterized by suffering and depression (in a television program devoted to the books, they are described as documenting "trauma").[57]

Such depictions contribute to the growing importance of therapeutic models in dealing with crises. After an accident in which tens of troops died on their way to deployment in South Lebanon, parents complained that commanders did not allow psychologists into units to help their sons in grappling with the tragedy.[58] In 2005, the media reported that four combat soldiers in an elite unit requested to be relieved from a mission because of fear, anxiety, and personal distress linked to post-traumatic phenomena. A public debate arose, with one camp comprising senior commanders deploring their feminine, timid response and the other involving civilians, soldiers, and parents contending that the army had neglected the mental health of its troops.[59] One outcome of this episode was a course given to commanders for identifying mental health problems among troops.[60]

The public debate on the question of soldiers' moral strength has been superseded by that of their emotional health. Kalman Binyamini, one of the founding fathers of educational psychology in Israel, has noted:

> During the Yom Kippur War [1973] we sat, a few psychologists, with the units in Egypt. There were guys there who were paralyzed; couldn't function; and we helped them to cry but that was after the action. There is a difference between that and the attempt to see the soldiers as children, as kindergarten children. Today soldiers are allowed to complain. . . . I think that psychology can hurt the power [of the IDF].[61]

The weeping of soldiers has become a subject for public debate[62] and is epitomized in the article "To Cry or Not to Cry" in the official journal of the IDF, *Ba-Machaneh*.[63] Among opinions from military men, academics, and psychologists are competing interpretations of soldiering and manhood in this debate. A journalist cynically characterized it as follows: "The stress on 'hitting at them' and 'we'll break their bones' is now replaced by weeping. . . . Spartan emotionality is transformed into exaggerated expressions."[64] An article expressing the dominant voice among psychologists quoted the IDF chief mental health officer, saying that "the IDF has turned from a body that automatically spits out weak people to an organization that extends its hand and gives legitimacy to tears."[65]

TRAUMA, CRITICAL FORMULATIONS,
AND MORAL RESPONSIBILITY

Psychological language, especially that which turns people into passive victims of circumstances, is often used to defuse criticisms. An example is the reaction to a mother who harshly criticized the IDF when her son was killed in a game of Russian roulette.[66] Through turning her into a "crazy" person because of her intense bereavement, the IDF attempted to silence her condemnation. The fact that she committed suicide on her son's grave only strengthened the attribution that mental instability was the cause of her disparagement of the IDF. An institutional expression of this pattern is related to the fact that conscientious objectors are very rarely recognized by Israeli authorities, and it was only in the late 1990s that special committees were established to grant such deferrals.[67] Nevertheless, even after establishing these committees, the IDF still makes great efforts to reduce the number of conscientious objectors. The most common pattern is for these individuals to receive exemption via a psychiatric discharge: a psychological reason is substituted for an ideological one.[68]

These processes are similar to the "therapeutic motif" constructed by U.S. Vietnam veterans as political opposition. This motif "renders veterans harmless by casting them in terms of metaphors of psychological dysfunction, emotional fragility, healing and personal redemption; it effectively silences the voice of the veteran as a source of legitimate knowledge about the nature of contemporary warfare, thus subverting a potentially effective challenge to discourses advocating the use of 'legitimate' state-sanctioned violence."[69]

By drawing attention to the suffering of individuals, the motif distracts us from wider concerns about the uses of war. Whereas in the United States many segments in society recognized collective wrongdoing, faced up to old accounts, and made amends for past wrongs by asking for forgiveness,[70] the dynamic in Israel is different because of the ongoing conflict. While there is an individualization and victimization of soldiers, there was also a move—during the last two Intifadas and the Second Lebanon War—to traumatize and treat the (predominantly Jewish) population. Sentiments of victimhood and the memory of trauma are basic elements in national identity and the creation of solidarity. A journalist cynically observed that "we are the unfortunate to whom everything is owed. In the morning we were King David and in the evening Anna Frank."[71] Thus, placing the self-as-victim at the center of attention blinds many Israeli Jews from seeing the "other" and how another people are occupied. Ironically, the therapeutic discourse has not only equalized the Israeli and Palestinian cases, but inverts them by turning (Jewish) Israelis into victims.

Organizational Psychology: Rationalizing Violence

The third discourse is rooted in organizational psychology. It, too, has substantial historical roots, although its concrete manifestations in Israel are more recent.[72] Historically, psychology in the military first developed out of a confluence of therapeutic care for shell-shocked soldiers and organizational sorting of recruits to different units and arms. Later it began to encompass other areas, such as training or psychological warfare.[73] In Israel[74] military psychology began to be institutionalized in the War of Independence and today can be found, as in the U.S. armed forces, in a variety of guises in all branches of the military as well as the IDF's School of Leadership.[75]

A Division of "Psychological Labor"

The "psychological" division of labor in the IDF is marked by a distinction between "mental health officers" (*kabanim*) and "psychologists" (*psichologim*). The former term is used for therapists, while the latter designates professionals who administer psychological tests or are organizational consultants. Over the past decade, hundreds of these consultants have entered the various branches of the IDF. The difference between the roles is institutional: the mental health officers are under the command of the chief medical officer and the organizational consultants are under the Behavioral Sciences Department. While the former are committed to use the therapeutic discourse, the latter are devoted to the organizational discourse focused on improved effectiveness and efficiency.

Within the discourse of the organizational psychologists, there is reference to combat. Rather than formulating the problem of combat in terms of violence, they emphasize finding ways to improve performance given the severe pressures it entails. Violence, or its synonyms, does not appear at all in this discourse in an article about leadership that develops a model of stress placed on soldiers in firefights.[76] In this model, violence is "translated" into pressures on individual soldiers and is linked to such variables as control or efficiency of the military organization.

Violence is not raised in the therapeutic discourse of mental health officers. The title of a book drawing a causal link between war and its psychological implications is *The Stress of Combat, the Combat of Stress: Caring Strategies towards Ex-Service Men and Women*.[77] Whereas in battles violence is wrought on others and experienced by soldiers themselves, in the post-traumatic literature the stress is almost wholly on the latter aspect. What is of interest is the violence inflicted *on* soldiers, or its long-term implications *for* the soldiers themselves. The problematics of effecting violence are individualized by turning soldiers into victims rather than perpetrators. In this way, the division of psychological labor is put into practice: behavioral sciences departments deal with danger and a general model of stress, while psychiatric units deal with the effects of violence on soldiers as victims. While the key question in the organizational literature concerns combat effectiveness, in the therapeutic literature, it is that of recuperation.

SCIENTIFIC MANAGEMENT

Psychology is central to the two major twentieth-century approaches to management: scientific and humanistic. While the former attempts to measure and coordinate the activity of employees through statistical information,[78] the latter centers on motivating employees through leadership and human relations.[79] Both variants exist in the IDF. Scientific management is part of "co-optive rational control"[80] carried out by matching soldiers to machines through testing, and the precise measurement of performance so that it can be predicted.[81] The underlying idea is to gauge to what extent people can be recruited to effectively perform military roles (for instance, with the motor skills necessitated by pilots or the emotional stamina needed by sea commandos). Closely allied with this emphasis are attempts to create predictive decision models within the military.[82]

Another example concerns motivation, a burning issue during the 1990s.[83] Psychological explanations were mobilized to account for the purported lack of motivation among some groups in the IDF. A former head of the IDF's Behavioral Sciences Department was the first to raise the issue and to pronounce that "the change is from a notion in which the individual serves the establishment and ideology to one in which the role of the ideology and the establishment is to serve the individual."[84] Phrasing the matter in this way, this expert formulates the problem by centering on what impels soldiers to serve: is it self-actualization or ideological commitment? Framing the issue as one of "motivation" detracts from the fact that this is an organization specializing in violence.

HUMANISTIC MANAGEMENT: "SOFT" SOLDIERING

An example of humanistic management is the new system instituted in paratroopers' basic training, in strong contrast to the previous one that included degradations and humiliations. In the new system,[85] mortifications, shouting noncommissioned officers, and incessant physical and emotional burdens are replaced by training soldiers according to systematically graduated programs of exertion. They are told about the pressures facing them and the difficulties of entering the military from civilian life. Recruits know their individual rights and plans for the course of training. Along the lines promoted by humanistic management, leaders act as role models and training is implemented by commanders but supported by organizational consultants. The term *internalize*—taken from the [IDF's] Behavioral Sciences Department—arises in every discussion with the commanders. An NCO who does not accept the system has "not internalized it yet." He will internalize or he won't be there.[86]

The system is accompanied by tests and questionnaires focusing on "morale" and attitudes, a part of humanistic management, which, through questionnaires and interviews gives soldiers (workers) a feeling that their needs and anxieties are being recognized and met.[87] The new scheme for the paratroopers is not an isolated case, as shown in the link between Total Quality Management (TQM) methods and humanistic management:

> The total quality management revolution is penetrating into the IDF. Instead of discipline, distance, and alienation between commanders and soldiers, today's enlistees are expected to come out and say what is wrong, even if this stands in contrast to what their officer thinks. The aim, it is said in the IDF, is to reach a situation in which progressive management methods will be used even in the field battalions.[88]

The primary agents in pioneering TQM methods were commanders who worked closely with organizational consultants, but their introduction, in turn, was closely connected to global psychological discourses.

"JUST LIKE ANY OTHER ORGANIZATION"

Common to the practices of organizational psychology is an assumed similarity between the army and other organizations. Organizational psychologists and consultants rarely direct their attention to the uniqueness of the military, with its specialization in effecting violence. The military is treated within this discourse in the same manner as schools or businesses.

In the American context, one commentator called this the MBA approach to soldiering, an approach in which bloodless euphemisms are used, like "servicing" rather than "killing" the enemy.[89] The discourse of organizational psychology obfuscates the fact that this is an organization specializing in violence. There is much self-reflection within militaries, but the focus is on managerial problems. Violence is trivialized again because a focus on such issues often means no real grappling with the price of violence and its victims, and the historical context perpetrating aggression. The primary aim of organizational psychology in the military (as in other organizations) is to aid in rationalizing performance, making troops more effective and efficient. Being mobilized for organizational aims and devoting attention to performance, the violent acts of the soldiers themselves are not scrutinized, but are sanitized and hidden away.

Conclusion: Some Wider Implications

We contend that the therapeutic, developmental, and organizational discourses regarding military service and war are "effective" in normalizing war. Three normalizing mechanisms cut across these discourses.

SOCIAL SOLIDARITY

Because Israel is torn by dissent and many of the hegemonic ideals are no longer automatically accepted, the common denominator linking many social groups has become human suffering associated with war. The Holocaust is now remembered less in heroic terms than through a stress on traumatic suffering.[90] Many Israelis emphasize universal aspects of human experience—pain and mourning—to escape contention and circumvent ideological splits. As Peter Erehnhous suggests, "[a] motif that celebrates unity (personal, relational, national) cannot abide discourse that engenders division. This is the tyrannizing power of the therapeutic motif."[91]

Suffering and mourning as bases of social solidarity create sentiments of equality in terms of dangers, fears, and the pain accompanying war. By placing individuals at its center and assuming universalistic criteria for assessing their pain, the therapeutic discourse silences the politics of identities, reproduces existing power relations, and reinforces the strength of the state. Commitment to the state, moreover, is strengthened through the developmental discourse that constructs a link between the individual life course and military service as natural and taken-for-granted, and validates the connection between maturation, adulthood, and war.

Our argument has been complex: while at first glance, the discourse of trauma appears to demilitarize sources of social solidarity, it actually strengthens the idea of war as fate and the centrality of the national state.

SOCIAL HIERARCHY

While the traumatic discourse produces social solidarity around suffering and mourning, it also creates an unquestioned hierarchy between those who have "paid" the price and those who have not. The demands of members of the Association of Bereaved Widows and Orphans not to let victims of "mere" terror attacks (civilian sufferers) into national ceremonies and monuments devoted to military dead should be seen in this light.[92] Their petition is an indicator of the kinds of hierarchy that seem to exist between different national sacrifices in Israel.

The contribution of psychological discourses to the stratification of men is expressed most clearly around the construction of military masculinity. Military service creates a hierarchy in which combat roles are defined as the apex for the inculcation of citizenship and membership. According to this conception, to be an Israeli in the "full" sense of the word implies that one has to be Jewish, male, and serve in the military to be granted full membership in the Israeli collectivity.

The three psychological discourses sustain the "superiority" of the combat soldier and define his version as hegemonic. The developmental discourse grants scientific validity to the "natural universality" of this masculinity. The organizational discourse stresses the functional improvement and professionalization of this masculine version. The therapeutic discourse establishes the social "authorization" given to it to voice the pain of war and express criticism. This logic underlies the Peace Now movement, which began with the political organization of reserve officers in the spring of 1978. Traumatic memories from the 1973 war were among the central motivations in setting it up, but its members' right to oppose government policy derived from their officership and from epitomizing the warrior ethos.[93] Combat service has been the source of legitimacy for conscientious objection from the time of the war in Lebanon.[94]

NEUTERING CRITICAL DISCOURSE

While traumatic discourse grants social sanction to voice criticism, all three discourses also neuter critical expressions about war and the military. The developmental discourse does this through de-contextualizing war while the organizational discourse neutralizes the violent dimension of the military organization. It is chiefly the therapeutic–traumatic discourse that does this through defining (Jewish) Israelis as victims of power and not the wielders of power repressing another people.

This discourse blurs the unequal power relations between Israel and its enemies, especially the Palestinians. It situates Israelis and the Palestinians as equals in a manner that turns them into competitors for suffering as a symbolic resource. As Arthur Kleinman and his associates note, "suffering has social use. . . . There is a market for suffering, victimhood is commodified."[95]

As the politics of victimhood accentuates, the traumatic discourse is, for many Israeli Jews, very effective in normalizing war and breaking down the dichotomies of good and evil, and of strong and weak. In this manner, the psychological discourses we have examined variously blur, conceal, sanitize, as well as naturalize issues related to violence, thereby "normalizing" the reality and effects of war and war-making.

Notes

1. Helena De Sevilia, Reuven Gal, and Michal Rotem, *What Do the Wars Do to Us?* (Zikhron Yaakov, 1992), 5–6 [Hebrew].

2. Neri Livne, "I Am Also Injured Mentally," *Ha'aretz,* November 17, 2000.

3. Yom-Tov Samia, "Organizational Climate in the Routine of Battle," *Ma'ariv,* March 30, 1998.

4. Charles Tilly (ed.), *The Formation of National States in Western Europe* (Princeton, N.J., 1985); Anthony Giddens, *The Nation-State and Violence* (Cambridge, 1985).

5. Edna Lomsky-Feder and Eyal Ben-Ari (eds.), *The Military and Militarism in Israeli Society* (Albany, N.Y., 1999).

6. James L. Nolan, Jr., *The Therapeutic State: Justifying Government at Century's End* (New York, 1998); Nicholas Rose, *Inventing Ourselves: Psychology, Power and Personhood* (Cambridge, 1996); Nancy Schnog, "On Inventing the Psychological," in Joel Pfisher and Nancy Schnog (eds.), *Inventing the Psychological* (New Haven, Conn., 1997), 3–4.

7. John Meyer, "Globalization: Sources and Effects on National States and Societies," *International Sociology* 15 (2000): 233–48.

8. Clifford Geertz, *The Interpretation of Cultures* (New York, 1973).

9. Graham Murdock and Robin McCron, "Consciousness of Class and Consciousness of Generation," in Stuart Hall and Tony Jefferson (eds.), *Resistance through Rituals* (London, 1976), 192–207; George L. Mosse, *Fallen Soldiers: Reshaping the Memory of the World Wars* (Oxford, 1990).

10. Eyal Ben-Ari (assisted by Galeet Dardashti), "Tests of Soldierhood: Trials of Manhood: Military Service and Male Ideals in Israel," in Daniel Maman, Eyal Ben-Ari, and Zeev Rosenhek (eds.), *Military, State and Society in Israel* (New Brunswick, N.J., 2001), 239–67; Liora Sion, "Images of Manhood among Combat Soldiers: Military Service in Israel's Infantry Brigades as a Rite of Passage," master's thesis, The Hebrew University of Jerusalem, 1997.

11. Oz Almog, *The Sabra: The Creation of the New Jew* (Tel-Aviv, 1997) [Hebrew].

12. David Biale, *Eros and the Jews* (New York, 1992); Daniel Boyarin, *Unheroic Conduct: The Rise and Fall of Heterosexuality and the Invention of the Jewish Man* (Berkeley, Calif., 1996).

13. Edna Lomsky-Feder and Tamar Rapoport, "Juggling Models of Masculinity: Russian-Jewish Immigrants in the Israeli Army," *Sociological Inquiry* 73 (2003): 114–37; Orna Sasson-Levy, *Identities in Uniform: Masculinities and Femininities in the Israeli Military* (Jerusalem, 2006) [Hebrew].

14. Lomsky-Feder and Ben-Ari, *The Military and Militarism.*

15. Yehuda Nuriel, "Relaxing the Self: Are You from Golani?" *Globes,* August 16, 2001.

16. De Sevilia, Gal, and Rotem, *What Do the Wars Do to Us?* 5–6.

17. Tsipi Ivry, "Pregnant with Meaning: Conceptions of Pregnancy in Japan and Israel," Ph.D. diss., The Hebrew University of Jerusalem, 2004.

18. Johan Fornas, "Youth Culture and Modernity," in Johan Fornas and Gorän Bolin (eds.), *Youth Culture in Late Modernity* (London, 1995), 1–11; Christine Griffin, *Representation of Youth* (Cambridge, 1993), 15–26.

19. Amia Lieblich, *The Spring of Their Lives* (Tel-Aviv, 1987) [Hebrew]; Edna Lomsky-Feder, *As If There Was No War: The Perception of War in the Life Stories of Israeli Men* (Jerusalem, 1998) [Hebrew].

20. Shlomo Abramowitz, "A Legend in His Time," *Yediot Aharonot,* November 1, 1996.

21. Lomsky-Feder, *As If There Was No War.*

22. Lieblich, *The Spring of Their Lives.*

23. Louise Wohllebe, "Military, Masculinity and the Family: The Intergenerational Perspective of Fathers," master's thesis, The Hebrew University of Jerusalem, 1999.

24. Hila Levy, "Bag Packers: Mothers of Soldiers in Israeli Society," master's thesis, The Hebrew University of Jerusalem, 2001.

25. Tamar El-Or, "Conditions of Love: The Work of Motherhood around the Camp," *Teoria u-Bikoret* 19 (2002): 79–114 [Hebrew].

26. Edna Lomsky-Feder, "The Bounded Female Voice in Memorial Ceremonies," *Qualitative Sociology* 28 (2005): 293–314.

27. Limor Even-Ari, "Programs for Preparing Israeli High-School Pupils for Military Service," master's thesis, The Hebrew University of Jerusalem, 2004; Noa Harel, "Playing Soldier: The Culture of Military Preparation in Private and State Frameworks," master's thesis, The Hebrew University of Jerusalem, 2002.

28. Sherry B. Ortner, "On Key Symbols," *American Anthropologist* 75 (1973): 1338–46.

29. Lea Kasan and Tamar Wittenberg, *The Stage of Take-Off—The Grappling of the Family with the Recruitment of Its Children into the IDF: A Review of the Professional Literature* (Jerusalem, 2001) [Hebrew].

30. Nissim Mizrachi, "'From Badness to Sickness': The Role of Ethnopsychology in Shaping Ethnic Hierarchies in Israel," *Social Identities* 10 (2004): 219–43.

31. Lomsky-Feder, *As If There Was No War.*

32. Chaim F. Shatan, "Bogus Manhood, Bogus Honor: Surrender and Transfiguration in the United States Marine Corps," *Psychoanalytic Review* 64 (1977): 586–610.

33. Yoram Bilu and Eliezer Witztum, "War-Related Loss and Suffering in Israeli Society: A Historical Perspective," *Israel Studies* 5.2 (2000): 1–32.

34. Amia Lieblich, *Tin Soldiers on Jerusalem Beach* (Tel-Aviv, 1979) [Hebrew].

35. Uri Ben-Eliezer, "Civil Society in Israeli Society: Politics and Identity in New Social Movements," *Israeli Sociology* 8 (1999): 51–98 [Hebrew]; Sara Helman, "Citizenship Regime, Identity and Peace Protest in Israel," in Maman, Ben-Ari, and Rosenhek, *Military, State and Society in Israel*, 295–318; Eyad Hallaq, "An Epidemic of Violence," *Palestine-Israel Journal* 10 (2003): 37–41.

36. Lomsky-Feder, *As If There Was No War.*

37. Sigalit Shakhor, "They Gave Their Soul," *Yediot Aharonot,* March 9, 2001.

38. Amnon Barzilai, "Ministry of Defense Has Formulated a New Process of Detecting Post-Traumatic Disorders among Battle-Shocked Veterans," *Ha'aretz,* February 23, 1998.

39. Uri Israeli, "Attitudes of Knesset Members to Battle Shock," master's thesis, University of Haifa, 1993.

40. Dan Inbar, "Attittudes of IDF Commanders to Battle Shock and Its Victims," master's thesis, Tel-Aviv University, 1987.

41. Amalia Argeman-Barnea, "The Paintings after the War," *Yediot Aharonot,* March 26, 2000; Uri Blau, "Ministry of Defense Recognizes Mental Injuries That Were Caused by Sharon's Assassination Units," *Kol Ha'ir,* May 25, 2001.

42. Eliezer Witztum, Ami Levy, and Zehava Solomon, "Therapeutic Response to Combat Reaction during Israel's Wars," *Israel Journal of Psychiatry* 33 (1996): 77–78.

43. David Bar-Gal, *Social Work As a Professional Career: Renewal vs. Erosion* (Jerusalem, 1982) [Hebrew].

44. Charles W. Greenbaum, Itamar Rogovsky, and Benjamin Shalit, "The Military Psychologist during Wartime: A Model Based on Action Research and Crisis Intervention," *Journal of Applied Behavioral Science* 13 (1977): 7–22.

45. *Psychologia,* 4 (1994).

46. Ruhama Marton, "The Psychological Impact of the Second Intifada on Israeli Society," *Palestine-Israel Journal* 11 (2004): 71.

47. Yossi Klein Halevi, "A Society in Shell Shock: Israelis Cope with the Routinization of Terror," *The Jewish Week,* 2002, at http://www.virtualjerusalem.com/jeisholidays/independence/53/jta.htm.

48. Avigdor Klingman, Amiram Raviv, and Bernie Stein (eds.), *Children in Stress and Emergencies: Psychological Characteristics and Interventions* (Jerusalem, 2000), 375 [Hebrew].

49. Dan Even, "A Rise in Demand for Psychological Help," *Kol Hazman,* July 6, 2001.

50. *Natal,* "Regarding the Emotions," *Bulletin of Natal* 2 (2001): 1–16 [Hebrew].

51. Argeman-Barnea, "Paintings after the War."

52. Galia Plotkin-Amrami, "On the Moral Boundaries of a Traumatized Community: The Disengagement and Construction of Self of Religious Zionism," paper presented at the Annual Meeting of the Israel Anthropological Association, June 2006.

53. Nolan, *The Therapeutic State,* 9.

54. Ruvik Rosenthal, *Is Bereavement Dead?* (Jerusalem, 2001) [Hebrew].

55. Doron Rosenblum, "Honey, the Soldiers Have Shrunk," *Ha'aretz,* January 4, 1994.

56. Boaz Neumann, *A Good Soldier* (Tel-Aviv, 2001) [Hebrew]; Orr Spivak, *My Golani* (Tel-Aviv, 2001) [Hebrew].

57. Tom Segev, "The Struggle for the Terrorism Memorial," *Ha'aretz,* April 24, 1998.

58. Gabi Zohar, "The Commander Is Your Therapist," *Ha'aretz,* February 14, 1997.

59. *Yediot Aharanot,* December 7 and 12, 2005.

60. *Yediot Aharanot,* February 19, 2006.

61. Avi Katzman, "Let's Talk about It Some More," *Ha'aretz,* March 8, 1991.

62. *Ma'ariv,* September 15, 1997; Tom Segev, "The Battle over the Monument to Terror," *Ha'aretz,* April 24, 1997.

63. "To Cry or Not to Cry," *Ba-Machaneh,* November 2000.

64. Aviehai Becker, "On a Clear Day You Can See Me Dead," *Ha'aretz,* September 25, 1998.

65. Ariella Eilon, "The Man Who Made You Mad," *Ba-Machaneh,* July 13, 2001.

66. Rosenthal, *Is Bereavement Dead?* 98.

67. *Ha'aretz,* May 22, 1998.

68. Amir Rapaport, "Sixty Percent of Those Released from the Army for Psychological Reasons—Are Healthy," *Yediot Aharonot,* July 19, 2001; Uria Shavit, "Profile Article," *Ha'aretz,* May 26, 2000.

69. Peter Ehrenhous, "Cultural Narratives and the Therapeutic Motif: The Political Containment of Vietnam Veterans," in Dennis K. Mumby (ed.), *Narrative and Social Control: Critical Perspectives* (Newbury Park, Calif., 1995), 78, 81.

70. Ibid., 77–96.

71. Arieh Caspi, "The Time Has Run Out," *Ha'aretz,* August 6, 2001.

72. Michal Frenkel, "The Hidden History of the Appearing Hand," Ph.D. diss., Tel-Aviv University, 2000 [Hebrew].

73. Gerald D. Page, "Clinical Psychology in the Military: Developments and Issues," *Clinical Psychology Review* 16 (1996): 383–96.

74. Uzi Ben-Shalom and Shaul Fox, "Military Psychology in the IDF: A Perspective on Continuities and Change" (unpublished manuscript, Ramat-Gan, 2006); Motty Safrai, "In the Spirit of the Army Lies Victory: The Beginnings of Military Psychology in the IDF," *Psychologia Tsvait* 3 (2004): 53–105.

75. Uzi Ben-Shalom and Henriette Kones-Fonte, "As Seagulls in a High Wind: Military Psychologists in the Yom-Kippur War," in Hagai Golan and Shlomo Shay (eds.), *Yom Kippur War Studies* (Tel-Aviv, 2002), 173–204 [Hebrew]; Micha Popper and Avihu Ronen, *On Leadership* (Tel-Aviv, 1989) [Hebrew].

76. Reuven Gal, "Leadership in Battle," in Itzik Gonen and Avihu Zakai (eds.), *Leadership and Leadership Development: From Theory to Practice* (Tel-Aviv, 1999), 199–231 [Hebrew].

77. Roy Brook, *The Stress of Combat, the Combat of Stress: Caring Strategies towards Ex-Service Men and Women* (Brighton and Portland, Ore., 1999). See also Joanna Bourke, *An Intimate History of Killing: Face-to-Face Killing in Twentieth-Century Warfare* (London, 1999).

78. Bourke, *An Intimate History of Killing;* Chris H. Gray, *Postmodern War: The New Politics of Conflict* (New York, 1997).

79. Richard Stivers, *Technology As Magic: The Triumph of the Irrational* (New York, 1999), 10.

80. Lawrence Radine, *The Taming of the Troops: Social Control in the United States* (Westport, Conn., 1977), 90ff.

81. Ibid., 89.

82. Dan Zakai, "An Analysis of Decision-Making Processes at the Level of Platoon Commanders," *Psychologia Tsvait* 3 (2004): 189–236 [Hebrew].

83. Avner Bernheimer, "Profile 96," *Yediot Aharonot,* April 19, 1996; Udi Lebel, "Rejected by the Army because of Lack of Suitability," *Yediot Aharonot,* April 4, 1997.

84. Ibid.

85. Alex Fishman, "After Me to Summer Camp," *Ha'aretz,* September 10, 1999.

86. Ibid.

87. Michal Frenkel, "The Hidden History of the Appearing Hand," Ph.D. diss., Tel-Aviv University, 2000, 156.

88. Erez Rotem, "Commander, Improve Your Appearance," *Ma'ariv,* January 19, 1997.

89. Fred Downs, "Death and the Dark Side of Command," *Washington Post,* August 16, 1987.

90. Tom Segev, *The Seventh Million* (Jerusalem, 1991) [Hebrew].

91. Ehrenhous, "Cultural Narratives and the Therapeutic Motif," 83.

92. Segev, "The Struggle for the Terrorism Memorial."

93. Michael Feige, "Social Movements, Hegemony and Political Myth: A Comparative Analysis of the Ideologies of Gush Emunnim and Peace Now," Ph.D. diss., The Hebrew University of Jerusalem, 1995.

94. Helman, "Citizenship Regime, Identity and Peace Protest in Israel."

95. Arthur Kleinman, Veena Das, and Margaret Lock, "Introduction," in Arthur Kleinman, Veena Das, and Margaret Lock (eds.), *Social Suffering* (Berkeley, Calif., 1997), 11.

THIRTEEN

Visual Representations of IDF Women Soldiers and "Civil-Militarism" in Israel

CHAVA BROWNFIELD-STEIN

In September 1949, during a period of "postwar" or "in-between" wars, the first Knesset discussed national military service and approved the Security Service Law (SSL).[1] This law laid the foundations for a phenomenon that was very unusual for its time: the *mandatory* conscription of both Jewish men and women over the age of eighteen. The SSL of 1949 has since proved crucial in shaping the distinctive features of Israeli society, the Israeli army—the Israeli Defense Forces (IDF)—and the complex relations between the individual, the military, political institutions, and the civil sphere in Israel.

The IDF was established in 1948 to "defend the existence, territorial integrity and sovereignty of the state of Israel" and "to protect the inhabitants of Israel and to combat all forms of terrorism which threaten the daily life"; the concepts of military, national security, and defense have been understood as fundamental to the very existence of Israel.[2] Ever since these public debates on women's conscription and the SSL, the terms *mandatory military service, draft,* and *women's conscription* have been integrated into every aspect of life.[3] Visual representations of women soldiers fascinated the media in Israel and around the world, and their photographs have been part of Israel's cultural codex. Photos of women in uniform filtered into the national memory, shaped the image of the IDF as "the people's army," and simultaneously formed the image of Israel as a "nation-in-arms."[4]

This chapter focuses on the visual representations of IDFWS (IDF women soldiers) and is the first to address the role of the visual field and

the significant impact of photographs of female soldiers on the militaristic character of Israeli society.[5] Focusing on the visual field represents
another step in the effort to widen the boundaries of understanding
the social and cultural phenomena that Israeli scholars defined by various terms, among them *Civic Militarism*,[6] *Materialist Militarism*,[7] and
Cognitive-Cultural Militarism.[8]

If militarization of society is achieved through the naturalization
of militaristic values, a study of Israeli militarism would be incomplete
without considering the visual ramifications of the SSL and the unique
phenomenon of women's conscription, and without discussing visual
representations of IDFWS in army camps, city streets, and military
parades. Although photos of IDFWS became icons for the new Israeli
state, their cultural militaristic influences and implications have thus far
remained invisible for academic research.

Through visual genealogy, this chapter analyzes and reconsiders the
process through which major organizational principles of Israeli society
"become controlled by, [dependent] on, or [derive] their value from the
military as an institution or militaristic criteria."[9] Military penetration
will also be discussed throughout Israeli culture, and attention drawn
to the visual aspects of the evasive and ever-changing processes of the
militarization of Israeli society.

Discussed are the cultural and aesthetic products of these informal, indirect, and hidden processes. Their pleasurable implications and
erotic aspects are illuminated using photos of IDFWS from the period
1948–1968 as a case study. Focusing on the visual aspects of the unique
phenomenon of women's conscription draws attention to the pleasurable
dimension of the connections between "technologies of the self" and
"technologies of domination"—what Foucault termed *governmentality*—
and illuminates the militaristic links between the constitution of the
subject and the formation of the state.[10] Photos are examined of IDFWS
from the first two decades of Israel's statehood, drawing on materials
found in Israeli archives. Building on Cynthia H. Enloe's theoretical
framework and definition of militarism, the chapter defines the unique
phenomenon of cultural militarism in Israel as "erotic militarism."

Following Enloe's ideas and those of other feminist scholars such
as Miriam Cooke, Angela Woollacott, and Madelain Adelman, the first
part briefly clarifies the differences and similarities between the terms

militarism and *militarization*.[11] It will expose the blind spots of the established perspectives, illuminate the visual aspects of mandatory women's service, and exhibit one informal practice through which Israeli society has become militarized.

Based on the study of visual culture, cultural studies, and broader interdisciplinary attempts to examine the cultural and social-political arena, I suggest that phenomena such as militarism or militarization cannot be adequately comprehended without adopting an interdisciplinary viewpoint. Only the interlinkage between seemingly diverse academic arenas can reveal the complexities of these phenomena and their strong implications on Israeli culture and society. Both descriptive and prescriptive cultural analyses have claimed that institutional analysis per se fails to take into account the cultural and historical conditions and the diversity patterns for civil–military relations. Rather than focusing exclusively on the military or decision-making process, cultural inquiries have pointed to the interconnections between individuals' experiences, cultural values, military structures, political configurations, and economic organizations. These studies describe the cultural and historical context and depict various procedures and practices by which societies become militarized.[12]

This study relates to visual and cultural studies that expose the political uses of visual representations that function in a social context and examines the production and reproduction of visual representations of collective memories and national identities.[13] With regard to Israel, I relate to studies that concentrate on the variety of state apparatuses, social practices, and hidden cultural mechanisms (e.g., rites, military parades, cinema, educational curricula, schoolbooks, and children's literature) by which the lives of ordinary Israelis are constructed and by which military values become "routinized" and "normalized."[14] The analytical tools used here, however, are "the gaze" as a source of pleasure and discipline, and Foucault's notion of the "political technologies of the body" and his concept of *governmentality;* these are employed to illuminate the latent affinities between mandatory women's service, photographs of IDFWS, and cultural fascination with militarism in Israeli society.[15]

The data employed are taken from the first two decades of Israel's statehood (1948–1968), which were also the formative years of the IDF. They consist of photos of IDFWS found at the IDF Archive (IDFA) and the National Photo Collection at the Government Press Office (GPO) Photography Department Archive, as well as archival material from the Israel State Archive (ISA), such as newspapers, government meetings, personal diaries, and biographies.

The discussion refers to three groups of photos taken in the public sphere; its main goals are the following: a) to examine the interdependency between the state apparatus and photography; b) to explore photos of IDFWS taken by official photographers; c) to expose, through photos of IDFWS, the military locus as a formative space of power and pleasure, domination and eroticism; d) to show the affinities between photos of IDFWS, *governmentality,* and the elusive ways by which *militarization* has slowly diffused into, and spread throughout, the entire social body in Israel.

One of the preferred goals of Israel and its mechanisms during those decades was the production of national memory via the visual field.[16] Hence, official photos are examined to focus on the mutual relationship between the state apparatuses and photography. Most of these representations were disseminated to the public; all were taken by male photographers of the GPO and IDF. Gender had a crucial impact on the ways the public perceived these images, and on the way the public icon of the "IDF woman soldier" was imprinted onto the collective memory in Israel.

Militarism, Militarization, and Visual Representations

During the last decade, several studies have claimed that the SSL and compulsory military service are among the institutional arrangements and social reproductive mechanisms that have constituted the IDF as the core of Israeli collectivity, and promoted the ideology of military power as the primary source of Israel's national security. They claimed that the army conscription system for men and women has produced and reproduced a predominance of military virtues and norms, and militaristic ethos. This social mechanism enables the smooth continuation and reproduction of militarism in Israel and militarization of Israeli society.[17]

The *Merriam-Webster Dictionary* defines *militarism* as "(a) predominance of the military class or prevalence of their ideals; (b) subordination of the civil ideals or policies of a government to the military; (c) a spirit which exalts military virtues and ideals; (d) policy of aggressive military preparedness." At the same time, *militarization* is defined as "the act of imbuing with military character or converting to military status."[18]

Although contemporary scholars and feminist researchers have exposed the traditional tendency to identify militarism with particular political and social formations other than those in Western countries, militarism is not synonymous with dictatorship or totalitarianism.[19] It tends to be defined as a political position based on the role of armed forces,[20] or as dominance of the military over civilian authority and a prevalence of warlike values.[21]

Studies of militarism have been principally and traditionally the domain of social sciences and political historians. Those analytical inquiries have focused on institutional and formal aspects and reflected the disciplinary boundaries and the political and social discourses of the early twentieth century. The ideological and institutional separation of "civil" and "military" found in Western countries was the model. Emphases were on the formal and institutional links between the armed forces and the military elites, the civilian institutions and the political structure, or, in other words, the theory of "civil–military relations."[22]

This research is based on Gender Studies and Enloe's theoretical framework, which rejects the structural paradigm of civil–military relations and the civil–military dichotomy. This theoretical standpoint argues that the fundamental distinctions into two established subsystems (such as military–civilian spheres, political–military elites, militaristic-pacifist, government–industry, private–public) have obscured deeper social processes.[23] These feminist perspectives refuse to accept the traditional concepts of militarism, the civil–military dichotomy, and the distinct tendency to identify militarism with particular political and social configurations (especially in South Asia, Latin America, and the Middle East, but *not* in the United States and Europe) as criteria for assessing a militaristic society. The studies also posit that the dominance of "specialists on violence" and their increasing influence on economic and social structures, as well as their impact on the arena of politics, are only one of the possible criteria for evaluating militaristic societies.

These studies offer the concept of "militarization" as a way to analyze the military's very existence and activities, and to emphasize that militarization processes are widespread and common to various sociopolitical groups and to both "developed" and "developing" countries. According to these approaches, the concept of militarization focuses on the direct and indirect influences of the military in terms of national, international, and transnational dynamic processes.[24]

One can draw the distinction between "militarism" and "militariza-tion" according to theoretical perspectives, time frames, and emphases. I differentiate them as differences—but not contradictions—between phe-nomenon and dynamic process, institutional and unintentional, struc-tural and coincidental, national and international, direct and indirect, formal and nonofficial or informal, conventional and contemporary, and recognizable and latent. I see "cultural militarism" as the naturalization of the violence of armies, the routinization of the disciplinary aspects of militaries, the predominance of military virtues, the amplification of potential threats, the domination of specialists on violence, and the intensification of military ideals and impacts.

Early analyses of Israeli society emphasized the reciprocal influences between the civilian sphere and the military sector, and accentuated the balance between these two established subsystems. Some underlined and highlighted a slight dominance of the civic sphere, which they referred to as "civilianization of the military."[25] Later works have highlighted the historical, cultural, and social constructions of militarization and mili-tarism in Israel. These "new critical studies" illustrate the nature of the citizen's army, which blurs the boundaries between the civilian and the military, as well as the centrality of the military ideals in Israeli society, and describe the dominance of the term *national security* within Israeli political structures.[26]

Some authors indicate that militarism is the central organizing prin-ciple around which Israeli society characterizes its boundaries and its identity. They claim that military service delineates the boundaries of the political collective of Israel and critically portray the continuing reliance of Israel on its military power for its national security. Most describe the weakness of the political level and the weakness in the structural mechanisms of civilian control over the military, and others posit that Israel can be considered "uncivil."[27] However, none of these approaches explicitly deals with the visual field, and none explores the impact of photographs depicting IDFWS on the militaristic character of Israeli society; this study bridges this conceptual and empirical gap.

Figure 13.1. David Eldan, "Chen Israel's Women's Army passes the flag-draped streets on Independence Day in Jerusalem," April 23, 1950. *D725-026, NPC, Government Press Office, State of Israel.*

Turning the spotlight toward IDFWS' photos and dealing with the political uses of visual representations help us to understand the unique historical conditions and cultural experiences that affect the specific militaristic character of Israeli society.[28] While previous studies discussed IDFWS' presence in the IDF, this study explores the ways they are represented to the public eye. Most studies have explored the IDF as a gendered institution and examined the incorporation of women into the military organization by observing the SSL and focusing on the women's marginalization and "semi-civilian" status as well as on other military practices and procedures.[29] The current discussion adds to this growing body of literature by addressing the visual representations of IDFWS as a case study of the latent ways of militarization of Israeli society.

Figure 13.2. Anonymous, "Women soldiers," *62\2112, B 1, 50, p. 6, IDF & Defense Establishment Archives*, Ba-Mahane.

Photographs of IDF Women Soldiers and Erotic Militarism in Israel

Three groups of photos were taken in the public sphere. The first group, *"On the Border": A Military Parade in the Civic Space,* includes photos of IDFWS marching in military parades through civic space and city streets (figure 13.1). A military parade, at that point, can be seen as a temporary military invasion into the public–civic space, while subordinating the latter to a firm set of institutional procedures and army rules.

The current conceptualization regards parades in terms of (liminal) *time* and (governed) *space,* but also as a *phenomenon in the field of vision* that can be observed from both spaces. These temporary relations between space, time, vision, and body enable a military expansion into the civic space, while at the same time marking the borderline between

Figure 13.3. Anonymous, "Afternoon Rest." *1094B, Chen, 145, p. 23, IDF & Defense Establishment Archives, IDF Photograph service.*

the two. The second group, *Closed Military Zone—No Civilians Allowed*, includes photos of IDFWS in the military–public space: the army camp (figure 13.2). The law of the state, the juridical system of sovereignty, and military institutional procedures define the boundaries of this space. They exclude all that is civic from the military space. The army camp is seen here as a space of inclusion and exclusion, and the military heterotopias is regarded as a "safeguard," keeping all illicit civilians outside, and thus defining the structure of citizenship and the borders of civil space.[30] The third and last group of photos, *Women's Dormitories—No Men Allowed*, includes photos of women soldiers in their own enclaves and dormitories. In this group two mechanisms organize the spatial and power relations (figures 13.3 and 13.4). The first includes and excludes civilians through the SSL. The second is of bureaucratic mechanisms and military codes of normalization. These army procedures include and exclude, inside the military zone, through the criteria of gender and duties.

Figure 13.4. (Bar-Am), in Cohen, *Bat Chen,* 38–39.

I suggest that there is a *structural affinity* among these three distinct groups of photos. What can be seen as polarities of aesthetic modes and spatial divisions (the first and third groups) are, in fact, manifestations of continuity. Moreover, despite visual differences, and notwithstanding representational dissimilarities, there are connections and continuations among the three groups and similarities in their impacts. Although one may distinguish between these three visual modes, during this period photographic images of IDFWS were shifting "on the fringe" and "in between" two poles of aesthetic representational systems (figures 13.5 and 13.6). Moreover, the hidden continuity between these visual groups was merely one of the more obscure conditions to smooth the way for cultural osmosis between military space and the civic one.

I suggest that despite these spatial divisions, IDFWS, who were "on the border" and "in between," are, in fact, in a "semi-civilian" status, as is expressed in the following statement: "A stranger immediately notices that military service does not cut off the female soldier from civil society. IDFWS are an inseparable part of our public landscape, adding variety and beauty to our streets."[31]

Figure 13.5. Anonymous, "War of Independence. In the photo: An IDF woman soldier brushing her hair in the Negev," December 3, 1948. *D284-090, National Photo Collection (NPC), Government Press Office, State of Israel.*

"WOMEN'S DORMITORIES—NO MEN ALLOWED"

See figure 13.4.[32] A photograph is a visual image that freezes a moment in time, describing objects, people, and places as they appeared within the frame view of the camera *at that given moment*.[33] This last term, borrowed from a lecture by Foucault,[34] indicates a parallel between a photograph and the military parade mentioned above. It is a selection of certain acts that operate through vision and through enclosing space and time. These acts produce and reproduce both power and pleasure relations. A photo is a conjunction of body–space–vision and time, and delineates power and pleasure relations as the core of it. Looking at this specific photo raises a series of questions characteristic of visual research: What was visible at that "given moment" captured by the camera's lens and exhibited to the public eye in this photographic image? What is the specific space? What is the "given moment"? Who is positioned and where? Who is observing, and who is being observed and from what angle? Whose body is displayed and is being looked at as an object of vision? How is the visual image related to the verbal? What is indicated and what is hidden by the image; namely, what do we see and *not* see? What does the dialectic shift between denotation and connotation allow? What are the interrelations between the linguistic message, the coded iconic message, and the noncoded iconic message?

Read the description of figure 13.4 and learn that the space is a military camp: "This is, no doubt, the most important phase in turning the new woman recruit into a real woman soldier. Here it is determined if she loses her individual identity under the army uniform or challenges it and remains an individual."[35] Those words clarify the context in terms of time and space and give a concrete meaning to the visual image. Despite often being regarded as a declaration of autonomy, photographs are frequently combined with the verbal. Only shifting between the two enables the construction of meaning. This complicated system allows the identification of the visible and at the same time escaping its fascinating blinding power. It is one of the factors that enable the pendulum-like shift of photographs from acting as seals of approval to tools of critique and back.[36]

The description shows that the frozen moment is a transitional moment between when the soldiers take off their civilian clothes and put

Figure 13.6. Anonymous, "One of the New Instructors, during the time of the parade," June 12, 1954. *D379-068, NPC, Government Press Office, State of Israel.*

on army uniforms. This transformational process is manifested on the bodies of young women. Theirs is the body we gaze at, gendered bodies of sexually mature women upon which *the political technologies of the body* are exercised.[37] The photo is a product of observational mechanism—the women represented seem unaware of the observer and of the observational act.

Two assumptions are neither contradictory nor mutually exclusive. The first is that the "panoptical" mechanism discussed by Foucault might have been so *obvious* that the women ceased to notice it. The second might indicate that even though everyone and everything are visible, the observing apparatuses seem to be invisible. Furthermore, it appears that interplays between visibility and invisibility guarantee order,[38] just as interplays between cultural modes of permission and prevention characterize eroticism:[39] "All women's dormitories are off-limits. . . . No men are allowed in the women's dormitories, not even in case of needed repairs, unless granted permission."[40]

This implies that the profession and the camera act as a "safeguard": they provide male soldiers with the privilege to enter a "no-entrance zone" and grant the lens the freedom to offer civilians legitimate voyeurism and an opportunity to peek inside a closed military space and gaze at IDFWS who are performing actions that are seen as intimate, daily routine.

The photographic view observing the women from behind raises another issue. It exposes the "observational look" as a voyeuristic and a scopophilic one (meaning pleasure in looking), and as Laura Mulvey[41] suggests, scopophilia is essentially active and erotic.[42] This exposes the panoptical schema as a conjunction of *looking as supervision,* and *looking as pleasure,* one manifestation of which is that of turning the bodies into docile bodies. The other is *representing* the bodies as erotic bodies. The photographer's eye and the lens of the camera take the role of seducers, creating a new form of collective voyeurism for civilians outside the military camps.

The following questions may be asked in relation to figures 13.3 and 13.4: Why was such a special permit given to the public eye via the cameras of the disciplinary mechanism or the photographic medium? Why was it allowed to peek at those IDFWS? What "public right" or "cultural practice" enabled the camera to enter a "no entry" domain and gather "there and then" visual "evidence"? Was it possible to raise these questions without the camera being used as a supervision apparatus, and without the interdependencies between visual mechanisms and disciplinary mechanisms? Does the "biased gaze" of the supervising eye create a "biased spectator"? What sort of exchange goes on through the field of vision—power, approval, or pleasure?

The two photos, which can be seen as two aggressive interventions into the women's dormitories to "copy" "objective" visual evidence, can be classified as part of "photo journalism" or the "documentary genre." Through them, parts of the invisible aspects of reality become visible, and fragments of the unknown become familiar. Under the mask of the documentary genre, our eyes can invade closed zones "out there" and enjoy the visual pleasure of looking at images of other bodies, while desiring to see what is not shown.[43] The simultaneity of "it was there" and "I was there" contributes to the aura of authority and authenticity associated with photographic images.[44] Daily routine events can be grasped as "natural," the space as "transparent," and the act of photography as "reflecting" reality and "re-presenting" the military domain. Nonetheless, what we see is the result of cultural construction: a process of framing and selection that is guided by cultural codes and expectations. What we are looking at are actually reproductions of traditional visual codes presuming a heterosexual male viewer observing "indoor domestic" spaces, thus providing an erotic quality.[45]

To name this visual pleasure a "male" gaze, and to analyze it as an exercise of power and gender relations is important, but nevertheless it is only partial. What distinguishes this gaze from the Hollywood Gaze described by Mulvey[46] is its unmistakable militaristic context. These visual images of IDFWS function as a "politics of truth," producing new forms of knowledge, and inventing new concepts that contribute to the "government" of new domains of regulation and intervention.

In a different context, images like these might be considered an individual's illegitimate voyeurism. In this particular context, however, these photographs provide *legitimate models for collective voyeurism attached to the military domain.* While exposing the daily life of IDFWS, these aesthetic representations are simultaneously wrapping the military apparatuses with an intensive libido. Throughout these images, the military space is represented and loaded with erotic imagination and sexual possibilities that are associated with "indoor domestic" places. While visual pleasures are provoked from watching images of IDFWS' bodies, they are, at the same time, indirectly perceived as enjoying military's norms and militarism. The singularity of the specific event is lost as it becomes accessible through photos and publicity to many viewers in diverse places. The publicity of these photos suggests that *the disciplinary mechanism might be invisible, but the power must be exposed and seen.* This description draws the interdependence and complex relations between photography and the state apparatuses, and describes the significant impact of photography on the mutual spillover between military and civil society.

Although it is important to indicate the ways in which these photos represent IDFWS' bodies, it is necessary to emphasize how this process—which is penetrated with erotic enjoyment attached to military images—"spills over" into everyday life outside military camps.

"CLOSED MILITARY ZONE—NO CIVILIANS ALLOWED"

The photograph in figure 13.7 depicts hundreds of men in uniform, young and old alike, eyeing one woman, examining her as an object. The young woman is shaking hands with an older senior officer leaning toward her. He wears a uniform. She is exposed, wearing only her swimsuit. The pleasurable gazes of the audience (which includes only four IDFWS in uniform) are focused on her. The caption of this visual representation is "IDF swimming contests," and it represents a military enclosed space.[47] The photo is part of a series of thirty taken by army photographer A. Z. Polsky on September 5, 1957, and published in the IDF journal, *Ba-Machaneh,* on September 13, 1957. The photographer's "mission" might have been to cover army swim contests, but the camera captured what Walter Benjamin defines as "optical unconscious."[48] Such photos were very common and totally acceptable, and because of their wide distribution it is important to relate to them in this context.

What these photos (figures 13.2 and 13.7) and a third photo, titled "Soldiers in the Field,"[49] offer to the public eye are more than just a new form of collective voyeurism for civilians outside the military camps. They offer, as well, military space as one of enjoyment and fantasy in the midst of an ideological structure. These representations delineate the *cultural position* of the public figure—"An IDF Woman Soldier"—as one of the different sort of little things around which individuals and community center their fantasies and their lives.[50]

The supposedly innocent photos, officially produced for a certain purpose, served another purpose, enabling us to examine them, in what Slavoj Žižek calls "looking awry."[51] "Looking awry" enables us to distinguish gaps or differences between the symbolic history of the collective and the hidden fantasmatic history confirming that on the surface.[52] In these photos, it reveals unconscious pleasurable layers melted into an egalitarian unifying aura of army service. The eroticism and excitement they provide help shape the pleasurable element in the linkage between the "military" and the "civil," and induce militarism as well. They are like "peepholes," beyond the bright aura of terms like *equality* or *liberalism*, the shady side of the law and its latent effects. They are like dark eyeglasses that enable us to look through the bright images of organized military parades that may blind our sight.

"ON THE BORDER": A MILITARY PARADE IN THE CIVIC SPACE

The spectacle of the military parade (figure 13.1) does not automatically invoke terms such as *eroticism, passion,* or *voyeurism,* which easily come to mind when watching photos of IDFWS in their dormitories (figure 13.4). Nevertheless, inspired by Gilles Deleuze and Felix Guattari and by Jacques Lacan, who contend that desire is the other side of the law, I argue that photos of IDFWS' quarters are the inevitable "other side" of photos of IDFWS marching through cities' streets.[53]

During the first two decades of independence, numerous military parades were held in Israeli cities. Spectators were fascinated and trapped by the "glamour effect" of IDFWS marching alongside men soldiers. Stimulated by Žižek's claims about object cause of desire, the psychic structure, and structural necessity of fascination, I assert that the performative mechanisms and the unifying process of military spectacles, as well as the mediation of photography, diminish the importance of the one (the soldier), and wrap the many and their visual representations in "a bond of desire."[54] The charisma and charm greatly exceed each individual's qualities and are not necessarily their own specific virtues, although they can be experienced as such. All the same, this bond is

Figure 13.7. A. Z. Polsky, "IDF swimming contests," September 5, 1957, 38. *1749/18, IDF & Defense Establishment Archives,* Ba-Mahane.

charging the disciplinary mechanism of the military with a surplus of desire and extra charm.

Conclusion

Collective memory is shaped not only by the uniqueness of singular experiences and special rituals but also by repetitive daily events or practices. During those first decades, the visual practice exposed to the public eye and infused into the collective memory the unusual photographs of IDFWS in their dormitories and during their daily routine. It also exposed the widespread photos of IDFWS in the unique event of a military parade marching through the civic domain. Thus, they attempted to inscribe their photos into the collective memory of Israeli society.

This chapter has suggested that during the early decades of Israel's statehood, photo images of IDFWS were modifying and shifting "on the fringe" and "in between" two poles of aesthetic representational systems. They combined the polarity of the "pure" and almost "clinical" representational principles referring to masculine and militaristic cultural codes with a more exposed erotic and feminized imagery. The visual images were shifting between representations of the public sphere using army uniform in parades, and between representations of the private sphere, suggesting eroticism and exposing feminine intimate acts and enclosed spaces to the public eye.

The transitional phases from voluntary to mandatory conscription carried with them the possibility of a number of configurations between the state, the military institution, and various women's groups. The SSL of 1949 was the legal name for the configuration that was chosen. The visual aspects of this unique phenomenon of women's conscription have been described here, the prevailing norms of national discourse as manifested in their photos outlined, and their cultural preferences and unconscious pleasures identified.

This chapter has suggested a deeper understanding of the institutional linkages that previous studies of Israel's pattern of civil–military relations—both traditional and critical—have identified. I argued that in addition to *institutional* linkages, the visual representations of IDFWS were one of the more vague conditions for the *cultural* osmosis between systems that characterize Israel's brand of "civil-militarism." The fact that Israeli women, like Israeli men, have been subject to compulsory service makes the military camp an important site for producing ratification and reproduction of erotic militarization. Their presence in army camps and, more precisely, the ways IDFWS were represented, thus make a crucial contribution to the eroticization of militarism in Israel, and for the social-cultural fascination of Israeli society with the IDF.

The visual vocabulary of photos of IDFWS that were distributed in the civilian sphere operated as a "shortcut" to erotic fantasy and, in turn, left civilian life with what Beverly Brown calls a "certain afterglow."[55] I would emphasize and re-term this impact as a "certain militaristic afterimage." The photos were like little implements of enjoyment moving from space to space, delivering visions from the open space of military parades and evoking desires out of the prohibition. All at once, they were leaving behind militaristic and erotic afterimages.

The critical reading offered in this chapter has helped reveal the unconscious layer of these visual texts. It has exposed how these photos have operated as visual instruments of legitimization, pleasure, and eroticization, which together created visual bridges that were "bridging" or "binding" processes of militarization. The contribution of this reading lies in discovering a certain kind of rational and underlying principle that the three groups of photos were using, and in exposing the role of legitimization that these bridges were playing. Photos of IDFWS were visual instruments of legitimization for an egalitarian ethos and military norms. Their photos in the public sphere and military parades were visual bearers for the ideology of the military rational–professional virtue of modernity, and they have helped promote the military service as a "source bond" of national identity. Simultaneously, photos of daily routines in military space have operated through the rational aspects of the documentary genre as a visual apparatus for voyeurism, fascination, and eroticism.

Looking at these unique images of Israeli–Jewish IDFWS is viewing visual traces of "social institution and mental machinery,"[56] which have intensified militaristic appeal and glorified military norms. Simultaneously, looking at them means looking at visual products that were constructed culturally as a modernist attraction and as a romantic attraction. Through them, hegemonic representations of the military were created as objects of desire, and military space appeared desirable.

By focusing on visual representations of IDFWS, I have attempted to call attention to the conscious and unconscious, the direct and indirect, and the pleasurable and disciplinary dimensions of the multiple meeting points between the state, the military, civil society, and individual citizens in Israel. Light was thrown on the "optical unconscious" of the connections between technologies of the self and technologies of domination, or what Foucault referred to as *governmentality*. I illuminated the militaristic links between the constitution of the subject and the formation of the state. The chapter has offered a new way of looking at the phenomenon of "cultural militarism" in Israel by describing the evasive and ever-changing processes of militarization of Israeli society in terms of an "erotic militarization" that constitutes a crucial part of this particular brand of militarism.

Notes

1. The first Knesset debated numerous issues on the War of Independence and its termination, the organization and functioning of the IDF, and regulation issues concerning the civic sphere such as education and marriage. See http://www.knesset.gov.il/index.html.

2. *Knesset Protocols,* August 15, 1949.

3. *Knesset Protocols,* August 15, 19, 24, 25, 30, 31; September 1 and 5, 1949.

4. Dan Horowitz and Moshe Lissak, *Trouble in Utopia* (Albany, N.Y., 1989), 195–230; Chava Brownfield-Stein, "Beautiful Group with a Gun: Visual Representations of Women Soldiers in Israel Defense Force Albums, 1948–1958," *Israeli Sociology* 6 (2005): 351–88 [Hebrew].

5. This chapter follows my master's thesis, "Beautiful Group with a Gun: Visual Representations of Women Soldiers in IDF Albums, 1948–1958" (Bar-Ilan University, 2002), which examined the reciprocal exchange between mechanisms and ideological state apparatuses and the role of photography in the construction of gender identities during the first decade of Israel's independence. The thesis indicated the correlation between political and military strategies and the visual presentation, claiming that photographs of women soldiers were an operative principal as well as a cultural mold and social ideology that included and excluded women.

6. Uri Ben-Eliezer, *The Emergence of Israeli Militarism, 1936–1956* (Tel-Aviv, 1995), 313 [Hebrew].

7. Yagil Levy, *The Other Army of Israel* (Tel-Aviv, 2003), 20–80 [Hebrew].

8. Baruch Kimmerling, "Militarism in Israeli Society," *Theory and Criticism* 4 (1993): 129 [Hebrew].

9. Cynthia H. Enloe, *Maneuvers: The International Politics of Militarizing Women's Lives* (Berkeley, Calif., 2000), 291.

10. Thomas Lemke, "The Birth of Bio-Politics—Michel Foucault's Lecture at the Collège de France on Neo-Liberal Governmentality," *Economy & Society* 30 (2001): 190–207.

11. Miriam Cooke and Angela Woollacott (eds.), *Gendering War Talk* (Princeton, N.J., 1993); Lois Ann Lorentzen and Jennifer Turpin (eds.), *The Women and War Reader* (New York, 1998); Joshua S. Goldstein, *War and Gender: How Gender Shapes the War System and Vice Versa* (Cambridge, 2001); Madelain Adelman, "The Military, Militarism, and the Militarization of Domestic Violence," *Violence against Women* 9 (2003): 1118–52.

12. Wendy Chapkis, "Sexuality and Militarism," in Eva Isaksson (ed.), *Women in the Military System* (New York, 1988), 106–14; Cooke and Woollacott, *Gendering War Talk,* 227–46; Val Williams, *Warworks, Women, Photography and the Iconography of*

War (London, 1994); Glenn D. Hook, *Militarization and Demilitarization in Contemporary Japan* (London, 1996); Enloe, *Maneuvers;* Michel Foucault, *"Society Must Be Defended": Lectures at the Collège de France, 1975–1976* (New York, 2003).

13. Stuart Hall, *Representation, Cultural Representations and Signifying Practices* (London, 1997); Arialla Azoulay, *Once upon a Time: Photography following Walter Benjamin* (Ramat-Gan, 2006) [Hebrew]; Irit Rogoff, *Terra Infirma: Geography's Visual Culture* (London, 2000); Liz Wells (ed.), *The Photography Reader* (London, 2003); Margarita Dikoyitskaya, *The Study of the Visual after the Cultural Turn* (Cambridge, Mass., 2005).

14. Edna Lomsky-Feder and Eyal Ben-Ari (eds.), *Military and Militarism in Israeli Society* (Albany, N.Y., 1999); Ella Shohat, *Forbidden Reminiscences* (Tel-Aviv, 2001) [Hebrew]; Raz Yosef, "Ethnicity and Sexual Politics: The Invention of Mizrahi Masculinity in Israeli Cinema," *Theory and Criticism* 25 (2004): 13–31 [Hebrew]; Ariella Azoulay, *The Civil Contract of Photography* (Tel-Aviv, 2006) [Hebrew].

15. Williams, *Warworks, Women, Photography;* Jean-Paul Sartre, *The Look,* trans. Avner Lahav (Tel-Aviv, 2007) [Hebrew]; Foucault, *Society Must Be Defended: Lectures at the Collège de France, 1975–1976;* Laura Mulvey, "Visual Pleasure and Narrative Cinema," in Jessica Evans and Stuart Hall (eds.), *Visual Culture: The Reader* (London, 1999), 381–89.

16. Yael Zerubavel, *Recovered Roots: Collective Memory and the Making of Israeli National Tradition* (Chicago, 1995).

17. Sara Helman, "Militarism and the Construction of Community," *Journal of Political and Military Sociology* 25 (Winter 1997): 305–32; Lomsky-Feder and Ben-Ari, *Military and Militarism;* Joyce Robbins and Uri Ben-Eliezer, "New Roles or "New Times"? Gender Inequality and Militarism in Israel's Nation-in-Arms," *Social Politics* 7 (2000): 309–43; Uta Klein, "Civil-Military Relations in Israeli Society," *Current Sociology* 50 (2002): 671–73; Levy, *The Other Army of Israel;* Rebecca L. Schiff, "Civil-Military Relations in Israel: Revisiting Israel as the 'Uncivil' State." Paper presented at the International Workshop on An Army That Has a State? The Role of Israel's Security Sector in a Comparative Perspective, The Van Leer Institute, Israel (Jerusalem, June 5–6, 2006).

18. *Merriam-Webster's Collegiate Dictionary* (Springfield, Mass., 1993), 1433.

19. Jennifer Turpin and Lois Ann Lorentzen (eds.), *The Gendered New World Order* (New York, 1996).

20. Michael Mann, "The Roots and Contradictions of Modern Militarism," *New Left Review* 162 (1987): 35–50.

21. John R. Gillis (ed.), *The Militarization of the Western World* (New Brunswick, N.J., 1989). On the concept of militarism, see Volker R. Berghahn, *Militarism: The History of an International Debate, 1861–1979* (New York, 1982); Michel Louis Martin and Ellen Stern McCrate (eds.), *The Military, Militarism and the Polity: Essays in Honor of Morris Janowitz* (New York, 1984); Martin Shaw, *Post-Military Society: Militarism, Demilitarization and War at the End of the Twentieth Century* (Philadelphia, 1991).

22. Yoram Peri, "The Political-Military Partnership in Israel," *International Political Science Review* 2 (1977): 303–15; Samuel P. Huntington, *The Soldier and the State* (Cambridge, Mass., 1957); Dan Horowitz, "The Israel Defense Forces: A Civilianized Military in a Partially Militarized Society," in Roman Kolkowicz and Andrzej Korbonski (eds.), *Soldiers, Peasants, and Bureaucrats* (London, 1982), 77–106; Moshe

Lissak, "Convergence and Structural Linkages between the Armed Forces and the Society," in Martin and McCrate, *The Military, Militarism and the Polity*, 49–61; Horowitz and Lissak, *Troubles in Utopia*.

23. Lorentzen and Turpin, *The Women and War Reader*; Enloe, *Maneuvers*.

24. Hook, *Militarization and Demilitarization in Contemporary Japan*.

25. Lissak, "Convergence and Structural Linkages"; Dan Horowitz, "Is Israel a Garrison State?" *The Jerusalem Quarterly* 4 (1977): 58–65; Horowitz, "The Israel Defense Forces," 77–106; Horowitz and Lissak, *Troubles in Utopia*, 195–230. On Israeli militarism, see Uri Ben-Eliezer, *The Making of Israeli Militarism* (Bloomington, Ind., 1988); Yoram Peri, *Between Battles and Ballots* (Cambridge, 1983).

26. See Kimmerling, *Militarism in Israeli Society*; Yagil Levy and Yoav Peled, "The Break That Never Was: Israeli Sociology Reflected through the Six Days War," *Theory and Criticism* 3 (1993): 115–28 [Hebrew]; Ben-Eliezer, *The Emergence of Israeli Militarism*; Lomsky-Feder and Ben-Ari, *Military and Militarism*. See also the chapter by Oren Barak and Gabriel Sheffer in this volume. Studies based on the following works, or influenced by postmodernist writings, have exposed clear militaristic attributes in Israel and have spoken of its "militaristic" society: Charles Tilly (ed.), *The Formation of National States in Western Europe* (Princeton, N.J., 1985); Anthony Giddens, *The Nation-State and Violence* (Cambridge, 1985); Christopher Dandeker, "The Bureaucratization of Force," in Lawrence Freedman (ed.), *War* (Oxford, 1994), 118–23. According to Kimmerling, in Israel "militarism penetrates both structurally and culturally into the collective state of mind . . . the essence of civilian militarism is that military considerations and considerations defined as 'national security' will almost always be privileged over other considerations." See his "Militarism in Israeli Society," 129.

27. Klein, "Civil-Military Relations in Israeli Society," 669–86; Levy, *The Other Army of Israel*; Yoram Peri, *Generals in the Cabinet Room* (Washington, D.C., 2006); Schiff, "Civil-Military Relations in Israel." The "Third Wave" or "the New Critical Approach," according to Barak and Sheffer, portrayed Israeli society as a "militaristic" society and Israel as a "garrison state." This approach also indicated the powerlessness of Israeli civil society, and its emphasis is, for the most part, on cultural aspects and informal exchanges and relationships.

28. Representation refers to the ways in which people, objects, places, and ideas are coded. The use of the term usually signs acknowledgment that images have histories, specificity interest, belief, values, and cultural context, and therefore carry ideological implications. Wells, *The Photography Reader*, 352.

29. Nancy Goldman and Karl Weignad, "The Israeli Women in Combat," in Martin and McCrate, *The Military, Militarism, and the Polity*, 201–30; Nira Yuval-Davis, "Front and Rare: The Sexual Division of Labor in Israeli Army," *Feminist Studies* 11 (1985): 649–75; Joyce Robbins, "Not Soldiers in the Ordinary Sense: The Israeli Women Soldier and the Politics of 'Non-Military' Roles in the 1950's," master's thesis, Tel-Aviv University, 1994; Dafna N. Israeli, "Gendering Military Service in the Israeli Defence Forces," *Israel Social Science Research* 12 (1997): 129–66; Robbins and Ben-Eliezer, "New Roles or 'New Times'," 309–43; Edna Levy-Schrieber and Eyal Ben-Ari, "Body Building, Character Building and Nation Building: Gender and Military Service in Israel," *Studies in Contemporary Judaism* 16 (2000): 171–90; Uta Klein, "Our Best Boys: The Gendered Nature of Civil-Military Relations in Israel," *Men and Masculinities* 2

(1999): 47–65; Orna Sasson-Levy, *Identities in Uniform: Masculinities and Femininities in the Israeli Military* (Jerusalem, 2006) [Hebrew]. These discuss inequality, sexual harassment, gender identities and gender roles, and different tasks and their impact on the status of women soldiers and gender-based hierarchies.

30. Foucault, *Society Must Be Defended.*
31. Zevia Cohen, *Bat-Chen* (Haifa, 1972), 9 [Hebrew].
32. Ibid., 38–39.
33. Wells, *The Photography Reader*, 1.
34. Foucault, *Society Must Be Defended*, 32.
35. Cohen, *Bat-Chen*, 30.
36. Azoulay, *Once upon a Time.*
37. Michel Foucault, *Discipline and Punish* (New York, 1979), 135–69.
38. Ibid.
39. Erotic mechanism always leaves something hidden ("no entrance zones") and parts unexposed to the senses. It requires mediation, space, and distancing. While eroticism is constructed by distinguishing and separating the allowed and the forbidden, the invasion of the camera lens into the "forbidden domain" indicates the suspension of the rule. At the same time, and only within classified space and measured time, this visual expansion is an approval or permission of looking as both enjoyment and erotic.
40. Israel Defense Forces Archives [IDFA], 501/1958, file 35.
41. Mulvey, "Visual Pleasure and Narrative Cinema," 381–86.
42. *Gaze* has become a widespread term to describe a particular way of looking. The voyeuristic gaze is used to describe the way in which men often look at women, as well as the way in which Western culture looks at the non-Western world. *Scopophilia* is the human drive to look, which in Freudian theory leads to voyeurism. *Voyeurism* refers to sexual stimulation obtained through looking, and in photography it refers to the image as spectacle used for the gratification of the spectator. See Wells, *The Photography Reader*, 350.
43. A photograph has a unique relation with what it represents and an immanent tension between "visible/invisible," "inside/outside" notions.
44. Susan Sontag, *On Photography* (Tel-Aviv, 1979) [Hebrew]; Roland Barthes, *La chambre claire* (Jerusalem, 1988) [Hebrew].
45. The erotic imagination also draws indirectly from the classification of spaces and social characters; physiognomy and garments indicate status and profession.
46. Mulvey, "Visual Pleasure and Narrative Cinema."
47. Photos in IDFA do not necessarily mean that the event actually occurred in a military space, since IDF photographers document many events in civil locations.
48. Walter Benjamin, *Kleine Geschichte der Photographie* (Tel-Aviv, 2004), 19 [Hebrew]. According to him, "photography with its devices of slow motion and enlargement, reveals the secret. . . . It is through photography that we first discover the existence of this optical unconscious."
49. Although the title is "Soldiers in the Field," the camera focuses on a woman soldier surrounded by men's eyes. She is sitting on a pillow, like a statue on a pedestal, surrounded by men. The many eyes gazing at her from close range create an atmosphere of siege. The caption reads: "Once you see the admiring looks following the platoon's clerk visiting soldiers on duty—you understand it all." By contrast, Israeli

poet Roni Somek presents a less-romantic approach. In his poem "Go for the Nipple," he writes about the secret erotic fantasies behind those gazes and the military's hierarchy attached to them.

50. Richard Rorty, *Contingency, Irony, and Solidarity* (Tel-Aviv, 2006) [Hebrew], 84.

51. Slavoj Žižek, *Looking Awry: An Introduction to Jacques Lacan Culture* (Tel-Aviv, 2005) [Hebrew].

52. Ibid., 25–26.

53. Gilles Deleuze and Felix Guattari, *Kafka—Pour une Literature Mineure* (Tel-Aviv, 2005), 94 [Hebrew]; Jacques Lacan, *Ecrits: A Selection* (London, 1977).

54. According to Žižek, "although any object can function as the object-cause of desire—insofar as the power of fascination it exerts is not its immediate property but results from the place it occupies in the structure—we must, by structural necessity, fall prey to the illusion that the power of fascination belongs to the object as such." *Looking Awry*, 40.

55. Beverley Brown, "A Feminist Interest in Pornography: Some Modest Proposals," in Parveen Adams and Elizabeth Cowie (eds.), *The Woman in Question: M/f* (Cambridge, Mass., 1990), 134–48.

56. See p. 18 in Christian Metz, "The Imagery Signifier," *Screen* 16 (1975): 14–76.

FOURTEEN

Contradictory Representation of the IDF in Cultural Texts of the 1980s

YUVAL BENZIMAN

Studying Society through the Prism of Its Culture

The Israeli poet Haim Gouri related a conversation with an Egyptian intellectual, Dr. Hussein Fawzi, who told him that every intelligence officer must study poetry. Had Israeli Intelligence read the Egyptian poetry written after 1967, he told Gouri, Israel would not have been surprised by the outbreak of the 1973 War.[1] This is probably an exaggeration: poetry, literature, and other kinds of cultural text do not contain military data. Yet such texts can tell us about the society in which they are written and read.

This chapter examines the ways in which the IDF is represented in Israeli cultural texts, arguing that this representation tells us a great deal about the role of the army in Israeli society. Since the underlying assumption of the chapter is that cultural texts have an essential role in society, focus is placed on significant, known, and canonical cultural texts of the 1980s that represent the function of the army in the context of the Israeli–Arab conflict, and not on marginal texts.

Nations are in an everlasting process of creating themselves through narratives, and there is a dialectical interchange between the nation that creates a master narrative for its cultural texts, and the cultural texts that provide a narrative for the nation.[2] Cultural texts have dual functions: they tell us the story of the society in which they were written by means of representing that society, and—simultaneously—they modify the perspectives and ways of thinking of the society that reads or watches them.

In addition, literature and other cultural texts provide an opportunity to examine social trends that cannot be manifested in public discourse and in social research, because fictional texts are not coerced to deliver a certain truth or to supply a mimetic representation of reality. Artists who produce such texts are thus allowed more freedom in addressing social issues. Their unconstrained position provides them with the ability to discuss topics not dealt with elsewhere, and to expose aspects of the social situation that no other discourse can reveal.

Discussing the interface between literature and politics, Fredric Jameson claims as follows: "There is nothing that is not social and historical—indeed . . . everything is 'in the last analysis' political."[3] Even those who resist this assumption would agree that cultural texts can reveal much about the unconscious social processes of a particular society and about the factors that mold its self-perception. In fiction that tends toward realism—as is the case with most texts dealing with the Arab–Israeli conflict—this observation is certainly valid. Moreover, in Hebrew prose fiction, which since the days of Hibat Tzion of the late nineteenth century has held a significant role in shaping the Jewish–Israeli social and national conscious,[4] this argument is even more powerful.

Benedict Anderson argues that printed materials in general, and novels (as well as newspapers) in particular have great importance in the shaping of modern societies, because they provide society with objects, notions, and representations that apparently help it imagine its common grounds.[5] If he is correct, we need to understand how Israeli cultural texts represent one of the most influential institutions in Israeli society—its army.

The 1980s, and the Israeli–Arab Conflict

The most significant years to be examined in a study of the representation of the IDF in Israeli cultural texts are the late 1970s and the 1980s. The IDF has had, for many years, a central role in the Israeli–Arab conflict. However, it was in this decade that the close relationship between society and its cultural texts resulted in recognizable changes both in the sociopolitical and national sphere, as well as in Israeli cultural texts.

The changes in the "real" conflict were manifest in the international realm: the Israel–Egypt peace agreement in 1979 proved that the Israeli–Arab conflict was no longer a threat to the existence of Israel; the notion that Israel could defend itself through peace agreements, and that the option of giving land for peace could be implemented, changed the way Israeli society perceived the conflict.[6] At the same time, the Lebanon War of 1982 altered the way the Israeli public viewed relations between Israel and its neighbors, as the war revealed that Israel was not necessarily only a peace-seeking state, but also an initiator of war.

Relations between Jewish and Arab citizens of Israel also changed. On March 30, 1976 (known as Land Day), a brutal clash took place between Israeli police and Arab citizens demonstrating against government expropriation of lands. Six Israeli Arab citizens were killed by the police in the demonstrations, and the Arab minority claimed that the police used disproportional force because the protestors were Arabs. The events of that day, perhaps more than any other event, emphasized the distrust of Israeli Arab citizens of the Jewish–Israeli state.

Israeli sociologists disagree about the causes for the outbreak of conflict between Jewish and Arab citizens in the late 1970s and the 1980s. Some believe it emerged because of the Palestinization of the Arab minority and the Jewish nationalization after the 1967 war; others maintain that the dramatic change in the Israeli government in 1977, ending the dominant one-party regime, brought the so-far silenced voices of Israeli society into the public discourse, with the Arab voice being one of them.[7] Regardless of the causes, the Jewish–Arab conflict inside Israel underwent an influential and essential transformation during this decade. Although the conflict might have seemed more tangible to the Jewish Israeli public, polls in 1976, 1980, 1985, 1988, and 1995 present a slow but steady decrease in the negative perceptions of the Jewish Israeli public toward the Arab minority.[8]

Relations between Israelis and Palestinians in Gaza and the West Bank also underwent changes, with a substantial increase in violent incidents involving Palestinians and Israelis, the IDF's harsher policy against the Palestinians, the crisis of the Palestinian economy, the establishment of a local Palestinian leadership (as opposed to the leadership in exile), and so on.[9] All these factors led to the first Intifada in 1987. However, as Baruch Kimmerling and Joel S. Migdal claim, the main change in the 1980s was the growing realization that the Palestinians could no longer be seen as sporadic groups fighting for local rights, but should be perceived as a people or a nation struggling for an independent and autonomous state.[10]

As expected, while dramatic changes regarding the "real" conflict took place, the representation of the conflict in cultural texts also underwent modification. It is impossible to determine what came first—modifications in cultural texts or changes in reality—but it is reasonable to assume that the changes occurred at the same time and had some mutual influence.

In the late 1970s, Ella Shohat[11] claims, there was a change in the way Israeli cinema illustrated the conflict: the Arab narrative received some expression, Arab actors began to star in films and had some influence on the story line, Jewish actors played Arabs while Arabs played Jews, and the Arab–Jewish conflict became a major topic in Israeli movies. All these led to a more balanced rendering of the conflict. Critics disagree on whether the dramatic change that occurred was real or artificial,[12] but all agree that a significant change did occur in the representation of the Israeli–Arab conflict at the end of the 1970s and throughout the 1980s.

Similar changes can be found in the way the Israeli–Arab conflict was manifested in Hebrew prose fiction of the 1980s. Compared with the decades before, a considerably greater number of texts that focused on the conflict were written. The preferred genre was now the novel, instead of the short story,[13] which allowed—at least theoretically—for a more polyphonic representation[14] of the conflict, in which the Arab voice could be heard. Some novels were written from a dual Jewish–Arab point of view, and thus presented the Arab position; Arab characters became rounder and complex[15] and no longer were stereotypes[16] that merely project on the Jewish hero,[17] but were now independent characters who exposed the reader to the Arab perspective.[18] Some texts ended the previous hierarchical dichotomy between Jews and Arabs, and proposed a more equal discourse,[19] and a few Arab novels became part of the canon of Hebrew literature.[20]

At the same time, as Dan Orian[21] shows, between 1982 and 1994 Arab characters appeared in more than one hundred plays in Israeli theater (which is more than all the plays with Arab characters in 1911–1973).

They played central roles, and placed the Arab Palestinian narrative of the hardships caused by the conflict in the forefront. Elie Podeh[22] shows that changes in the depiction of the Israeli–Arab conflict in Israeli textbooks also began in the mid-1970s and continued through the 1980s. A similar phenomenon can be seen in other cultural modes of representation.

The IDF, a key component in the representation of the conflict, is represented in a majority of these cultural texts. In most of them it is not merely represented, but has a central role. It is therefore important to see how the army is represented, what role it plays in cultural texts dealing with the conflict, and how its representation is influenced by the fact that the rendering of the conflict as a whole diminished, in the period discussed, the authority of the traditional Jewish–Zionist narrative.

The representation of the IDF in cultural texts dealing with the conflict seemed so important in the 1980s that the IDF's army filming unit (probably for reasons of propaganda) cooperated in making Eli Cohen's movie *Ricochet* (also known as *Two Fingers from Sidon*, 1986) about the Lebanon War of 1982, a film that was very popular in Israel. This represents an example of the tangled relations between fiction and reality: senior generals such as Shaul Mofaz (who later became CGS) and Yitzhak Mordechai (who later served as a brigadier general) played themselves as officers.

The Function of the Army

A distinction should be made between cultural texts dealing with the conflict between Arabs and Jews inside of Israel, and cultural texts on the conflict between Israel and the Palestinians in Gaza and the West Bank. Although similar phenomena can be observed in the two sets of texts, the function of the IDF is different in each. Whereas the conflict between Israel and the Palestinians has been represented in a variety of texts, the conflict between Arabs and Jews inside Israel is dealt with less often. In spite of the difference between the two types of conflict, only through observing them together can we provide a full picture of the role of the army in the Israeli–Arab conflict and of its overall function in Israeli society.

The Role of the Army in the Relationship
between Israel and the Palestinians

Although different kinds of civilian relationships have existed between Israelis and Palestinians, and although cultural texts can construct whatever relations they wish, they almost always tell stories of the conflict in which the interaction is between the Israeli army and Palestinian civilians. The IDF is represented as the only institution in Israel that has direct and permanent dealings with the Palestinians. Only the IDF knows their way of living, only it can explain their way of thinking, and only it seems to possess an exclusive understanding of Palestinian society. Whether in South Lebanon or in Gaza and the West Bank, the kinds of interaction described—love stories, violent incidents, war, personal acquaintances—all involve soldiers. The IDF is, therefore, seen as the overall representative of Israel and its interactions with Palestinians.

Even in the few texts that tell stories about types of interaction that are nonviolent and nonmilitaristic, the IDF is still represented as an important factor. In Haim Buzaglo's *Fictive Marriage* (1988), for example, the Israeli Jewish protagonist deceives his wife when he tells her that he is leaving for New York, because he actually stays in Israel. In his suitcase, which he leaves at the airport, he puts his army uniform. He eventually ends up employed with Palestinians who enter Israel in order to work, while pretending to be deaf so as to conceal from them the fact that he is not a Palestinian himself. The army uniform, shown for only a few seconds at the beginning of the movie, tells us that his supposed trip, which turned out to be an intense encounter with Palestinians that arouses his (and Israeli society's) entire set of national stereotypes, is actually a part of what should be seen as military service. Therefore, even in a film that has nothing to do with the IDF but deals with civilian interaction between Palestinians and Israelis, the IDF has a small but meaningful role.

The central role of the IDF in almost all such depictions results in a Palestinian understanding of the IDF as the sole representative of Israeliness, dominating every aspect of Israelis' daily lives. It sometimes seems as though the characteristics of the sovereign state that owns this army are unimportant, because the Palestinians only interact with this agent.

In Avi Valentin's novel *Shahid* (1989), the Palestinian terrorist says, "These were the Jews I knew. All of them were soldiers. I couldn't imagine Jews without army uniform and high shoes. . . . I only saw soldiers in khaki clothes with accouterment and weapons."[23] In Nissim Dayan's *A Narrow Bridge* (1985), the IDF seems to be so well established inside the Palestinian society that it takes part in defending certain Palestinian people in that society and knows everything that goes on inside it—even more than the local Palestinians do. It is not surprising that the reserve officer tells Laila, the Arab widow with whom he is in love, "with me you can do anything you want; I am the Law here"—"here" meaning both inside Israel and in the Territories.

The most significant example of the IDF's function in intervening in every aspect of Palestinian social life, and at the same time being seen by the Palestinians as the embodiment of Israel, is found in David Grossman's novel *The Smile of the Lamb* (1983).[24] Hilmi, an old Arab, holds Uri—an Israeli officer—hostage, threatening to kill him if the IDF does not evacuate the entire occupied territories. Not surprisingly, it is not Israel or its government to whom he addresses his claim, but the IDF—the only institution that interacts with Palestinians, and the governing body that rules their world.

Not only do the Palestinians see the IDF as the only representative of Israel, but the IDF is also regarded as the only institution that can change Israel's attitude toward them. The cultural texts tell us a story in which it is not the government that shapes policy; nor can any civilian have any influence in this area. Only the IDF has such influence. The IDF changes its attitude toward the Palestinians at will, and practically decides how to act. Civil leadership is rarely mentioned, and when it is, it is treated with disappointment and scorn; this, in its turn, leads the army officers to decide by themselves how to treat the Palestinians.

In Yitzhak Ben-Ner's *Ta'atuon* (1989), Chrul, the Israeli General Security Services person, says that his job is "one of the few jobs in which an individual can significantly influence reality,"[25] and adds that if people like him disappear, "the Israeli nation will be lost"[26]—as if the field officers alone determine the fate of Israel. *The Smile of the Lamb* constructs a similar pattern, as we are told that the main reason why the two Israeli officers, Uri and Katzman, decided to do military service is because they hope that through this job they will be able to change reality and assist Palestinian society. The implication is that no civil act can achieve the same effect.

Two further examples illustrate this phenomenon. In Yoram Kaniuk's novel *A Good Arab* (1984), it is mentioned that in 1948, "every Israeli officer decided what his policy was."[27] In Amos Kenan's allegorical novel *The Road to Ein Harod* (1984),[28] the brigadier general says that he had captured and killed the CGS, the ministers, and the PM because they had ruined everything, and that he is looking for a new prime minister.

These aspects of the all-inclusive, omnipotent role ascribed to the IDF in cultural texts are also relevant to the question of how the Palestinians are shown to be treated. Here lies the most important and interesting aspect of the army's representation in Israeli culture: the IDF is presented as a cruel, harsh, violent military that abuses Palestinians. The relations between the soldiers and the Palestinian population seem to be almost intimate: the soldiers walk in their streets, enter their houses, and watch every move they make, and at the same time the soldiers keep a distance from the Palestinians, enabling the soldiers to act harshly against them.

Despite the almost unlimited power granted to the IDF, the soldiers themselves seem to be frustrated about the violent acts that they perform. They behave cruelly and feel bad about it, hit Palestinians and cannot handle the violence, and perpetuate the harsh attitude toward Palestinians while speaking against it. The soldiers' acts are not meant to be abusive, and they apparently do not mean to be violent; the situation in which they are involved leads them to these acts. It might be the IDF's violence in retaliation for Palestinian violence, which gets out of control, or the tense atmosphere that leads to unconstrained acts—but the outcome is that this is the way the soldiers act. Reading the novels or watching the films reveals how the situation leads them to act the way they do, and so their violence does not appear to be merely evil; yet, the IDF is still portrayed as cruel and violent, although inadvertently. This representation seems schizophrenic since the IDF is represented as having both the power and the ability to change reality while deciding how to act toward the Palestinians.

Examples of this phenomenon can be found in *The Smile of the Lamb,* in which the abuse seems so natural to the army's behavior that it is the reason behind Katzman's recruitment to his job—he wants to change this behavior. However, he soon becomes part of it, and so he recruits Uri, who is supposed to be in charge of changing the conduct toward the Palestinians, but learns that he has no power to do so either. This is also the case with Holy of *Ta'atuon,* who seems to be a perfectly educated young soldier with good intentions, who finds himself abusing an Arab without realizing the horror of his deeds, which are regularly performed as part of his unit's daily work.

A schizophrenic situation exists in which soldiers abuse Arabs but their acts seem to be forced upon them by the reality in which they operate. The fact that the soldiers do not want to act violently—although the army has complete power to do whatever it likes, but doesn't make any change—also leads to a denial and silencing of every opinion put forth against the army's behavior. Although the soldiers are not happy with their abusive acts, and have a hard time acting in that manner, they are not willing to hear any word against the army, or to allow any criticism of their own behavior. One would expect that with the IDF's apparently enormous power, the soldiers could alter the reality that makes them feel so uncomfortable, but nothing of this sort happens. Even though the soldiers are unhappy with the situation in which they have to act, they still silence any criticism.

This schizophrenic situation is also demonstrated by the soldiers' only partial understanding of why they act the way they do, what their job exactly is, and in what political situation they are involved. Even as they make and implement rules as they go, the soldiers sometimes seem not to know why they are participating in these confrontations, and almost always seem to have reservations about their own behavior. In *Ricochet,* for example, set in Lebanon, Gadi—a new officer—asks one of the soldiers to tell him more about the situation in Lebanon. Although he has been there a long time, the soldier says that he hadn't understood anything until an expert Orientalist had come to give the soldiers a lecture. Only then were they told about the nature of the place in which they were spending practically all their time. In Eran Riklis's *Cup Final* (1990), a reserve soldier captured by a group of Palestinians in Lebanon tells his captors: "We didn't want to go into this war," and the head of his captors answers him: "All Israeli soldiers say that, and yet you keep on making one war after another."

Most of the military characters in Israeli cultural texts on the conflicts of the 1980s end up losing their minds. Being abusive but also believing that they should not be so, not fully comprehending why they need to act the way they do but performing every order, not understanding why they have to be placed inside Palestinian cities but in fact invading people's houses and operating inside them, being in apparently intimate relationships with Palestinians but also being quite distinct from them, feeling as if they are the rulers of the world but not being able to live and act as they believe they should—all these contradictions lead to a state in which the soldiers can no longer carry on with their ordinary lives, and so they lose their minds. This is the case with films about the Israeli–Lebanon War, such as *Ricochet,* in which all the soldiers are on the verge of insanity, and Buzaglo's *Time for Cherries* (1990), in which the main protagonists go out of their minds. In Rafi Bukaey's *Avanti Popolo* (1986), the entire situation is hazy as to the degree of madness; this is also the case in *The Smile of the Lamb,* where Uri collaborates with his own captor. In *Ta'atuon* the two soldiers, Holy and Michael, are hospitalized in a mental institute, and Chrul does not distinguish between imagination and reality. *The Road to Ein Harod* tells the story of a hallucinated reality, in which the brigadier general seems as deranged as his captor.

The Role of the Army in Jewish–Arab Relations in Israel

The texts describing connections between Jews and Arabs inside Israel also tell a story in which the IDF has a crucial role, this time within Israeli society. Texts approaching the conflict between Jewish and Arab citizens of Israel show the IDF's significant role in determining national identity. Since cultural texts of the 1980s mainly dealt with the Israeli–Palestinian conflict and the Lebanon War, and not with the discord between Jewish and Arab citizens of Israel, focus is placed only on the two main novels that approach this issue (although some other texts will also provide examples): Sammy Michael's *A Trumpet in the Wadi* (1987)[29] and *A Good Arab,* both describing love stories between a Jew and an Arab inside Israel.

Israeli cultural texts tell us that no normal relationship can persist between Jewish and Arab Israeli citizens. Romantic relations and other kinds of ties simply fail to prevail, as the conflict between the two societies emerges and ruins personal connections. Although the reason for the failure of interpersonal contacts seems to involve differences in nationality and the inability of the two societies to allow one of their members to have any kind of close relationship with a member of the out-group, it is the IDF that functions as the "instrument" that separates the two national groups. On the Israeli side, it seems that rejection of cross-national relationships originates in racism and that the IDF is brought to the forefront since Arabs cannot be part of it and it serves to separate them from the Jews who do get recruited.

In order to become part of Israeli society, one has to be recruited to its army. Those who are recruited are Israelis, and those who are not recruited—because of their Arab affiliation—are not really considered to be part of Israeli society. In *A Good Arab,* Yosef is half-Arab, half-Jew, but is brought up as a Jew. As an adolescent, he writes Zionist manifestos, believes that the Jewish people have a right over the Land of Israel even if this means that Arabs should be killed, reads the protocols of the Eichmann trial, and forces his family to celebrate his bar mitzvah. When he is not inducted into the IDF because his father is an Arab, he understands that he will no longer be able to be a part of his friends' society, and struggles against the authorities in order to be recruited—but in vain. His ostracism from the IDF leads to his removal from society. When his friends want to talk among themselves about their service, they cannot do so in his presence. The topics of conversation that they can share with him dwindle, leading eventually to a separation between him and his fully Jewish friends.

A similar pattern appears in *A Trumpet in the Wadi:* the only way in which Alex, the Jewish Russian immigrant, can become part of Israeli society is by serving in the army. In all other respects he does not belong: he does not speak Hebrew, lives in an Arab neighborhood, and has an Arab girlfriend named Huda. It is only through his military service that he "officially" becomes a member of Israeli Jewish society. At the end of the novel he is killed during his service in the Lebanon War, and his death renders him a full member of Israeli society. Huda is left alone, pregnant, with doubts about whether to keep their child: "If I would raise him in the Jewish neighborhood, in eighteen years . . . I will have to give up my son to another war. He will want to go to an elite unit. All his life he will try to show how dedicated he is, just because he has an

Arab mother."[30] Huda doesn't know that her son, as half-Arab, would probably not be recruited at all, but she understands that if she chooses to raise him in a Jewish environment, the only way for him to become a member of this society will be to serve in the army.

These novels also tell stories in which the IDF's presence in Israeli society is so powerful that it even undermines romantic relations between Jews and Arabs. Although these interpersonal relations seem very strong, and although the characters do not seem particularly attached to their nationality, the Jewish characters find themselves committed to the army to a degree that threatens relationship with their lovers. In the dilemma that they confront—whether to become part of the IDF or to remain with their lovers—the Jews choose the IDF. Eventually, the romantic ties continue, but not after the protagonists' declarations that they prefer the Jewish Israeli army.

In *A Good Arab,* after Dina's recruitment, she and Yosef talk: "I told her, with all your liberal and leftist ideas, the thing you really want is for you to have a strong army, and she said, yes, that is right, and I told her, my people are at war against my country and vice versa, and what am I? And she said, you are my love, but I am a part of something, I belong to its genetic code."[31] In *A Trumpet in the Wadi,* after Alex's recruitment Huda says that she was suddenly afraid that "deep in his heart he was an Israeli soldier that is commanded to keep a secret, and I suddenly was an Arab in his eyes."[32] In *Ricochet,* loyalty to the army is stronger than commitments to lovers, friends, and family and can be seen even when the conflict is not between Jews and Arabs: the love affair of Rauf, the Druze Israeli soldier, and his fiancée from South Lebanon ends when he avoids answering her family's question about whether he will fight against them if the South Lebanese stop cooperating with Israel. He is then mysteriously murdered.

Since Israeli Arabs are a minority in a Jewish state, and since the only way for one to be part of this society is to serve in the IDF, even Arab characters are portrayed as willing to collaborate with the Jewish army. Yosef of *A Good Arab* is led for that reason to cooperate with the General Security Services. Since he is only a collaborator and not a homogeneous part of the security institutions, he does not find his way back to the Israeli society to which he belonged before turning eighteen. In *A Trumpet in the Wadi,* although Huda and her mother pray for a Palestinian victory in Lebanon and even have a cousin who is killed there, they find themselves supplying Alex with food and clothes before he goes to fight in a war against their relatives; they wish him a safe return, even though this means that members of their own people would be killed.

This phenomenon is also found in novels written by Arabs, including Anton Shammas's *Arabesques* (1984)[33] and Emil Habibi's *The Opsimist* (1984).[34] The Opsimist tries to survive in Israeli society by collaborating, and in *Arabesque,* Arab characters collaborate with the IDF. Both novels present cases of Arabs who want to be part of the society that rejects them, and who realize that to be accepted they must play a part in the security institutions. Yet since the conflict is between Jews and Arabs, and because the IDF is a tool in the hands of the Jewish people, Arabs will never be equal partners in the security services and therefore will never be part of Israeli society.

In cultural texts dealing with the conflict between Arab and Jewish Israeli citizens, the IDF is presented as possessing the power to decide who can be a part of Israeli society and who cannot. The IDF has enormous power in shaping that society, and is regarded by Israelis with such admiration that characters are willing to be recruited even if it means ruining their relationships with Arab friends who must remain outside. Having the role of a "legitimacy tool" that separates Jews and Arabs, the army becomes an entrance key to Israeli society, one that guarantees that Arabs are not allowed inside.

The Ultimate Attribution Error

To overcome the enormous psychological pressures that nations and groups experience in conflicts, groups go through processes of delegitimizing and dehumanizing the other society, enhancing patriotism and being ready for sacrifice, being self-persuaded about the rightness of their thoughts and ideas, and enhancing feelings of victimization.[35] In order to go through these processes, both individuals and societies, consciously and unconsciously, become biased and distort information they perceive, analyzing it in ways that reinforce their existing narratives.[36]

One of these biases is known as the "fundamental attribution error"–"ultimate attribution error."[37] When a good performance is given by a member of one's "in-group," she or he will attribute it to her or his personality traits, whereas a good performance by a member of the "out-group" will be attributed to external circumstances: a situation that made her or him act well, or an easy task that she or he was asked to perform, rather than a compliment to her or his skills or character. On the other hand, a negative performance by a member of the "in-group" will be attributed to external circumstances rather than to her or his character, while a negative performance by a member of the "out-group" will be attributed to her or his character.[38]

Israeli cultural texts that deal with the conflict provide a vision biased by the ultimate attribution error. They do not describe the IDF positively, but there is always an external reason justifying this representation. The soldiers abuse Arabs, but do not mean to do so: it is the stressful situation or the provocation of the Arabs that leads to these acts. They decide how to act and what policy to implement, but feel as if they don't support this policy and believe that they were forced into it, as they are the only Israeli Jews who have contact with Arabs, a factor that leads to their mental breakdown. They do not want to be prejudiced or racist, but the fact that Arabs are not inducted forces them not to accept them into their society either. They apparently prefer their personal love to the love of their country and army, but they cannot help being a part of a "genetic code" materialized in the army.

Although representations of the IDF in Israeli cultural texts are often critical, they eventually excuse its actions and justify its role. External factors lead the IDF as a whole, and its soldiers as individual characters, to impossible positions and circumstances. The IDF is then forced to act in ways that seem inappropriate. Apparently, the army does not want that much power to act the way it does, in determining the nature of Israeli society—but circumstances force it to take on its roles. Eventually, it seems as if the IDF acts in the best way it can in the given situation into which it is forced.

Conclusion

The representation of the IDF in cultural texts dealing with the Israeli–Palestinian conflict in the 1980s shows it to have unconstrained power: it rules the Palestinians, it takes on the job of civilian institutions, it acts in harsh and abusing ways, and it is not open to criticism although it is not happy with its own behavior. These circumstances contribute to the soldiers' mental breakdown. The representation of the IDF in cultural texts dealing with the Jewish–Arab conflict inside Israel in the 1980s illustrates that it is granted too major a role: it decides who and who cannot be part of society, it is considered to be so important that Jewish characters are willing to lose their lovers in order to serve in it, and Arab characters are willing to collaborate with it. In performing the unpleasant task of excluding Arabs from Israeli society, the IDF is represented as both the agent that decides and implements the Israeli attitude and Israeli policy toward Palestinians in the territories, and the chief factor that shapes Israeli society from within.

No representation, either in the public discourse or in academic studies, can provide a precise, complete, and full picture of reality. Therefore, as with other representations of the army, the way that cultural texts envision it is probably not fully accurate. However, these representations do tell us something about certain aspects of Israeli society's perception and understanding of the army. Not surprisingly, these representations bear the flaw of the ultimate attribution error, and by that reveal another aspect of Israeli society's perception of the army: the IDF can be criticized severely and depicted pejoratively, but there is always some justification for its actions, and in spite of all the condemnations that might be made against it, in the last analysis it is still portrayed as doing the best it possibly can in the difficult circumstances that are apparently forced upon it.

Notes

1. Haim Gouri, "The Blood and the Azure Rock," *Ha'aretz,* July 16, 2003.

2. Homi K. Bhabha, "Introduction: Narrating the Nation," in Homi K. Bhabha (ed.), *Nation and Narration* (London, 1990), 1–7.

3. Fredric Jameson, *The Political Unconscious: Narrative as a Socially Symbolic Act* (London, 1981), 20.

4. Dan Miron, *If There Is No Jerusalem* (Tel-Aviv, 1987) [Hebrew].

5. Benedict Anderson, *Imagined Communities* (London and New York, 1991).

6. Dan Horowitz and Moshe Lissak, *Troubles in Utopia* (Albany, N.Y., 1989).

7. Shmuel Noah Eisenstadt, *Israeli Society in Its Changes* (Jerusalem, 1989) [Hebrew]; Sammy Smooha, "Class, Ethnic and National Splits in Israeli Democracy," in Uri Ram (ed.), *The Israeli Society: Critical Aspects* (Tel-Aviv, 1993), 172–202 [Hebrew]; Baruch Kimmerling, "The New Israelis: Cultural Multiplicity without Multi-culturalism," *Alpayim* 16 (1998): 264–308 [Hebrew].

8. Sammy Smooha, "Arab–Israeli Relations in Israel as a Democratic-Jewish State," in Efraim Ya'ar and Ze'ev Shavit (eds.), *Trends in Israeli Society* (Tel-Aviv, 2001), 1:231–363 [Hebrew].

9. Baruch Kimmerling and Joel S. Migdal, *Palestinians: The Making of a People* (Jerusalem, 1999) [Hebrew].

10. Ibid.

11. Ella Shohat, *Israeli Cinema: East/West and the Politics of Representation* (Austin, Tex., 1989).

12. Ella Shohat, *The Israeli Cinema: History and Ideology* (Tel-Aviv, 1991) [Hebrew]; Judd Ne'eman, "The Empty Tomb in the Postmodern Pyramid: Israeli Cinema in the 1980s and 1990s," in Charles Berlin (ed.), *Documenting Israel* (Cambridge, Mass., 1995), 117–51; Yosefa Loshitzky, *Identity Politics on the Israeli Screen* (Austin, Tex., 2001); Nurith Gertz, *A Different Chorus* (Tel-Aviv, 2004) [Hebrew].

13. Gilad Morahg, "Loving and Shooting: The Image of the Arab in Israeli Fiction," *Moznayim* 71 (1987): 15–18 [Hebrew].

14. Mikhail M. Bakhtin, *The Dialogic Imagination* (Austin, Tex., 1981).

15. Shimon Levy, "Captured in Fantasy," *Moznayim* 57 (1983): 70–73 [Hebrew]; Gilad Morahg, "New Images of Arabs in Israeli Fiction," *Prooftexts* 6 (1986): 147–62.

16. Gila Ramras-Rauch, *The Arab in Israeli Literature* (Bloomington, Ind., 1989).

17. Ehud Ben-Ezer, *Sleepwalkers and Other Stories: The Arab in Hebrew Fiction* (Boulder, Colo., 1999).

18. Menachem Perry, "The Israeli–Palestinian Conflict as a Metaphor in Recent Israeli Fiction," *Poetics Today* 7 (1986): 603–19.

19. Nurith Gertz, "Grossman's *The Smile of the Lamb*: In Quest of Authentic Humanity," *Hebrew Studies* 34 (1993): 79–98.

20. Hannan Hever, *Producing the Modern Hebrew Canon: Nation Building and Minority Discourse* (New York, 2002).

21. Dan Orian, *The Image of the Arab in Israeli Theatre* (Tel-Aviv, 1996) [Hebrew].

22. Elie Podeh, *The Israeli–Arab Conflict in Israeli Textbooks (1935–1995)* (Jerusalem, 1997) [Hebrew].

23. Avi Valentin, *Shahid* (Tel-Aviv, 1989), 27 [Hebrew].

24. David Grossman, *The Smile of the Lamb* (Tel-Aviv, 1983) [Hebrew].

25. Yitzhak Ben-Ner, *Ta'atuon* (Tel-Aviv, 1989), 185 [Hebrew].

26. Ibid., 199.

27. Yoram Kaniuk, *A Good Arab* (Tel-Aviv, 1984), 63 [Hebrew].

28. Amos Kenan, *The Road to Ein Harod* (Tel-Aviv, 1984) [Hebrew].

29. Sammy Michael, *A Trumpet in the Wadi* (Tel-Aviv, 1987) [Hebrew].

30. Ibid., 231.

31. Kaniuk, *A Good Arab*, 97.

32. Michael, *A Trumpet in the Wadi*, 201.

33. Anton Shammas, *Arabesques* (Tel-Aviv, 1986) [Hebrew].

34. Emil Habibi, *The Opsimist* (Jerusalem, 1984) [Hebrew].

35. Nadim Rouhana and Daniel Bar-Tal, "Psychological Dynamics of Intractable Ethnonational Conflicts: The Israeli–Palestinian Case," *American Psychologist* 53 (1998): 761–70.

36. Walter G. Stephan and Cookie W. Stephan, *Intergroup Relations* (Boulder, Colo., 1996).

37. Thomas F. Pettigrew, "The Ultimate Attribution Error: Extending Allport's Cognitive Analysis of Prejudice," *Personality and Social Psychology Bulletin* 5 (1979): 461–76.

38. Miles Hewstone and Jos Jaspars, "Intergroup Relations and Attribution Processes," in Henri Tajfel (ed.), *Social Identity in Intergroup Relations* (Cambridge, 1982), 99–127.

FIFTEEN

Military and Society since 9/11: Retrospect and Prospect

CHRISTOPHER DANDEKER

9/11: A Turning Point in War and Conflict?

The militant Islamic, terrorist outrage in Mumbai in late November 2008 was immediately referred to by some commentators as "India's 9/11." This was because, inter alia, the attacks were on symbols of Indian capitalist cosmopolitanism, such as the Taj Mahal Hotel; there was targeting of Westerners and Jews; a ruthless, violent pursuit of objectives with no moral or humanitarian scruple; and an attempt to leverage regional and global political effects (including a conflict between Pakistan and India) through these acts of "symbolic violence." Apparently Blackberries were used by some of the terrorists to monitor how successfully their efforts had been in producing spectacular effects via what Martin Shaw has termed "global surveillance."[1]

Looking back at September 11, 2001, we can state that the piquancy of that day was rooted in three considerations: first the ways in which real time 24/7 media coverage enabled most of the rest of the world to join the U.S. East Coast morning audiences and become connected with terrorism as a "spectator sport";[2] second, the attacks appeared to provide the clearest empirical demonstration of the predictions and warnings about the risks of "asymmetrical warfare" for contemporary Western liberal capitalist societies (and the potential of the Revolution in Military Affairs [RMA] to counter them);[3] and third, the terrorist attacks were focused—deliberately so, and not for the first time, as was evident in the earlier failed attempts to destroy the World Trade Center—on highly symbolic targets. Their value was to be measured less in U.S. dollars and more in what those buildings—the World Trade Center, the Pentagon and, so it would seem, the White House—*signified,* not only to U.S. citizens but also to most of the world's population.

September 11 helped to further crystallize already existing debates about the changing nature of war and conflict, and the possible decline of major interstate war. Discussion has focused on the nature of asymmetric threats to contemporary democratic states, including analysis of "wars amongst the people," "three and four block" war, "hybrid warfare," and how to respond to the challenges they pose.[4] For example, so far as "hybrid warfare" is concerned, Frank Hoffman argues that such contests are likely to involve a "hybrid blend of traditional and irregular tactics, decentralized planning and execution and non-state actors . . . using both simple and innovative tactics in innovative ways."[5]

This suggestion is not unrelated to another U.S. naval commentator's influential concept of "three block warfare."[6] Charles Krulak argues that it would be possible for members of a military unit within one urban setting to be involved simultaneously in different kinds of missions: in one block delivering humanitarian relief, in another, separating conflicting parties and dealing with tactically high-intensity exchanges of fire with insurgents. This rapid tempo of events is likely to be exposed to media scrutiny during which tactical and subtactical decisions can have major operational and even strategic consequences, as when an apparent war crime can damage the mission of an intervening state and its international reputation. Lower-level decisions by junior personnel mean that the "strategic corporal" becomes more significant, with major implications for recruiting and educating these soldiers to deal with this increasingly sensitive political environment.

The concept of Three Block War has been extended recently to Four Block War by James N. Mattis and Frank Hoffman. They argue that

> [t]he additional block deals with the psychological or information operations aspects. This fourth block is the area where you may not be physically located but in which we are communicating or broadcasting our message. The Four Block War adds a new but very relevant dimension to situations like the counterinsurgency in Iraq. *Insurgencies are wars of ideas, and our ideas need to compete with those of the enemy. Our actions in the three other blocks are important to building up our credibility and*

establishing relationships with the population and their leadership. Thus, there is an information operations aspect within each block. In each of the traditional three blocks our Marines are both "sensors" that collect intelligence, as well as "transmitters." Everything they do or fail to do sends a message. They need to be trained for that, and informed by commander's intent. The information ops component is how we extend our reach and how we can influence populations to reject the misshaped ideology and hatred they are offered by the insurgents. Successful information ops help the civilian population understand and accept the better future we seek to help build with them. Our Marine ground and air forces must have the tools and capabilities to get the message across in each block [emphasis added].[7]

Two key inferences can be drawn from these ongoing discussions. First, it is by no means obvious that, in the context of ideological and resource conflicts, it would be prudent for states to discount the possibility of future interstate war, and therefore they need to plan and invest accordingly. Second, in responding to new forms of conflict, it is becoming clear that states cannot afford to do without the techniques of fighting interstate war. Recent events, illustrating the relevance of the concepts of three–four block and hybrid warfare, point to the likelihood that the nonstate actors with whom, for example, the UK armed forces are likely to engage in armed conflict will have the capacity to conduct or sponsor a range of operations—some sequential, some simultaneous. These will probably include small- to medium-scale terrorist attacks but with the capacity to produce spectacular, symbolic effects that magnify the immediate physical and psychological damage to regional and global dimensions—Mumbai, for instance. Such activities can extend to insurgency operations with the support of local populations (Iraq, Chechnya, and Afghanistan) through to major combat operations such as conducted against the IDF from and in Lebanon in 2006, although the relative success of these operations against Israel owed as much to the slow and inadequate response of the IDF as to the efforts of Hizbullah. The latter was compounded by the capacity of Hizbullah to tap into IDF military communications as well as to mount an information campaign that made the most of its successes in regional and global opinion.[8]

To meet the challenges of this strategic landscape, states encountering it will need their armed forces, especially their armies, to be configured for full-spectrum warfare. From the point of view of the British army, for example, not least in its ongoing operations in Afghanistan, the above analysis renders obsolete the idea that the British army would be able to specialize in and be equipped for stabilization and/or reconstruction operations, as these will have the inherent risk of turning quite quickly, and unexpectedly, into a contest in which war-fighting skills come into prominence. Clearly some force packages will be able to be configured for relatively low-risk peacekeeping operations, but there will be a need to plan for reinforcements if necessary and to reconfigure a deployment, drawing on a wider full-spectrum capability in the army as a whole.

The above two points provide an opportunity to examine some military society issues in Western democracies that emerge from the changing nature of war and conflict.

After 9/11: Implications for the Military and Society

MILITARY ASPECTS

Whatever doubts that some Western countries have had about U.S. policy responses to 9/11—especially the intervention in Iraq, with the focus now shifting to the imbroglio in Afghanistan and public support of contributing states for the mission there rather fragile—it is still very much in their interests for them to develop the capacity to be able to cooperate militarily with that country. This will continue to be the case even if, as seems likely, the Obama administration in the United States will seek to recalibrate its security policy to focus more on diplomacy and soft power than on military means. Assuming it does, it will still wish to use the military instrument, as it deems appropriate, and to continue to invest in the means of sustaining its global military preeminence. Moreover, the new administration's focus on restoring the moral international authority of the United States will make it keen to make sure it will be able to operate successfully with others in "coalitions of the willing": the United States cannot do without the material, political, and symbolic support of its allies.

For other Western democracies, it is imperative that, for this cooperation to happen, they must ensure that the already existing technological gap between the United States and its friends and allies does not become an unbridgeable gulf, even if some—not least France—want their own and wider EU military capacities to be developed as the basis of a European counter-weight to U.S. power in the world. However this may be, European states have to face the fact that they need to spend more, and more wisely, on their defense. The question is whether this imperative will clash with public opinion's priorities for spending, with the pressing claims of education, health, transport, and other valued services.

In providing more resources for defense, there will be a continued drive for more flexible armed forces among Western industrial states.[9] National states will be constrained to work more and more cooperatively with one another: multinationality is as important as "jointery" (the close cooperation among individual armed services of a single national state) as future trends for the armed services. In developing multinational approaches to flexible forces, issues of role specialization will need to be addressed. This process will allow national and historical differences to come into play as to where comparative advantage lies among national members of the NATO alliance, the EU, and "coalitions of the willing." For new as well as older members of NATO and the EU, there will be delicate issues of choice to be handled in regard to war fighting, peace support operations, gendarmerie functions, and other military roles.

The current position in the UK illustrates some of the dilemmas and controversies. Some argue that there needs to be a rise of 1 percent of GDP from 2.5 percent to 3.5 percent in order to meet the needs of the overstretched armed forces, particularly in light of the ongoing commitment to Afghanistan as well as the costs of force modernization and sustaining the UK's capacity to mount expeditionary warfare and other campaigns. However, the condition of the defense budget, especially the triple costs of investment in human resources, large capital projects—especially the two new aircraft carriers (now delayed for two years to defer costs)—and ongoing operations in Afghanistan, means that if there is to be a commitment to the army's need for full-spectrum capability, then either there has to be an increase in the defense budget or a review of priorities so far as future capital investment projects are concerned.

Much will depend not just on national political and economic calculations but also on consideration of what role the UK wishes to play internationally, especially as a future partner of the United States and other states in coalitions of the willing. It is well known that the UK will have to make a judgment as to how much (interoperable) capability it will need to have to be more than a symbolic coalition partner and be able to exercise influence in the planning and decision making of operations—something that was lacking in the buildup to the invasion of Iraq in 2003.

In adding momentum to the trend toward flexible, quick reaction forces with global and precise reach, 9/11 gave states much to think about in terms of the balance between expeditionary operations and homeland defense and security. To take the case of the UK, in its *Strategic Defence Review* of 1998, the primary role of armed forces was conceived as "going to the crisis before the crisis came to you," which became a key theme in the current Labour government's foreign policy.[10] Yet some modification of this kind of thinking was required after 9/11: the crisis can come to you before you go to the crisis, as a response to interventions abroad, as was evident on 7/7 in London 2005 and Glasgow in June 2007. Defense planners now have to think even harder about securing the home base while projecting power abroad or threatening to do so to deal with crises.[11] This will involve ensuring that not only regular (including Special Forces [SF]) but also reserve forces are organized and distributed appropriately to meet both power projection and homeland defense needs.

Against this background of the need to balance expeditionary efforts against the imperatives of homeland defense, in the United States and other states, we are witnessing greater priority being given to homeland security. In the case of the United States, this means a twin effort of maintaining a technological edge in the military means of power projection abroad as well as in the means of detection and prevention of intrusions into the homeland.

Effective homeland defense demands even closer cooperation between military, border, and other police agencies as well as other security agencies as states recognize that the boundaries between internal and external security have become even more blurred. These security organizations and agencies are becoming more and more concerned with developing effective means of cross-border international cooperation: one example in this regard is the close and quite effective links between the United States, the UK, and France on antiterrorist intelligence and policing. Just now, the need for such links between the UK, Pakistan, and India (Israel has close links with the latter) is very evident. Of course, this is not to underestimate the pressing need for sharply focused, quick-reaction, and specialized military forces for expeditionary warfare; even these depend increasingly on cooperation with other nonmilitary security agencies, for example in acquiring intelligence about targets and indeed in attacking them—as has been evident, for example, in the cases of Kosovo and Afghanistan.

With regard to cooperation among the wide array of security organizations focused on the war on terror, there remain serious issues of interagency cooperation that need to be addressed. As the United States recognizes, simply providing more resources does not, of itself, overcome problems of bureaucratic competition and cultural boundaries among competing agencies; in this regard, it may be inferior to some of its friends and allies.[12] Yet it would be mistaken to view the interagency issues only through the prism of the efficiency of the apparatus of national security: 9/11, and in the UK after 7/7 especially, have posed the traditional problem of national security and democracy in an acute fashion. How is it possible to exercise democratic oversight and accountability over the organizations of national security while maintaining the necessary degree of secrecy about what they do and how they work?[13] For states like Israel, this question has piquancy, as the military is such a key player in shaping national security policy, sometimes in the face of significant opposition from civil society.[14]

One of the problematic consequences of investing in quick-reaction forces for the wider defense organization concerns what can be referred to as a "two-speed," or "two-tier" military. This can add to difficulties to do with ensuring compatibility between the technologically superior United States and its less-developed friends and allies, as well as those to do with the role specialization mentioned earlier. A few years ago, in the UK, for example, there was evidence of an emerging "two-speed" or "two-tier" army: the ready forces earmarked for deployment especially focused on the higher-intensity operations, with the rest either home-based or on other missions including the forms of peacekeeping or "sweeping up" after the more dangerous missions have been executed. While some kind of distinction between rapidly deployable spearhead forces and other formations might be inevitable, it would be most unwise if the latter were configured in such a way in terms of equipment, ethos, and employment policy that they were unable to turn their hand to higher-intensity operations should they be required. Of course, and this is quite another point, the distinctions (more or less justified) between elite and other fighting forces is an inevitable feature of any army. A two-speed military might not only lead to social divisions and tensions within the armed services, especially ground forces, but might also lead to recruitment and retention difficulties in those segments that might be considered by potential recruits as second-class.

However, this situation is much less significant now than it was three years ago: one key reason is that the requirements of deployment abroad in Iraq and especially Afghanistan mean that all contingents are likely to be rotated because of the sheer demand for personnel—including reserve forces. It is also instructive to note that women play a key role in these deployments, with the percentage serving in Afghanistan (20 percent approximately) being about twice their overall contribution to the personnel of UK armed forces. It is likely that the nature of "360 degree warfare," with the increasingly fluid boundaries between combat and noncombat zones, together with the need to overcome general recruitment and retention problems will mean the current deployment rules for women (which exclude them from infantry and armor) will be reviewed again in due course. As before, the perceived lessons of the IDF will have a bearing on such a review, including the performance of women in armed units such as border police, and, so it would seem, the shared UK and Israeli experience that when female soldiers die or are injured they do so as soldiers and not as women in the eyes of the military and the wider civilian community.[15]

In addition to tensions between different segments of the military of a flexible quick-reaction force, there are also signs of strains *within* the segment most engaged in the war against terror, namely Special Forces and those specialized units that work closely with and support them.[16] It is currently not easy to establish whether these problems are just an exaggeration of already well-documented problems that have emerged over the past decade, as smaller armed forces have had to deal with an increased operational tempo: doing more with fewer can place all sorts of strains on personnel (and their families and friends) as well as their equipment.[17] The impact of deployments on stress within military families in different parts of the armed forces, including the incidence of violence, is a subject deserving of closer scientific scrutiny.

SOCIETAL ASPECTS

A final set of issues with regard to the effects of 9/11 on the military and society concerns risk perceptions by different groups of citizens and their influence on behavior. Today, citizens in the Western states that have abolished conscription (the great majority excluding Israel) are, in the main, spectators of rather than active participants in the actions of their countries' intervention forces. Indeed, much of what they do see constitutes relatively little of the shadowy operations that, perforce, are conducted in secret against terrorist groups, their state, and nonstate supporters.

However much or little they see or are allowed to see, the public's views can play a significant role in the decisions of political elites to commit forces to particular operations and to sustain that commitment over time, as we witnessed in respect to the military preparations for the invasion of Iraq in 2003 and ongoing concerns in the UK and France about the level of sacrifice in terms of (combatant and noncombatant) casualties in Afghanistan relative to perceived successes. Public opinion matters: governments since the intervention in Vietnam have to consider key questions, namely, is an intervention in the national interest and one that can be portrayed as such to the public in a convincing fashion? What level of sacrifice can be sustained by the public relative to the perceived success being achieved? How is success being defined and is there momentum in the process of achieving it? In this regard, it is important to note that much will depend on whether a state believes in absolute victory or has a more pragmatic idea of success in terms of an acceptable condition, produced by military and nonmilitary means that allow for the intervening state(s) to withdraw. So far as Afghanistan is concerned, some of the tensions between the United States and the UK can be understood in terms of this distinction, which in turn is connected with the civil–military relations perspectives of Samuel Huntington and Morris Janowitz, respectively.[18]

As 7/7 for the UK, 9/11 for the United States, and Israel's dealing with Lebanon, for example, have all illustrated, citizens cannot only constrain governments in their use of armed forces as a means of furthering their security policies; in addition, they *are* in the front line of terror attacks whether or not these are on so-called military targets: here they are *not* "spectators" of the war on terror but are very much involved as potential targets. In this connection, it is worth noting that civilians suffered more casualties than the military in the September 11 attack on the Pentagon (these included Department of Defense civilians).[19] The attacks on Bali and Mombasa, and now Mumbai, together with those that are anticipated involving weapons of mass destruction entailing threats to civilian populations, show how far civilians are involved directly in the current war on terror, even though they are so distant from attacks on foreign targets by their own state's intervention forces where, as some commentators have argued, they are spectators of "virtual war."[20] Thus, the idea of virtual war seems even more one-sided after the events of September 11, and 7/7, and Mumbai in November 2008.

At work here is a traditional feature of terrorist attack: less the infliction of material damages per se but more the securing of a psychological effect. This has always posed interesting dilemmas for governments and other agencies. The principal one is how to reassure the public about the seriousness of the risks they face without conveying an impression of complacency or overconfidence about the capacity of government to protect the population. This is despite the fact that one important feature of the contemporary scene is the perceived need of government to be doing and *to be seen to be* doing "something" about the control and management of risk. Governments also have to avoid generating feelings of anxiety—or even panic—which is precisely one of the key objectives of those who use terror as a weapon.

Especially in democratic states, there is the related question of how much information about risks associated with terrorist groups and counterterrorist activities should be released (directly by government or by nongovernmental agencies, including the media) to the public. Achieving the right balance is crucial: for example, giving detailed advice on what to do in the face of bioterror attacks, the chances of which may be infinitesimally small, may well generate feelings of anxiety all out of proportion to the true nature of the risk involved. As a result of recent terrorist attacks and the public discussion about the possibility of bioterrorist attacks in the UK, for example, a number of journalists have reported a sense of edginess and anxiety as governments try to steer a course between the poles of the dilemmas highlighted above. Thus a climate of heightened risk can lead to both "warning fatigue" on one hand and an exaggerated sense of fear on the other.[21]

Conclusion

Democratic states across the world face the challenges of hybrid war and need to design armed forces fit to face them, to invest in their military capacity to be useful contributors to coalitions of the willing, the most important member of which for the near future in terms of global politics will be the United States, although other powers, such as China and India, will be likely to acquire a higher profile in the next two decades. Military investments will pose difficult choices in terms of the level and shape of public expenditure.

Governments also need to think about how best to integrate military and nonmilitary instruments when they intervene in hybrid wars (to balance use of force, hearts and minds, and state construction or reconstruction efforts, for instance). Furthermore, governments have to clearly define for their domestic and international publics why they are intervening and what constitutes the basis of achieving success and how long they propose to be engaged in a mission to counter a threat posed by hybrid war. In this regard they will need to acquire and engender in their publics qualities such as "strategic patience"—operations may take longer and be more difficult than both publics and governments may foresee—resilience in the face of terrorist objectives to unnerve, as well as a facility for controlling strategic narratives. In a fast-moving media environment, with a diversity of providers and media of communications—not least via the Internet—it is important that military and other security agencies are sure-footed, able to provide effective, proactive counter-responses to terrorist information operations: to ensure that successes on the ground are converted into successes in the information war. As outrages from 2001 to 2008 illustrate, an essential response to them is one that is not confined to military means but engages in the struggle for ideas. And this struggle should not be restricted to ends—defending the values of democracy—but must extend to the means through a convincing narrative, including short- and longer-term steps about how the struggle is being waged, how setbacks are being dealt with, and how political will is being deployed on objectives that can be achieved as well as being valuable on their own terms.

Notes

1. Martin Shaw, *The New Western Way of War* (Cambridge, 2005), 36–41, 47–70.

2. The use of the term *spectator sport* in the context of war can be traced to Michael Mann: see his essay "Capitalism and Militarism" in Martin Shaw (ed.), *War, State and Society* (London, 1984). For a useful general discussion see Colin McInnes, *Spectator Sport War: The West and Contemporary Conflict* (Boulder, Colo., 2002), and Shaw, *The New Western Way of War.*

3. Laurence Freedman, *The Revolution in Strategic Affairs* (Oxford, 1998); *The Transformation of Strategic Affairs* (Oxford, 2006).

4. Rupert Smith, *The Utility of Force: The Art of War in the Modern World* (London, 2005); Herfried Münkler, "What is Really New about New Wars?" in John Andreas Olsen (ed.), *On New Wars* (Oslo, 2007); Frank Hoffman, *Conflict in the 21st Century: The Rise of Hybrid Wars* (Arlington, Va., 2007); James N. Mattis and Frank Hoffman, "Future Warfare: The Rise of Hybrid Wars," *US Naval Institute Proceedings* 132 (2005): 233.

5. Hoffman, *Conflict in the 21st Century,* 7, quoting U.S. National Maritime Strategy.

6. Charles Krulak, "The Strategic Corporal: Leadership in the Three Block War," *Marines Magazine,* January 1999, at http://www.au.af.mil/au/awc/awcgate/usmc/strategic_corporal.htm (February 12, 2008).

7. Mattis and Hoffman, "Future Warfare."

8. These points emerged in a recent seminar in the Department of War Studies at King's College London. I am particularly indebted to comments by Professors T. Farrell and L. D. Freedman.

9. Christopher Dandeker, "Building Flexible Forces for the 21st Century: Key Challenges for the Contemporary Armed Services," in Giuseppe Caforio (ed.), *Handbook of the Sociology of the Military* (New York, 2003).

10. Christopher Dandeker and Laurence Freedman, "The Armed Services," *Political Quarterly* (October–December 2002): 465–75.

11. Speech by the UK Secretary of State for Defence, the Rt. Hon. Geoffrey Hoon QC, "Strategic Defence Review: A New Chapter (Cm5566)," at http://www.mod.uk/DefenceInternet/AboutDefence/CorporatePublications/PolicyStrategyandPlanning/StrategicDefenceReviewANewChaptercm5566.htm.

12. Some years ago Tom Ridge, Assistant to the U.S. President for Homeland Security, commented that he thought the UK was superior to the United States in handling these interagency issues. This might be connected with the UK's own long-standing war against IRA terror. Speech delivered to the Centre for Defence Studies, King's College London on November 7, 2002, "Protecting against the Global Threat: Strategies from American Homeland Security."

13. Christopher Dandeker, "National Security and Democracy: The United Kingdom Experience," *Armed Forces & Society* 20 (1994): 353–74, and the other essays in that issue of the journal.

14. See the chapter by Avraham Sela in this volume.

15. Personal communications between author and Professor Eyal Ben-Ari, The Hebrew University of Jerusalem.

16. Philip Jacobson, "When Wives Become the Enemy," *Sunday Times Magazine,* October 6, 2002, 52–56.

17. Christopher Dandeker, "The United Kingdom: The Overstretched Military," in Charles Moskos, John A. Williams, and David R. Segal, *The Postmodern Military* (Oxford, 2000), 32–50. Matthew Hotopf, Lisa Hull, Nicola T. Fear, Tess Browne, Oded Horn, Amy Iversen, Margaret Jones, Dominic Murphy, Duncan Bland, Mark Earnshaw, Neil Greenberg, Jamie Hacker-Hughes, Rosemary Tate, Christopher Dandeker, Roberto Rona, and Simon Wessely, "The Health of UK Military Personnel Who Deployed to the 2003 Iraq War: A Cohort Study," *Lancet* 367 (2006): 1731–41.

18. The idea of "condition" is developed in Smith, *The Utility of Force.* For a discussion of this theme, see Christopher Dandeker, "The End of War? The Strategic Context of International Missions in the Twenty First Century," in Kobi Michael, Eyal Ben-Ari, and David Kellen (eds.), *The Transformation of the World of Warfare and Peace Support Operations* (Westport, Conn., 2009).

19. I owe this point to David R. Segal, University of Maryland.

20. Michael Ignatieff, *Virtual War: Kosovo and Beyond* (London, 2000).

21. For a related discussion, see M. Brooke Rogers, Richard Amlot, G. James Rubin, Simon Wessely, and Kristian Krieger, "Mediating the Social and Psychological Impacts of Terrorist Attacks: The Role of Risk Perception and Risk Communication," *International Review of Psychiatry* 19 (2007): 279–88.

APPENDIX A

Israeli Ministers of Defense since 1948

David Ben-Gurion	*May 1948–January 1954*
Pinhas Lavon	*January 1954–February 1955*
David Ben-Gurion	*February 1955–June 1963*
Levi Eshkol	*June 1963–June 1967*
Moshe Dayan	*June 1967–June 1974*
Shimon Peres	*June 1974–June 1977*
Ezer Weizman	*June 1977–May 1980*
Menachem Begin	*May 1980–August 1981*
Ariel Sharon	*August 1981–February 1983*
Menachem Begin	*February 1983*
Moshe Arens	*February 1983–September 1984*
Yitzhak Rabin	*September 1984–March 1990*
Yitzhak Shamir	*March 1990–June 1990*
Moshe Arens	*June 1990–July 1992*
Yitzhak Rabin	*July 1992–November 1995*
Shimon Peres	*November 1995–June 1996*
Yitzhak Mordechai	*June 1996–January 1999*
Moshe Arens	*January 1999–July 1999*
Ehud Barak	*July 1999–March 2001*
Binyamin Ben-Eliezer	*March 2001–November 2002*
Shaul Mofaz	*November 2002–May 2006*
Amir Peretz	*May 2006–June 2007*
Ehud Barak	*June 2007–*

Chiefs of Staff of the Israeli Defense Forces since 1948

Yaakov Dori	*June 1948–November 1949*
Yigael Yadin	*November 1949–December 1952*
Mordechai Maklef	*December 1952–December 1953*
Moshe Dayan	*December 1953–January 1958*
Chaim Laskov	*January 1958–January 1961*
Tzvi Tzur	*January 1961–January 1964*
Yitzhak Rabin	*January 1964–January 1968*
Chaim Bar-Lev	*January 1968–January 1971*
David Elazar	*January 1971–April 1974*
Mordechai Gur	*April 1974–April 1978*
Rafael Eitan	*April 1978–April 1983*
Moshe Levy	*April 1983–April 1987*
Dan Shomron	*April 1987–April 1991*
Ehud Barak	*April 1991–January 1995*
Amnon Lipkin-Shahak	*January 1995–July 1998*
Shaul Mofaz	*July 1998–July 2002*
Moshe Yaalon	*July 2002–June 2005*
Dan Halutz	*June 2005–February 2007*
Gabi Ashkenazi	*February 2007–*

Important Dates

November 1947–July 1949

Israel's War of Independence (the Palestine War, the First Arab–Israeli War).

May 14, 1948

Termination of the British Mandate in Palestine, Israel declares independence.

May 15, 1948

Several Arab States intervene in the conflict in Palestine.

May 26, 1948

The Israeli army, the Israeli Defense Forces (IDF), is officially established and absorbs members of the pre-state Jewish militias.

October 21, 1948

Israeli imposes a military government over most of its Arab Palestinian citizens. The military government was abolished in 1966.

February–March 1949

Israel and each of Egypt, Lebanon, Jordan, and Syria (but not Iraq and the Palestinians) sign Armistice Agreements.

April–September 1949

The Lausanne Conference is convened by the United Nations Conciliation Commission for Palestine (UNCCP), with representatives from Israel, Egypt, Jordan, Lebanon, and Syria. The conference is, however, unsuccessful.

September 8, 1949

The Knesset (Israel's parliament) passes the Defence Service Law. Later versions of this law were adopted in 1959 and in 1986.

September 24, 1950

The Israel Army Radio officially starts to broadcast.

April 1953

The Israel Border Police is established.

May 3, 1956

The first Druze and Circassian Soldiers from among Israel's Arab Palestinian community are recruited to the IDF. Later, Bedouins are also recruited, but most Muslims and Christians are exempted.

October–November 1956

The Suez Crisis (the Tripartite Aggression, Operation Kadesh, the Suez War). During its war with Egypt, Israel, which is joined in the war by Britain and France, occupies Sinai but is forced to withdraw in 1957.

October 29, 1956

The Kfar Kassem Massacre. After a curfew imposed during the Suez Crisis, scores of Arab Palestinian citizens of Israel, mostly laborers returning from work, are killed by Israel Border Police.

June 5–10, 1967

The Six-Day War (also known as the third Israeli–Arab War). Israel defeats Egypt, Jordan, and Syria and occupies the Sinai Peninsula and the Gaza Strip from Egypt, the West Bank and East Jerusalem from Jordan, and the Golan from Syria.

March 21, 1968

The IDF attacks the Jordanian town of Karameh and becomes embroiled in a full-scale battle with Palestinian forces and the Jordanian army.

March 1969–August 1970

The War of Attrition between Israel and Egypt.

October 1973

The October War (Yom Kippur War) between Israel and Egypt and Syria. The Arab States, chiefly Saudi Arabia, effectively employ the oil weapon.

April 1, 1974

The issuing of the interim report of the Agranat Commission, the Official National Commission of Inquiry appointed by the Israeli government to investigate the circumstances leading to the outbreak of the October War.

September 1975

Israel and Egypt sign the Sinai Accord under U.S. auspices.

March 30, 1976

The first Land Day organized by Israel's Arab Palestinian citizens in response to the confiscation of lands. Six demonstrators are killed by security forces.

July 3, 1976

The IDF launches Operation Entebbe (the Entebbe Raid or Operation Thunderbolt; retroactively named Operation Yonatan) to rescue hostages taken by Palestinian factions to the Entebbe Airport in Uganda.

November 1977

Egyptian President Anwar al-Sadat visits Israel, paving the way to the Camp David Accords (*September 1978*) and the Egyptian-Israeli Peace Treaty (*March 1979*).

March 1978

The IDF launches Operation Litani in South Lebanon.

June 1981

The IDF launches Operation Opera, a long-range air strike that destroys the Osirak nuclear reactor in Iraq.

April 1982

Israel evacuates all of its settlements in Sinai according to the terms of the Egyptian–Israeli Peace Treaty.

June 1982

Israel launches the Lebanon War (Operation Peace for Galilee), designed to crush the PLO forces in Lebanon and facilitate the election of its local ally, Bashir Gemayel, as Lebanon's president.

September 1982

Following the Sabra and Shatila Massacre, perpetrated by Israel's ally, the Lebanese Forces, the Kahan Commission of Inquiry is formed. Its report (*February, 1983*) leads to the removal of Defense Minister Ariel Sharon from office.

June 1985

The IDF withdraws from most parts of Lebanon, leaving a self-declared "Security Zone" under the control of its forces and their ally, the South Lebanese Army.

December 1987

The First Palestinian Intifada begins in the West Bank and the Gaza Strip.

January–February 1991

During the Gulf War Iraq fires thirty-nine Scud missiles at Israel.

October–November 1991

The Madrid Conference, held under the auspices of the United States and the USSR, brings together delegations from Israel, Syria, Lebanon, and a joint Jordanian–Palestinian delegation. Following the conference, bilateral talks commence.

June 1992

The Leftist-Centrist bloc wins the Israeli elections and Labor Party leader Yitzhak Rabin forms a new government.

July 1993

The IDF launches Operation Accountability against Hizbullah in South Lebanon.

September 13, 1993

Israel and the PLO sign the Oslo Agreement (the Declaration of Principles on Interim Self-Government Arrangements) under U.S. auspices.

May 1994

Israel and the PLO sign the Cairo Accord (the Gaza–Jericho Agreement).

October 26, 1994

Israel and Jordan sign a formal peace treaty.

September 24, 1995

Israel and the PLO sign the Interim Agreement on the West Bank and Gaza Strip.

April 1996

Israel launches operation Grapes of Wrath against Hizbullah in South Lebanon. Israeli fire kills more than one hundred Lebanese civilians in Qana.

September 1996

Israel opens a tunnel in the Old City of Jerusalem, setting off deadly clashes between the IDF and Palestinians.

January 1997

Israel and the Palestinians sign the Hebron Agreement (Protocol Concerning the Redeployment in Hebron) under U.S. auspices.

October 1998

Israel and the Palestinians sign the Wye River Memorandum.

May 2000

Israel withdraws from its self-styled "Security Zone" in South Lebanon and its local ally, the South Lebanese Army, collapses.

July 2000

The Camp David Summit between Israeli Prime Minister Ehud Barak and PLO leader Yasser Arafat ends in failure.

September 2000

The Second Palestinian Intifada begins in the West Bank and the Gaza Strip.

October 2000

13 Israeli Arab Palestinian citizens are killed by the security forces during riots, leading to the establishment of the Or commission of inquiry.

March 29, 2002

Israel launches operation Defensive Shield in the West Bank.

September 2005

Israel completes its disengagement, a unilateral withdrawal from the Gaza Strip and certain areas in the West Bank that includes the dismantling of all military bases and settlements.

July–August 2006

The war between Israel and Hizbullah (the Second Lebanon War).

September 2007

Israel launches a long-range air strike that destroys a suspected nuclear reactor in Syria.

April 2, 2008

The Knesset passes the Army Reserve Law.

December 2008–January 2009

Israel launches operation Cast Lead against Hamas in the Gaza Strip.

CONTRIBUTORS

Oren Barak is a senior lecturer in political science and international relations at the Hebrew University of Jerusalem.

Amir Bar-Or teaches in the political science department at The Hebrew University of Jerusalem and in the army and security studies program at Ben-Gurion University of the Negev.

Eyal Ben-Ari is a professor of sociology at The Hebrew University of Jerusalem.

Uri Ben-Eliezer is a senior lecturer at the department of sociology and anthropology at the University of Haifa.

Yuval Benziman is a lecturer in the program for conflict management at The Hebrew University of Jerusalem.

Chava Brownfield-Stein is a lecturer in gender studies at the interdisciplinary studies graduate program at Bar-Ilan University.

Samy Cohen is the research director of political sciences at the Centre d' Études et de Recherches Internationals (CERI) in Paris.

Stuart A. Cohen is a professor in the department of political studies at Bar-Ilan University.

Christopher Dandeker is a professor of military sociology in the department of war studies at King's College London.

Yuval Feinstein is completing his doctoral studies in the department of sociology, University of California, Los Angeles (UCLA).

Noa Harel completed her master's thesis, "Playing the Military: The Culture of Preparation for the Army in a Private Course and in the Gadna," at The Hebrew University of Jerusalem.

Yagil Levy is an associate professor in the department of sociology, political science, and communication at The Open University of Israel.

Edna Lomsky-Feder is a senior lecturer in the school of education at The Hebrew University of Jerusalem.

Kobi Michael is a senior lecturer in the Program of Conflict Resolution at Ben-Gurion University of the Negev.

Amiram Oren is a research fellow at the Van Leer Jerusalem Institute.

Yoram Peri is head of the Rothschild Caesarea School of Communication, director of the Chaim Herzog Institute for Media, Politics and Society, and a professor in the department of communication at Tel-Aviv University.

Avraham Sela is an associate professor in the department of international relations, and a senior research fellow at the Harry S. Truman Research Institute for the Advancement of Peace at The Hebrew University of Jerusalem.

Gabriel Sheffer is a professor of political science at The Hebrew University of Jerusalem and a fellow at the Institute for National Security Studies, Tel Aviv University.

Zalman F. Shiffer is an independent economic consultant and served on the National Security Council at the Prime Minister's Office.

INDEX

Abramovich, Amnon, 107
Adelman, Madelain, 305
aesthetic representational systems, 314f13.5, 316f13.6, 322
Afghanistan, 349, 350, 353, 354
Al-Aqsa Intifada. *See* Second Intifada
al-Asad, Hafiz, 86
Algerian War, 22, 240–41, 243
Almond, Gabriel, 262
Amal (Shiite militia), 76, 78
Aman (Israeli intelligence), 243, 249, 255
Anarchists against the Wall (AATW), 200, 210n35
Anderson, Benedict, 330
Anti-Wall Movement, 195, 200–206
antiwar movement, 82–83, 297
Arab Israelis: army service and, 339–41; as collaborators with IDF in cultural texts, 340–41; Druze, 74, 76, 146, 340, 364; impact of Israel State land uses and, 185, 187, 331; Israeli citizenship and, 339–41; Land Day (March 30, 1976), 331, 364; Palestinization of, 331
Arafat, Yasir, 65n48, 194, 195, 196, 249, 250, 251, 366
Arens, Moshe, 250
Arusi, Ratson, Rabbi, 136–37
Ashkenazi secular middle class: challenges to, 162–63; economic

bargaining, 150–51, 159–61; military recruitment, 147–48; motivation for sacrifice, 145, 149; perceptions of citizenship, 161–62; youth's contractual militarism, 145–46, 165n6
Association of Bereaved Widows and Orphans, 297
Avanti Popolo (Bukaey), 338
Aviner, Shlomo, Rabbi, 131–32, 142n32
Azulai, Uri, 283–84

Ba-Machaneh, 104, 124, 291–92, 319, 321f13.7
Barak, Ehud, 48, 86–87, 98, 195–96, 248, 249, 251, 366
Barak, Oren, 259
Bar-Or, Amir, 10
Bar-Tal, Daniel, 47, 48
Bat Chen (photograph), 314f13.5, 315
Begin, Menachem, PM, 16, 108–109, 125, 248
Beilin, Yossi, 83, 86
Beit Surik, 199, 207
Ben-Ari, Eyal, 10, 139
Ben-Bassat, Avi, 224
Benda, Julian, 112
Ben-Eliezer, Binyamin, 242, 250
Ben-Eliezer, Uri, 8, 97
Ben-Gurion, David: apparat control by, 23, 24, 36t1.1; authority of, 10,

16, 254, 259, 272–76; on building
a power base, 272, 274–76; CGS
tensions with, 249; on dissident
military organizations, 272; Mapai
party and, 18, 23; on use of force for
gaining political objectives, 275–76;
Yishuv and, 272–76; on Zionist ide-
ology, 265–66, 274
Benjamin, Walter, 319, 327n48
Ben-Meir, Yehuda, 53
Ben-Ner, Yitzhak, 335–36, 337, 338
Bennett, Lance W., 111
Benziman, Yuval, 11–12
Bil'in (village), 201, 204, 205
Binyamini, Kalman, 291
British Mandate, 275, 363
Brodet Committee Report (David
Brodet), 232–34
Brown, Beverly, 232
Brownfield-Stein, Chava, 11
B'Tselem, 209n22
Bukaey, Rafi, 338
Buzgalo, Haim, 334, 338

Camp David Summit, 97, 98, 107, 366
Carmi, Raad, 250
CGS (Chief of General Staff), 47, 50;
Aman (Israeli intelligence), 243; on
conscientious objection to disengagement policies, 123–24; influence in public sector, 48, 242–43;
influence of, 56–57, 68, 69; as information source on Arab affairs, 102;
as outspoken, 242–43; on peace negotiations, 106; on peacetime army,
98; reconstruction of Israeli sovereignty, 196–97, 209n19; tensions
with political leaders, 249, 250; on
troop deployments in security zone
in southern Lebanon, 76. See also
individual names
Christian Lebanese communities,
73–74, 77–79
cinema, Israeli, 332, 333, 337, 338, 340
citizenship: Arab Israelis and, 339; contractual militarism, 7–8, 145–46,
156–63, 167n37, 285; and military

service, 147, 148–49, 282, 297,
335–43, 339
civilian sector: epistemic communities in, 35; French army relations
with, 242; French expertise on
strategic issues, 243–44; government reaction to terrorist attacks,
355; Hagana and, 263, 264, 267–73;
knowledge of military affairs,
231, 235, 239–41, 250–53; military parades in, 310f13.1, 311, 315,
320–21, 322, 323; military relations with, 29–30, 238–41, 245–46,
257n13, 326n26, 353–54; relations
with intelligence community,
243–46; retired officers in, 18, 28,
31, 36t1.1, 55, 242–43, 248–49, 250;
role in defense budget preparations,
216–18, 221–24, 231–35; Security
Network's influence in, 31–32,
36t1.1; traumatic influence of war
on, 10, 11, 287–94, 297, 353–55;
weakness of, 22–27, 33, 45–46, 71.
See also land use; military land use;
military sector; political sector;
public opinion
civilian-military relations: in defense
budget negotiations, 216–18,
221–24, 231–35, 236n16; epistemic
authority, 5, 35–36, 43, 47–48,
56–57; militarization of public
space, 310f13.1, 311–12, 311f13.2,
315–23; weakness of civilian sector,
22–27, 33, 45–46, 71. See also memorial ceremonies; protests; public
opinion
Clausewitz, Carl von, 240, 241, 246
Clemenceau, Georges, 239
Clinton, William, President, 195, 196
Closed Military Zone--No Civilians
Allowed (photograph), 311f13.2, 312
Cohen, A. Eliot, 43
Cohen, Eli, 333, 337, 338, 340
Cohen, Samy, 9
Cohen, Stuart A., 7, 238, 259
combat units, 121, 136–38, 156–57, 161,
282, 288–89, 294, 353

Kaniuk, Yoram, 336
Katyusha rocket attacks, 79, 80, 81
Kenan, Amos, 336, 338
Kimmerling, Baruch, 262, 326n26, 331–32
kippah serugah/kippot serugot: contractual patterns of exchange, 163; deployment during disengagement, 126–27, 141n17; gender relations in combat units, 136–38; group identity of, 136–39, 163; motives for participation in disengagement, 130, 131; national-religious rabbinate's influence on, 127; observance of religious lifestyle, 136–38; rabbinic opinions on disengagement, 127–31, 142nn28,29, 163; reported opposition to disengagement policies, 123–24; settlers' associations with, 123, 126; teacher-disciple relationships, 127, 128, 131, 141n24. *See also* national-religious soldiers; responsa on military life
Kleinman, Arthur, 299
Knesset: in budget preparation process, 229; in defense budget negotiations, 217, 221, 229–30, 234; disengagement from Gaza Strip and northern Samaria, 122; executive relations with, 229–30; Foreign Affairs and Security committees, 53; military relations with, 66n56, 83, 247, 304, 363; prime ministers' relations with, 254
Kohn, H. Richard, 64n25
Kosovo, 244, 352
Kruglanski, Arie W., 46–47
Krulak, Charles, 347

Labor party, 76, 83, 85, 149, 195
Lacan, Jacques, 320
Lahad, Antoine, Gen., 77
Land Day (March 30, 1976), 331, 364
Land of Israel (Eretz Israel), 17, 99, 125, 128, 129, 135, 137, 152, 265, 266–68, 274, 339
land use: academic research on, 171–75, 183–84; annexation for separa-

tion barrier construction, 198, 199, 209n25; civilian ownership, 169, 171–75, 177–78, 187; frameworks for discussion, 188; geostrategic aspects of, 171–72; JNF Institute for the Study of Land Policy and Land Uses, 174–75; KKL-JNF Institute for Land Uses, 174–75; Land Day (March 30, 1976), 331, 364; legal aspects of, 177–78; minority population interests in, 187
Lebanon War (first), 71; casualties, 79–80, 82–83; erosion of IDF prestige, 149; films on, 333; Israel as initiator of war, 331; Israeli public awareness of, 28, 75, 76, 77, 79–84, 88–89, 331; Naqura negotiations, 77; Peace for Galilee Operation, 75, 365; protection of northern Galilee, 67, 75, 76, 77, 78, 80–81, 84–86; Sabra and Shatilla massacre, 75, 365; South Lebanon Army (SLA), 77, 78, 79, 83, 84, 86, 87, 365; Syria, 76, 77, 80, 81, 85, 86, 363. *See also* Security Zone (Southern Lebanon); withdrawal from Southern Lebanon
Lebanon War (2006), 1, 232, 252, 253
Levy, Hila, 284
Levy, Yagil, 7, 98
Levy, Yair, 146–47
Lieblich, Amia, 287
Lipkin-Shahak, Amnon, CGS, 146, 242
Lissak, Moshe, 259, 273
Lomsky-Feder, Edna, 7, 10, 139, 287
"looking awry" (Žižek), 320, 328n54
looking for pleasure, 306, 307, 317, 318–19, 320, 321f13.7, 327n49
Low Intensity Conflict (LIC), 43–45, 44(chart 2.1), 48–52, 60–61, 68, 98
Lubrani, Uri, 76
Luckham, Robin, 15

Ma'ariv, 104
Machsom Watch, 200, 210n34
management strategies: conflict management, 42–43, 46, 63n7; emotional management, 159; hu-

Orian, Dan, 332–33
Oslo peace process, 83, 97–98, 107, 129, 194, 197, 249

Palestinian Authority, 57, 60, 65nn47,48, 251
Palestinian National Movement, 206
Palestinians: al-Aqsa Intifada, 88, 89, 114, 145, 206, 212n58, 215–16, 225, 289; Amal (Shiite militia) relations with, 78; in Anti-Wall Movement, 195, 200–204; Yasir Arafat, 65n48, 194, 195, 196, 249, 250, 251, 366; in cultural texts, 333, 334–41; demonstrations against barrier construction, 200, 201, 211n36; elections, 114; Hizbullah, 88; and IDF as sole representative of Israeliness, 334–35; International Solidarity Movement (ISM), 200, 211n36, 212n54; in Israeli public discourse, 102, 108–10, 116, 197, 333–40; Land Day (March 30, 1976), 331, 364; putative measures against, 196–97, 199–200, 331; reconstruction of Israeli sovereignty, 196–97; Sabra and Shatila massacres, 75, 365; and Separation Barrier construction, 199–200, 202–205, 206–207; struggle for self-determination, 114–15, 199–200
panopticon (Foucault), 317
parades, 310f13.1, 311, 315, 320–21, 322, 323
Parliamentary Investigation Committee (France), 239
Peace for Galilee Operation, 75, 365
Peace Now movement, 298
Pedatzur, Reuven, 261–62
Peres, Shimon, PM, 76
Peretz, Amir, 231, 252, 254
Peri, Yoram, 6–7, 238, 239, 251, 259
photography: afterimages of, 322–23; Walter Benjamin on, 327n48; defined, 315; gendered space in, 312f13.3, 313f13.4, 315, 317; as legitimate models for collective voy-

eurism, 318; "looking awry" (Žižek), 320, 328n54; phenomenon in the field of vision, 311–12; voyeurism, 312f13.3, 313f13.4, 315, 317
Plotkin-Amrami, Galia, 290
Podeh, Elie, 333
Polanza, Nicos, 97, 112–13
political sector: in discourse space model, 43–45, 44(chart 2.1), 55–56, 61; EOS (Estimation of the Situation) process, 49–52, 60–61; FMM (Four Mothers Movement) interaction with, 84; generals' roles in public debates, 242–43; geography of security, 170–72; as goal of Jewish nationhood, 274–75; Hagana, 268–71; Israeli public's mistrust of, 46; media involvement in, 104–106; meetings with antiwar groups, 84; military knowledge of, 54–55, 57–59, 60–61, 84–86; political-security culture, 259–63, 260, 262; on Post-Traumatic Stress Disorder (PTSD), 288; of the Yishuv, 272–73. See also Knesset; political-military relations
political-military relations: allocation of security resources, 53, 225, 226, 232–33; army as interest group, 209n19, 245, 251; challenges to political leadership, 239–42; directives to the military, 46, 63nn7,9,10, 246–47, 249–51; discourse space concept, 43–45, 44(chart 2.1), 55–56, 61; in France, 239–43; knowledge base in, 54–55, 57–61, 81–82, 84–86; leadership in, 10, 16, 243, 245, 248, 254, 259, 272–76; National Security Council (NSC), 217, 227, 228, 231, 236n24, 244; retired security personnel in political office, 18, 28, 31, 36t1.1, 55, 242–43, 248–50; weakness of civilian sector, 22–27, 33, 45–46, 71
Post-Traumatic Stress Disorder (PTSD), 280, 287–89, 294
praetorianism, 23, 36t1.1, 68, 238

withdrawal from Southern Lebanon, 366; decision of PM, 249; diplomatic initiatives, 77, 85–86; evaluation of operational alternatives to, 78–79; public opinion on, 6, 82–86, 249; security implications of, 78–79, 86, 103; SLA personnel in, 87; Syria and, 85

Wohllebe, Louise, 284

women soldiers: in Afghanistan, 353; conscription of, 11, 304, 305; the gaze, as source of pleasure, 313f13.4, 315, 316f13.6, 317; gender relations in combat units, 136–38; from national-religious community, 121, 135–38, 140n6; participation in disengagement operation, 125; transition from civilian to military identity, 313f13.4, 315, 317; uni-forms, 313f13.4, 315, 316f13.6, 317. *See also* IDFWS (IDF women sol-diers), visual representations of

Woollacott, Angela, 305

Workshop on Israeli Security and Society, 2

World Zionist Organization, 269, 270

Ya'alon, Moshe, MG: on Estimation of the Situation (EOS) process, 49–52, 60–61; on the Intifada, 98; on Israel as "warring society," 98; on Israeli sovereignty, 196; on Israeli withdrawal from Gaza Strip and Northern Samaria, 125, 249; on the Israeli-Palestinian conflict, 114;

knowledge generation of military echelon, 56, 57, 58–60

Ya'ar, Ephraim, 262

yad le-achim. See disengagement

Yamit, evacuation of, 125, 129

Yanai, Shlomo, Gen., 174

Yavin, Haim, 107

Yesh Gvul, 83

Yeshivat Merkaz Harav Kook, 122

yeshivot hesder, 121–22, 123, 128, 133, 136, 140n6

Yishuv: clash between Zionist Movement and Arab Nationalist movement, 268; goals of Jewish nationhood, 265, 274–75; Hagana, 263, 264, 267–73; Labor movement, 70; national security system, 10, 259–60, 263, 270–72; paramilitary organizations (dissidents), 270, 272; Parity High Command, 273; politi-cal culture of, 260, 262, 266, 276

Yom Kippur War (1973), 7, 103, 149, 215, 243, 287, 291, 297, 364

Zeevi, Rahaveam, 105–106

Zionist Movement: binding mecha-nisms lacking in, 266–67, 271; debate on use of force, 265–66; Diaspora life, 265–67, 282; expan-sion of political power base, 274–76; Hagana, 263, 264, 267–73; Jews' return to Palestine, 267–68; role of military in, 268–70; sovereignty, 265–66, 274

Žižek, Slavoj, 320, 328n54